SO-BFE-130

FLORIDA STATE
UNIVERSITY LIBRARIES

OCT 23 1995

Tallahassee, Flo.

BACKWOODSMEN

"Bear Tine" Withers as a young man. Valentine Withers got his nickname from an enthusiasm for bear hunting. (Jasper County Historical Commission, Jasper, Texas)

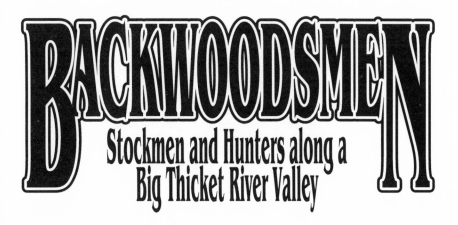

BACKWOODSMEN

Stockmen and Hunters along a Big Thicket River Valley

by
Thad
Sitton

University of Oklahoma Press : Norman and London

F
392
N35
S57
1995

Books by Thad Sitton

The Loblolly Book (Austin, 1983)

(with G. L. Mehaffy and O. L. Davis, Jr.) *Oral History:
A Guide for Teachers (And Others)* (Austin, 1983)

(with James Conrad) *Every Sun That Rises:
Wyatt Moore of Caddo Lake* (Austin, 1985)

(with Lincoln King) *Loblolly II: Moonshining, Basketmaking,
Hog Killing, Catfishing, and Other Affairs of
Plain Texas Living* (Austin, 1986)

(with Milam Rowold) *Ringing the Children In: Texas
Country Schools* (College Station, Texas, 1987)

Texas High Sheriffs (Austin, 1988)

(with Sarah Sitton) *Austin's Hyde Park:
The First Fifty Years, 1891–1941* (Austin, 1991)

*Backwoodsmen: Stockmen and Hunters along a
Big Thicket River Valley* (Norman, 1995)

Published with the assistance of
the National Endowment for the Humanities,
a federal agency which supports the study of
such fields as history, philosophy, literature, and language.

Library of Congress Cataloging-in-Publication Data

Sitton, Thad, 1941–
    Backwoodsmen : stockmen and hunters along a Big Thicket River
Valley / by Thad Sitton.
        p.   cm.
    Includes bibliographical references (p.   ) and index.
    ISBN 0-8061-2742-2 (acid-free paper)
    1. Neches River Valley (Tex.)—Social life and customs. 2. Logging—
Texas—Neches River Valley—History. 3. Outdoor life—Texas—
Neches River Valley—History. I. Title.
F392.N35S57 1995
976.4'276—dc20   95-3681
                                                                         CIP

The paper in this book meets the guidelines for
permanence and durability of the Committee on
Production Guidelines for Book Longevity of the
Council on Library Resources, Inc. ∞

Copyright © 1995 by the University of Oklahoma
Press, Norman, Publishing Division of the University.
All rights reserved. Manufactured in the U.S.A.

1   2   3   4   5   6   7   8   9   10

For Edward Elias Cochran, 1883–1970

CONTENTS

This book describes the way of life of a sizable group of southeastern Texans who persisted in a subsistence life-style of herding, small farming, hunting, trapping, fishing, and gathering well into the twentieth century. To echo writer Edward Hoagland, their accounts seem "notes from the century before."[1] Little has been written about these people. In truth, there is a gap in the historiography of the rural South where the story of the southern backwoodsmen, the "Cracker Natty Bumpos," should have been, and this is one historian's attempt to fill it.

The woodsmen of the Neches River valley were traditionalists, and at the end of the country roads and the edge of the river bottoms their nineteenth-century lifeways lasted until the coming of the stock laws in the 1950s. Growing up during that decade, a "town boy" from Lufkin in Angelina County, I knew little of their world, although some of my own family had come from it. At the hunting club we belonged to on the Neches River, only the occasional faraway sound of trailing hounds or the dark shape of a foraging razorback hog hinted at a lifeway different from the one I knew beyond the club's boundary fences.

Most townsmen a generation older than myself were as oblivious of that rural world as I was. Especially before World War II, town and country were very different places. Isolated by bad roads from their county seat towns, countrymen along the Neches lived lives as medieval as modern. Animal and human muscle powered their occupations, and kerosene and lighter pine illuminated their homes. On the same winter mornings in the late 1940s when my mother let me out of the family car to attend Kurth Elementary School in Lufkin, some of the last generation of rural schoolchildren followed pine-knot torches through dark winter woods to one- and two-room schools.

This book has several roots—strands of circumstance that powerfully coalesced to lead me to a study of the place I grew up in but really did not know. For one thing, during a trip through upstate Mississippi in the 1970s I discovered that the Gothic world of William Faulkner's "Deep South" was virtually indistinguishable from the world I knew back in "Deep East Texas." During the 1980s, my research for a study of Texas rural schools fired a continuing fascination with the lost world of the countryside, and my readings of the oral history accounts in Campbell Loughmiller and Lynn Loughmiller's *Big Thicket Legacy* showed me where to go next. Recorded in the 1960s and 1970s, the testimonies in *Big Thicket Legacy* suggested the historical topics explored in detail in this book: southern stock-raising practices, the southern subsistence life-style, and the traditions of the free range. These voices clearly hinted at a rural lifeway as yet poorly documented by historians, and I embarked on a quest for information with which to describe it. Most of that evidence resided in living memory and only there, and I began the research task none too soon. As C. L. Sonnichsen once observed, "The grassroots historian must do his work before the night cometh, in which no man can work."[2]

Finally, something more personal and intangible compelled the Neches research; a persistent "sense of place" related to my childhood experiences of the big woods and wild river haunted my imagination. Over the decades, I returned to the Neches again and again. As J. A. Baker wrote of his own special countryside in the south of England, the Neches bottoms were "a land to me as profuse and glorious as Africa—a dying world, like Mars, but glowing still."[3]

Big woods and free-flowing river yet remain, although the U.S. Corps of Engineers plans huge reservoirs, and major timber companies (repenting of a half century of self-proclaimed "stewardship of the bottoms") now clearcut the great hardwoods for wood chips and paper pulp. Nonetheless, at Big Slough, Devil's Bayou, Alabama Creek, Forks of the River, and a hundred other places, the bottomland forests still stretch unbroken as far as the eye can see. Only the backwoodsmen are gone.

The introductory chapter of this book chronicles southerners' initial adaptations to the great forest that covered most of the landscape and explores the limited historiography of the southern stockman and hunter—the backwoodsman. This lifeway, based on feral livestock, subsistence farming, and free use of the "open woods," developed during the eighteenth century and spread westward with the moving frontier.

Chapter 2, "A Flow in Time," is an environmental stage-setting for the rest of the book. Since this is an environmental history, it is important for the reader to understand something of the workings of the river in its valley, the ecology of the hardwood bottomlands, and the ten-thousand-year history of the adaptations of Native American peoples to the woods and river.

Chapter 3, "The River-Bottom Strain," gives a general description of the lifeways of Anglo settlers in the communities along the Neches Valley from settlement times to the early twentieth century. In many ways the life-styles changed very little over these years. I discuss patterns of migration to Texas, considerations involved in choosing a homeplace, house building, and communal work occasions. The purpose of the chapter is to provide a cultural background for the following, more detailed descriptions of subsistence activities.

The subsistence chapters—chapter 4, "River Traffic, Timber Work, and Moonshining," chapter 5, "Hunting, Trapping, and Fishing," and chapter 6, "Rooter Hogs and Woods Cattle"—form the core of the book. In them I describe these important activities in detail, making heavy use of the informants' own words.

Finally, since virtually every aspect of the old subsistence life-style depended on the use of the woods as commons, chapter 7, "Closing the Woods," tells how that life-style came to a bitter end along the Neches during the middle twentieth century. It offers a historical account of the prolonged struggle to end the traditions of the southern open range and to assert full common-law rights over private property and the rights of the state over wildlife. Thus, "Closing the Woods" deals with the coming of the game laws, stock laws, and fire-control laws, the posting and fencing of land, and the end of using dogs to hunt for deer (no small matter in rural southeastern Texas).

Many people helped me during my research and deserve my thanks. First and foremost, I owe a debt of gratitude to the interviewees, who endured a stranger's many questions and gave forthright information about touchy topics, even when they were not quite sure what I was up to. Among these memoirists, I single out pasture rider Charlie Harber for special thanks. Charlie not only sat still for several lengthy interviews but also caught wild hogs in his hog traps and demonstrated, right before my eyes, how to make barrows from boars.

Ecologist and historian Daniel W. Lay read the entire manuscript, as did the two anonymous scholars recruited by the University of Oklahoma Press, and all made helpful suggestions. F. E. Abernethy, James H. Conrad, and Dan K. Utley read and commented on various chapters. Despite all this helpful criticism, however, any remaining errors of fact or interpretation are my own responsibility.

Thanks also go to the staffs of the Barker Texas History Center in Austin, the Texas Forestry Museum and the Museum of East Texas in

Lufkin, and the Jasper County Historical Commission. Nancy Wilson, Bertie Bryant, and Anne Hildebrand helped me with the photographs, and my friend Vick Hines, of Austin, drew the excellent locator map of the Neches country.

Thanks finally, and most emphatically, go to my wife, Sarah Clydette Sitton, who supported and encouraged this lengthy hunter's quest through libraries, archives, and the thickets of memory.

THAD SITTON

Austin, Texas

BACKWOODSMEN

I don't know how Pap came to this part of the country, but Uncle Auss, his brother, started out with an ox wagon and one of the oxen died, and he lost his temper and knocked the other one in the head and walked back to Georgia. He came here later. I describe Uncle Auss's bunch, not all of them, as people who made their own rules as they went along. They didn't go by anyone else's rules; they just rigged up a set. I always called them the river-bottom strain.

—Arden Hooks

1
INTRODUCTION

Even before 1820, American settlers were drifting in small numbers across the Sabine River into southeastern Texas. Far away in San Antonio and Mexico City, the government of New Spain did not approve, but it had no real power to stop them. South of the small Spanish settlement of Nacogdoches, the lands between the Sabine and Trinity rivers lay largely unsettled and almost unknown. Native American societies originally occupying the land had been reduced to scattered remnants by more than a century of exposure to European diseases. Small grasslands created and maintained by generations of Indian fires occasionally punctuated the landscape, but these were lost in a vast forest stretching east to the coastal plains of the Atlantic.[1] A mixed growth of pines and hardwoods covered the uplands, with a great wedge of longleaf pine woodlands extending across the South into southeastern Texas almost to the Trinity River. Periodic fires started by man and lightning swept the uplands, helping to maintain the pure pine stands, but the fires stopped at the well-watered bottoms of the Trinity, Neches, and Sabine rivers and their many tributaries. Here, a diverse climax forest of giant oaks, gums, hickories, magnolias, cypresses, and scores of other hardwood species held sway, as it had for eighteen thousand years.[2]

Small wonder, then, that the American newcomers spoke of southeastern Texas as the "Big Thicket" and the "Big Woods."[3] In 1835, Andrew F. Smyth, who would end his days running steamboats on the Neches River, sent a letter from the family home in Moulton, Alabama, to a brother, recently arrived in what later became Jasper County, and addressed the letter, "To George W. Smyth, Esq., Texas, In the Western Woods."[4] That was how southeastern Texas seemed to the new settlers and settlers-to-be from the old southern states of Georgia, Mississippi, Alabama, and Louisiana farther east—a vast, primal forest.

By long before 1835, however, the great southern woods had become familiar to Anglo-Americans and the moving frontier had become a way of life. William A. Owens, who interviewed the children and grandchildren of the Big Thicket pioneers in the 1930s, described a typical arrival:

> Camping out under trees while they worked, they built log houses, covered them with hand-split boards, and chinked and daubed them with red clay. They built stick-and-dirt chimneys. Fireplaces were for heat and cooking, and for light at night, the only light except for the red smoky glare of a lightwood knot. They cleared only as much land as they could work with one horse hooked to a Georgia stock or Kelly turning plow, enough land for a little cotton, a little corn— for a patch of sweet potatoes and black-eyed peas. Their cattle grazed on the open range. So did the razorback hogs. There was elbow room and to spare. They had no wish to obliterate the wilderness.[5]

This adaptation to the new environment had come swiftly, but for the first generation of southerners, there had been a price to pay. At Jamestown, in the Virginia colony, settlers had died in the midst of an incredible plenty because they lacked the necessary knowledge to exploit the wilderness. Historians Ray Allen Billington and Martin Ridge noted:

> The forests were teeming with wild life: deer, buffalo, bears, and other animals in profusion, turkeys that weighed seventy pounds or more, and ducks so numerous that flocks seven miles long shut out the sunlight as they passed overhead. Streams swarmed with fish so large that ordinary nets would not hold them and so plentiful that a horse could not wade across a river where they were running. Sturgeon twelve feet long were killed with axes, and oysters thirteen inches across were seen along the coast. Once the Englishmen learned to use their resources they were assured a bountiful living.[6]

The learning process took too long for some. Jamestown was settled in May 1607 by three shiploads of settlers sent out by the London Company to transfer England's civilization to the New World, but the knowledge of that civilization proved inadequate in the American wilderness. By the spring of 1608, only 38 men remained alive of the original 105.

By the end of a decade, the Englishmen had learned a "rudimentary knowledge of frontier technique." Friendly Indians taught them how to plant corn, hunt deer and wild turkeys, catch fish, and clothe themselves in the warm skins of animals. A half century later, the forest adaptation had progressed much further, and the southern frontier was producing real woodsmen. Billington and Ridge concluded:

In 1682 both Virginia and Maryland began employing patrols of mounted border rangers to ride constantly along the frontier, ready to fend off minor raids or give warning of major attacks. Clad in buckskin, carrying guns and long knives, mounted on spirited ponies, and steeped in the lore of the Indian and the forest, these rangers were true frontiersmen whose wilderness skill testified to the amount learned by the English since the first colonists starved to death amidst plenty at Jamestown.[7]

The settlers who moved into southeastern Texas in the early nineteenth century were the inheritors of over two centuries of accumulated experience of hunting, fishing, gathering, farming, and stock raising in the southern forest. Far more than most of them realized, they owed this knowledge to the southeastern Indians.[8] A thousand details of woodcraft had Indian origins, and even the practices of Anglo-American farming differed from Indian farming practices only in degree. The new settlers prepared forest lands for agriculture in the old way—by girdling, selective clearing, and burning. They worked their early crops of maize, beans, and squash with hoes in between the tree stumps, just as the Indians had done. Even the frontier cash crops of tobacco and cotton began as a hoe agriculture.[9]

Indians had been exploiting the resources of the southern woods and rivers for many generations. Some of their hunting, fishing, and gathering techniques dated to the Archaic Era and were more than nine thousand years old.[10] The Anglo settlers' fine-grained adaptation to the bottomland forests, as described by historian Thomas Clark, doubtless owed much to Indian examples.

The southern hardwood forests made an indelible impression on the folkways and life of people who dwelt beneath their canopies. These woods produced an almost endless variety of fruit-bearing shrubs, of berries, and nuts. Some of the giant black walnut, chestnut, and hickory trees yielded enormous annual crops of edible mast, and the heavy oak cover littered the forest floor with layers of acorns to provide food for wild game and domestic hogs. Matting the ground as low-growing underbrush were shrubs compatible with the heavy overstory. Most of these flowered, bore berries, and had aromatic roots that could be converted into specifics for the folk treatment of the ills of man. . . . Folk of the deciduous timber region colored their homespun cloths with natural vegetable dyes, regulated their blood and bowels with natural teas, and even eased the pains of childbirth and death with herbal concoctions gathered from the floor of the woods. In no other portion of the nation was human life so thoroughly integrated with natural forest resources as in the hardwood areas of the South.[11]

This dependence on the resources of the hardwood bottomlands was one of the reasons that new settlers in southeastern Texas preferred to locate along the Neches, the Sabine, and the major tributaries of these two rivers. In choosing a location, they looked for the juxtaposition of "openings," small areas of naturally treeless land, with good timber and river access.[12] They avoided swamps and bottoms as building sites but used these areas to hunt, fish, gather, and provide food for their stock. As ecologist Daniel W. Lay noted, "The river bottoms attracted the people that had nothing." In the beginning most of the settlers fell into this category. Lay explained: "They were living off the land like the Indians were, and the hammock land next to the bottom was best for their crops and gave them access to more diverse ecosystems than any other location. Just as the Indians had before them, they had access to the resources available in uplands, hammock lands, bottomlands, river, sloughs, oxbow lakes, and the lower reaches of all the creeks that flooded in the spring."[13]

This subsistence period often lasted for years in southeastern Texas as the settler built a log house, put in a large garden, and gradually cleared land for his cash crops. While he cleared his land, he made a living by running stock, hunting, trapping, fishing, and perhaps harvesting cypress. A location on the river also held out the promise of easy transport of cotton and other cash crops to market, as well as import of supplies. Sometimes, this herding and subsistence period continued indefinitely; settlers often learned that local soils were marginal for cotton and that more wealth could be accumulated by running hogs and cattle in the river bottoms.[14]

The system of livestock raising used by southerners moving to southeastern Texas was already two centuries old. In the winter of 1611, Jamestown colonists, desperate because they had nothing to feed their stock, had turned the cattle and hogs into the forest to fend for themselves. The colonists assumed their animals would die of starvation or exposure, but they found most of them fat and healthy in the spring. The virgin forests provided adequate protection from the mild southern winters. Hogs fattened on mast from the oaks, hickories, and other hardwood trees, and the cattle prospered on grass growing under the pine forests and on switch cane in the bottoms.[15]

Rather quickly, a tradition of stock raising developed based on using the woods as unfenced open range. The common-law doctrine that confined livestock to one's property did not apply in the Old South. There, the traditional practice required the farmer to fence *in* his crops and fence *out* foraging stock. The burden of fencing was on the farmers, not the stockmen, and landowners were liable for damage to stock when their properties were not properly fenced. As early as 1632, the

Virginia colony passed a law requiring farmers to fence in crops "or else to plant, uppon theire owne perill," and the colonial governments of Maryland, South Carolina, and Georgia later established similar laws.[16] The royal colony of Georgia, for example, passed a law in 1755 requiring a farmer to have fences of a specified height; otherwise, any "trespass or damage so ever he shall receive or sustain by hogs, cattle, or horses shall be his own loss." In the early nineteenth century, the territories of Mississippi and Alabama and the Republic of Texas followed in the same pattern. They "preserved the free range by requiring only a mark or brand for stock to run free."[17]

The southern livestock tradition that settlers brought to southeastern Texas was very different from the Hispanic tradition developing far to the west on the arid brushlands and prairies of southern Texas and northern Mexico. In its most essential characteristics, the southern livestock tradition was an adaptation to the great forest. Earmarked and branded, a man's hogs and cattle ranged with the animals of other stockmen across miles of woods, fending for themselves against the big predators—bears, wolves, and cougars—that were the only check on their numbers. In the winter the hogs ate mast, and the cattle ate switch cane in the bottoms. In the summer they moved into the pine uplands in search of grass and forage.[18] Traveler after traveler commented on the South as a paradise for livestock. The forest trees dropped tremendous crops of mast. The interspersed prairies and open pine forests "billowed with wild oats and grasses, wild vetch, and pea vines 'tall enough to reach the shoulders of a man on horseback.'"[19] Bottomlands and swamps were covered with a rich pasturage of cane. In 1850 an anonymous observer of East Texas stock raising commented: "The cost of raising cattle amounts to nothing more than the time consumed in marking and branding. Cattle require no feeding. . . . Hogs are never fattened upon corn, from the fact that they fatten themselves in the woods, upon acorns, which, of course, is the cheapest method of producing pork and bacon."[20]

East Texans and other southerners defined "good range" in terms of adequate access to both hardwood bottoms and pine uplands, and if the uplands were open enough, this could be an entirely forested environment.[21] Southern "rooter hogs" and "woods cattle" had poor meat quality by modern standards, but they were adaptable, aggressive, range-wise, and capable of fending for themselves in the big woods. They were at least semiferal, and this wildness was essential to their survival. Once or twice a year, in operations referred to as "hog hunts" and "cow hunts" rather than "roundups," the stockman took his dogs and went out to locate his animals in the woods, drove them to the closest stock pen, "worked them"—earmarking, branding, and castrating—and then set most of them free once again, keeping some for butchering.

Nothing was so essential to southern stock raising as the tradition of the open range. Arriving in Texas in 1832, Sherrod Wright claimed a league of land just east of the Neches River in what is now Jasper County. This was only his home base: a decade or so later his cattle and hogs ranged over eighty thousand acres of forest.[22] Thousands of other southern stockmen did the same. They moved in, bought or homesteaded a few hundred acres of land, then turned their seed stocks of hogs and cattle into the woods to multiply and spread. Most of the land was owned by someone, but the commons tradition gave every man usufruct rights of trespass, hunting, fishing, gathering, and stock raising on the lands of every other man, with the exception of fenced fields and homeplaces. Some men followed the tradition of the commons to its logical conclusion and eschewed landownership altogether. A critical observer of Hardin County stockmen-farmers noted in 1887:

> Very few of the descendants of the old settlers own any land. For the last forty years they have been in the habit of settling upon any land fit for cultivation. . . . After working someone else's land for two or three years, he sells the improvements and his squatter's claim to one of his neighbors, and then hunts up another place or piece of land to improve and sell in a like manner. . . . The people have been in the habit of using every man's land as their own for so many years that they have come to believe that the land has no owners.[23]

Some contemporary observers saw the southern stockman-farmer in an objective way. Among them was John F. H. Claiborne, a Natchez journalist, who traveled across the Pine Belt of the South in 1840 and commented on the richness of the open range, the large numbers of hogs and cattle, the independence and hospitality of the people, their dietary dependence on the sweet potato, and the close association of stock raising with predator hunting.[24] Most, however, were like the 1887 visitor to Hardin County, who was offended by the stockmen-farmers' use of other men's land and their "monotonous diet of cornbread, bacon, sweet potatoes, and venison" and who found them "very primitive in their habits." Implying a racial distinctiveness as well as a primitive life-style, this man observed, "Nearly all the children born and reared in the pine woods have light hair."[25]

Probably the contemporary observer with the greatest effect on historical interpretations of the pioneer stockmen-farmers was Frederick Law Olmsted. He traveled extensively among the southern herdsmen in the 1850s and had almost nothing good to say about them, criticizing their diet, agricultural practices, houses, and preference for a leisurely life-style. Of one East Texas homestead (which had graciously offered him shelter for the night), he remarked: "There were several windows, some of which . . . were entirely open. There was not a pane of glass. The doors were closed with difficulty. We could see the stars, as we lay in bed, through the openings of the roof; and on all sides, in the walls of the room, one's arm might be thrust out."[26]

For more than a century after Olmsted's travel books about Texas and the "cotton kingdom," historical interpreters of the southern backwoodsmen dismissed these people in terms hardly different from their popular stereotypes as "poor whites," "crackers," or "pineys." For example, in the 1974 edition of *Westward Expansion*, for long the standard work on the subject, Ray Allen Billington wrote:

> Far below the yeoman farmers in the South's social scale were the poor whites who, as "crackers," "hillbillies," or "sandhillers," were scattered in small communities through the poorest southern lands. . . . They depended for food less on their weed-choked fields than on omnipresent hogs who cared for themselves and on game they brought down with their long rifles. Unkempt, illiterate, shiftless, and lazy, these miserable byproducts of the plantation system were condemned to their squalid existence by more fortunate neighbors who pushed them onto unproductive lands.[27]

Most commonly, however, historians simply ignored the southern herdsmen. They often discussed Anglo society in the antebellum South as if it had included only two classes, slaveholding planters and the "yeoman farmers" who wished for nothing so much as to become slaveholders and planters themselves. The rest were just "poor whites" and unworthy of attention. Julian A. C. Chandler's thirteen-volume opus, *The South in the Building of the Nation* (1909–13), dismissed the region's livestock industry in just fifteen pages while devoting only 125 words to hogs. Similarly, Ulrich Bonnell Phillips's *Life and Labor in the Old South* (1929) spent less than a page on southern stockmen. To Frederick Jackson Turner in *The Frontier in American History* (1920), southern stock raising was only a passing phase as the line of the moving frontier pushed west. According to this view, first came the woodsmen, fur traders, and miners, then the stock raisers, and then— rather closely behind and quickly displacing the stock raisers—the farmers and plantation owners.

In truth, the herdsman was rarely if ever displaced by the farmer, since he had the customary right to range his stock on the farmer's land. The works of history reassessing the southern stockmen, the southern subsistence life-style, and the backwoods South in general still make up only a short list, but already the previous negative viewpoint has been outmoded. In *Plain Folk of the Old South* (1949), Frank L. Owsley marshaled evidence for the existence of a southern rural middle class of stockmen and small farmers, who had remained largely outside the plantation economy. He studied church records, wills, county court records, mortgage books, deed books, county tax returns, the manuscript returns of the federal censuses, and a variety of little-used local and family histories to draw a portrait of this "lost social class" of the rural South. These records revealed a southern rural society of great complexity: "But the core of the social structure was a massive body of plain folk who were neither rich nor very poor. . . . The great majority secured their food, clothing, and shelter from some rural pursuit, chiefly farming and livestock grazing." At another point Owsley noted, "A grazing and farm economy rather than a plantation economy was practiced by nearly all the non-slaveholders and by 60 to 80 percent of the slaveholders." By "farm economy" he meant "a diversified, self-sufficient type of agriculture" and stock raising.

After a lapse of over a quarter of a century, other scholars began to follow Owsley's lead in a reassessment of the southern livestock tradition and the southern stockmen-farmers. In an important article in the *Journal of Southern History* in 1975, Forrest McDonald and Grady McWhiney offered a reinterpretation of the antebellum southern herdsman and discussed the reasons for the historical neglect of the southern livestock industry. They described a tradition of long-range drives of hogs and cattle to market utilizing overnight holding pens, or "stock stands," spaced at intervals along the route. They noted the possible Celtic origins of many southern stock raising practices and pointed out that in 1860 hogs and other southern livestock were worth half a billion dollars—more than twice the value of that year's cotton crop.[28] McWhiney later returned to some of these same matters in his *Cracker Culture: Celtic Ways in the Old South* (1988).

In 1981 cultural geographer and historian Terry G. Jordan, in his book *Trails to Texas*, argued that western cattle ranging had "southern roots." Contrary to what Walter Prescott Webb implied in *The Great Plains* (1931), the Anglo stockmen were not tabulae rasae when they moved out into the open country and encountered Hispanic livestock practices. They had their own stock-raising tradition, formed far to the east, in South Carolina—a forest tradition carried west along the line of the southern pine uplands. Southern stockmen ran both hogs and cattle on the wooded commons, made extensive use of stock dogs, burned the upland forests on a yearly basis to encourage the growth of new grass, went on twice-yearly "cow hunts" and "hog hunts" to work stock in widely scattered pens, earmarked both hogs and cattle, and engaged in other practices unlike those of the Hispanic tradition. After the American stockmen moved out beyond the line of the forest, the open-country Hispanic methods seemed more appropriate and came to predominate. The hog, a forest animal, disappeared from the Anglo free-range tradition altogether.

Southern stock raising and the rural subsistence life-style in general were based on the commons, on the open range, but only recently have historians begun to appreciate the historical importance—and staying power—of this tradition of usufruct rights over other people's land. In a 1982 article in the *Journal of Southern History,* J. Crawford King presented an overview of the prolonged social and political conflicts involved in the coming of the stock laws and the "closing of the southern range."[29] In two important works, Steven Hahn explored the historical roots of the traditions of the commons and the importance of these traditions for a subsistence life-style based on "hunting, fishing and foraging."[30]

This persistent subsistence life-style of hunting, fishing, gathering, stock raising, and small farming has been largely ignored by historians of the twentieth-century South, although those people in actual contact with rural southerners were always aware of its importance. A retired game warden from central Texas, trying to identify the sources of the cultural shock he experienced after being sent to enforce unpopular game laws in "deep" East Texas during the 1950s, summed up regional cultural distinctiveness with two related points: the survival into the middle twentieth century of a tradition of "living off the land," and the "Indian idea that the land belongs to everybody." In this he was exactly right.[31]

Nevertheless, only a few scholars have bothered to study southern ideas and practices of hunting, fishing, and gathering. In 1991 anthropologist Stuart A. Marks published *Southern Hunting in Black and White,* a serious analysis of the social and cultural significance of hunting in rural North Carolina. Texas folklorist F. E. Abernethy has discussed the social practices and traditions associated with fox and deer hunting.[32]

Generally speaking, however, southern novelists have done a better job of interpreting southern hunting than have the scholars. In *Home from the Hill* (1958), Texas writer William Humphrey explored the complex relationship between hunting and the southern male psyche. William Faulkner's wonderful hunting tale, "The Bear," in *Go Down, Moses* (1940) went deeper into the cultural meanings of southern hunting than any other source and is far more a work of social realism than most of its interpreters recognize.[33]

The present study follows Owsley's "plain folk" of stockmen-farmers into the twentieth century in and along the Neches River valley of southeastern Texas. Its purpose is to use oral history accounts and documentary sources to create a detailed description of the southern subsistence life-style as adaptation to environment. To accomplish this, I collected information on the topics of hunting, fishing, farming, stock raising, and such bottomland activities as log rafting, stave making, tie making, and moonshining.

Such practices persisted very late along the Neches River, a typical silt-laden, slow-moving, southern lowland stream, which flows in its shallow, heavily timbered valley from a headwaters in Van Zandt and Smith counties 260 miles southeast to the Gulf of Mexico. The river takes its name from the Neche Indians, a group of the Hasinai Caddos who lived along its banks. The Hasinai Indians themselves called the stream *Nachawi*, "Osage orange," naming it for the tree from which they made their excellent bows.[34]

The Neches is a county boundary stream all the way to the Gulf, and the counties that border it have many things in common. Moving south along the upper and middle river, the Neches counties included in the research area were Smith, Cherokee, Houston, Angelina, Trinity, Polk, Jasper, Tyler, and Hardin. These counties are all heavily wooded, with relatively poor soils and low population densities, and are dominated economically by major timber companies.

With the exception of the city of Lufkin in Angelina County, the county-seat towns of the Neches area have a sameness about them. Arranged around the typical southern courthouse square, they are deceptively quiet places of a few hundred to a few thousand inhabitants, springing to a quickened life only on weekends, when citizens come in from the hinterlands. A visitor who walks the streets of Crockett, Jasper, Livingston, or Groveton on Saturday afternoons and who looks about and listens to the topics of conversation and turns of speech finds little to distinguish these places from a hundred others across the Piney Woods South. This was true in the 1920s, 1930s, and 1940s, the decades that form the chronological focus of this book, and it is true today. This is Texas, but it might as well be upstate Mississippi, or Louisiana, or Alabama.

Logically, if one seeks to collect information about the southern subsistence life-style—about Owsley's "plain folk" of stockmen, farmers, and woodsmen—one should go to where this lifeway persisted the longest. This is emphatically true of the Neches counties of southeastern Texas. The southern free range was the economic linchpin of this way of life, and in most of these counties the stock laws abolishing it were not voted in until the 1950s. In his study of the closing of the southern range, King found that the southern counties that resisted

THE NECHES RIVER

the stock laws the longest had a high percentage of independent small landowners, relatively low population densities, little tenancy, not much cotton, relatively few African Americans, and a lot of razorback hogs. In fact, "the greater the number of hogs per capita a county had the greater was the likelihood of that county's remaining open range."[35] The Neches counties fit this model in every parameter.

Hogs were certainly everywhere along the Neches until the 1960s. They foraged in the woods, napped in the dust of country roads, caught and ate chickens from people's yards in the county-seat town of Jasper, and more than once broke into the Hardin County Courthouse. Nor did they immediately disappear with the coming of the stock law. When game warden Billy Platt was assigned to Jasper County in the early 1960s, only a few citizens yet had dared to build perimeter fences around their properties to keep out other people's stock, even though the stock law had been passed several years before.[36] Hogs, cattle, stockmen, hunters, and other trespassers wandered across an unfenced landscape of other people's land into the 1960s and beyond. As J. R. Cockrell, of Polk County, summed it up, "The woods were full of people in those days."[37]

The people interviewed for this book were born and grew up in many rural communities along the edge of the Neches Valley. Many of these places were not listed on the official maps of their own time, and many more have disappeared from the maps of today. Scattered across miles of landscape, these were informal communities, created and perpetuated by the beliefs of the rural people that belonged to them. Like the North Cedar Creek community in Trinity County and the Bellview and Weaver's Bend communities in Angelina County, they centered on a country school, a church, and a graveyard. Sometimes, in the case of warring churches, only the common school unified the community. As one woman told me, "Churches divide a community; the school brings it together."[38]

These rural communities along the Neches were not all the same— far from it. Tracing their roots well back into the nineteenth century, isolated from the county-seat towns and from nearby communities by bad roads and slow transportation, they were little social worlds unto themselves. Among their number were a few all-black communities settled by freedmen after the Civil War, communities that blacks sometimes called "colonies" and whites "independent quarters," and all-white settlements where no black person could go except at risk of attack. Godly communities founded by ministers and centered on a church existed side by side with settlements associated with moonshining, timber theft, and other real or imputed deviancies. There were communities dominated by a single extended family, communities locked in a perpetual state of feud between families, and others so plagued by violence that people called them "killing communities." As woodsman Charlie Harber told me, "For years those men in that community of Possum Walk [Trinity County] all wore outside guns on their hips."[39] Some rural communities even had their economic specializations. More than one was known for the quality of its ribbon-cane syrup or the efficiency of its water-powered gristmills, and one place in Jasper County won renown for building excellent cypress coffins.

The families that lived in the rural communities along the Neches Valley practiced a wide range of subsistence strategies dependent on the uplands, bottomlands, and river. The late Charlie Havard, whom I interviewed on several occasions in 1986, was an excellent case in point. Charlie's family had moved into southern Angelina County on the edge of the Neches Valley before the Civil War. Until the stock law passed after the end of World War II, Charlie and his brothers and cousins continued the family's traditional subsistence life-style. He raised corn for his hogs and other stock, along with a little cotton, but his main money crop was sugarcane. Charlie had a syrup mill on his place, made syrup for his neighbors and himself, and sold the excess to the commissary of a nearby sawmill town. Charlie ran a trapline with his brother in the nearby bottoms, night-hunted for venison with a carbide head lamp, and fished the river with nets and trotlines in the spring, selling buffalo and catfish by the wagonload in Lufkin and Old Manning. As his foster son told me about Charlie's fishing and hunting, "The law didn't have much to do with the way he done his business."[40] Charlie was a solid citizen in other ways, but—like many other rural East Texans—when his family needed deer, or duck, or fish, or money from the same, he went out and got it.

But above all, Charlie Havard ran hogs and cattle in the Neches bottoms. Charlie was in some respects a poor man, but he had hundreds of hogs and cattle scattered for miles up and down the river. His father and his brothers had the same, and so did other neighbors in the Bellview and Weaver's Bend communities of Angelina County and across the river in Polk County.

Charlie and his relatives went out several times a year with their stock dogs to locate, drive, pen, and work their animals. Hogs and cattle were treated in much the same way. Stock pens were placed in strategic locations up and down the river and were used by different men. All the stockmen along Charlie's stretch of the Neches cooperated, since it was in their own best interests to do so. Hogs in particular often roamed for miles in search of acorns, wild fruits, and other food, swimming the Neches into Polk County whenever they felt like it. Charlie and the other men kept each other informed about the movements of their respective herds and sometimes earmarked, castrated, and inoculated each other's animals. After the stock law began to be effectively enforced around 1950, Charlie Havard rounded up and sold his hogs and cattle and went to work as a timber scaler for Carter Lumber Company. In this too he was entirely typical, since, more than anything else, it was the stock law that forced southern drovers and woodsmen along the Neches into mainline employments.

Typical also was Charlie's refusal entirely to give up the old ways. He still tied his excellent hoop nets and fished and hunted on his days off with a determination motivated by something stronger than a simple desire for recreation. Without much thinking about it, Charlie was determined to keep part of his old subsistence life-style alive. Many former stockmen and woodsmen along the Neches felt and did the same; the pull of the old ways was strong. James May, of Lufkin, a generation younger than Charlie Havard but born and raised in the same rural traditions, dutifully punched a time clock five days a week for decades at Lufkin Foundries, but when the whistle blew on Friday afternoons, he reverted to the old lifeway. In a plywood motorboat of his own design, May spent the night tending his nets and trotlines and light-hunting deer over the banks for forty miles downriver to Diboll, often not returning to town until Monday morning.[41] To the game wardens' enduring sorrow, there were many men like James May in the counties along the Neches.

Another reason that the subsistence life-style persisted along the Neches counties is that the environment itself persisted. At a time when so many southern bottomlands have been drowned by reservoirs or drained and converted to soybean fields or slash pine plantations, much of the Neches bottoms remains in old-growth hardwood forest. Little altered by the two small reservoirs along its course, the river still rises in late winter and early spring to spread for miles across its wide, shallow valley and—like the Nile—to deposit a layer of fertile silt. Two national forests, two of the state's six wilderness areas, several wildlife areas, and the eighty-mile-long Neches corridor of the Big Thicket National Preserve lie along the river. At the Big Slough Wilderness, the Upland Island Wilderness, the "Forks of the River" country above the confluence of the Neches and the Angelina rivers, and elsewhere, the bottomlands remain somewhat as they were at the time of the arrival of the first American settlers. Human use has altered the bottomlands over time, but remnants of the environmental past linger.[42]

This study combines the theoretical perspectives of cultural geography and ecological history with the research method of oral history in an attempt to reconstruct and describe the "cultural knowledge," the subsistence tricks of the trade, of the Neches Valley stockman-farmer-

Angelina County family scene, c. 1920. (The Museum of East Texas, Lufkin, Texas)

woodsman during the early twentieth century. Documentary sources were used whenever appropriate, but the reconstruction of the old subsistence lifeways would not have been possible without the assistance of the many people interviewed between 1985 and 1992. Strangely (or perhaps not so strangely, since they were all "woodsmen"), the most enlightening information came from either retired "outlaw hunters" or retired game wardens. Few men alive in the late 1980s had as much of the full repertoire of the subsistence life-style as "Little Charlie" Havard of Angelina County, Jess Wells of Houston County, Roy Smith of Trinity County, or Walter Cole of Jasper County, but many people had practiced or observed some of the old ways. For the most part, it was a matter of picking up a detail here and a detail there, then confirming those practices with other informants.

To any social historian worth his or her salt, there are no small details. Former U.S. Senator Ralph Yarborough first told me of the "deer stake," the practice of planting a sharpened wooden stake inside the rail fence protecting the family garden or field to kill or disable white-tailed deer leaping inside. People knew that deer were creatures of habit and that they always leaped rail fences at the lowest points. A person studied the ground to determine a deer's customary landing area inside the fence, then set a sharpened stake to pierce the animal in the "sticking place" on its next foray into the garden.[43] This was nei-

B. E. Whitaker and family of Jasper County posed in front of giant oak tree. (Jasper County Historical Commission, Jasper, Texas)

ther an idle cruelty nor an insignificant matter. A family depended on its garden to provide vegetables for the entire year. Before the turn of the century, deer often were so numerous as to be serious threats to gardens and crops—pests, unless a family happened to need venison. The deer stake was a simple thing, but it could simultaneously keep raiding animals out of the sweet potato patch and put meat on the table. What is more, the technique of the deer stake was very old. It was carried across the South from Virginia and the Carolinas with migrating settlers. As in the case of many other techniques for making a living in the southern forest, the settlers had learned about the deer stake from the southeastern Indians, who may have been using it for a thousand years.

The cultural book of knowledge for getting a living from the woods and river is almost lost. Most of it never reached the printed page. Only the rare exception like Solomon Wright's autobiography, *My Rambles as East Texas Cowboy, Hunter, Fisherman, Tie-Cutter* (1942), gives us some inkling of what might have been included. Most of the cultural tricks of the trade for hunting, fishing, timbering, stock raising, trapping, and other woods occupations were part of oral tradition, passed down from generation to generation by example and word of mouth. Therefore, it is reasonable to seek this information in the memories of living men and women by way of oral history. In the river bottoms, at the ends of the country roads, the old ways were still closer than I had dared to hope. This book is the result.

2
A FLOW IN TIME

When Frederick Law Olmsted crossed the Neches River during the early winter of 1854, he found it only "three rods in width." He remarked of this unimpressive stream, "Like all the eastern rivers of Texas it is thick with mud." On his way back east later that year, he encountered a very different river—an almost impassable, mile-wide torrent of brown water flowing "bluff to bluff" across a heavily timbered valley. The "muddy ditch" had become "a Mississippi."[1]

For twenty thousand years the Neches has risen to claim its ancient valley in the late winter and early spring. In October or November the autumn rains begin. Slowly at first, then more rapidly, the current quickens, the water level rises within the riverbanks, and finally at scour channels and creek mouths the river breaks forth to flood the bottoms. It flushes out and refills the backswamps, oxbow lakes, and overflow channels it deserted a few months before. It begins a slow tour of the river courses it left behind and—with sharper and more purposeful current—resumes the cutting away of the land along the channels of new courses. At high water the river's true intentions become revealed. The observer sees that a giant black gum on the edge of the cutbank is undercut and doomed and will crash into the river during the first spring thunderstorm. Judging by the speed of the current roaring across a river bend, the observer surmises that the long meander soon is destined to be cut off and left behind as the river shortens its course.

As the water rises and the current speed doubles, the river's power to transport materials downstream increases from eight to sixteen times. With awesome force it slams into cutbanks at the sharp bends, collapsing the banks and carrying their materials downstream. At these especially turbulent places, corkscrewing vertical eddies scour the river bottom into deep pits. Larger and larger sand and gravel particles are carried by the current, and even heavier materials bounce and roll downstream along the bottom. At the surface, downed trees accumulate in drifts, thrashed by the current. Channels cutting across the necks of meander bends deepen in a matter of hours, as the river quickly moves to adjust its course.[2] Along the straight stretches, the river slides by in silence, almost as fast as a person can run. It is swiftest at its center, where water literally flows on water with little friction from bottom or bank. Here in midstream, as a physical sign of its speed and power, the surface of the water bulges upward ever so slightly in a convex curve.[3]

Ruled by the power of the river, the valley through which it flows is in a state of constant change. The river shifts its course even within the finite span of a human lifetime. Much of the route that Captain Andrew Smyth floated on his first keelboat trip to Sabine Pass in 1846 now lies on dry land. Over hundreds of years, the river constantly moves back and forth in great loops across the shallow trough of its valley, occasionally impacting and eroding the valley sides. The meanders of the ever-shifting river march downstream, like the loops of a shaken garden hose. The meander loops have a certain size and spacing—an amplitude and wavelength—determined by the average width of the river at any given point.[4]

Meanwhile, as the river meanders back and forth in its valley, the whole substance of the valley flows toward the sea. Whatever particle of sand the river drops today at an accumulating point bar to become part of the forest floor under great oaks and gums will be picked up again by the river a hundred years or a thousand years hence. The constituent elements that make up a giant black gum tree are in temporary residence only. In time the tree will fall and decay, and the river will return to move its elements farther downstream.[5]

The river is both creator and destroyer of its bottomland universe, and at the apex of every meander bend both forces can be observed in action. On the cutbank side, the outside of the bend, a mature forest of oaks, gums, and other hardwoods is destroyed as the river undercuts its bank. At the same time, on the inside of the bend, a point bar builds up from sediments carried down from cutbanks destroyed farther upstream. Soon, this new ground created by the river is colonized by black willow and river birch. Across every sharp bend, a world coming into being faces a world coming to an end.[6]

Meander bends themselves have their cycles of life and death. For reasons that geologists still argue about, a meander begins as a slight curve in the course of the river, then develops laterally in a deeper and deeper bend. As the meander bend moves off at right angles to the overall course of the river, the point bar builds out to follow it, leaving behind a series of shallow ridges that become covered first with birch and willow, then with ever-larger hardwoods. Eventually, the meander curve develops into a nearly complete loop—a gooseneck bend that the river begins to cut across in high water. Usually this shortcut comes about a third of the way up the meander bend, and after a flood season or two or ten, it leaves behind a crescent-shaped lake at the apex of the former meander. Occasionally, the river does something much more dramatic, cutting across the neck of the meander to leave the entire loop behind as an oxbow lake. Like memories of what the river used to do, these remnants of former river courses are scattered down the valley on both sides of the present river channel.[7]

During high water, the processes of both erosion and deposition accelerate. Cutbanks and the riverbed itself are eroded by the current, and new layers of sand and silt are deposited on the point bars. As the river moves over the top of its flooded banks, the current slows, dropping fine silts to form "natural levees" bordering the river on either side, and even finer silts are carried and deposited far across the backswamps and flats that parallel the course of the river.[8]

Where major tributaries like Cochino Bayou, Shawnee Creek, or Alabama Creek intersect the river, floodwaters expand far inland, creating long corridors of bottomland reaching back into the pine hills. Creeks often reach the river in a tangle of channels, creating situations in which people and their stock may be easily cut off by rapidly rising waters. More than one tributary along the Neches is called "Devil's Bayou" because of its history of drowning men and animals.

At any given location along the river, the processes of erosion and sedimentation creating the immediate riverside landscape of meanders, point bars, cutoffs, natural levees, and backswamps are usually fairly clear. Farther away from the river, however, things get complicated. The river has visited every place in its valley not once but many times, often leaving remnants from one visit superimposed on remnants from earlier ones. It is like a criminal who has returned to the scene of the crime again and again, confusing all the evidence. Only the culprit's last footprints are very clear. Sometimes deep oxbow lakes created ten years ago lie beside marshy oxbows of two centuries before. Low ridges left from former natural levees, ghosts from old river courses, wind across the wooded bottom in every direction.

At certain places where the river presently is located far to one side of its wide, shallow valley, a maze of overflow channels parallels its course. Are these old river channels in the process of abandonment or new channels into which the river is preparing to change its course? It is often difficult to tell. Certainly, the Neches has altered its course drastically many times in the past, sometimes shifting for miles from one side of its valley to another in a relatively short time. A whole series of divided channels (usually called "Old River" and "New River" by local people) occur along the Neches and doubtless are intermediate stages in the process.

All life in the Neches Valley, plant and animal, is adapted to the ebb and flow of the yearly river floods. To the casual eye, the river bottom appears basically flat, but slight elevation changes left by the river's ancient travels back and forth across its valley have major consequences for bottomland vegetation. This vegetation is extremely sensitive to the duration and frequency of river floods, and the slightest rise and drop along the floodplain floor creates strikingly different combinations of dominant trees and other plants. Buried deep beneath the surface of the river in times of flood, black willows and river birch colonize the developing point bars on the river's edge. Cypress and tupelo gum stand in the edges of sloughs and oxbows. Sycamore, willow, and water hickory grow on the sandy river benches up from the normal water level. Higher up still are linden, black walnut, cherry-bark oak, sweet gum, and ash, and above them the giant loblollies stand on bottomland ridges where the floods seldom if ever reach. Finally, where the land slopes up at the edges of the valley, grow forests of loblolly, beech, and southern magnolia.[9]

The result of the river floods and the sensitivity of plant species to elevation is a large diversity of different plants existing side by side. In the Forks of the River bottoms just above the confluence of the Neches with its major tributary, the Angelina River, botanists have distinguished 24 distinctive community types made up of different combinations of species from 189 kinds of trees and shrubs, over 800 herbaceous plants, 42 woody vines, and 75 grasses.[10]

This complexity of plants is vertical in space as well as horizontal across the surface of the land. The climax-growth bottomland forests along the Neches exhibit what botanists refer to as "forest layering," somewhat like the Amazon rain forests. As William Bray observed in 1906, any forest will have three layers—the tallest trees, the understory trees, and the ground vegetation—but forests along the Neches have five or even six layers. Bray eloquently explained:

> In this forest there are the masterful, dominant, species like the white and the red oaks, hickories, ash, walnut, gums, magnolia, and the loblolly pine, which demand the best illumination and so overtop the others. They make the top story. Others like beech, hornbeam, ironwood, lin, and holly content themselves with less of the direct sunlight and submit to, perhaps even depend upon, the dominance of their superior neighbors. They constitute the second story counting from the top.

Others yet, of normally still smaller stature and perhaps positively dependent upon the shade and protection of their superiors, constitute a third layer or story. Such would be the flowing dogwood, hawthorn, mulberry, witch hazel, etc.

Lower in stature than these and correspondingly more shaded and dependent, are shrubs like the swamp honeysuckle, Virginia willow, corkwood, sweet leaf, blueberry, bay-gall holly, and others. Still beneath these stories of woody vegetation is a stratum of herbaceous plants such as wood-fern and partridge-berry, with, finally, the carpet stratum of sphagnum, green mosses, and liverworts.

Now all these plants are, in a sense, messmates at a common table. They share the soil space and the air space together, and the sunlight, each according to its needs.[11]

This diversity of plants within the Neches bottoms supports a corresponding diversity of wildlife. The bottomland hardwood forest contains a great variety of trees, shrubs, and vines, often growing close together and differing from each other in height, branch pattern, fruit, foliage thickness, and shade tolerance. Since these produce fruit or nuts at different times of the year, and send out leaves and buds on different schedules, food and cover are available to wildlife year round. Insects survive the winter in the shelter of trees and vines that keep their leaves all year, and these provide food for flocks of overwintering, insect-eating birds. Wild fruits like mayhaws, mulberries, blueberries, paw-paws, and scores of others are produced at different times in the spring, summer, and fall, and a prodigious autumn mast drops from the thirteen species of oaks, seven species of hickories, and other nut-bearing trees that dominate the bottoms.[12]

Along with the many food sources, bottomland hardwoods offer shelter to wildlife in the form of cavities in the wood of standing or fallen trees. Few hollows occur naturally in the upland pines, but in hardwoods broken-off branches, fire scars, insect invasions, or other injuries provide an opportunity for fungus to enter and develop a cavity, and the hardness of the wood means that the cavity may last a long time. Wood ducks, screech owls, flying squirrels, raccoons, opossums, and gray squirrels use high cavities in standing timber. Mink, otter, and bears use hollow downed logs and butt rot cavities in tree trunks for shelter and winter denning sites.

The availability of food and of den or nesting sites explains why the bottoms support several times the populations of birds and other animals found in nearby mixed pine and hardwood forests. And as ecologist Larry Harris noted, the return of the yearly river floods makes the fallen mast available to other species and sets off a new chain of life in the shallows of the flooded forest.

Winter floods cover much of the mast with water, making it available to millions of dabbling ducks, those that feed in shallow water. On slightly higher ground, deer, squirrels, wild hogs and turkeys rely on mast for food. The presence of nuts and fruits from many different plants means that a reliable food source is generally available throughout the year and at different levels of the forest, from bottom to top. . . . Seasonal flooding produces shallow, warm water areas where many kinds of water life spawn and feed on the submerged mast and other dead matter. Flooded bottomlands are nurseries for many valuable fish. Small invertebrates, snails and crayfish become food for larger animals like frogs, fish, young wood ducks and wading birds. Some of these provide food for still larger creatures like otter, mink, herons, egrets and many other water and land animals. In this manner, the richness and high productivity of the forest translates into a comparable richness of wildlife.[13]

Some animal species live in the Neches bottoms throughout the year; others use them as a seasonal resource. Two centuries ago, groups of buffalo occasionally grazed in the small prairies and openings along the edges of the valley. Cougars, bobcats, gray fox, bears, red wolves, and an occasional solitary jaguar or ocelot prowled the forest. Depending on the season of the year and the availability of food, the valley was home to deer, turkeys, wild hogs, and black bears, which moved from river bottoms to pine uplands and back again. Bears in particular loved the dense switch-cane thickets of the deep bottoms, using them for food and cover for many centuries before settlers' cattle began to eradicate the cane. Besides the many kinds of river fish, creatures of the bottoms were the gray squirrel, otter, beaver, mink, heron, duck, and other water birds. The green-and-purple wood duck dabbled in the fall backwaters for acorns, beechnuts, and the fruits of the black gum. By day the red-shouldered hawk soared across the bottoms, looking down on woods, backswamps, and oxbow lakes. By night the shift changed, and the same areas were patrolled on silent wings by the barred owl, the brown-eyed raptor that settlers called "old eight-hooter."[14]

In the deep woods, giant woodpeckers bounded on short flights from tree to tree, demolishing dead limbs and unsound tree trunks in their endless quest for grubs. The crow-sized, pileated woodpecker sometimes foraged on the ground as well, but the even larger ivorybill woodpecker remained aloft in the dead and dying hardwoods that harbored the insect grubs, its primary food. From time to time the ivorybill gave its startling call, which some people compared to the harsh tooting of a child's tin horn, and the raucous laugh of the pileated woodpecker also sounded across the deep bottoms. To early settlers the pileated was a bird of many names: "Indian Hen," "Lord God," "Good Gracious," and "Johnny Good God," among others.[15]

When the mast ripened in the fall, immense flocks of passenger pigeons swept down from the Northeast to forage in the oaks and hickories as they had for millennia. These were large pigeons with pointed tails, red eyes, and loud voices to make themselves heard in the uproar of the flock. They came by the hundreds of millions— perhaps by the billions—in such numbers that they darkened the sun overhead, broke off the limbs of the trees they roosted on, and challenged the powers of description of those who witnessed them. One observer told how the "scouts" would come in October to reconnoiter the acorn crop, soon followed by the rest of the flock.

> Two or three days later the birds would come in . . . like a sand storm and would cast a shadow over the earth. We could not see either edge of the flight, nor through them the birds highest above the earth. The low ones would cover the treetops and the higher ones would fly farther on. Then the birds would feed and thrash down the acorns for about two hours, when they too would fly on northward. . . . They would continue this for a few days, then alight on the ground and clean up what food there was there. This would last for about twenty or thirty days, which would be the last that we would see of them until the next year.

Another man recalled: "A humming sound would begin in the northeast without warning, and in almost no time the horizon would be covered by such a dense cloud of birds that it completely covered the sky east, north, west, and south, with not a white spot of sky showing. So dense was the flight that it made twilight of the morning."[16]

The first Native American inhabitants of the Neches Valley may have exploited the great roosting flocks of wild pigeons in the same way that southeastern Indians and American settlers did later. Hunters went to the roosts after dark with torches of cane or lighter pine and thrashed the befuddled birds out of the trees with long poles.[17]

No one can say for sure when the first humans came to the Neches country or exactly what they found when they got there. The bottomlands may have looked much as they did in the early nineteenth century. Scientists estimate that the hardwood climax forests developed very early. Beyond the bottoms, however, the mixed upland forests of twelve thousand years ago may have been broken by more prairies than they are today.[18]

Even before human intervention, the uplands were the domain of fire. Fuel was abundant in the form of grass and pine needles. Pine needle fall was heavy, and the grass accumulated in places because there were no native grazers except the occasional buffalo. In this environment, lightning from the thunderstorms of late summer and early fall could ignite numerous fires. Once started, a natural fire might survive the rainfall and dews by smoldering for days in the resin-rich heartwood of pine snags and roots, then break out and run great distances after winds rose and humidity fell. Life in the uplands was adapted to these periodic natural fires. The pure stands of fire-tolerant longleafs were maintained by fire. Red-tailed hawks soared along the edge of the moving flames, watching for game to flush, and bobwhite quail flew in just after the fire had passed to feed on dead insects in the smoking aftermath.[19]

Fires stopped on the edge of the Neches bottoms, the domain of river floods. Here, the first humans found a great hardwood forest broken only by the small openings left by the death or toppling of some giant tree, the excavations of the river at meander bends, or the occasional tangled swath left by a passing tornado. The size of the bottomland trees can be guessed at only from the evidence of scattered survivors: at Bee Tree Slough, a bald cypress 9 feet through the trunk above the butt swell and a 5-foot-thick black gum; near the mouth of Graham Creek, a shagbark hickory 16 feet in circumference and a cherry-bark oak 165 feet tall.[20]

As surmised from the evidence left by their projectile points (virtually all the evidence we have), the first people to see the Neches bottoms were big-game hunters of the Clovis tradition, who began to wander through the area around 10,000 B.C., give or take a millennium. We still know little about these "Paleo-Indians," but their essential nature is revealed in the tools they made. These were few in number, as befits a people often on the move, but were exquisitely made and efficient. Paleo-Indians brought down game with flint-tipped, feather-guided darts thrown with hand-held spear-throwers and butchered the game with flint choppers, scrapers, and knife-edged flakes. Nothing in the rest of their limited tool kit was quite like the dart points, which were made with the greatest care and precision. Farther west on the Great Plains, the Paleo-Indians specialized in hunting such huge Ice Age animals as the mastodon, mammoth, giant ground sloth, and species of giant bison, and the Paleo-Indian dart points appear to have been made by people who knew their lives depended on their tools. The flint points are large, precisely shaped, delicately flaked, and undoubtedly efficient and seem made with an almost religious adherence to tradition. The several styles of Paleo-Indian dart points remain constant across great stretches of time and American landscape. The Clovis point found embedded in the vertebra of a dead mammoth in New Mexico is virtually indistinguishable from points found in Alaska, on the Atlantic Coast, and at Holly Bluff along the Neches.

From what we know of the ancient environment, the Clovis hunters who wandered the Neches country twelve thousand years ago would have found few if any of the big-game animals they specialized in farther west. Perhaps somewhat dryer than today, with uplands perhaps more broken by small prairies, the Neches area would have been good game country for white-tailed deer, black bear, and turkey but would have contained little to challenge a race of elephant hunters. The Clovis point found at Holly Bluff is more likely to have been lost in a wounded deer than in a mastodon. That the Paleo-Indian hunters lacked a close adaptation to the East Texas environment is suggested by the scattered and seemingly random nature of the sites at which their artifacts have been found. There is no obvious patterning to these sites and no concentration along the edge of the river bottoms. These plainsmen and big-game hunters from farther west may have found the thick hardwood bottoms an unfamiliar landscape, one to avoid rather than to exploit.[21]

Eventually, some Paleo-Indians passed on their way, while others stayed and evolved into many different regional lifeways. Beginning about 6000 B.C. and continuing for thousands of years, there is evidence of an increasingly finer-tuned adaptation to environment along the Neches, as elsewhere across North America. Hunting and gathering groups remained in place, exploiting the same environments for many generations, and year by year, lifetime by lifetime, they accumulated knowledge about their surroundings. Along the Neches, people learned that the crushed roots of a certain plant would stop bleeding, and that red oak acorns, bitter with tannic acid, could be made edible by leaching with boiling water, and that certain species of river fish might be clubbed or speared in the shallow backwaters during spring spawning runs.

Instead of one kind of dart point in use across enormous distances, the hunting and gathering peoples of the Archaic Era evolved dozens of different kinds adapted to local preferences and circumstances. The tool kit of stone tools began to include pitted stones used in the processing of nuts and seeds. A person might place several nuts in the indentations in one stone and use another nut to crush them all at once. For the first time, the tremendous mast production of bottomland oaks, hickories, and other trees was processed for human use.[22]

As Archaic cultures along the Neches shifted toward a more balanced hunting and gathering life-style, populations grew, and villages increasingly were located on sandy, well-drained sites just inland from the edges of the river valley. This site preference began as early as 6000 B.C. and continued for thousands of years. A home base just inland from the edge of the bottoms gave a hunting and gathering people access to the widest range of ecosystems. It was a strategic location from which to exploit the resources of river, tributaries, backwater lakes, bottoms, pine uplands, and the rich "ecotones," or environmental transition zones, that lay between them.[23] Centuries later, the first Anglo pioneers often chose the same sites, for most of the same reasons. (As old rivermen told me, "A good place to camp is a good place to camp.")

With little doubt, these Archaic hunting and gathering societies along the Neches heavily influenced their immediate environments by their use of fire. Periodic burning of the woods was virtually universal among the Native American societies of eastern North America at the time of their first contact with Europeans, and this practice doubtless was very old. Indians told early settlers that they burned the woods in fall and spring to eleminate ticks, fleas, snakes, and other vermin from around their villages, to keep the woods free of underbrush to facilitate hunting and traveling, and to make fire drives for game. The degree to which Indians recognized the larger environmental consequences of their burning of the woods is an open question, but periodic fires also helped maintain open areas (increasing the "edge effect"), encouraged the growth of various edible wild plants, and created ideal habitats for such primary game species as deer and turkey.[24]

West of Alto on the edge of the Neches bottoms is a sandy, level prairie, about a mile across, that early settlers called Mound Prairie and modern archaeologists know as the Davis Site. It is just the sort of location Archaic peoples liked to choose for their camps. A few Paleo-Indian dart points have been found here, along with a much wider range of artifacts, which show that Archaic hunter-gatherers used the area off and on for thousands of years. Gradually, the Neches hunter-gatherers learned new tricks. About 200 B.C., fragments from the first crude pottery begin to show up in campsite debris otherwise indistinguishable from Archaic sites thousands of years older. Around A.D. 800 or 900, small, finely chipped projectile points appear, attesting to the arrival of the bow and arrow, and new forms of pottery show up. Clearly, something had changed; some other people had come to live on Mound Prairie, on the edge of the Neches Valley.[25]

Archaic peoples usually are lost in the anonymity of prehistory, but in the case of the Neches hunter-gatherers we know with some likelihood who they were. They probably were the ancestors of the Atakapan speakers, groups who called themselves the Bidai, Dedose, Patrici, and Akokisa. By historic times these people were scattered throughout southeastern Texas along the edges of river valleys and creeks.

Continuing a long tradition, they gathered plant foods from the bottomlands, grew some corn, hunted deer, bear, and small animals, and occasionally went west to the plains to hunt buffalo. They used the bow, and perhaps the blowgun, for hunting and probably spent the winters in huts covered with bison hides.[26]

The Bidai and the Dedose were old allies of the people who had come to Mound Prairie around A.D. 800, whose language they spoke and whom they considered their "kin." These bringers of the bow and of agriculture were the Caddos, the westernmost pioneers of a great tradition of forest cultures extending far to the east and north.

The Mound Builder cultures had been evolving in the woodlands of eastern North America since about 1000 B.C., and the Caddos were part of the last and greatest phase of this expansion. Since this cultural tradition was centered along the Mississippi Valley, it is usually called the Mississippian. Its ceremonial centers were located on the edges of river valleys from present-day Georgia to Oklahoma, with the largest known settlement at Cahokia, Illinois, on the Mississippi across from St. Louis. One hundred and twenty temple and burial mounds are scattered across the landscape for miles at Cahokia. The population that built them up, a basket of earth at a time, certainly numbered in the many thousands.

The Mississippian phase of the Mound Builder culture is also called the "Late Woodland," with good reason. It was a lifeway grew from the resources of the forest. The Caddos and the other Mississippian peoples combined an efficient hoe agriculture cultivating corn, beans, and squash with the ancient legacy of hunting and gathering. Their centers had large populations, stratified societies of priests and commoners, temple and burial mounds, and trade networks that reached from the Atlantic Ocean to the Rocky Mountains and from the Gulf of Mexico to the Great Lakes.[27] The flat-topped mounds, traditions of human sacrifice, fire temples, design motifs on the elegant, line-engraved pottery, and a hundred other things of the Mississippian culture remind archaeologists of Meso-America.

The Caddo village at Mound Prairie was a true frontier outpost, probably settled from earlier centers in current-day Oklahoma and far northeastern Texas. It was located near the western edge of the forest environment, the farthest southwest of known ceremonial centers of Mississippian culture, but for centuries it remained part of that larger world. Luxury trade items like fine flint blades, effigy pipes, copper ceremonial objects, stone earspools, and other luxury goods show that long-distance trade networks continued to operate. The burial mound, two temple mounds, and remains of a fire temple at Mound Prairie show that Mississippian traditions were being maintained.[28]

The Caddos burned the temples at the top of the mounds at intervals of about eighty years, then laid down a fresh layer of earth and constructed a new temple. The burial mounds were also constructed in stages. Several people would be interred, probably priests or other elite persons and their servants, then at a later time a new layer of earth would be added and more people buried in the mound. Evidence at Mound Prairie clearly suggests a two-class society. An elite ruling class controlled the functions of government, including religious ceremonies. A class of commoners produced the majority of food and provided the labor force necessary for community activities, such as mound building and temple construction. This division clearly shows up in the structure of the village, as revealed by the archaeological evidence. The inner village contained the burial mound and temple mounds; the elite ruling class lived in and around the temple mounds, where they conducted ceremonial functions of government and religion. The outer village consisted of the scattered houses, shaded work areas, and farming plots of the commoner class.

Around A.D. 1100, for reasons that are unclear, the Mound Prairie ceremonial center began to decline. The luxury trade goods from the Red River country and the Mississippi Valley no longer reached the frontier outpost. No new mounds were built, and the old ones ceased to be added to. Caddo agriculture was still effective, and the environmental resources of river, bottomlands, and uplands were as rich as before, so archaeologists conjecture that the reasons for the decline were cultural. Perhaps the ruling class was losing its grip. After 1300 the Mound Prairie center was abandoned. Well-organized and methodical as always, the Caddos' leave-taking was orderly. They added a last, thin layer of fresh earth to all of the mounds.[29]

After abandoning their ceremonial center, the Caddos did not leave the area but moved out into scattered farming hamlets, or villages, made up of beehive-shaped thatched huts, which usually housed two or more related families. They soon forgot about their mound-building past. In 1779, the Spanish Indian agent Athanaze de Mézières, a Frenchman in the service of the Spanish crown, noted the presence of the already ancient village at Mound Prairie. He asked a Caddo group living nearby about the mounds, but they knew nothing of the origin of the village or who had lived there.[30]

This social change from ceremonial centers to scattered farming hamlets probably did not mean a drop in population. In fact, it may have meant very much the opposite. At the time of their first sustained contact with Europeans in the late seventeenth century, Caddo groups were scattered down the Neches and Angelina valleys to the confluence at Forks of the River, and more Caddos were located to the northeast. In 1690, more than two dozen Caddo groups were loosely united into two or more confederacies, all sharing a common language. The largest confederacy was the Hasinai, which occupied the Neches and Angelina valleys and included the Neche, Hanai, Nacogdoche, Nacomo, Namidish, Nasoni, Anadarko, and Nebedache tribes.[31]

From the Spanish perspective, these Hasinai tribes were the Tejas, or "friendly," Indians. The Spaniards' first missions in present-day East Texas were located among the Hasinais of the Neches Valley in the general vicinity of the Mound Prairie site in 1690. The French, who placed greater emphasis on the fur trade than on the winning of souls, approached Caddo country from the east. Their first contacts were with the Natchitoche and other eastern Caddos, but by 1714 they had established direct trade relationships among the Hasinais.

Early descriptions of Caddo lifeways along the Neches came from these Spanish priests and French fur traders. Their comments are biased and partial but still full of intriguing details. For one thing, Caddo personal appearance differed greatly from tribe to tribe and sometimes astonished European observers. Hair was worn in various ways, faces and chests were heavily tattooed, and skulls were deformed by systematic binding during infancy to make them "taper off towards the top." One observer noted of the Caddo men: "They cut their hair in many different ways, but in every case the hairless spaces alternate with those with hair. The most striking of these hair cuts are those in which the wearer pulls all the hair out by the roots, leaving only a band or strip along the top of the head from the forehead to the base of the head, imitating the comb of a rooster."[32] Another European described the hairstyle of the Caddo women: "They always wear their hair tied, carefully combed, and dressed like a queue. After gathering it into a knot, they tie it into a curious knot at the neck with a red rabbit skin which they have colored for the purpose with an herb which grows throughout the whole region."[33] Both sexes tattooed and painted their bodies and wore a variety of ornaments. Shells, bones, feathers, and pretty stones were worn in the nose, ears, hair, and as necklaces, armlets, wristlets, and at the knees. European trade items soon were added to the mix. A Spanish observer noted: "They are fond of bells. They also like hats, glass beads, and everything in the shape of ornaments; and things which make a noise."[34]

Perhaps most disconcerting to European visitors was the Caddo custom of weeping and wailing with joy when they met strangers. Both women and men did this, and the Caddos wept at other happy occasions as well. Women also wept in anticipatory grief when unfortunate events were about to befall, and French and Spanish visitors soon learned to watch for this behavior as an early warning of trouble.[35]

Hasinai political life was probably simplified from the grand old days of ceremonial centers and temple mounds, but it was still complicated. The Hasinai Confederacy was made up of eight, or perhaps more, tribes, loosely associated under a single leader known as the *gran xinesi*. He was both the civil and the religious head of the confederation. His office was hereditary and passed at his death to his closest male relative. As high priest, he was custodian of the principal fire temple, where he maintained a perpetual fire, and was the intermediary, through the channels of two legendary divine children, between the Hasinais and their chief deity, an immortal being called *Ayo-Caddi-Aymay*.[36]

However, most activities we would consider political were conducted at the tribal level. Tribes were led by the chief, or *caddi*, assisted by messengers and attendants called *canahas* and by other officials. Each tribe maintained its sacred fire temple and perpetual fire, the latter transferred at some point in the far distant past from the fire of the *gran xinesi*. Fires were of great religious significance to the Hasinais, and they clearly distinguished between ordinary fires kindled on a daily basis for secular purposes and the perpetual temple fires, which were never allowed to go out.

The Hasinais were excellent gardeners, growing two kinds of corn and several kinds of beans, as well as sunflowers, squash, and probably other vegetables, on the light, sandy soils of the upland terraces. In their agriculture, as in their other endeavors, they were highly organized. A Spanish observer noted:

The crops which the Asinais plant are also community crops. They begin first at the house of the *chenesi,* who is their leading priest and the person who takes care of their fire temple. . . . They then plant for the principal captain *[caddi]* and afterwards for all the rest in their order as fixed by the captains in their assemblies. What the Indians do is to clear the land and dig it about the depth of a handbreadth. They do this first with wooden hoes of seasoned walnut, and then with iron hoes which they have acquired from the Spaniards and from the French who live in Natchitoches. This work is finished in two or three hours and the owners of the house give them an abundance of food. They then move to another spot to do the same thing. The planting of the corn and the beans and the other seed is the duty of the householders. . . . They plant the beans in an odd way. In order that the vines may run and be protected from small animals and from mildew, they stick a forked cane at each hill. Then the vine bears more abundantly and it is no trouble for them to gather the crop because they pull up the cane and carry the whole thing home. In their houses they have large baskets made of heavy reeds, into which they place their shelled corn and beans.[37]

The large storage baskets were only one of many useful objects the Hasinais made from river reeds and the plants Anglos would later call switch cane. Spanish and French observers doubtless commented about only a fraction of the Caddos' intricate material culture, but they mentioned reed flutes, reed baskets of various shapes and sizes, reed sifters used for winnowing corn and acorn meal, handsome reed panniers used as saddle bags, reed eating platters, and reed mats and screens used in the household. Inside the large, beehive-shaped Caddo houses thatched with reeds, the Spaniards observed "very brilliantly colored" pieces of reed matting on the beds and "very curious rugs of reed of different colors which could be used in ladies' drawing rooms." Nor was this all; the Hasinais also made reed torches to light their way around at night and reed rafts to cross the river on.[38]

Various other aspects of Hasinai material culture were occasionally noted. The Europeans remarked on the beautiful and varied pottery, hoes of fire-hardened walnut, wooden mortars and pestles, men's clothing of tanned and dyed deer hides so beautifully finished that they looked like black velvet, and strong rope made from the bark of walnut saplings. No mention is made of dugout canoes, trotlines to catch fish, cloth made from pounded mulberry bark, or the blowgun, though these were common among other Caddoan peoples and may well have been used along the Neches.[39]

The Spanish priests often commented about the Hasinais' agricultural activities but had much less to say about their hunting and gathering techniques. Caddo agriculture was a hopeful sign from the Spaniards' point of view. Such settled gardeners seemed preadapted for conversion to Christianity and the mission life. First impressions proved misleading, however. The Hasinais exchanged gifts with the priests, listened politely to what they had to say, then quietly continued the ancient worship of *Ayo-Caddi-Aymay*.

Furthermore, as the Spaniards gradually realized, the Hasinais were still as much hunters and gatherers as they were settled gardeners. Men hunted deer in the fall and turkey all year round, and in the winter they went on long trips to the north to hunt bears and to the west to hunt buffaloes. Hickory nuts and acorns gleaned from the woods along the Neches proved to be as important staples of the Hasinai diet as corn and beans. Acorns had a caloric value greater than that of any of the cultigens and greater than that of any other wild nut except the pecan. White oak acorns, which were extremely low in tannin and required no special preparation except cooking, were a staff of life in the Hasinai diet. It is probably significant that in their central creation myth the high god, *Ayo-Caddi-Aymay*, first came to earth as a drop of blood within an acorn shell.

The findings of modern archaeological research have confirmed the importance of hunting and gathering in the Caddo life-style. One ethnobotanist conducted a careful analysis of the plant resources—acorns, hickory nuts, and other plant foods—within gathering distance of the Caddo ceremonial center at Mound Prairie. He estimated that if only 5 percent of the plant resources of the area had been used, the site could have supported a population of 13,755 people at 2,900 calories a person per day.[40]

Centuries after Mound Prairie was abandoned, a Spanish observer of the Hasinais noted that they collected "many species of acorns, all of them good, and some of them as sweet as chestnuts." He added, "From the other kinds the Indians make a kind of food which serves as bread, just as if it were corn." A Frenchman reported that he and his companions had been served "a kind of soup made of acorns which they had cooked in the juices of meat," and a second Spaniard noted that the Caddos gathered "quantities of thick-shelled nuts and acorns to last a whole year" and made use of hickory nuts, chinquapins, persimmons, wild cherries, red and white mulberries, and various kinds of plums.[41] Another man reported that the Indians gathered "many kinds of herbs, very good to eat" and "edible roots which, like sweet potatoes, grow under ground." Another saw them roasting "the seed of reeds, which is the same size as that of wheat, and when it is well parched, it contains much nourishment."[42]

As these notes attest, Spanish and French observers saw clearly the Hasinais' heavy use of hickory nuts, acorns, and other nuts and fruits from the forest but beyond that suggested only the merest smattering of what must have been an extensive usage of wild plant species. If the Hasinais were like other Native American peoples of the eastern forests, they probably recognized and used for food, medicine, or some other purpose literally hundreds of different plants.[43]

The Hasinais were delighted to obtain colorful breeds of European chickens, primarily to use the feathers as ornaments, but in the beginning they had no other domestic animals except the dog. Consequently, they got all their flesh, fish, or fowl from the woods and river by a variety of hunting and fishing techniques that are poorly described in the European accounts. One man noted: "This country contains various kinds of animals that are good to eat, such as wild hogs, which are quite large and savage like those in New Spain. There are many deer, prairie chickens, and wild ducks." Another stated: "The animals that are most abundant in these woods are deer from which the Indians secure their staple food, together with wild ducks. To these are added during the winter months many bustards and cranes, while partridges and quails are abundant during the entire year."[44] At a later date

(1768), another observer gave an even longer list of wild game species hunted by the Caddos and, significantly, placed Spanish stock animals right at the top. In "the woods they live on horses, mules, mares, deer, since there are many, bison which abound, bear, wild boar, rabbits, hares, dormice, and other quadrupeds, with snakes, vipers, wild turkeys, geese, ducks, hens, partridges, cranes, quail and other birds that are on the beach or on the lakes and margins of the rivers, with fish of all kinds, which abound."[45]

The eclecticism of Caddo tastes shows through in this list, as does the Caddos' willingness to add European domestic work animals to the pot. Even the wild hogs, which were "quite large and savage like those in New Spain," had European origins. Their ancestors probably had been lost a century before from the large herds of swine driven along as provisions by Hernando de Soto and his men in their explorations of the Southeast.

The Spanish and French sources were not very informative about the specifics of Hasinai fishing and hunting methods. Fishing was probably more important to the Hasinais than the sources suggest. Even without the help of hooks and trotlines (which they may have had), buffalo fish could be clubbed or speared in the shallows during the spring spawning season. In late summer many fish were trapped in drying backwater pools, where they could be easily speared, seined, shot with harpoon arrows, or poisoned by readily available plant toxins from green walnuts or buckeyes. When the Neches fell to its lowest level in the late summer, freshwater mussels could easily be gathered from riffles at midstream and along the edges of sandbars.

At least in later times, the Hasinais made yearly horseback excursions west to hunt buffaloes in open country and north to hunt black bears. Of the buffalo hunts, a Spanish source remarked: "At various times in the year, the Indians come together for the purpose of going out to hunt buffalo. The nearest place they can be found is about four days' travel from this place. The reasons for their going in bands to hunt the buffalo is fear of other Indians, their enemies."[46] The Hasinais also traveled considerable distances in the winter to hunt bears, probably with the aid of their small, sharp-nosed breed of dog, which they called the *jubine*. The bears were a source not only of meat but also of bear oil—the cooking oil and seasoning so important to the Caddo diet. Another Spanish source reported: "Usually in the winter, they are accustomed to kill a great number of bears toward the north and they bring home a great deal of bear fat rolled up in moss and loaded on their horses. After rendering it out they keep it in pots for seasoning the whole year."[47]

The Hasinais' primary game animal, however, was the white-tailed deer. Like other Indians of the Southeast, they used the deer as fully and completely as the Plains Indians did the buffalo, making use of its flesh, hide, horns, hooves, tendons, teeth, and doubtless other body parts. The Hasinais had a special ritual preparation for a deer hunt, which one Spaniard described.

> Before they go out to hunt deer, they put on a post in their thatched huts the dry head of a deer including the neck and horns, while they pray to their *caddi ayo* that he will put the prey into their hands, while at intervals they throw pinches of the tobacco that has been provided into the fire. When they have performed this ceremony— which lasts more than an hour—they put its head at the door of the hut and with another just like it they go out in the woods to hunt, covering their naked bodies with white dirt.[48]

Whether or not the ritual preparation was effective, the Hasinai deer-hunting method was highly so. The white clay masked human body scent, and the dried deer head was used as a decoy. The hunting method used by the Caddos was practiced all across the Southeast. Indians would make a deer-head decoy by removing the skin from the head and neck of a deer. They cured the skin and stuffed it, stretching the neck over a framework of cane hoops, then hollowed the antlers out in back so that the whole apparatus would be extremely light. The hunter carried it tucked into his belt, and when he sighted a deer he leaned over and put the decoy over his head and shoulders. He held his bow or gun in his left hand, sticking his right arm through the neck of the decoy to manipulate the head. He then imitated the motions of a deer with the decoy head, moving it rapidly from side to side, lowering it to browse on the grass, and occasionally reaching back to lick as deer often do when they are nervous. In addition, he would sometimes imitate a deer's call or rustle the limb of a tree, so that aggressive bucks would approach looking for a fight. When the deer got close enough, the hunter dropped the decoy and shot.[49]

As early as 1700, Hasinai skills in the chase were being redirected to supply raw materials for European markets. Deer hides were one of the basic commodities of the Hasinais' trade exchange with the French and Spanish, and the fur and hide trade grew throughout the eighteenth century. In 1830 Swiss botanist Jean Louis Berlandier estimated that Indians had supplied 40,000 deer hides, 1,500 bearskins, 1,200 otter pelts, and 600 beaver pelts to Nacogdoches merchants in the few months that he had observed the local trade.[50]

Until the late seventeenth century, the area of current-day East Texas existed as a sort of territorial no-man's-land claimed by Spain, coveted by France, explored by both, and settled by neither. In 1686 the Frenchman La Salle, by design or accident, entered the area and by so doing set off the first surge of Spanish exploration and colonization. The surge of Spanish interest had no other purpose than denying the area to the French and was apparently predicated on the belief that this could be accomplished by eliminating the French-Indian trade relationship. The first step in such a procedure was the establishment of missions and the Christianization of the Indians of the area, especially the Caddos.

Accordingly, in March 1690, Alonso de León, governor of Coahuila, and Fray Damian Massanet, a Franciscan, accompanied by 110 soldiers and 5 priests, set out to establish missions among the Hasinais. They reached the Neches River in late May of that year and laid claim to the ancient territories of the Hasinais in the name of Charles II, king of Spain. Two missions were established, though they were little more than log huts. Mission San Francisco de los Tejas was founded on San Pedro Creek west of the Neches near a settlement of the Nebedache Hasinais. A few months later, Mission Santísimo Nombre de María was established among the Neche Hasinai across the river four miles to the east.[51]

Relations with the Hasinai were cordial at first but soon deteriorated. The Indians proved far less interested in Christianity than the missionaries had hoped. As the novelty of their strange visitors wore off, the Hasinais grew tired of supplying the Spaniards with food, irritated at the soldiers' attentions to their women, and suspicious that the Europeans were the source of deadly new diseases sweeping their villages. In October 1693 the Spanish missionaries and soldiers buried the mission bells, burned the missions, and returned to Coahuila. The first attempt to establish missions in East Texas had ended in abject failure.

The Spanish returned in 1716 to found new missions; this initiative too was in response to actions of the French. In 1713 the French government had dispatched Louis de St. Denis with orders to establish a settlement among the Natchitoches Caddos on the Red River and to establish trade agreements with other friendly groups westward to Coahuila. The first task was easily accomplished, and by fall of 1714 the resourceful St. Denis was sitting down with Hasinai leaders to barter guns, beads, knives, and cloth for cattle and buffalo hides. Then he moved west to make contact with the Spaniards, setting off a wave of alarm in Coahuila and Mexico City.[52]

In response to the new French threat, a second expedition to establish missions soon was launched. The saving of Indian souls was a real motive (as was the quest for gold, something neither Spanish nor French ever quite forgot), but the political purpose of the second attempt to found missions was the same as that of the first.[53] The Spanish hoped that Christianizing the Caddo and centering their lives around mission communities would serve to protect them against the temptations of French trade. This was not to be, though the Spaniards put far more energy into their second missionary attempt than they had into their first. This time six mission communities were established, extending from the general area of the first missions near the Neches all the way to a final outpost only a few miles west of the French at Natchitoches. These missions proved little more successful in attracting Caddo converts than had the first ones. However, they did help to hold the French at bay until the end of the Seven Years War in 1763, when France was forced to give Louisiana over to the control of Spain. Their political purpose gone, the East Texas missions now seemed only a financial burden. The Spanish government soon chose to abandon them once again and withdrew priests and soldiers to San Antonio.

By the 1770s, however, not everybody was willing to leave. At the time of the closure of the missions there were approximately five hundred civilian settlers living in the area of the Los Adaes mission, the one closest to Natchitoches. This was a mixed population of Spanish, French, Indian, and black settlers who had congregated around Los Adaes when it was the provincial capital. Led by a settler named Antonio Gil Y'Barbo, a Spaniard of mixed race who had been born at Los Adaes in the 1730s, the settlers first obeyed their government and relocated to San Antonio, then petitioned it to be allowed to return to East Texas. Eventually, they did this, and a mixed settlement grew up around the site of one of the old missions that had been established near a settlement of Nacagdoche Hasinais.

By 1800, Nacogdoches, as the town came to be called, had grown to become one of the three centers of Spanish power in Texas, though it was very different from the other two. San Antonio was the administrative center and included a town, a presidio, several missions, and a number of outlying ranches. Goliad (La Bahía) was much the same on a smaller scale. The environment around both these places was open grasslands with scattered trees and was readily adaptable to Spanish ranching culture. Nacogdoches, however, lay deep in a very different kind of country, near a poorly defended frontier. Spanish ranching culture never adapted very well to the deep woods of the area, nor did many Spaniards learn to like the landscape.[54] A Spanish traveler's observations from the early nineteenth century were typical and referred to "immense woods where the sun barely penetrates" and "terrible floods caused by the rivers which form horrible marshes and lakes where immense numbers of mosquitoes, ticks, red bugs, gadflies, and etc., breed."[55]

Not surprisingly, Nacogdoches failed to attract the usual sort of

Spanish colonists and never became very much like a typical colonial town of northern Mexico. Most of its population had just accrued, rather than colonized under the usual procedures, and consisted of a polyglot group of adventurers, refugees, and drifters from many countries. The largest number came from French (and later Spanish) Louisiana, but even these were a mixed lot. The chief attractions of living around Nacogdoches were freedom from homeland authorities and the excitements of illicit trade. The town had a set of officials but was never formally designated as a pueblo or a presidio. Its civic and social life had little of the normal stability, and although the surrounding countryside included some prosperous ranchers, it was mostly occupied by a scattering of squatters, Indian traders, and smugglers. Already by 1800, as if matters were not confused enough, settlers from the United States were beginning to arrive.

Caddos from various tribal groups of the Hasinai Confederacy were also scattered around Nacogdoches, but by 1800 their numbers were on the decline. For almost a century the Caddos had played French traders against Spanish ones to get a better deal. They bartered furs and hides for guns, beads, knives, axes, hoes, and cloth, and they came to favor the French, who were more willing to supply them with firearms and liquor. As the numbers of domestic stock around the mission settlements increased, the Caddos showed themselves willing to steal from the Spanish in order to trade with the French. One man observed: "The Indians steal as many as they can; the bulls, cows, and calves for eating, the horses, mules and mares (of which there is a drove) for their commerce and traffic with the French to get whiskey, sugar-cane whiskey, vermillion, beads, cloth, powder, balls, guns, tobacco, and other things."[56]

From the time of St. Denis, the French proved skillful at establishing and maintaining good trade relations with the Caddos. Toward the end of the eighteenth century, an observer noted: "In each of the friendly pueblos or tribes of Texas and tribes of the North, there resides a merchant from Louisiana, who is always instructed in the language of the nation where he is; one who knows how to read and write, and is very prudent to make himself loved by the natives. He has to maintain commercial relations and peace between the nations, [and] the friendship which they have for us, watch their movements with care, and give notice of the least news he learns."[57]

From the perspective of the Caddos, Europeans had provided them with iron tools, guns, alcohol, and many beautiful objects for personal adornment and had filled their woods and prairies with feral cattle, hogs, and mustangs that were there for the taking. That was not all, however. The Europeans had also brought new diseases that doomed the Caddos as a people.

Because of their long sojourn in the New World, Native American societies had been blessed by the absence not only of the diseases that Europeans ordinarily experienced in childhood but also of the more lethal pathogens that were epidemic in the Old World: smallpox, influenza, plague, malaria, yellow fever, tuberculosis, and several others. Thus, they had little or no resistance to these diseases. Early Spanish sources attest that European illnesses struck Hasinai villages with terrible force. Speaking in general of the initial effects of these diseases on Indian populations of eastern North America, historian William Cronon wrote: "Mortality rates in initial onslaughts were rarely less than 80 or 90 percent, and it was not unheard of for an entire village to be wiped out. From the moment of their first contact with an Old World pathogen, Indian populations experienced wave upon wave of epidemics as new diseases made their appearance or as new nonimmune generations came of age. A long process of depopulation set in, accompanied by massive social and economic disorganization."[58]

Social disorganization compounded the biological effects of disease. An epidemic might cause a village to miss a key phase in its annual subsistence cycle—the corn planting or the fall hunt—and so bring about a food shortage that weakened people's resistances to other diseases. Something like this certainly happened to the Hasinais, since Spanish sources began to mention crop failures, unsuccessful hunts, and famines soon after epidemic diseases began to sweep the villages.

Signs of cultural breakdown and social disorganization were everywhere among the Caddos by the late eighteenth century. Many former village sites lay abandoned, their fields untilled. Because of falling numbers, several different tribal groups of Hasinai and other Caddos now coalesced in mixed villages, sometimes joined by non-Caddos like the Bidai and the Dedose. With the decay of the old society and its status system, Indians were drawn more deeply into the fur trade to exchange pelts and hides for European prestige goods. The alcohol they obtained from these transactions accelerated social breakdown.[59]

In the Neches country, as elsewhere in the eastern United States, the rapid depopulation and social disorganization caused by epidemic diseases often made Indians more willing to sell their lands to whites. Something like this may have lain behind the first document on record in which land in Angelina County was conveyed. Signed in Nacogdoches on October 21, 1797, and witnessed by, among others, Don Jose Maria Guadiana, lieutenant governor of the town, it stated:

[Before the assembled witnesses] appeared the Indian known as the son of the deaf Indian, Surdo, of the Bedias nation, the Captain of the Ays nation named "Negrito" being present, which says that he has sold and does actually sell to Vincente Michili, the land that will be found situated on the Neches, extending from the creek of the Bedias to the place where the said Surdo will be found, as the same was held by their father, and belongs to them by possession, granting the same for the consideration of one blue undershirt, one white shirt, eight brass bracelets, one handful of vermillion, one fathom of red ribbon, which the said Surdo has received from the aforesaid Vincente Michili; and the Captain "Negrito" has received a gun and fifty charges of powder and ball.[60]

A historian estimated this land sale at approximately seventeen thousand acres. The Indians involved were Atakapan-speakers, inheritors of the ancient cultures of the Archaic peoples. Michili, born in Venetia, Italy, about 1770, ended his days in one of the missions in San Antonio. He was part of that shadowy company of European refugees, frontiersmen, and adventurers who frequented Spanish East Texas before settlers from the United States began to arrive.[61]

The most interesting question, however, is what did the son of Surdo think he was selling for a blue undershirt, a white shirt, and assorted other goods? Like the Hasinais and other Native American peoples, the Bidias had a clear notion of private property rights over guns, horses, and other movable property and doubtless even recognized personal ownership of intangible property, such as songs and spells that were sung or recited before a hunt. Rights over land, however, were different. Indians of eastern North America recognized tribal ownership of territory (in the European sense of "sovereignty"), but as a general rule land and things on the land within that territory, even the cultivated fields, were held by usufruct right only. The land was there for the use of whatever member of the society was using it at the moment. Rights over land were not absolute and forever, as were European land rights. William Cronon has argued that in most cases Indians, like the son of Surdo, conveyed possession of the land in the only way they knew to possess it. "What they conferred . . . was a right of ownership identical to their own: not to possess the land as a tradeable commodity, but to use it as an ecological cornucopia."[62]

In any case by 1800 most of the lands along the Neches lay empty. Already half American in culture, the displaced Indian peoples from the Southeast—Cherokee, Shawnee, Delaware, Alabama, Coashatta, and other groups—drifted in and settled, often choosing old fields left by the Hasinais. So did early Anglos like Peter Ellis Bean, who was awarded a league of land for his services to the Mexican government.

Bean shrewdly chose land that was close to the Neches and that included the site of the famous Neches Saline, a source of Indian saltmaking operations for centuries. After approaching the site on trails beaten deep into the earth by the Hasinais and other Native Americans, Bean arrived at the land with a official from Nacogdoches and took ownership in the old Spanish way. While the official watched, Bean symbolized and proclaimed his absolute and total possession by "shouting aloud, throwing stones, pulling herbs, and setting stakes and landmarks in evidence of the legitimate and true dominion which he . . . acquired over said land."[63]

3

THE RIVER-BOTTOM STRAIN

By 1828, when Peter Ellis Bean claimed his lands along the Neches, Nacogdoches was still Hispanic in political organization and architecture, but Anglo-Americans were beginning to dominate social life. The government official who escorted Bean to his land was himself a case in point, an Anglo named James Guiens. Like earlier settlers, the Anglo-Americans had been lured to Spanish and (after 1821) Mexican East Texas by the possibilities inherent in a poorly policed border zone. The international boundary between Texas and the United States served as a selective social screen for the restless westward-moving population of the southern frontier. The border blocked Americans with strong attachments to the institutions of their homeland and powerfully attracted those who had good reasons to escape its laws. Before 1836, the percentage of social irregulars in East Texas—outlaws, drifters, adventurers, Indian traders, smugglers, and land speculators—was very high, and this was well-known back in the United States, where East Texas had developed an unsavory reputation.[1] When the God-fearing Zuber family crossed the Sabine in 1830, William Zubers' mother instructed him not to drink the water. As William explained, "Later I heard a popular saying that 'when a man drinks Sabine water, he becomes a thief.'" Another saying current at the time of the Zubers' arrival was, "There is no God in Texas."[2]

After the Texas Revolution of 1836, settlers coming to East Texas became much more typical of those who had been moving west for generations along the southern frontier. Settlers traveled west by ox-cart or ox wagon in groups united by family, community, or congregational ties "back in the old country" of Alabama and Mississippi. Fragmentary records of the trips survived in family oral traditions for a century. The family of Solomon Wright's mother came to Jasper County in 1834 in a two-wheeled cart drawn by a yoke of oxen. The wheels of the cart were made of single thin blocks sawed from a large blackgum log, and since "matches were expensive and hard to get, they didn't have any and carried fire in the pith of corn cobs."[3] Brown Wiggins's people came to Hardin County from Mississippi in a train of a dozen ox wagons, with milk cows and saddle horses following behind. "They all had ox wagons, generally two yoke of steers to each wagon, with a cover on it. Some had a little tent packed away on it. Half the time they was traveling by compass and little wagon roads."[4]

Although the selective screen of the Hispanic border was gone, the settlers willing to pull up roots in the old country and come to Texas were perhaps more restless, adventurous, ambitious, contentious, or unsuccessful than their neighbors who remained behind. The desire for cheap or free land drove many, as did the hope of a new start. In Texas, personal tragedies, failed marriages, harassing lawyers, old vices, and the law could all be left behind. So could creditors; many a would-be bill collector found "GTT" (gone to Texas) scrawled on the door of a cabin when he came to call. As historian Frank Owsley noted, "A debtor might flee into the wilderness and divest himself of his debts as a cow rids herself of the swarms of tormenting insects by dashing through a thicket of bushes." Going from the old communities "into the new country was, to many a migrant, like passing through a doorway which closed behind him and through which he returned no more."[5]

As in the past, a move into the wilderness was selected by an independent sort of person, as Arden Hooks's recollection of some of his family testified.

> I don't know how Pap [his grandfather] came to this part of the country [Hardin County], but Uncle Auss, his brother, started out with an ox wagon and one of the oxen died, and he lost his temper and knocked the other one in the head and walked back to Georgia. He came here later. I describe Uncle Auss's bunch, not all of them, as people who made their own rules as they went along. They didn't go by anyone else's rules; they just rigged up a set. I always called them the river-bottom strain.[6]

However, for even the most independent of the "river-bottom strain," moving west was rarely a solitary action. The pattern of migration and settlement in the South, for rich and poor, was remarkably uniform during the antebellum decades. Typically, friends and relatives living in the same or neighboring communities would form one or more parties and move west together. When they reached the promised land, they would form a new community, usually called a "settlement." Firstcomers would space out rather widely, then later-comers from the old community would fill in the gaps.[7]

Extended families sometimes were scattered by westward migration, but more often than not they migrated and settled together. After some time had passed, older family members who had initially remained behind might pull up their roots and move west to be near the families of their children and grandchildren. One man wrote his son, who was preparing to migrate: "I wish you to go where you think it will be best for you to go—where you can be more prosperous and happy. I will go where you go and stay where you stay." As Owsley observed, "The rural environment of the Old South where the whole family worked together, hunted together, went to church and parties together, and expected to be buried together and to come to judgment together on the Last Day, helps explain the closely knit family."[8]

Another factor behind family settlement was young people's respect for their elders—a deference based on practicality. On the moving southern frontier, older settlers' experience and knowledge of the tricks of the trades of stock raising, farming, hunting, house building, and homemaking never became obsolete. Young people, even after they had families of their own, often chose to remain close to their parents in extended apprenticeships.

The main influx of settlers to East Texas began after 1836. Migrants came from both the Upper and the Lower South, since important immigrant roads from those two regions met at Nacogdoches. From the north came Trammel's Trace, a major route followed by Arkansans and Tennesseans into East Texas. Settlers from the Lower South—Alabama, Mississippi, and Georgia—entered East Texas by way of an old Spanish road leading westward from Natchez, Mississippi, to Natchitoches, Louisiana, and on to Nacogdoches.

These immigrant tracks were general lines of travel across the landscape rather than sharply defined roads. Like the strands of an unbraided rope, alternative paths of travel twisted about, diverging from and converging into each other. The traveler was never entirely certain which trail was the main trace nor free of the fear of taking the wrong turn and getting lost. In his 1857 account *A Journey through Texas*, Frederick Law Olmsted described the route west of the Sabine River between Natchitoches and San Augustine, in terms that could apply to nearly all the early roads through the Piney Woods: "The road could hardly be called a road. It was only a way where people had passed along before. Each man had taken such a path as suited him, turning aside to avoid, on high ground, the sand, on low ground, the mud. We chose, generally, the untrodden elastic pavement of pine leaves, at a little distance from the main track."[9]

Not surprisingly, immigrants often relied on following the routes of others who had recently gone before, a practice called "plumbing the track," or else they abandoned the roads altogether to follow streams or to run compass courses to their destinations.[10] This latter option was particularly common in the open longleaf woods that began south of Nacogdoches. There, compass travel was easy. Walter Cole explained, echoing the recollections of many: "When I was a boy I could ride a horse a hundred miles cross-country through Louisiana and Texas in virgin timber, pine timber. And it was longstraw—we called it long-haired pine, longleaf pine—wasn't a limb on it maybe for fifty feet. You could see a deer a half a mile across the Piney Woods."[11]

Whether settlers came to the Neches country by way of Nacog-doches, by the more obscure East-West trails south of Natchitoches, or by compass course through the longleaf zone, they soon got their fill of stream crossings. The Sabine, the Angelina, the Neches, and their many tributaries formed major barriers across the general line of travel. Set-tlers forded all the streams they could, and when the streams were too deep to ford, they floated their carts or wagons across on rafts or with logs lashed alongside. Sometimes crossing was impossible, and flood-waters delayed them for days or even weeks. Ferries were available at some major river crossings, but the ferrymen were notoriously unde-pendable and certain to raise prices to exorbitant levels when the rivers flooded. The costs of "pilotage" could compound the ferry fees. After Olmsted crossed the lower Neches in 1853, he found the ferry landing still separated from dry land by a mile of flooded bottoms; he was forced to "engage a pilot to take [him] out by the saddle channel."[12]

Once they had crossed the rivers and "plumbed the track" into Texas, immigrants set about finding a homeplace. As a general princi-ple, they sought land in environments most like those they were famil-iar with back home. Wealthy, slaveholding planters usually rejected the poor soils of southeastern Texas for the settled lands of the Brazos and Colorado drainages farther west or else moved into the more fertile country of the "Texas Redlands" east and west of Nacogdoches. Only a few planters chose to clear the giant hardwoods and establish cotton farms along the Neches bottoms, and some of these quickly repented of their decisions. On the sediment-enriched bottomland soils, cotton might grow eight feet tall among the blackened stumps, but all too often it did not get a chance. River floods in spring and early summer repeatedly destroyed the crops.

Stockmen-farmers from the southern Piney Woods found the pine uplands and hardwood bottoms of southeastern Texas more to their liking than did the cotton planters. Here was a familiar environment, where their subsistence tricks of the trade would work. They settled on hammocks and bluffs along the river valley, ranging their stock in the bottoms and raising corn and garden crops on the lighter soils of the uplands.

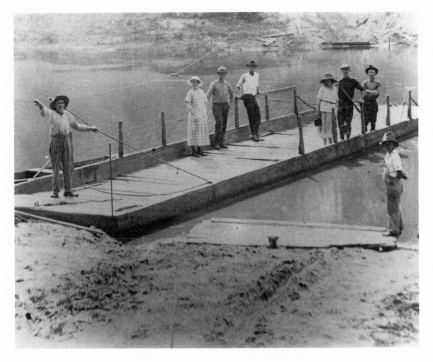

Bohler Ferry on the Neches, Jasper County, c. 1922. Ferryman John Bohler is on the left. (Jasper County Historical Commission, Jasper, Texas)

For the stockman-farmer, the general pattern was a long-range migration to southeastern Texas, the establishment of a homeplace, then more often than not one or more short-range moves as the settler tried to find the best of all possible locations in the new land. A family's log cabin and partially cleared fields could always be sold to a newcomer.[13] Unimproved timberland was incredibly cheap well into the nineteenth century, often selling for $.50 to $1.50 an acre, but some people preferred to pay nothing at all.[14] Brown Wiggins explained: "If you went in and settled on a place and went to living there, anywhere in these woods, if you paid taxes on it and they didn't bother you for ten years, the court would give you a title to 160 acres. Timber wasn't worth anything, wasn't any way of getting it out of here, and they didn't watch it real close, and some of these squatters would get 160 acres off of most any big land owner before he would know it."[15] In the backwoods of the Neches counties, this sort of speculative internal settlement continued into the twentieth century as people moved to the remaining local wilderness to establish homesteads.

When the stockman-farmer set out to find the perfect homeplace in the mid-nineteenth century, he looked at the landscape through the lens of a different set of values than those of twentieth-century southerners and took different things into consideration. Land itself was cheap or free, and the stockman needed only a hundred acres or so for a home base for his wide-ranging livestock operations. Certain social considerations were very important to a new settler: the presence of family and friends in the area to provide help in getting established and social support thereafter; access to markets; and the location of the land relative to roads, ferries or fords, gristmills, churches, and schools. The river was both a blessing and a curse, and a family needed to make sure that it chose land on the appropriate bank. The Neches held the possibility of cheap transportation to the Gulf for cash crops— cotton, hides, furs, cypress shingles—but it was also a barrier, cutting a family off from the other side. In floodtime, a ferry might charge more to take a family's wagon across the river than a steamship would charge to transport a bale of cotton to the port of Sabine Pass.

Most important of all considerations, however, were the resources of the land itself. The firstcomers usually chose "openings" or old Indian fields on the edge of the river valley for their homesites, setting their log cabins at the border of the woods and their cornfields and gardens in the clearings. Later-comers had to clear their homesites from the forest—often preferring mostly hardwood stands, since these were judged indicative of better soils and since hardwood stumps rotted faster after clearing. Ideally, the nearby river bottoms and pine uplands offered excellent livestock range for hogs and cattle: plenty of room, freedom from competition with other men's stock, plentiful mast and switch cane under the bottomland hardwoods, and grass under the pines.

The new settler also looked at the landscape with the eye of a hunter-gatherer, evaluating its resources in wild animals and useful wild plants. Plentiful wildlife, especially such primary game species as deer and turkey, was considered to be an important indicator of the fertility of the site. Wildlife was also critically important during the first period of occupation, when hunting and gathering played a major role in providing food for the family. The presence of wild greens, hickory nuts, pecans, chinquapins, and such commonly used fruits as mayhaws, grapes, blackberries, and persimmons was noted. Also important were tree species needed as sources of wood for establishing a homeplace: pine logs of the right diameters for cabins and outbuildings; good-splitting oak for rail fences; cypress for pickets, *pieux* ("plank") fences, and board roofs; post oak, mulberry, and fat pine for fence posts; hickory and dogwood for the handles of tools.[16]

Lost long ago from Spanish or Indian herds, wild hogs, cattle, and mustangs (usually called "prairie ponies") roamed woods and "openings" at many places along the Neches, and settlers regarded them as free for the taking, part of the natural resources of the wilderness. Settlers shot wild cattle for beef and made the hides into shoes and chair seats, but they also took advantage of the potential cash resource of wild cattle. In fact, the settler evaluated a potential homesite with the eye of an entrepreneur as well as that of a hunter-gatherer. Cattle hides and tallow, deerskins, otter and couger pelts, bear oil, honey, and cypress shingles were all basic resources that could be sold down the river in the years before the family's cattle, hogs, cotton, and sugarcane came into production.

The desire to make money is easy to understand in the twentieth century, but some other important nineteenth-century considerations involved in choosing a homesite are perhaps less familiar. Settlers also evaluated a potential homeplace in terms of the availability of fat pine, salt, and good drinking water and the distance of the site from the miasmas of decaying vegetation.

Fat pine (also called lighter pine), the resinous heartwood of decayed pine trees, was a basic resource of the rural life, and many settlers from the Piney Woods could not conceive of settling anywhere that it was not available. Fat pine was used to start fires and was burned for illumination in fireplaces, torches, and woven-iron fire pans carried on long wooden handles. It provided the fierce heat under black iron pots to wash clothes, scald hogs, dye cloth, cook syrup, make salt, and perform a score of other household operations. It was heated to exude pine tar, and the pine tar was distilled for turpentine—a necessity for home medicine, among other things.

Another consideration was the local availability of salt at salt springs or salt licks. In the former case, salt was present in the water from springs or shallow wells and could be obtained by evaporation from boiling; in the latter, it was scraped off the surface of the ground. Salt was an absolute necessity, required for human and animal consumption, for preserving pork, for pickling, for use as a mordant in dyes, and for many other household needs.

In addition, in their evaluations of a potential homesite, settlers prized the availability and quality of water in nearby springs and running creeks. People settled in some places because they liked the taste of the water, and they rejected others for the opposite reason. If settlers thought they had a particularly good water source, they bragged on its fine taste and healthfulness to neighbors.

A final important consideration involved in the choice of a homesite related directly to the healthiness of the location. Malaria, in its various forms, was the scourge of the lowland South. People believed that deadly vapors, or miasmas, arising from decaying vegetation and stagnant water, caused malaria, yellow fever, cholera, and other deadly diseases—another important reason to choose well-drained sites on the edge of the bottoms. When people moved into the Neches country, old settlers warned them: "If you live on a river, you better get on a big bluff where you get the breeze both ways and away from that old green water. Malaria will kill you if you don't."[17]

The clearing of land and the building of new homes went on for a century as settlers gradually filled in the interstices between the lands of others in dispersed rural communities; the experience of settling the big woods was repeated many times, across several generations. Lance Rosier's great-uncle, D. F. Jordan, left his home in Hardin County to homestead new lands farther out in the Big Thicket sometime before the Civil War. He built a small, temporary log cabin, which lacked enough room for his large family to sleep inside. They had killed some hogs the first day, and that night the Jordan children (including Rosier's Aunt Dose) were kept awake by cougers crunching hog bones, snarling, and fighting. When the children tried to crowd into the cabin, their mother told them, "Well, Josie, you girls might as well go right on back out there, because you've got to get used to it."[18] Several generations had to get used to it. When former U.S. Senator Ralph Yarborough was a boy in the decade before World War I, the smoke from settlers clearing "new ground" along the Neches still hung in the fall air.[19]

Across a time gap of three quarters of a century, A. R. Fillingim, of Hardin County, remembered the hard labor of clearing virgin land. "We chiseled out—I say chiseled out, because it was a pain to put that land in cultivation—a little field, with virgin timber on it and no market; we had to cut and burn it. The Big Thicket wasn't touched except for a few acres each family whittled out for growing corn for the horses and hogs."[20]

In the beginning, settlers cleared land for houses, gardens, and fields as the Indians had done. Brush was cut, stacked, and burned; in the fall, after the leaves had fallen, trees were girdled and left standing. Settlers planted their first crops of corn, sweet potatoes, and turnips among the great trunks in the ghost forest of this "deadening" and cultivated them with heavy hoes. During the first year, or the second, the deadened trees gradually were felled with axes or by the Indian method of continuous fires burning at the bases of the trunks. Severed limbs were moved into brush heaps, preparatory to burning. Trunks were sawed into approximate twelve-foot lengths and left where they lay, since they were usually too heavy for the men of a single family to move unassisted.

At this point, the settler usually sent word to his neighbors that he had been clearing new ground and wanted to hold a logrolling, one of several community work events that also served as social occasions and parties. On the appointed day families arrived from miles around, the women bringing food and the men tools for the logrolling. While the women prepared a big meal, men worked in teams to move the heavy logs to brush heaps. Specially prepared handsticks or handspikes, often made with drawing knives from dogwood or hickory, were thrust under each log at several points with a man on each side. Then, as Walter Cole recalled: "Someone would hit his leg with his hat and holler, 'Give light!,' and them head men out yonder at the butt end of it would straighten up. And another'n would get up, and another'n. And they'd lift that log off of that ground, and maybe two or three big niggers in there, too. And they'd rare back and lay their shoulder on that log, and some of em would holler, 'Walk ye, while I let ye!'"[21] At this point, walking in step and keeping their backs straight like weight-lifters, the men carried the log to the nearest log pile, set it down, and went back for another one. Logrollings often went on for days, and every night the logs piled up that day would be "chunked up" and set afire.

The logrolling was a community work event, a social occasion, and a competition among men. The person in charge matched workers for size and estimated strength, but if one man proved stronger, the other would be "pulled down" when they lifted, his hand jammed igno-miniously in the dirt. Walter Cole captured the spirit of these affairs. "They would pull one another down, show what they could do, and they knowed who was the stoutest man was [sic] in the country. And they had a quart of whiskey in every fence corner, a-drinking it. They'd get drunk about twelve o'clock, and they'd have a big dance all night. Dance all night, too."[22]

On another occasion, the community might pitch in to help a just-arrived settler, a newly married couple, or a local family victimized by fire to build a new log cabin or log house. These house-raisings, as they were called, continued into the 1930s in some communities.

When settlers rolled onto their new lands in oxcarts and ox wagons in the mid-nineteenth century, their tools were few, but their skills were considerable. Most men were capable of building a crude log cabin as temporary shelter with only ax, broadax, auger, and froe-and-maul. Pioneers clearly distinguished the log cabin from the log house, a much more elaborate permanent home, which in the Neches country often took the form of a two-room structure with a central hall or breezeway up the middle and a porch or gallery across the front. Log cabins were minimalist, one-room affairs with dirt floors, "mud daub" chimneys, rived-board roofs weighted down with poles, and puncheon doors and window shutters (if the cabin was so grand as to have windows) pinned together from rived boards. Never intended for extended occupation, log cabins were commonly used for a year or perhaps two as the family settled in and made preparations for building a permanent log home. Sometimes a family built its log cabin by itself; sometimes several families who had come to Texas together pitched in to build each of them a cabin in turn.[23]

Builders made much use of rived boards in these temporary structures. The froe-and-maul was the poor man's sawmill, and southern woodsmen were highly skilled in its use. Good-splitting wood of oak, pine, or cypress could be sawn into lengths, split, and "bolted up" and boards up to eight-feet long rived off the bolts. Rived boards covered the roof of the log cabin, sealed the cracks between the logs, were pinned together to form the door, and often covered the sides as well. Brown Wiggins, of Hardin County, noted of his grandfather's time: "When they settled that way they generally built them one of those board houses. You could split a big board out of the timber we had then."[24] The need for temporary log and rived-board cabins persisted into the twentieth century. When a young Angelina County preacher named Tom Laird married a girl from the Little Rock community of Hardin County, the young couple "stayed there with Uncle Warren while they built a split-board house about 600 yards from the Brown home. They put a fireplace in it, with a mudcat chimney, and Mirtie and Tom lived there till the first child was born."[25]

Like this couple, people got out of their cramped and uncomfortable log-and-board cabins as soon as they could—even if there was room enough inside for them to sleep away from the panthers. The settler chose a well-drained house site on a hammock or small hill, open to the prevailing southeastern winds and close to good water. Then he cut pine logs of the correct diameter, sawed them into proper lengths for the sides of the log "pens" of his proposed house, hauled them to the house site, and stripped them of bark.

Some families had the skills—and necessary manpower—to build their own log houses, but most did not. At this point, when all the raw materials were on hand and the cypress or longleaf pine foundation blocks set in place, most families either called for a community house-raising or hired professional housebuilders. These professionals sometimes lived in the community, but more often they traveled about plying their trade. They worked in teams, often of three and four, and many of them were excellent builders. Three professionals could construct a standard two-pen log house in less than a week for under one hundred dollars.[26] The other alternative, the community house raising, had its own costs in terms of the reciprocal obligations set up between the family building the house and all community participants. The people who helped build a house expected to be able to call on the owner at a later date for help at logrollings, rail splittings, crop workings, hog killings, and a variety of other chores.

On the chosen day, neighbors from the surrounding countryside arrived for another occasion of work, play, and socializing. Experienced builders directed the younger men in the placement of the large sill logs, front and back, which rested directly on the foundations and would support most of the weight of the structure. Then logs called "sleepers" were placed at two-foot intervals from front to back and were inset and pinned into the sills. Later, the rived boards of the puncheon floor would be fastened from center to center on these.

Then the "corner men" were chosen and took their station at each corner of each of the house's two log pens. A two-pen house with a center hallway required eight corner men. One after another the logs, left round or previously hewn flat on two sides or four sides by the landowner, were set in place. Working at each end of a log, the two corner men notched their respective ends to fit the logs beneath them. They chopped the square notch, half square notch, or the more difficult locking notches of the full or half dovetail—whatever the homeowner wanted or enough people knew how to do. After chopping their notches, the two men tested the fit, flipped the log over to make minor adjustments, locked the log into place, and called for another one. As one early participant recalled, this went on with "a constant run of social chat, hunting feats, stirring incidents, interesting exploits, or political matters [which] made the time pass pleasantly, and more like a good natured social gathering than the hard work it was."[27]

The noon meal was a feast, prepared by all the women but with major contributions from the smokehouse, pantry, garden, and chicken yard of the family hosting the house-raising. Thereafter, the men got back to work, often cutting the windows and doors and setting the rafters into the plates, the large squared-off logs at the top of each wall, by the end of the day. At dusk another great meal was served, normally followed by a dance or other festivities. If work remained to be done, participants went home and returned to finish up the next day.

Usually, the new homeowners were left to put on the board or shingle roof, to pin the puncheon floor into place on the sleepers, to seal the cracks between the logs of the walls with inside boards, and to ceil the rooms. The neighbors might reconvene for another communal work event, the chimney daubing. The lower part of the Neches country lacked rock for chimneys, so "mudcats" were commonly used. Chimney builders gathered mud from post oak flats or mayhaw flats (each type of mud had its supporters), carried it to the house on "ground sleds" or wagons, then mixed it with a binder material, such as gray moss, to form mud bricks of the proper consistency to build the chimney. Workers on the ground wrapped mud around binder material to form "mudcats," then tossed these to workers on the scaffolding, who plastered them onto the wooden frame of the chimney. The risers forming the rectangular vertical structure of the chimney often were hewn poles of heart pine, and the cross pieces, or "sticks," were narrow rived boards pegged or nailed into place. The inside structure of the chimney in the "fireplace room" was also of stick and mud, often with a worn-out crosscut saw blade forming the arch over the hearth.[28]

Southeastern Texans strongly preferred cypress for roofing material, since it could be easily split into roof boards, shakes, or shingles. Known as "the wood eternal," it resisted rot for many decades.[29] The McGalin homestead on the edge of the Neches bottoms in southern Jasper County clearly demonstrated not only people's preference for cypress but also the dominance of rived-board construction. Built in the early twentieth century, this log house had a rived-board cypress roof, rived boards backing and sealing the cracks in the log walls, a rived-board floor and ceiling, rived-board puncheon doors and window shutters, a rived-board "drop kitchen" on one side, and several rived-board outbuildings. It was surrounded by a rived-board picket fence.[30]

In many Neches Valley homesteads, nineteenth-century technologies persisted well into the twentieth century or revived when money got short and modern conveniences ran out. Furniture was crude and minimal in the first-generation homes and remained so for many years. A pair of benches, an "eating table" (sometimes made of rived boards), a few stools and chairs, and a couple of one-legged rope beds with the back sides braced into cracks in the log walls sufficed for many. Gradually, people replaced such crude homemade furniture with beds, chairs, and tables made by community craftsmen or purchased in town. Until the advent of the iron cookstove, housewives prepared their families' meals at large open fireplaces in log kitchens often separated from the main house because of the danger of fire. Iron bars suspended pots over the fire, and three-legged dutch ovens allowed cooking directly in the coals. Neches Valley settlers illuminated their kitchens and homes with pine-knot fires in the fireplaces, lard (or bear oil) "saucer lamps," and homemade beef-tallow candles long after coal oil lamps became available after the Civil War. When it became necessary to move around outside at night, pine torches or fire pans lighted the way.[31] Matches were expensive; thus the household fires were banked to survive the night or were kept burning in outside stumps. If the stumps went out, a child had to be sent to a neighbor's house for fire. Such visits were

A communal work occasion—building a "mudcat" chimney, Jasper County, c. 1900. (Jasper County Historical Commission, Jasper, Texas)

necessarily brief. Guy Croom, of Angelina County, recalled an old country saying about a visitor who refused to tarry: "He acted as though he had come for a coal of fire."[32]

Even before a family's log house was completed, family members bustled about putting in a garden, building fences, and constructing necessary outbuildings. Cow sheds, chicken houses, cotton houses, corn or peanut cribs, sweet potato bins, springhouses, and smoke-houses might be constructed, all built of logs and rived boards and with varying degrees of care. The most attention often went to the smokehouse, the all-important repository of the family's preserved pork. Neches Valley smokehouses were often tightly fitted, hewn-log structures as large as the room of a house, with roofs covered with cypress shingles two or three layers deep. Sometimes shingles covered the sides as well. Crude saddle notching might be good enough for the cow shed, but logs in the smokehouse were likely to be locked tightly in place with careful notchings of the full- or half-dovetail varieties.

Another important outbuilding was the lowly "potato bank," in which the family's sweet potato crop was stored, often in thick beds of pine straw. Sweet potatoes, along with turnip greens, were true settlement foods, usually the earliest garden crops planted after settlers reached a new home. People broadcast turnip seeds by hand, then covered them lightly with a rake, harrow, or crude tree branch drawn by a mule. Even if planted in the fall or winter, turnips produced leaves for greens in a very short time—a trait that made the plant perfect for the new settler.[33] Settlers carefully transported seed sweet potatoes to the new homeplace, sprouted them in compost, and planted the slips in beds in the late spring. New land covered with timber was painfully hard to clear, but sweet potatoes made the most out of a small space, producing four or even five hundred bushels to the acre.[34] The sweet potato was highly nutritious, productive, relatively easy to store, and one of the mainstays of the rural southern diet. It was baked, boiled, fried, and used to make pies, cakes, and even beer. Hunters and stockmen took baked sweet potatoes with them when they left for the woods.[35] Brown Wiggins, who had observed the arrival of the Barney-castle family from Alabama, returned six months later to see what progress the family had made in settling in. Typically, it seemed that sweet potatoes had been one of their priorities. "[Old man Barney-castle] had cleared him up a place there and raised some sweet potatoes and was digging them. He had built a furnace out of clay and called it a dirt oven. He'd build a fire in there and wait till it got good and hot, and then drag nearly all that fire out and put a couple of bushels of sweet potatoes in there and shut the door, and go on to work, and he'd have baked sweet potatoes for three or four days. So when we rode by the old man gave us a big one right out of the oven."[36]

Sweet potatoes had little chance to mature unless the family fenced them off from deer and feral hogs with a split rail or *pieux* fence, and garden fences were always one of the early priorities. Rail fences were constructed of split lengths of oak or pine, stacked in a zigzag pattern. Immune from the plow, blackberry vines and other wild plants soon sprung up in the angles of the zigzags, a fact that explains why some rural people called these "briar fences." Well-made rail fences were "hog proof," especially if the worm of the fence was built tighter and the angles between the cross-stacked rails were made more acute.[37] Of Acadian origin, *pieux* fences were characteristic of the lower Neches counties, where bald cypresses were common along the edges of sloughs and backwater lakes. *Pieux* boards up to nine feet long could be rived off horizontal cypress logs with long-handled froes and used to make an excellent fence.[38]

Rail and *pieux* fences stopped rooter hogs and woods cattle, but only the best of them were real impediments to the white-tailed deer, which could jump obstacles up to seven feet high, or to the powerful black bears, raccoons, and possums. A new garden and a new fence meant that battle was joined with the wild creatures of the nearby woods and bottoms. The settler placed deer stakes at low places in the fence, set traps for raccoons and other varmints, and launched a campaign of night-hunting with fire pan and rifle to try to thin out the wildlife enough to "make a crop."

The settler's dogs often played a key role in this home defense system. Some immigrants came to Texas with coonhounds like black and tans, blueticks, and redbones, but more often than not the stockman-farmer in the Neches counties arrived with an old folk breed of uncertain origin, the "black-mouthed cur." This was an intelligent, medium-sized, strongly built stock dog with a yellow or brindle coat and a black mouth. Courageous and fierce, it could stop a charging bull by grabbing its nose or a boar hog by a grip on its ear. In fact, a man could not work stock in the woods without such a dog. Back home in the evening, the cur dog turned to home defense, keeping raccoons away from the corn, deer away from the sweet potato patch, and unannounced strangers away from the door. Several people recalled how their fathers or grandfathers had activated the canine security system at dusk with a single command of "Watch him, Joe!" or "Look out now, Coaley!," with the dog padding away to begin its patrols.

Black-mouthed curs also made good hunting dogs, though they lacked the fine noses and long-distance staying power of blooded hounds. They were important tools of the trade during the long phase-in period when the new settler got many of the family's needs by hunting, trapping, fishing, and gathering in the pine woods and river bottoms. Dogs were important to rural southeastern Texans to a degree hard for the historian to credit until—over and over again—he hears the way people's voices change when they talk about their dogs. A. L. "Leak" Bevil, former county judge, stockman, and bear hunter, summed it up wonderfully well in an interview with Campbell Loughmiller and Lynn Loughmiller.

> Folks in this country had to have dogs and had to have vicious dogs. A good cur dog, properly trained, was worth just about whatever you had to pay for him, for you used your dog every day for everything. A man used his dog to pen his cattle; he used his dog to pen his hogs; he used his dog to protect him at night; and he used him to hunt. He was used for hogs, bear, deer, cattle, panther, everything. Then the kids would get out and run rabbits with them. A lot of people used them to tree squirrels. Take them out at night and they'd tree possum and coon. But when the daddy took them out, it was either hog or cattle, bear or deer, and they dare not run a rabbit, or fool with a possum or coon.[39]

During the early hunting and gathering phase of settlement, bear hams and bear bacon swung in the smokehouses on grass cords almost as commonly as did hog meat. Hunters shot bears in winter after they had grown fat from eating acorns, and their fat was rendered into bear oil, a cooking oil preferred by many over hog lard. The lard and the bear fat often were stored in the smokehouse in large gourd containers. Deer were the most common source of wild meat, however, and were so numerous until the late nineteenth century that people killed them more or less whenever venison was needed, sometimes shooting them from the house porches. Wild turkeys and ducks also were taken in large numbers. Hunters lured gobblers with calls during the turkeys' spring breeding season and "jump shot" or potshot waterfowl on river eddies and backwater pools. The normal procedures of hunting and trapping to protect a family's garden and fields provided additional wild flesh for the pot.

Bear meat could be cured like pork, and turkey breasts and venison could be smoked and dried in the old Indian way, but the hot, humid climate of southeastern Texas caused problems with meat preservation. Fish were easily taken with bankside set hooks at every river bend, slough, and backwater lake, but—except when kept alive in the river current in rived-cypress boxes—fish had to be immediately cooked and consumed. People went out often to fish or hunt and stopped when they had enough meat for the next day or so; then they went out again. When a large number of fish were caught, a steer was killed, or some other windfall occurred, a family distributed the excess among neighbors, in certain expectation that the neighbors soon would do the same for them. Neither overkilling nor stinginess made much practical sense.

Nineteenth-century settlers used wild plant species for food, raw materials, dyestuff, and medicines less extensively than had the Hasinai Caddos, but they still relied on many species. However, the medicinal part of this knowledge did not survive as far into the twentieth century as did many other subsistence techniques. In 1990, a good many southeastern Texans still knew how to "grabble" catfish from under river logs with their bare hands, to set "standers" and drive deer with dogs, and to find and rob bee trees, but few of them knew more than a small fraction of the once-formidable folk pharmacopoeia of wild medicinal plants. Much of that knowledge passed away with their grandparents' generation, and its true extent can only be guessed at.[40]

A smattering of the old plant lore was recalled, however. For example, folk healers used a preparation from the bark of the understory tree called the granddaddy graybeard as a blood purifier, a general tonic, and a diuretic to cure kidney stones. They prepared an extract from the bark of the witch hazel to cure skin irritations, a tea from the leaves of the southern bayberry to relieve dysentery, and concoctions from the black willow, goldenrod, and American holly to reduce fever. Some plants, like the red buckeye and the sassafras, had many uses in pioneer folk medicine. Folk practitioners administered a bark tea from the red buckeye to treat fever, used its powdered bark to soothe aching teeth, and made a preparation from its seeds to bring relief from hemorrhoids. Carried in the pocket, the seed also was regarded as a preventative for rheumatism. Sassafras had an even greater reputation as the prime "Indian cureall" and was even exported to England. It served as a pain reliever, stimulant, diuretic, antipyretic, and laxative, among other things.[41]

Some of the edible plant resources of the bottoms, the old legacy of the Hasinai Caddos, were used more heavily than others. On a sunny afternoon in late fall sometime around 1900, a group of women from the Shooks Bluff community in northern Angelina County went walking across the Neches bottoms to methodically gather hundreds of pounds of hickory nuts. As self-taught botanist Lance Rosier noted, it was a common practice in the fall for people along the Neches to gather large amounts of hickory nuts (the scaly-bark variety was preferred), chinquapins, beechnuts, pecans, and walnuts and to store them for the year.[42] A survey of the subsistence activities of certain rural families during the Great Depression found that during these hard times each family gathered, on the average, several hundred pounds of nuts each fall.[43] Mayhaws, blackberries, dewberries, persimmons, highbush blueberries, and several kinds of wild plums and grapes were also regularly used in jellies, preserves, pies, and cakes. Harold Snelson's family, typical of many along the Neches, gathered large quantities not only of scaly-bark hickory nuts, walnuts, and chinquapins but also of "persimmons, mayhaws, sloe plums, dewberries, mayberries, blackberries, summer grapes, muscadines, possum grapes, and fox grapes."[44] Wild greens also were important, and Rosier noted that Hardin County people commonly ate dandelion, poke salad, peppergrass, sour dock, and perhaps a few other species.

Rural people might have used the wild nuts, fruits, and greens of the woods even more had it not been for competition from their feral hogs, which shared many of the same tastes in vegetable foods. Hogs were the ultimate omnivores, consuming everything a human would eat, animal or vegetable, and much, much more. Hogs eagerly devoured fallen mayhaws and beat trails across the bottoms in search of persimmons, which they loved. On still fall mornings, squirrel hunters commonly heard hogs crunching hickory nuts under the big scaly barks from hundreds of yards away, the nuts popping like pistol shots in the cold air.

Hogs ate almost everything, but sometimes it seemed to the early stockman that almost everything liked to eat his hogs as well. Some settlers arrived in southeastern Texas with seed stock, but most purchased them from earlier settlers or caught, earmarked, and branded wild hogs and cattle already on the range. Standards were loose, particularly in the early days when wild, unmarked stock were common. People with animals on the range customarily claimed all the unmarked cattle and hogs they could catch. Solomon Wright told a story about a man who came to the Neches country in an oxcart pulled by one old block-headed ox, turned him loose in the woods that fall to range and reproduce, and the next spring branded a hundred yearlings. This was perhaps only a slight exaggeration.[45]

However a family obtained its first hogs and cattle, the stock increased rapidly on the rich resources of the virgin range. If the bears, panthers, wolves, and bobcats did not get too many, the minimal "two or three brood sows on the creek" became a herd of hundreds in only a few years. In the beginning, however, many stockmen found they were mainly "feeding the varmints" and soon launched programs of predator control. Just as raising a garden made one a trapper, running stock in the woods along the Neches made one a big-predator hunter. A stockman's cur dogs also did hazardous duty in the early days as bear, panther, wolf, and jaguar hounds. For some, the hunt for the big predators became almost an obsession, and a few stockmen killed hundreds of bears and panthers during their careers. Solomon Wright's grandfather let his dogs run free at night to hunt big game, and he had a rule that whenever they treed a bear or panther, he would rise from his bed and go to kill the animal, "no matter if it was the dead hour of midnight."[46] Many other early stockmen followed the same rule.

Bears loved pork, and in the lean season of spring and summer of the year they would follow the rooter hogs out of the bottoms into the pine hills as the hogs foraged for food. As Sam Houston Cain stated: "Bears were bad to eat pigs. . . . They'd catch a fat hog, and eat its neck the first thing, bite him at the back of the neck, and his head would drop down and they'd just eat him alive."[47] To try to protect their animals, early Hardin County stockmen killed many bears in the summer uplands and let them lie, the meat and fat inedible at that season of the year.[48]

Even without this assistance, woods hogs and cattle protected themselves far better than modern breeds of stock. When a bear attacked a big boar or barrow, sometimes it was the bear that lost the fight. With pigs and shoats on the inside (a "shoat" is an adolescent hog of either sex), the old sows that led each herd would rally and form a tight defensive circle to face a big predator, squealing and "popping their teeth" in threat. By night, they raked pine straw into a bed and took up defensive positions facing out. Some people called them "rake-straw hogs" because of this habit. After many generations in the wild, woods cattle showed some of the same adaptations. Cows fiercely defended their calves, and such cattle also would rally—would rush in, bellowing, from all around at the scent of blood or trouble.

While their herds increased in the bottoms and pine hills, settlers gradually cleared and fenced all the land they needed for field crops of corn, peas, peanuts, sugarcane, and cotton. For some stock raisers, like Brown Wiggins's people in Hardin County, this meant only a few acres—enough to produce a few garden crops and corn for the family, hogs, and horses—but others went much more deeply into the farming life.

In many ways, the system of subsistence agriculture practiced by settlers along the Neches resembled that of the southeastern Indians. They cleared their fields in the same way, by girdling and burning, and like the Indians, they began with a hoe agriculture, cultivating crops among the great stumps. Only after the stumps decayed could they use the plow. Corn was their main field crop, as it had been for the Indians, and they also grew beans, squash, and gourds and practiced intercropping, as the Indians had done.[49] Squash and gourds grew around the edges of the cornfield, and after the corn was hoed for the last time in early summer—after it was "laid by"—people commonly planted field peas between the rows and left them to grow and twine up the cornstalks. Settlers grew the same varieties of bottle gourds that Indians had grown for a thousand years and used them in many of the same ways. Different sorts of gourds functioned as dippers and other household utensils and as storage containers for lard, bear oil, salt, and honey. Other "birdhouse" gourds, placed on long poles around the edges of gardens and fields, attracted purple martins, which ate garden insects and drove blackbirds and crows from the sprouting corn. This too had been learned many generations ago from the Indians of the Southeast.

If sweet potatoes, okra, and turnips ruled the gardens in the settlements along the Neches, corn, peas, and sugarcane dominated the fields. Eaten in nearly all the ways that the Indians had prepared it, corn was roasted in coals, boiled whole, made into hominy or grits, or ground into meal and processed into a bewildering array of dishes and breadstuffs that were baked, boiled, or fried.[50] Field peas—crowder, black-eyed, purple-hulled, and all the rest—appeared so commonly on East Texas eating tables at noon and dusk that some people reported that their stomachs turned and their hearts fell when they saw the peas. Alongside the cornbread and peas on the family table very likely sat a half-gallon bucket of cane syrup, processed from sugarcane grown in the family's field, to be liberally administered to cornbread or biscuits. Families consumed a prodigious amount of ribbon-cane syrup, one of the high-calorie survival foods of the southeastern Texas diet. A family with several children often tried to keep around fifty gallons a year for home use, selling any surplus. Workingmen and schoolchildren carried several-ounce bottles of syrup with them every day in their lunches to eat with cornbread or pour into the holes they punched in the tops of "cathead" biscuits.

Rural households along the Neches had to be autonomous and self-sufficient in food and in as many other necessities of life as was possible. In the beginning, this self-reliance came from sheer necessity—the nearest source of resupply was often several days' travel away. Before the Civil War, Soloman Wright's grandfather made two round trips a year to Alexandria, Louisiana, for flour, sugar, coffee, salt, and ammunition, but that was all he bought.[51] The family grew its own food and made its own clothes, and these were the only things it could not produce at home. Over a half century later, Ellen Walker's family in Hardin County went the Wrights one better. Her father and mother made not only the family's shoes and clothing but also its soap, salt, and sugar—in fact, everything they needed except coffee, which they purchased in bulk as green beans and roasted in the wood stove themselves.[52] This self-reliance and household autonomy became important again during the economic hard times of the Great Depression, but it was always almost as much a matter of pride as of poverty. During the 1930s, C. W. Gandy's uncle and grandmother prided themselves on maintaining the old family homeplace with nothing needed from town but coffee, flour, clothing, and a few odds and ends. This elderly uncle, who never married, even went so far as to grow and cure his own chewing tobacco and regretted for the rest of his life the time he forgot his chew and had to buy a dime plug of tobacco in Jasper.[53]

Around the rural homestead, household chores and technologies divided along the lines of men's and women's work, although some wives and daughters crossed over into masculine precincts because of necessity or personal preferences. My own maternal grandmother, Eva-rilla "Jonnie" Sitton, played a boy's role on her family's farm: plowing, picking cotton, working stock, and helping at her father's brick kiln. Both reasons were involved in this instance; she preferred it, and her father did not have enough boys. Ellen Walker spent several decades helping her husband make crossties. She "score hacked" with a double-bit ax while her husband followed along behind with his broadax, knocking out the chunks.

Maintaining the household garden, as well as cooking and preserving vegetables, was chiefly the woman's job, and was a big one. Charlie Havard's wife, Alpha Omega Havard, was always diligent about this, filling one side of the smokehouse with cans and jars of garden produce and stacking the overflow, three quart jars deep, around the walls of their bedroom.[54] Similarly, home medicine tended to be more the province of the wife than the husband, though he might take her orders for medicinal plants and go out in the woods to collect them. Oscar Allen's mother in Angelina County distilled the family's medicinal turpentine from pine rosin, using it, along with kerosene, coal oil, and medicinal plants, to concoct a variety of household remedies.[55]

Women spun, wove, and dyed their families' clothing until around the end of the nineteenth century. As Mrs. Rankin Laird, of Polk County, recalled in 1937, her family had made not only their own clothing but their own starch, bluing, and dyes. Plum roots were used to make a copperas-colored dye, dogwood roots for purple, and hickory roots for brown. Wild indigo plants made both blue dye and bluing.[56] Long after store-bought cloth became common, women still sewed their families' clothing, often tailoring girls' dresses, men's and boys' shirts and underwear, and many other items from the free fabric of feed sacks.

Most of the technologies that centered on the use of the black iron pot fell within the women's domain. Although boys from the household might be commanded to draw the water from the spring or well and to get the fat-pine fire roaring, the weekly boiling and washing of family clothing and bedding was women's work and was a serious matter. Lye soap used to wash clothes also was made in the yard pot, as was lye hominy, and hogs were scalded in it. When clothing was dyed, or re-dyed, it was usually in the yard pot. One old formula for the color red was a gallon of red clay in a cloth sack, ten gallons of water, and a cup of salt boiled in the pot with the items to be dyed. Women also boiled water in the pot for a variety of in-house cleanings. Kitchen floors were often covered with white river sand, but periodically the sand was swept away, the floor scoured with homemade cornshuck scrubs and scalding water, and fresh sand laid down.

Although hogs and cattle were the business of men and boys, women often did most of the work involved in caring for domestic animals around the place—cows, chickens, guineas, domestic turkeys, geese, and others. Like a lot of rural livestock, the southern barnyard chicken had become at least half feral. It often could fly like a pheasant, and if there was no chicken house, it roosted high in trees, safe from raccoons and foxes. Hens hid their eggs so well they were hard to find. Milk cows and the milk and butter they provided were vital to the family diet, and it was a time-consuming daily chore to watch over them, let them out and in, feed them, and milk them.

Whereas women made the clothing on the nineteenth-century farmstead, men made the shoes. Ellen Walker explained: "[Daddy] made our shoes out of wild cow hide; used a wooden trough for tanning. Soak the hide in alum water and red oak bark, bark turn it yellow. Lay the hide on a log and beat it with a club, while it is wet, to get the hair off and make it soft. Don't dry it in the sun; this would make it stiff. Daddy made the sole first and then put the top on with wooden pegs. Had an awl, punch a hole and put a peg in there, and them pegs didn't come out, neither."[57]

Men took the lead in stock raising, home-building projects, various necessary crafts, heavy field work, and planting, cultivating, and gathering corn, sugarcane, cotton, and other crops. Several times a year, men rode out for days at a time to locate, mark, neuter, and butcher their stock. Letting stock animals range free in the open woods seemed to some a lazy man's occupation, but in fact it was not. True, the animals fended for themselves, but someone still had to work the stock, and to work the animals he had to find them, scattered across miles of bottoms. Even when it was not time to mark or butcher, stockmen often wandered the woods in hog or cow hunts, checking on the whereabouts and status of their animals. For one thing, without this periodic showing of the flag to other free-range stockmen, one's animals tended to disappear.

On the remote farmstead or stock range, men had to know how to do many things, had to be or become the jacks of many trades. Blacksmithing often was required to fix old tools or to devise new ones, and most stockmen-farmers along the Neches had a small forge and could repair plows and wagons, shoe horses and mules, make hinges, and do other basic work. Many often made their own charcoal, stacking split oak blocks into a conical pile, covering it with a layer of dirt, and setting it afire to smolder for many hours. Only when fueled with charcoal did a home forge get hot enough to make iron red-hot and workable.[58] Worn-out metal tools were repaired if at all possible, but if they could not be fixed they were recycled as other useful objects: files became knife blades, crosscut saws became homemade machetes called "hack knives." Men repaired broken wooden tools, furniture, and other items with rawhide, a basic fix-it material and the "bailing wire" of the nineteenth century.[59]

Usually the men took the lead in the techniques of meat preservation at hog killing time in early winter, when the animals necessary for a year's meat supply were caught, killed, scalded, scraped, butchered, soaked in salt brine, and hung in the smokehouse over a slow hickory fire. Men made the gourd containers in which lard and salt were stored in the smokehouses. They made other gourd utensils, white oak and hickory baskets, beehives, household furniture, shoes, treenware, animal traps, and dugout canoes. Not everyone knew how to do everything, but a person was always learning new techniques from his neighbors. On the isolated farmsteads along the Neches, a premium was placed on doing everything for yourself that you possibly could. Once again, the twin reasons were a pride in self-reliance and a lack of ready cash.

The southern free range—the customary usufruct rights on other people's land in river bottoms and pine uplands—provided family subsistence and sources of cash income for many families along the Neches for over a century. The most basic usufruct right and the underpinning of all the others was the right to range livestock. As a good neighbor, you fenced your fields to make them hog and cow proof, then you let your animals roam with everyone else's across hundreds of square miles of open range. Other stockmen's animals came on your land to eat your acorns, switch cane, and grass, but your animals did the same on theirs. Any stock raiser could travel anywhere in hills and bottoms to work his stock and could build stock pens wherever he thought they were needed, no matter whose land he was on.

In the early days such woods-raised stock provided one of the few sources of ready cash, since they could be compelled to walk to market. As Solomon Wright noted, major cattle trails ran east from the Neches country to markets in Louisiana. The Opelousas Trail passed through Beaumont on its way to Opelousas and New Orleans. Farther north, the Beef Trail went through Jasper, crossed the Sabine at

Nix's Ferry, and split to terminate at either Natchitoches or Alexandria. Commercial "stock stands," places where drovers could rent pens for their cattle or hogs, buy hay or corn to feed the animals, and secure lodging for themselves, were spaced out about every ten miles.[60] Particularly in the early days, stockmen also drove hogs relatively long distances to market. A major slaveholder living in eastern Angelina County left every year with his slaves on a hog drive to Louisiana,[61] and Jasper County resident Walter Cole recalled, in some detail, a hog drover of eighty years later: "Old man Will Wright drove hogs a-horse-back from here to Orange and shipped em, two or three hundred head of em at a time. I've seen him drove hogs out of that old Neches River bottom here, bunches of hogs that covers five acres of ground. They penned em up, they had places along the road there ever eight or ten miles, you know, pens to put em in. When he'd drove a bunch of hogs all day, he was ready to lay down in the bed."[62]

Other sources of family income also came from the open range, but these products had to be rolled out in wagons or shipped down the Neches on flatboats, keelboats, or steamboats. Flatboats and keelboats began to run on the Neches and the Sabine in the 1830s, and they continued through a half century of the steamboat era, finally dying out with the steamboats soon after the coming of the railroads in the early 1880s. Just as a man had the customary right to run his stock anywhere in the woods, so did he have the right to add to his family's income by hunting, trapping, and gathering. Furs, deerskins, wild cattle hides and tallow, bear oil, and honey all traveled down the Neches alongside the planters' cotton. With these items went cypress shingles and white oak barrel staves also taken from other people's lands on the free range. These had a more dubious status, however, since cutting another landowner's bankside cypresses or fine white oak stave trees and selling them in Beaumont was not only illegal but of doubtful morality in terms of the customs of the southern common range. Nevertheless, such practices went on almost everywhere. High-quality cypress logs were being rafted or free-floated down the Neches to Beaumont as early as the 1840s, and not all of these came from the timbermen's lands. After 1882 a major market developed for hewn railroad ties, and many of these had "free range" origins as well.[63]

As people exploited the resources of woods and river, and as generation followed generation living along the Neches, the stockmen-farmers developed a web of place-names to identify and describe locations on the open range. After a while, a man could tell another that he had seen his hogs near Peach Tree Point, or had found a bee tree just upstream of the mouth of Burnt Slough, or had located a good cypress on the edge of the old oxbow lake called Gourd Vine Eddy. Charlie

Havard could even explain to his brother exactly where he had hidden a new trap in the midst of their several-hundred-acre trapping range, and the brother could go there and find it. Someone always owned a given stretch of Neches bottoms—legally and on paper—but the special no-man's-land status of the bottoms as open range clearly showed up in the place-names. In the pine uplands, features such as creeks and hills often were named for the individuals who first settled on or around them. In the bottoms, as in the maze of twisting river channels, sloughs, and backwater lakes west of Buna in Jasper County, natural features rarely were named for specific people. Names were purely descriptive, often suggesting the kinds of natural resources to be found at those places: Little Black Creek, Big Pine Hammock, Tobacco Box Slough, Possum Lake, Buck Lake, and Bear Man's Bluff.[64]

The "bear man," whomever he may have been, lived for years on a Hardin County river bluff adjacent to the Neches and sold bear meat to the crews of passing timber rafts, flatboats, keelboats, and steamboats, the last with their decks stacked high with bales of cotton. A good many families arrived in the Neches country harboring the old southern dream of wealth through cotton and often settled along the river because that seemed the only practical way to get the crop to market. Major successful cotton farms were operated before the Civil War by the Bonner, Ewing, Stovall, and Chancy families of Angelina County and by others along the Neches, but these were the exceptions.[65] Upland soils in southeastern Texas proved mediocre cotton land at best. If a family had the resources in slaves, sons, or hired hands to clear the hardwood bottoms, the bottomland soils could be productive, but one year out of three the Neches rose in June to drown the cotton in the field. Many people soon concluded the crop was not worth the trouble and—like the Rawls family, of Jasper County—shifted over to livestock operations.

Many of the stockmen-farmers along the Neches raised some cotton as a money crop right up to World War II, but few of them ever depended on it for family survival. They made a few bales in a good year, and their children rode the cotton wagons down miles of dusty roads to the nearest mule-, water-, or steam-powered gin. Many of them recalled the smell and feel of the cotton, the scent of the road dust, and as they approached the gin, the tortured squeal of the animal-powered cotton press or the thundering whistle of the steam gin.[66]

Many men in the Neches country were like Charlie Havard's father, who distrusted cotton and seldom grew it in the family's bottomland field. If the river rose in late spring to flood corn or peanuts, he could always replant, and if it staged a surprise rise in early fall before the crops were gathered, he could always turn the hogs in to salvage the spoiled crop by converting it to pork. Flooded cotton, or insect-destroyed cotton, on the other hand, was a total loss. Cotton was labor-intensive and too big a chance to take for the Havards, who, like many others, made a living by dividing their eggs among several baskets.

The Havards' preferred bottomland crop, and the choice of many others as well, was sugarcane. Cane grew ten feet tall in the deep, moist soils of the creek and river bottoms. It loved water, resisted disease, and in a good year produced hundreds of gallons of syrup an acre. Cane syrup was not only a survival food, packing an enormous number of calories into a small space, but a ready source of cash. Syrup had been an item of exchange, along with deer or cattle hides, from settlement times. Charlie Havard and his family sold all of their excess syrup to the commissary of the lumber mill at nearby Old Manning, and most other growers had similar ready markets.

In a pattern repeated at hundreds of rural communities up and down the Neches, the Havard family also made syrup for others. Most people raised some sugarcane, but usually only one or two people in a community had a syrup mill or had the special knack and know-how to make excellent syrup. Syrup making was as much an art as a science, and community people had definite opinions about who among them did it the best. Usually, as in the Havards' case, the owner of the cane mill was also the syrup maker; Charlie's father had a reputation for cooking syrup known far and wide. Every year in the late fall, he and his family would begin milling cane and cooking syrup, starting with their own crop, then taking the crops of each of their neighbors in turn. For pay, Havard took a cut of the finished product.

"Seed cane" was carefully saved from cold damage through the winter, then planted edge to edge in the row in early spring. A new stalk sprouted from each joint. After a season of vigorous growth, the nine- or ten-foot-tall stalks were cut next to the ground, stripped of leaves, and carried by wagon to the local cane mill. Especially in the earlier years, these syrup makings were often community social events as many people dropped by to help out, watch the syrup being made, chew cane, drink the fresh cane juice, and visit with friends. At least one person supervised the cane mill, feeding stalks of cane into the rollers of the mill and keeping the horse or mule plodding around and around. Other crew members fed pine knots into the cooking fire and skimmed the syrup, while the syrup maker watched over the whole operation. In settlement times, syrup makers had poured the juice into huge, sixty-gallon syrup kettles and dipped it from kettle to kettle with long-handled gourd dippers as it cooked. By Charlie Havard's day, cane juice cooked into syrup in evaporator pans using a continuous-flow process; after the operation was well under way, raw cane juice would be running into one end of the long evaporator pan at the same time that finished syrup was being tapped off the other. From first to last, however, whether in black iron kettles or modern evaporators, making good syrup depended on the fine eye, nose, taste, and judgment of the syrup maker. White males were usually in charge, but not always. Syrup making was a meritocracy, and if someone's grandmother or a black man from a nearby community was the best, she or he got the job.

For the days or weeks that it operated, the community syrup mill provided one of those occasions in which the whole dispersed rural community came together. People gathered at the mill each afternoon and weekend, sampling cane juice and conversing about crops, stock, weather, and politics. Families in the vicinity held taffy pulls for local young people; boys and girls divided into couples to stretch and stretch the overcooked syrup until it solidified into creamy white taffy. After a little benign neglect and time for fermentation, the "skimmings barrel" at the mill produced "cane beer," a potent party beverage for adult males.

The rural community also assembled at other times—at weddings, logrollings, pea thrashings, and a score of other occasions—far more commonly than conventional interpretations of rural southerners would suggest. As historian Frank Owsley noted, since Frederick Law Olmsted the historiography of the rural South has been haunted by the image of the "cracker" or "redneck": isolated, suspicious, hostile, and individualistic to a fault, ready to move farther west or farther into the wilderness whenever he saw the smoke from other men's chimney fires. Like most stereotypes, the redneck parody contains elements of truth. As one Hardin County historian observed, people liked to live there because in Hardin County, "they could do anything they damn well pleased," and they liked to settle far enough from their neighbors to indulge in the male perogative of urinating unobserved in their own front yards.[67] However, it is equally true that Hardin County pioneers also seized on every reasonable excuse to get together for a social occasion or a party. Beside the example of the clannish backwoodsman should be set the truer example of the master Hardin County fiddle player, who was so much in demand for social events that he sometimes went around with his hand in a phony bandage as an excuse not to play.[68]

Many other examples could be chosen from the oral testimony to make the same point: backwoods folks along the Neches were highly social. Ellen Walker and her mother regularly took off their shoes and waded miles through the backwater to attend church on Sunday mornings, and not just to hear the sermons. Ellen once wore her only good

*Making syrup at the M. K. Withers home in Cairo Springs community, Jasper County.
(Jasper County Historical Commission, Jasper, Texas)*

dress to a social occasion several nights running, each day dyeing the dress a new color.[69]

As the rural world of the Neches communities in which Ellen Walker and Charlie Havard grew up slips farther away, it is sensible to review certain facts about that world. The communities were dispersed, diverse, and separate from each other, but each of them united around different elements of an infrastructure of schools, churches, water mills, and crossroad stores. Most of these communities were scattered across miles of landscape, although some, like the Weaver's Bend community in Angelina County and the McGalin community in Jasper County, were localized in a single end-of-the-road settlement. In an era of animal transport, they were often isolated from the nearest courthouse town by many hours of travel, a gap that persisted—because of bad roads—long after the coming of the automobile. In many cases the names of the communities suggest their origins: Weaver's Bend was started by a single extended family; Shooks Bluff in Cherokee County, a river port on the upper Neches, was first settled by a man named Shook; Boykin Springs in Angelina County was settled by the Boykins around a particularly good water source; Black Creek people all lived along a certain creek drainage in Hardin County; and the nearby Pine Ridge community not only was located on a pine ridge but was founded in close association with the Protestant church of that name.

Watermelon party on the front porch, Angelina County, c. 1903. (Kurth Memorial Library, Lufkin, Texas)

Communities were diverse, and the relationships between neighboring ones could be problematic. According to a former Black Creek boy, the citizens of the church-centered Pine Ridge community looked down their noses (as well as downhill) at dwellers along Black Creek, whom they believed to be irreligious moonshiners with a tendency to allow dogs in the house. Such antagonisms often came to the fore when boys from one community tried to date girls from another and the sexual jealousies of boys from the girls' community were aroused.[70] More than one courting male emerged from a school dance or a church program to find that his reins or wagon seat had been covered with axle grease, and more than one was waylaid and "chunked" by unseen assassins somewhere on his way home. On rare occasions these conflicts between communities (and between races) became serious, with each community a forbidden area for people from the other. A man from Angelina County remembered seeing a black family's car limping down the shoulder of Highway 94 near Hudson, driving on its rims; they had had a flat in a place where a man from the Nigton community could not afford to stop.

Few African Americans resided along the Neches Valley, but in rare instances blacks gathered in isolated communities and lived very much like the Anglo stockmen-farmers.[71] Usually white stockmen, like Charlie Havard, of the Bellview community, and black stockmen neighbors, like Wesley Boykin, of Boykin Springs, got along with each other.

Only when whites moved close by, or when the woods filled up with competing livestock, did relationships turn acrimonious, and in these cases the blacks often lost out.

Sometimes, as apparently was the case in the Pine Ridge community, a single church was the center of community life, but more often than not, different Protestant churches contested for community allegiances. This could be divisive, and thus the community school became the only neutral ground for the meeting of warring theologies. When Carl Havard grew up in the Bellview community of Angelina County, the preachers of the nearby Baptist and Pentecostal churches had more or less consigned each other's congregations to the fiery pit. Both churches had their baptizing places on Neches sandbars, with the Baptists some miles upstream of the Pentecostals. Some Baptists thought this might mean that a few Pentecostals would be saved, since the water sanctified by the Baptists flowed down to them.

The Baptists who said this were serious. As Carl Havard told me, "They wasn't a-joking like you and I doing now." In a time of deep conviction, religious differences could be serious, even leading to violence. Likewise, old antagonisms between extended families smoldered from generation to generation. Trinity County had a special reputation as a "feud county," with good reason, but others were not far behind. Sometimes these old family antagonisms had their roots in an ancient land deal, an old conflict over stock ownership, or a more recent conflict between young men courting the same girl. In particular, the no-man's-land of the open range bred misunderstandings and grievances that simmered for years and occasionally erupted into violence. Often these old conflicts lay behind a fight that broke out during some occasion where many people from the community got together. As Ellen Walker and others remembered, the violence often was triggered by "fighting" whiskey. "Now and then somebody'd have a logrolling. They'd pile logs all day, then have a big dinner and dance. Some of em would get drunk and fight, fight worse than dogs. I was at a logrolling one time and just before dinner two of the boys got in a fight over a girl and one knocked the other in the head with a hand spike and killed him just as dead as a doornail, right there in the field. He was drunk, how come him to do it."[72]

A dark thread of violence persisted in the counties along the Neches and was often recognized and regretted by the local people themselves. Sometime in the 1930s, an old man in Hardin County told folklorist William Owen, "There's a heap of bad blood in here that ain't never been bred out yet."[73]

Nevertheless, the thing that seems most impressive about the Neches communities is the cohesiveness of community bonds, the intensity of

Baptism at Jack Creek near the Neches, Angelina County, 1912. (The Museum of East Texas, Lufkin, Texas)

community social life, and the collective willingness of community members to provide support for others. The community was the only social net anyone had, and everyone recognized that fact. Beyond altruism lay practicality: a family had to help others to ensure similar help for themselves. If a family's fences burned in a woods fire, or its house was destroyed by a tornado, or someone got sick and could not work the fields at some crucial point in the crop cycle, neighbors almost always showed up for a rail splitting, a house-raising, or a crop working.

What is more, they were sure to socialize, eat, drink, dance, and otherwise have a good time while they did the work. The modern dichotomy between work and play was alien to the social world of the communities along the Neches, where all community work occasions combined both elements in differing degrees. Some occasions were more work than play, some more play than work; some were mainly men's events, some mainly women's; some were of benefit to only the individual or family for which they were performed, setting up recip-rocal obligations for the future, some of benefit to all participants. People gathered together to help or be helped at house-raisings, fence buildings, barn buildings, chimney daubings, crop workings, logroll-ings, pea thrashings, syrup makings, salt makings, woods burnings, spinning bees, quiltings, hog killings, corn shuckings, hickory nut gath-erings, and predator huntings. Even funerals drew the support of the community as well as of the extended family. People brought food to the wake, laid out and prepared the body, built the coffin, dug the grave at the cemetery, and helped transport the corpse to its final resting place—doing whatever was needed to assist the bereaved family.

Later, members of that family would help other people in the com-munity in the same way. There were many reciprocities in this rural world. Once they were "caught up" with their own labors, farmers "swapped work" with neighbors who needed help, working for them to build up a store of reciprocal workdays in the future. Stockmen sharing the open range exchanged information about the whereabouts of stock, rescued other men's animals along with their own when the stock were trapped by the rising river, and sometimes even marked and vaccinated the animals of other stockmen. When a family butch-ered a steer or killed several deer or caught a large poundage of fish, they carried the excess meat around to the neighbors in a wagon cov-ered with sweet gum leaves to keep the flies off. A man might come in from the field at noon to find a piece of beef or a haunch of venison hanging from the meat hook at the back of his dog run. Sometime soon he would return the favor. If someone broke his leg or was taken sick in the night, three long blasts on a "blowing horn" would bring all the neighbors within hearing to the rescue. It was the universal alarm, ignored by no one.

In these small, face-to-face communities everyone depended on ev-eryone else, and the rare family that failed to live up to its social obligations faced social criticism, ostracism, or something even more drastic. Frank Ashby told of one such incident from Houston County, as described to him by his grandfather.

> Grandpa said a stranger would move in, or somebody, and they'd build him a house. Every one of em! They'd go in and tote them logs—some of em would peel em, and some of em would notch em. Well, they'd have the house built. And he said they built this one old man a house over there, helped him clear a pretty-good-sized patch for a garden and everything. And he said that old bastard wouldn't do nothing but fish and hunt a little. They kept a-watching him and a-watching him and telling him he better plant a little corn or something. Never did plant a seed, [though] they'd given him all the seed he wanted. He said they got tired of farting with that man—a grown man, too! They carried him out there and put him over a log and whupped his ass till it stung. And he left there. They never did know where he left to, he just got his wagon and left. They couldn't put up with that kind of a man in their community.[74]

Between the occasional logrollings and other community work events, individual families were isolated on their farmsteads, separated from their nearest neighbors by the requirements of daily work and by long stretches of bad roads. In a time before radio and television, when few rural families received the county newspaper, sources of daily amusement could be few and far between, and people grasped at whatever possibilities were available. People walked for miles across the countryside to view the flames shooting out of the Harrel family's brick kiln at night. Every evening after their work was done, Guy Croom's parents sat on their front porch in Angelina County to sing old hymns together, and much later the Crooms learned that their neighbors had often slipped up and hidden close to the house to listen.[75]

A great many entertainments took place in and around the one-, two-, and three-room common schools that served the communities along the Neches. The community attended Friday afternoon spelling contests and public recitals, and major school programs at Christmas and "school closing day" drew large audiences for student poetry readings, plays, singing, and song-and-dance performances. Communities expected their schools to stage entertainments, and woe unto the teacher who failed to put on good ones. As Weldon Hutcheson noted, the Christmas pageant was especially looked forward to.

> Well, gosh, you wouldn't have room to seat everybody, because everybody came! They didn't have nowheres else to go, and after all, they either had kids, grandkids, or nieces or nephews in school anyway. Out in those little old country schools, usually, every darn

kid that was in the school performed. At a Christmas program there'd be songs and maybe some kind of a little skit. You know, we were rather easily entertained back then. Then, sometimes, they'd be some kind of little comic something done. In other words, those little first graders, well, they got up and sang some kind of damn little old song, just to give them something to do. And then somebody'd memorized some little ditty and get up and say it, and everybody would just set there like they were having the biggest time!

Hutcheson concluded: "You're talking about times that's just so different than now that there's no comparison. People just didn't get out and go very far, and any activity that was in the community, everybody turned out for it."[76]

Among these activities were church events, which also were heavily attended. The humble Sunday sermon had entertainment value, and so emphatically did the occasional wedding, baptism, funeral, graveyard cleaning, singing school, protracted meeting, or camp meeting. Camp meetings in particular drew people from miles around. At these brush arbor revivals, lasting several days, the major preachings took place at night by the flickering light of fire pans or fat-pine torches. At the camp meeting, minister after minister rose to assail the crowd with visions of heaven and hell; the biggest guns, the most blood-chilling speakers, were always saved for last. People also camped out, visited, and socialized at these meetings, so much so that certain denominations denounced camp meetings and refused to hold them. Some ministers were known to unexpectedly leave the platform during the meeting to vanquish the card games, whiskey parties, teenage romances, and other secular activities going on nearby. There was even an old country saying about "camp meeting babies."

Families with teenagers sometimes held taffy pulls, singings, play parties, and dances for the young people of their communities. Singing was involved in most of these affairs, but communities were divided about the proprieties of dancing. At the conservative extreme, only singing was allowed. Play parties were compromises that allowed some dancing, but only to the sound of human voices. Real dances had fiddles, guitars, banjos, and all the rest. Many people reported that the best part of all these occasions came at the very end, when boys escorted girls home across the dark countryside.

Chaperoned by an adult or two, young people also went out at night on courting hunts—usually possum hunts or bird thrashings. Former participants report that the possum hunts rarely lasted very long: someone would claim to be tired, and the party would stop, build a fire, talk, and perhaps sing some songs. Boys and girls at bird thrashings carried torches into the woods, cut long cane poles, thrashed sackfuls of befuddled robins and blackbirds from their brushwood roosting sites, then roasted them over open fires. This was, by all accounts, very romantic.

The extended family was the social core of many common recreations. One of these was the simple family visit, in which one branch of the clan came to visit another branch. On the prearranged date the visitors, accompanied by children and dogs, rolled up in their wagon or drove up in their Ford. Then for a day or perhaps two, punctuated with feasts at breakfast, dinner, and supper, the adults visited and the children played. Another common family occasion was the family fishing trip, often arranged as a reward after crops were laid by in the early summer. Accompanied by other family members or neighbors, the family piled food, quilts for sleeping, and other gear into the wagon and rolled down to the Neches to camp out and fish for several days and nights.

Unlike most of the family, youth, and courting recreations, men's amusements often had a hard edge of competition to them. In the very early days men took part in shooting contests to see who could "thread the needle" by shooting through an augur hole, drive a nail, snuff a candle, or "bark" the most squirrels, (To bark a squirrel, you shot into the tree bark just under it, killing the animal by concussion but leaving it otherwise untouched.) Men also competed to see who could find the most bee trees in the course of a single day.

Hunters sitting around a fire on a hilltop and listening to their hounds run foxes or wolves also were competing, though this time vicariously through the performance of their animals, which they followed through the noises made by the hounds. Other men "heard the truth" and secretly rejoiced when a competitor's hound "trashed" (went off after a deer or raccoon) or "potlickered" (got left behind or gave up). Horse racing was a passion of many sporting types along the Neches into the early twentieth century, and cockfights, dog fights, and dog hunts for deer persisted into the 1990s—despite the fact that they were all illegal.

In the communities along the Neches, the old subsistence life-style of the stockmen-farmers lasted a long time. The people whom Arden Hooks called the "river-bottom strain" were traditionalists and indeed inclined to rig up their own set of rules and to stick with these rules, despite progress in state and local laws. River hermits like Uncle Boy Dykes, of Tyler County, and others like him lived a nineteenth-century existence into the 1960s and beyond. A consummate woodsman, Uncle Boy hunted, fished, and ranged hogs in the bottoms, just as his ancestors had done. He and his wife lived in a log cabin without electricity and got their water from a nearby spring until the stock laws, game laws, and old age put them out of business.[77] Dykes was an extreme case, but in 1990 many men and women along the Neches remembered growing up in a world more medieval than modern, a world still powered by animal muscle and illuminated by lighter pine. They recalled spending twelve-hour days in the field, traveling on overnight trips to town, sleeping in wagonyards, rescuing hogs from the flooded backwaters in dugout canoes, and taking turns holding the fat-pine torch while their families ate dinner on winter evenings.

On the edge of the river bottoms, at the end of the country roads, many elements of the old way of life survived even while younger members of families went to work at Ratcliff, Diboll, Bessmay, Kirbyville, and dozens of other huge sawmill operations. Like many others, the Gandy children had a base in the countryside at the family homeplace still run by their grandmother and uncle. Uncle Dave Gandy farmed only twenty acres, but he ran hogs and cattle on a hundred square miles of Neches bottoms. Each fall, the mill-hand sons and grandsons returned home to help with the yearly hog butchering, which provided pork for all of their families.[78]

As Ralph Yarborough recalled, the first automobiles that traveled the country roads caused milk cows to break fences, horses to throw riders, and frightened dogs to crash through screen doors, but they did not immediately transform the isolation of the rural world.[79] Many Neches folk could not afford cars; in addition, for months of the year the local roads could not be traveled by car. Many of these roads had mudholes so permanent and well known that they had names. Social distance is a function of travel time, and by that measure many Neches families remained far from their county-seat towns until after World War II.

During the prosperous 1920s, many sons and daughters of the Neches stockmen-farmers left the rural world for twentieth-century employments in cities, factories, and mill towns, but during the Great Depression many of them moved back home again. After this breakdown in the twentieth-century economy, young people revised their opinions about the value of learning how to build log houses, or can vegetables, or run stock in the woods. Hunting, fishing, and gathering became a mainstay of many families—often supplemented by the federal dole. People sold mayhaws and hickory nuts on the highways and peddled them door to door. Families moved to the river and camped out in circumstances where the food might become monotonous but at least nobody would starve. During the 1930s, when people were in dire need and the game law lacked teeth, the populations of deer, raccoons, and other wildlife species reached their lowest ebb in the twentieth century as people stripped the last resources of the bottoms for food.

Wildlife populations recovered somewhat during World War II, the watershed event of the rural world along the Neches. Many young people left the Neches communities during the war, never to return. The failure of cotton prices after the war pulled out one of the economic underpinnings of the rural communities, and the coming of the stock laws in the 1950s, which ended free-range stock raising, destroyed an even more important one. Not only were stockmen fenced off from their former ranges, but for the first time other people's woods were closed to their hunting, trapping, and trespassing. The school was the institutional core of the rural community, and in 1949 the Gilmer-Akin Act set new standards that made its continued existence impossible. And as rural people once said, "When the school dies, the community dies."

4
RIVER TRAFFIC, TIMBER WORK AND MOONSHINING

Commercial uses of the resources of woods and river began with the first settlement, but they increased enormously in scale of environmental impact after market access improved with the coming of the railroads in the 1880s. For a half century after Anglo-American settlement, however, people along the Neches got their goods to market (if they got them there at all) over terrible wagon roads or down a difficult river plagued with shoals, snags, sandbars, log jams, shifting channels, collapsing banks, and "deck-raker willows."

Only the wretchedness of the roads can explain southeastern Texans' determined—even desperate—attempts to make the Neches and the Sabine work for river transport. At the best of times, the big freight wagons drawn by three to five yokes of oxen took several weeks to transport settlers' cotton, tobacco, hides, furs, and other products to Shreveport or other shipping points on the Red River and additional weeks to bring back supplies. Freighters generally charged one cent a pound for a one-way trip—a price contemporaries regarded as exorbitant bordering on ruinous. Freight wagons carried five four-hundred-pound bales of cotton or around two thousand pounds of other goods as a standard load, so the cost for transport of a single bale to market was four dollars and up. To put this in perspective, during the 1850s it cost four dollars to get an average bale of cotton from Jasper County to Shreveport, but only one dollar more to ship it the rest of the way to England.[1]

The teamsters usually were honest men, but the roads of mud and slush they traveled were bad in the best of conditions and impassable in the worst. The three-month round trip to Shreveport in the dry season might take six months or even more after the rains began. Travelers on horseback could depart the main track in mud time to choose parallel courses through the pine forest, but the freight wagons had no option but to go right down the middle. The yokes of oxen, bellies sunk almost to the surface of the mud, groaned and heaved their way through enormous mudholes under the curses and whip-cracks of the teamsters. If the oxen got stuck, the teamsters had no option but to "whip them out." Freighters often descended from the wagons and wallowed in the mud alongside their oxen and mules, a practice that led one veteran to remark that he knew the Crockett-Nacogdoches road "from one end to the other and six feet down." In wet seasons, teamsters sometimes traveled together in extended wagon trains so that they could pool their teams to get their wagons through mudholes and across boggy bottoms. Nevertheless, flooded streams often blocked them for days or even weeks at a time as they waited for the water to fall and ferries to resume operation.[2]

Travelers from the older southern states were accustomed to bad roads, but they often remarked on the roads of southeastern Texas as terrible beyond anything in their experience. Local farmers sometimes gave up on wheeled vehicles altogether and used "mud sleds" to transport goods to and from nearby market towns. Bad roads occasionally paralyzed the economic life of the infant Texas Republic. During the summer of 1839, President Mirabeau Lamar's advisers told him that if the roads did not improve, no provision wagons would reach the frontier capital of Austin before winter.[3] Five years later, Englishman William Bollaert remarked about another terrible mud season during a visit to southeastern Texas: "Some waggons [sic] have arrived today at Huntsville only 3 *months* from Houston. Water navigation forever! Hauling is no go!"[4]

Having learned this lesson farther east, many new settlers along the Neches were of the same opinion. Newcomers chose their lands with an eye to river access, and many of the first commercial centers were river ports (or would-be river ports) on bluffs along the Neches and its major tributary, the Angelina River. Shooks Bluff on the upper Neches was one, though settlers there soon learned, to their sorrow, that steamboats could reach that far upriver only at times of extreme high water. Rockland, one hundred river miles downstream, was the usual head of steamboat navigation on the Neches. Marion, on the Angelina, was the first seat of county government in Angelina County. Earlier known as Mose's Bluff and McNeill's Landing, in 1846 Marion had a general store, apothecary, blacksmith shop, river ferry, and several houses.[5]

Bevilport, on the Angelina just above its confluence with the Neches, was the most important river port in northeastern Jasper County. Surveyed by Captain Andrew Smyth's brother George W. Smyth and incorporated in 1836, Bevilport developed a major street and a number of stores along the waterfront. The stores and a large hotel (built in the 1850s) faced the river, with large porches extending for several feet beyond the bank. Travelers could pace the porches at their leisure, gazing down at the busy wharves where flatboats, keelboats, and steamboats loaded and unloaded their cargoes. In the decades before the Civil War, flatboats and keelboats carried most river cargoes. After the war, steamboats like the *Laura, Camargo,* and *Sun Flower* moored alongside the waterfront, unloading the latest fashions from Galveston and loading the various crops to be shipped downriver. Downstream the steamboats stopped at the major ports of Town Bluff, Wright's Landing, Weiss's Bluff (Bear Man's Bluff), and Beaumont, as well as many places in between. Then they entered Sabine Lake and made one last stop at Sabine Pass before going on to Galveston or New Orleans.[6]

In the first decades of the twentieth century, a few men and women still recalled the steamboat era on the rivers of southeastern Texas. A certain Captain Weiss testified, "I desire to say that I have helped to wear out two steamboats on these rivers, and as I have run a four-hundred-bale boat as high up the Angelina as Patonia in Nacogdoches County to Rockland on the Neches and to Bellzoria on the Sabine, I feel I am competent to speak on these matters."[7] Captain Andrew Smyth's daughter Minty remembered: "It was a great sight when the whistle would blow for some of the landings to see all the people hurrying to the riverbank. I can see now the Negroes carrying sides of bacon and other goods on their heads from the deck of the *Laura* to the shore and just as if it were yesterday I can hear them singing their favorite song: 'I'm all the way from Phil-a-del-fee-ah.'"[8]

Other contemporaries took a less sanguine view of the romantic Neches steamboat era, however. Professional rivermen from the Mississippi drainage regarded the Neches, Angelina, and Sabine as shallow, dangerous, and marginal rivers, plagued by cycles of flood and low water and full of boat-killing obstacles. The Rockland Shoal on the Neches, Blue Buck Shoal on the Sabine, and Devil's Racetrack Shoal on the Angelina threatened to tear the bottom out of any vessel whose captain had lingered too long upstream while the river fell. At any water level, "planters" (unseen snags firmly planted in the bottom), "sawyers" (snags sawing up and down in the current and breaking the surface), and "sleeping sawyers" (snags sawing up and down beneath the surface) lay in wait, ready to pierce the thin hulls of unlucky or unwary steamboats. When steamboats first began running on the southeastern rivers in the 1840s, many made only two or three trips before being snagged and sunk, and periodic sinkings continued to the end of the steamboat era. Visible at low water, the wrecks remained on the bottom for many years, and old rivermen in the 1920s and 1930s could still point out to historians the remnants of the *Pearl River* (snagged and sunk near Spurger) and other sunk steamboats.[9]

Perhaps because of the dangers, many of the early southeastern

Texas steamboats seem to have been a far cry from the floating palaces that plied the mighty Mississippi. An unimpressed English traveler described her Texas steamboat as having the appearance of a wooden shack on a large raft, and another disgusted passenger dismissed his craft as a "small, filthy, horribly managed concern" serving only tough beef, Irish potatoes, and coffee.[10] Passengers on the latter boat supplemented this monotonous diet by hunting and fishing during the considerable periods when their boat remained grounded on sandbars.[11] Early steamboats on the Neches were sometimes underpowered as well. A descendant of the captain of the *Camargo*, a ninety-two-ton square-nosed boat that began operating before the Civil War, later recalled his boyhood experiences aboard the vessel: "The power was insufficient to push it up against the current and likewise not enough to hold it back going downstream. It was not unusual, when the water was high, for the boat to hang up on a sweet gum tree or a cypress even though the thing had been going forward in reverse all the time to slow her up! Then followed the business of saving the cotton that had gone overboard with the impact."[12]

Captain Andrew Smyth, of Bevilport, whose career encompassed nearly the whole era of river transport on the Neches, was one of the last captains of the wayward *Camargo*. Smyth and two other investors bought the boat in Galveston in 1869 for the bargain price of three thousand dollars, and Smyth ran it on the Neches until 1871. The partners got their money back and a little more, but in 1871 on a trip downriver the steering mechanism of the *Camargo* broke, and the boat went on a tear from one bank to another, ramming into logs and narrowly missing underwater snags that would have sunk it. After the boat came to rest by accident in a cypress backwater, Captain Smyth swore "Never again!," and he and his partners sold the *Camargo* and set out to find a real steamboat.[13]

Andrew Smyth had come to Texas around 1840 and taken a job as overseer on his older brother's plantation, Walnut Run, near Bevilport. Although he soon owned his own lands and might have emulated George's agricultural example, Andrew drifted into the riverman's life. To raise cash to develop his property, he built a flatboat from timber on his own land and floated a load of cotton downriver to Sabine Pass in 1844. Evidently he enjoyed himself and liked the ready cash this produced, since in 1846 he hired three "Congo Negroes" from a neighboring farmer and built and floated three rafts to the coast. Local farmers booked space on Andrew Smyth's rafts even before Smyth and his men finished constructing them. River transport to Sabine Pass cost Jasper County farmers only one dollar a bale in the 1840s and 1850s, but their problem was finding a riverman whom they could trust not to sink their cotton to the bottom of the river or run off with the money. A reputable and dependable local man like Andrew Smyth had no trouble getting business.

Smyth and his crew floated the first of the three rafts to the Gulf in April 1846, carrying ninety-two bales of cotton at a cost to Smyth of ten dollars. The trip took about three weeks. By the third trip of that year, Smyth and the "Congo Negroes" had become skilled raftsmen, deftly handling the long poles with which they kept their ponderous crafts off drifts, sandbars, and cutbanks. The river raft was a rectangular box of heavy hewn timbers with sloping ends, a rough deck covering the cargo, and a board shack or tent perched on top as shelter for the crew. After a one-way trip, rivermen sold their raft for its timber in Sabine Pass for nearly as much profit as they made in freight.[14]

On these trips people asked various favors of Smyth, giving him lists of things they wanted him to buy in Sabine Pass and Galveston and asking him to make arrangements to have the goods shipped upstream on the next keelboat. This demonstrated to him the profits that might be gained from a two-way trip and set him to thinking about building a keelboat. There were keelboatmen on the southeastern rivers, but few dependable ones. Most went into "merry retirement" at the end of each trip, going back to work only when their money ran out. Rafts were temporary crafts and seldom given names, but not so keelboats. In 1846 Smyth built a keelboat, which he called the *Jasper.* Like others of its kind, it was designed to move large quantities of freight up and down western rivers. Looking rather like Noah's ark, the *Jasper* was a long narrow oval, pointed at both ends, with a stout keel running from bow to stern and strong ribs sheathed with caulked planking. A large, decked cargo box filled most of the hull and rose above the gunwales, and on top of it was built a small cabin. An enormous rudder, perched on a bent pole, could be moved to either end of the two-ended craft as needed. The crew cabin had a table, a hearth located under a smoke hole in the roof, a couple of bunks attached to the walls, and an odd-shaped window with wooden shutters.[15] Not the least of the virtues of the keelboat was the right of the man who ran one to style himself "captain." In June 1846, Captain Smyth took the *Jasper* on the first of many runs down the Neches. Nimble and maneuverable craft compared with rafts, keelboats often descended the Neches from upstream of Shooks Bluff and descended the Angelina from upstream of Patonia, so Smyth's trip from Bevilport to Sabine Pass was relatively easy. With its hold full of cotton, most of the time the *Jasper* just drifted with the current, but when Captain Smyth needed to maneuver, a few thrusts on the poles or several pulls on the oars gave the keelboat the momentum to answer its rudder. At Sabine Pass the farmers' cotton was unloaded and the hold filled with orders for everything from pins to parlor stoves; then the *Jasper* took on extra crew for the hard trip back upstream.

Keelboats were driven by sails, current, or manpower, but on the trip back up the twisting, tree-lined Neches only manpower worked. Keeping to "eddy water" and the slower current next to the bank, the *Jasper* plodded its way back upriver under power of oars, white ash poles, or towlines. The long poles had metal "shoes" at one end and rounded knobs on the other and probably were used most of the time on the relatively shallow Neches. On either side of the cargo box lay a narrow wooden catwalk that the French called the *passe avant*. Wooden crosspieces—cleats—were nailed to it a foot or so apart to give the polemen traction when they walked from bow to stern. In a cycle repeated thousands of times in the course of a day, crewmen walked forward, faced astern, set their poles in the river bottom, put the round knobs in the hollows of their shoulders, then bent over their poles and walked to the stern in unison, thrusting the boat upstream. With a strong current, head winds, or heavy cargo, the polemen bent over so far they sometimes used their hands as well as their feet on the deck cleats. While this process went on, a rope might be used to snub the *Jasper* to a tree trunk on the bank to prevent it from slipping farther downstream. At some point the crew resorted to the towrope, usually pulled by men because the banks were too obstructed to use animals.

Eventually the *Jasper* reached Bevilport, but the trip upriver was slow and hard going, and the rivermen needed diversions. The man whose turn it was to operate the rudder (the easy task) might improvise a song, sing it until he was tired or ran out of imagination, then let it be picked up by other improvisers in the crew, the African Americans included. Few other vessels traveled the river, and most of the professional rivermen knew each other, so another keelboat or raft coming downstream often signaled the end of work for that day. The rivermen pulled over to the bank, built a fire, socialized, and tapped their whiskey kegs.[16]

On the way upstream the *Jasper* stopped to transact business at almost every river landing—to unload goods or to pay off a client for his cotton. Farmers who did not have river landings met Smyth at Bevilport to collect their cotton money and pick up their goods. Smyth's account books might record that he owed one man a certain amount in cash from the sale of cotton, less the cost of four sacks of salt, a portion of the cost of the trip from Sabine Pass to Galveston to purchase a bellows, and the cost of hauling the salt and the bellows aboard the *Jasper* to Bevilport. The bookkeeping differed for every client.[17]

Captain Smyth ran keelboats and flatboats on the Neches for twenty years after he built the *Jasper*. In 1866, following the relative inactivity of the Civil War years, he took six flatboats downriver filled with cotton at two dollars a bale and cleared a profit of nine hundred dollars. While at Sabine Pass, Smyth made his usual trips to Galveston to place orders for goods to be shipped upriver on the steamboats *Pelican State, Early Bird, Rough and Ready,* or *Sun Flower.*

Although keelboats and flatboats continued to run on upper sections of the Neches and Angelina after 1870, steamboats were taking over most of the river traffic downsteam of Rockland and Bevilport, and Smyth and his Jasper County business partners soon made the transition to steam. Captain Smyth operated the steamboat *Camargo* from 1869 to 1871 and the steamboat *Laura* from 1871 to 1879. Purchased in Evansville, Indiana, for eleven thousand dollars, the *Laura* was as different from the earlier boat as daylight from dark. Nattily painted in green and white, the *Laura* was 115 feet long and 32 feet wide and was powered by an efficient forty-horse engine. Above a broad cargo deck of six-hundred-bale capacity was a passenger deck with five small cabins down each side of a central saloon. The saloon featured such amenities as sofas, mirrors, a big mahogany sideboard, a grand piano, and a long dining table with chairs. A tall iron stove served to heat the saloon in winter, and doors with louvered inserts opened to the deck in summer to let in every breeze.[18]

After a safe descent of the Mississippi and a trip along the Louisiana coast, the *Laura* ascended the Neches to its new home port. A small but respectable steamboat on the Mississippi seemed a floating palace on the backwaters of southeastern Texas, and the *Laura* impressed all who saw or traveled on it. Smyth's business partners also expressed pleasure— after they got over their initial shock at the price. The captain had spent two thousand dollars more than the nine thousand dollars allotted for purchase.

The *Laura* soon began its run from Bevilport to Sabine Pass, carrying cotton and other produce downsteam, supplies upstream, and passengers both ways. Passage with a private cabin, meals, and saloon privileges cost fifteen dollars; deck passage cost six dollars. On the run downsteam the *Laura* stopped at the major ports of Town Bluff, Work's Landing, Wright's Landing, Yellow Bluff, Bear Man's Bluff, Bunn's Bluff, Concord, and scores of private landings in between. At every river community, farmers, merchants, and townspeople rushed to the wharves to do business or just to see what freight and passengers were aboard. When they heard the *Laura*'s whistle, field hands ran to the edge of the river fields to see it go by. Occasionally a small group of travelers stood on the bank and waved handkerchiefs, signaling the boat to come over and pick them up.

The Steamboat Laura, *1880s.* (The Museum of East Texas, Lufkin, Texas)

"Packet day," the first riverboat visit after the low-water season, was an especially momentous occasion as people hurried down to the landing with their accumulations of things to sell. On either side of the Big Thicket, bear oil sold well, as did deer hides, tallow, wild honey, home-made palmetto hats, and bear, otter and panther furs. Sellers packaged their bear oil and wild honey in large gourds that were often polished, beautifully decorated, and sealed with whittled wooden corks.[19]

The *Laura* proved extremely profitable, and by 1875 the partners had recouped their purchase price. Captain Smyth operated it until his sudden death in 1879, and others ran the steamboat into the 1880s, but the end of the Neches riverboat era was just over the horizon. For one thing, a ruder race of rivermen now occupied the scene, floating logs and log rafts to the new sawmills at Beaumont and Orange. An old Mississippi River saying held that "the raft is king of the waters," since the largest steamboat had to give way to its ponderous passage.[20] As the 1870s passed into the 1880s, riverboat captains had more and more trouble dodging the increasing numbers of rafts and free-floating saw-logs and picking their way through logjams and other obstructions. The Neches had always contained more than its share of snags, sand-bars, and overhanging trees, but now the river trip was becoming impossible. At the same time as the rivers filled with logs, the railroads built across the Neches country from south to north and west to east;

they offered a cheap, swift, year-round transport, with which the steamboats could not compete.

Even at this late date, some people kept the riverboat faith, however. At the insistence of local politicians, the U.S. government authorized studies and proposals for navigation improvements on the Neches and the Sabine in 1882 and 1892.[21] Steamboat backers launched the *Neches Belle* in 1889 and ran it on the Neches and the Sabine for a decade. A thousand-bale boat far more grand than the *Laura*, the *Neches Belle* featured luxurious cabins and a gilded saloon with not only a piano but also a live band. Ornamental coops housed chickens in the *Neches Belle's* pilothouse to supplement the wild game that was the steamboat passenger's usual fare, and there were other amenities, but none of these could save the *Neches Belle* from the general fate of steamboat transport. On its last trip up the Sabine to Logansport in 1898, the steamboat carried bridge timbers for one of the railroads that soon replaced it.[22]

Interviewed in 1986, timberman and raftsman R. J. Rawls, of Woodville, never saw a Neches steamboat in operation, though he recalled from childhood the thunderous whistles of the last boats echoing across miles of silent bottoms. Just as Andrew Smyth's career spanned the riverboat era on the Neches, that of R. J. Rawls spanned much of the boom era of cut-and-get-out logging. As a boy, he went to work with timber contractors cutting valley-side timber, drying it, dragging it to the river, and dogging it into rafts bound for Beaumont. Later, he labored in the woods crews of major timber companies as they cut the virgin timber along log tram rights-of-way. For fourteen years Rawls worked as a "flathead" in a two-person felling team, pulling one side of a man-killing "Simon saw" opposite the same African-American partner. After rising to positions of higher responsibility in the woods crew, he ended his logging career as a jack-of-all-trades in the small "peckerwood" mills that came in for the leavings after the big companies had cut out.[23]

In the beginning, all the mills were small. The first settlers in southeastern Texas supplied all of their needs they could with the rived boards made by the poor man's sawmill of the froe-and-maul. If they had to have sawn boards of a considerable length, they slowly and laboriously used the pit saw—a two-man ripsaw in which one man (the less fortunate one) stood in a pit underneath the log being sawed and "ate a lot of sawdust."[24]

The pit saw cut only two or three hundred board feet a day, but the water-powered sash saw, which soon replaced it, could cut twenty times that much. The sash saw had a blade fixed in a wooden frame that moved up and down with the action of a crank attached to a large, overshot waterwheel. The log moved against the saw, being either pushed by hand on a wagon or drawn by a pawl-and-ratchet gear working off the wheel. A water-powered sash saw cut up to three thousand board feet a day, but it was still leisurely in operation; one man recalled that the person who fed it "could read the Bible or the *Galveston News* while the saw was cutting."[25]

Water-powered sash saws spread across southeastern Texas as the country filled up with settlers. Every little community soon had a multipurpose water mill that ground corn, ginned cotton, and ran a small sash saw cutting wood for local consumption. In the 1960s one old Newton County settler named and described no less than twenty-six former county water mills for a feature writer of the *Beaumont Enterprise*.[26]

While the Neches Valley stockmen-farmers wielded their froes and broadaxes and while the water-powered sash saws nibbled at the forest, serious timbering operations began on the coastal reaches of Buffalo Bayou, the San Jacinto River, the Neches, and the Sabine. Around 1830 the Harris family built a steam-powered, two-sash-saw mill at the head of navigation on Buffalo Bayou. William Zuber, who observed the mill in operation, recalled: "This was the first steam mill I ever saw— the first built east of the Sabine River. . . . Much of the land owned by the Harris brothers was a forest of noble pines growing within two hundred yards of Bray's Bayou. These were cut down for saw stocks, hauled to the bayou, floated to the mill, and sawed into lumber. The Harrises boarded their employees, the number of whom, including choppers, haulers, floaters, sawyers, and cooks, was generally twenty men."[27] Others followed the Harris brothers in their sawmilling north of Houston. By the late 1850s, fifteen steam sawmills operated on Buffalo Bayou and the San Jacinto River, some of which cut at the respectable rate of twenty-five thousand board feet a day.[28]

Meanwhile, major timber industries developed at Beaumont, using logs floated down the Neches. Cypress, the wood eternal, served as grist for the mills of the first timber boom. Beaumont was laid out in 1837, and the first shingle-making operations began at almost the same time. In the beginning, the shingle makers used only a slightly more systematic version of the old folk shingling methods. Cypress logs were floated down the river or obtained from the disassembly of flatboats. Workers sawed the logs by hand into shingle lengths, split the lengths into blocks, and rived the blocks into shingles using froes. Then, using "shave horses" to hold the shingles, men "dressed them down" with drawknives, always thinning the bottom edges, and boys tied them into handy lots. Machinery and the first real shingle mills soon replaced the slow hand labor, and production soared.[29]

The first prosperity of the Beaumont lumber industry was based on hardwood: cypress shingles and lumber, white oak staves, hickory barrel hoops, and furniture-grade walnut planking. Meanwhile, a similar industry developed at the Orange side of Sabine Lake. In the prewar boom year of 1859, U.S. Customs at the port of Sabine Pass registered the combined export of 11,919,000 shingles, 97,000 staves, 7,000 hoop poles, and 1,099,000 board feet of lumber.[30]

Beaumont's first steam sawmills began operations by the 1850s—at first using sash saws, then the much more efficient circular saws. Loggers floated both cypress and pine down to feed the sawmills, but the 1870s were the heyday of cypress drives as an incredible amount of the wood came down the river. By the 1870s Beaumont had five sawmills, collectively sawing about 200,000 board feet a day, three shingle mills producing 250,000 a day, and three planing mills. The sawmills included the Reliance Lumber Company, Long and Company, the Beaumont Lumber Company, and a few smaller mills. All logs were supplied by timber "rafted or floated loose." Every rise in the river brought tens of thousands of logs from upstream, and the mills began operating, using existing stocks, as soon as they got word that the rise was coming and the logs were on the way. The *Beaumont Enterprise* noted in 1880: "The logging business is being pushed extensively at all the camps up the river. When a rise does come, there will be a very heavy booming of timber. Log men have at last grasped the idea that the demand for pine timber at Beaumont means fifty million [log?] feet yearly, and they are going to do their level best." By 1883 the timbermen, raftsmen, and log drivers approached the expectations of the *Enterprise*, since well over two million log feet were coming down the Neches each month.[31]

As Beaumont boomed, even more exciting things happened in Orange, the gateway to the Sabine. Having cut out in the white pine forests of the Northeast and Midwest, the Yankee lumbermen were on their way, and their primary target was the 230,000-square-mile longleaf forest sweeping like an enormous crescent across the upland South. Pennsylvania lumbermen Henry J. Lutcher and G. Bedell Moore reconnoitered southeastern Texas in 1877, noting with growing excitement the virgin forests, the suitability of the Sabine and the Neches as float streams, and the ridiculously low land prices, which began at fifty cents an acre for prime timberland. They decided to build a big mill at Orange on the Sabine, since they judged that river a somewhat better float stream than the Neches and prime pine lands were available closer to the mill. At first entirely supplied by river transport, the Lutcher and Moore mill in Orange cut one hundred thousand board feet of lumber a day, more than doubling the production of the next-largest Texas mill. It was the first big mill, but other northern lumbermen soon established even larger ones.[32]

As they had done on the rivers of Wisconsin and Minnesota, the lumbermen at Beaumont and Orange built catchment "booms" halfway across the Neches and the Sabine to trap the loose logs and log rafts floating down. The companies constructed the booms by driving pilings into the river at points about thirty feet apart, then chaining high-floating logs dogged together to the pilings, much as one might build a fence. After interviewing several people in Beaumont and Orange in 1940 about the former operations of the booms, lumber industry historian Hamilton Easton offered this explanation of how they had worked:

> A place was left open at the top [of the boom] to let the logs in. The logs were let out at the lower end of the boom as needed. These operations corresponded to opening and shutting gates for cattle, and the boom itself corresponded to a stock corral. Commercially, these booms were operated on the principle of a bank clearing-house, in that the logs of other companies were scaled and milled and at the end of the month checks were sent to the other firms for the correct amount due them. Logs were branded by means of a stamp iron. A star and crescent was the mark or brand of the Lutcher and Moore Company.[33]

Lutcher and Moore Company had its own logging camps, as did many others. In 1882 the Texas Tram and Lumber Company of Beaumont maintained a logging camp on Wright's Creek in Jasper County. The lumbermen cut the timber, skidded logs to the creek with oxen, floated them several miles downstream to Wright's Landing on the Neches, then launched them down the river to the mill near Beaumont. At about the same time, Bear Man's Bluff farther downriver was the headquarters of a major float-logging operation of the Beaumont Lumber Company.[34]

Most companies in Beaumont and Orange had their own timber camps and sent down logs stamped with the company marks, but the river transport system also lent itself to the participation of many independent timbermen. The booms awaited the branded logs of large operators and small, by the hundreds or by the tens of thousands. The river served as a common highway, free for any man's use. Filed in dusty record books in county courthouses all along the Neches and the Sabine, hundreds of registered log brands testify to the large number of southeastern Texans who availed themselves of the "float road" to other men's mills.[35] Beside the "star and crescent" of Lutcher and Moore and the "star and circle" of the giant Kirby Lumber Company were listed the "SA" and "111" log brands of the families of Louis Bingham and Bob Allen.

By the time, around World War I, when the Binghams and the Allens were floating rafts on the Sabine and the Neches, rafting had become much more common than log drives. Log drives—the free-floating of logs to the mill—worked best on larger rivers of higher gradient, higher current speed, and unrestricted flow. Northern rivers were well suited to this method, and Lutcher and Moore and other early lumbermen accustomed to log drives tried to make them work on the Neches and the Sabine, but with indifferent results. The Sabine perhaps worked better than the Neches for loose-log drives and probably saw more of them. However, both rivers were plagued with log-trapping eddies, brush obstructions and tight places that became the sites of major logjams, and side channels that led sawlogs into mazes of sloughs and bayous and then hung them up. A great many free-floated logs never made it to the mills, and as time went on and prime timber became more valuable, timbermen on the lower river usually chose to fasten their sawlogs into rafts.[36]

On the narrow, constricted upper Neches, well above the economic reach of the Beaumont lumber companies, only single-log floating usually was possible. Ironically, Bob Allen's last float job on the upper river during the 1920s was an exception to the rule—a hewn-log rectangular raft of oak ship-building timbers put together far upriver near Diboll and destined for Beaumont. Equipped with a stern-facing oar to help keep it aligned with the current in places where the river was too narrow for it to turn sideways, the raft nonetheless had exhausted its builder by the time it reached Rockland. There, he hired the experienced Allens to run it the rest of the way down.[37]

Upriver from Rockland, various individuals and small mills floated small numbers of single logs down the river. The Kirby Lumber Company mill at Rockland took some floated logs, though not from a great distance upriver.[38] At the other extreme, the people of the riverside communities of southern Angelina County sometimes cut a single big cypress tree (no matter on whose land it grew), let it dry in the woods all summer so that it would float, then, when the river came up in the fall, guided it to the edge of someone's bottomland field. Here they left it, returning to saw, bolt, and rive it into roofing boards after the water went down.[39]

Other float operations, small and not so small, went on all the time. Roy Smith, of Trinity County, and Carl Havard, of Angelina County, recalled logs coming down their stretches of the upper river, though the ultimate destinations of the logs often remained obscure. Timbermen skidded logs into the river above Highway 94, perhaps intending them for a mill near Diboll, and a man in a rowing skiff made periodic trips downstream to nudge the ones that had hung up on their way. Farther downriver Carl Havard remembered two men walking the riverbank on opposite sides of the Neches, using long "jam poles" to accomplish the same purpose. The Nick Crain Log Landing, Tom Havard Log Landing, and a hundred similar place-names along the upper river attest to bluff bank locations where lumbermen either skidded logs into the river or took them out of it. In low water ancient sawlog "sinkers," many branded with the timber marks of long-dead lumbermen, can still be seen on the river bottom.[40]

Below Bon Weir on the Sabine and Rockland on the Neches, rafts of cypress and pine floated down the Sabine and the Neches for almost a century. Around the time of the establishment of New Orleans in 1718, the Louisiana French developed a method for logging cypress trees from their boggy home along bayous and backwater lakes. The giant heart cypresses, five hundred to one thousand years old and commonly five to six feet thick, were girdled in the spring and left to dry in the woods all summer. This made them buoyant enough to float. Then, after the river rose in the late fall, loggers went in and felled them, floated them to the river, and dogged them into rafts.[41]

From the swamp to the mill, the logging of cypress was a watery business. Logging crews paddled into the flooded bottom in boats. They built scaffolding above each tree's giant butt swell, from which to fell it, or if the water was higher, they plied their eight- and nine-foot crosscut saws from the decks of tippy paddle skiffs. This was hard, dangerous work, and when the ancient tree finally began to topple, the fellers scrambled down from the scaffolding and ran off through the backwater or frantically paddled their boats away in what they hoped was the correct direction. Once down, the cypress was "limbed" and "bucked" (cut into sawlogs) by men working in and even under the water. Then they floated it through the flooded bottom to a slough and down the slough to the staging area for the rafts. Sometimes men pulled the great cypress logs to the collection point with rowing skiffs; sometimes wearing hobnailed boots, they balanced on the logs and maneuvered them through the woods with jam poles; sometimes they worked as "swampers," pushing the logs as they waded through the water. Cypress timbermen had to be nearly as comfortable in the water as otters, but often this was not easy. As Wesley Smith recalled from his logging days: "Levi McDaniel bought the timber rights to a league of land near Fairdale, from A. W. Canfield. He had to have land that overflowed at least six months of the year. That was about 1885. I helped to cut that timber and my feet stayed wet and cold so much they swelled and almost rotted off."[42] F. R. McDaniel, the son of Levi

McDaniel, told what happened after the cypress timber reached the river:

We made "cribs" by laying five or six logs side by side and using a "binder," a heavy pole with holes bored in it with strong white-oak pins driven into each hole with a "ring maul," across each end of the crib. Twelve or fifteen cribs were buckled together with a binder pole to make a "raft." A "ring-dog" was driven into the outside pole and a rope used to fasten one raft to another. In this way several rafts could be floated down the river side by side, snaked out behind, and close to one hundred thousand feet of timber could be taken to market at one time. Our camp stood in the middle of a big raft with a tent or shed over it. We wore hob-nailed boots and carried a sixteen foot jam pole with a spike in one end and a hook in the other to push or pull the rafts about.[43]

Timbermen constructed log rafts of cypress, pine, or sweet gum in much the same way on the Neches and the Sabine, though there were interesting variations in the methods used to float them down the rivers. The Bingham family on the Sabine and the Allen family on the Neches ran log rafts on their respective rivers for decades around the turn of the last century, but neither clan of raftsmen chose to tether its rafts together in long strings, like those McDaniel described.[44] However, there is no doubt this was sometimes done; the cover of the *American Lumberman* of October 8, 1910, displays a rafting operation of the Miller and Vidor Lumber Company of Galveston in which a long chain of ten-log cribs, tethered together, is snaking down the river.

Both the Binghams and the Allens were private operators, buying timber from riverside landowners, hiring crews to log it and haul it to the river, then taking over, with family members, to raft it up and float it to the booms. By around World War I, the Binghams ran only pine rafts, but on the Neches the Allens rafted pine, cypress, and sweet gum, often from as far upriver as their home base of Rockland.

Like many other pine loggers using river transport, the Binghams hauled logs to the river with ox teams and accumulated the logs in great stacks on a high bank to dry and await the rafting season. Without this several-month period of drying out, many more of the logs would go to the bottom as sinkers. After the river rose in early winter and the time seemed ripe, the "chocks" holding back the logs were pulled, and the logs tumbled down a skidway into the river, ready to be rafted up.

Perhaps because the Allens rafted bottomland cypress and sweet gum as well as pine, they used a somewhat different method. They deadened the cypress trees in the spring and cut them in the fall in the usual way. Sweet gum was cut, peeled of its bark to facilitate drying, and left in the woods where the backwaters would be certain to reach. Pines logged in the uplands were skidded down to the bottoms and left to cure in staging areas where winter floodwaters were sure to come. Whether rafting pine, sweet gum, or cypress, the Allens worked the logs in the same way. After the river rose, they donned hobnailed "corked shoes" and stood on the logs; using long jam poles, they pushed and poled the logs through the flooded woods to the river, there to be fastened into rafts.

Except for some differences in the size of the finished rafts, the Allens and the Binghams built their timber rafts in much the same way. Rafts were often constructed in the eddy water where a slough or big creek entered the river. Family members, even those too young to ride the rafts, scrambled about on the floating logs, pushing and pulling them into place with the hooks and spikes of the jam poles. After a certain number of matched logs (eight to sixteen, depending on their size) had been assembled into a crib—the basic building block of the raft—loggers placed pine binder poles about nine inches in diameter across both ends and fastened them into place with white oak pins. Then, loggers used shorter binder poles and additional white oak pins to fasten crib to crib and form the raft. Operating on a larger river and farther downstream, the Binghams assembled ten or twelve cribs into a large, oblong raft. Like other upstream raftsmen on the Neches, the Allens fastened four cribs into a perfectly square raft, which they called a "block."

On the Neches, the Sabine, and everywhere else, the humble white oak pin was the key element of log raft construction. Raftsmen split four-inch blocks from the "butt cut" of young white oaks, then used drawknives to carve the blocks into one-and-one-quarter-inch diameter pins with two-inch heads. Pin makers took great care in selecting the wood and carving the pins, and Louis Bingham's father, the leader of the family rafting operations, often did this job himself. Unbelievably tough, the white oak pins "broomed" and frayed under the action of the logs but never gave way. Raftsmen used a larger-sized augur to bore the hole in the binder pole than was used to bore the hole in the log beneath it, so that the pin (kept from slipping out of the binder by its oversized head) fit loosely through the binder pole, tightly in the log. This, and the strength of the white oak, allowed the raft to "give" to absorb its enormous impacts with cutbanks, snags, and other rafts.

Once launched on the river, however, the Binghams and the Allens handled their rafts in very different ways. The Binghams manned each raft with a crew, kept their rafts together, and tied them up at night, much as Andrew Smyth had done with his flatboat fleets eighty years

Steamboat Laura *blocked by log-raft jam on Neches, c. 1880. (Jasper County Historical Commission, Jasper, Texas)*

earlier. The Allens placed all hands on a trailing "camp block," which ran drag for their operation, and let the other rafts go, free-floating, night and day, pinwheeling toward Beaumont.

The Binghams normally floated five to eight large rafts, each with a crew of two men outfitted with a cypress dugout and a 150- to 200-foot "checkline" coiled and ready in the bottom. Most of the time the raft drifted along in the central current and required no handling. Small snags and midstream brush did not halt the huge raft, which smashed through and over them with ease. Periodically, however, members of the raft crew spied potential trouble up ahead in the form of a major logjam, a dangerous cutbank bend, or some other obstacle, and they sprang into action. Launching the dugout, one man paddled to the bank while the other played out the rope, which was attached to the raft. Once at a strategic location on the bank, they snubbed the rope to a tree to control the raft and keep it in a good position past the danger point. Then they jumped back in the dugout and paddled back to their raft, coiling the rope for the next run to the bank as they went.

If the raftsmen felt they were getting too far ahead or too close to the raft in front of them, they snubbed off to allow a proper distance of a few hundred yards. At the end of the day all the rafts were tied to the bank wherever they were, and the crews took their dugouts and paddled upstream—sometimes for miles—to the kitchen raft, which was always the last raft in the drive. The kitchen raft had a tent and a cooking fire, which burned on a dirt-filled log frame centrally located on the raft. Food was simple—bacon, eggs, biscuits, and the like—usually prepared by Louis Bingham's uncle. Sometimes the crewmen from the lead raft did not reach the kitchen raft to get their supper until nearly midnight, and most of the time all the rafters spent the night on the kitchen raft or on the bank alongside. Before dawn, however, they left and paddled back to their assigned rafts. As Louis Bingham said, "They'd start on time the next morning soon as the crack of day."

Sometimes there were delays. Despite all that a raft crew might do, a raft might get hung up and have to be jerked loose by the next raft behind or be nudged on its way by a portable winch-like contraption called a "rassle jack." This simple but effective device involved only two poles and a rope. To operate the rassle jack, two men held one pole in a vertical position on the bank while one or two other men went around it with another pole "like on a sugar mill." This wound the rope "like a windlass" to pull the raft free. Sometimes a raft got caught in a big eddy going around and around on a river bend, but Bingham's father carried a rowing skiff along for just this eventuality. He ran the nose of the skiff up on the raft and waited while the raft cycled upstream through the eddy. Then, as the raft began its closest approach to the downstream current, he rowed as hard as he could toward the central current to nudge the raft out of the eddy and on its way.

As Louis Bingham noted, "It took em anywhere from seven to nine days to get to Orange, according to how high the river was." After the Binghams' rafts were all safely caught in the Lutcher and Moore boom and the timbermen paid off, the crew, cypress dugouts, ropes, pulling skiff, and other gear were carried on a company tugboat to a certain bluff, where there was a tramway, then shipped home in a railroad car.[45]

Bob Allen's family did things very differently on the Neches, and so did the Neches rafting operations described by Bert DuBose and R. J. Rawls.[46] Drives on the Neches River involved a greater number—perhaps twenty or more—of small, square, four-crib rafts, or "blocks," followed by a larger six-crib camp block. The Allens' four- or five-person crew normally stayed on the camp block, which had the tent, a rectangular frame of logs with dirt inside for the cooking fire, the paddle skiff, the ropes, and a large stationary wooden winch called a "bull wheel," which was mainly used to ensure that the camp block never got stranded.

If the Binghams ran their log rafts like a fleet of flatboats, the Allens ran theirs like cows driven along a fenced roadway—roped or goaded ahead from time to time but otherwise left to travel on their own. The key strategy of the Allens' operation revealed itself in the size and shape of the rafts. They kept the four-crib blocks small, so that the blocks could pass through the narrowest places in the upper river, and square, so that the blocks resisted hanging up. One end of a block might jam into a cutbank or a bankside willow, but the other end remained in the current; thus the block was almost certain to spin around the obstacle and go on. Occasionally some blocks hung up, and the trailing camp raft attended to them. Other blocks in this loose raft drive drifted on their way day and night and might reach the Beaumont boom several days ahead of the crew. The Allens worried very little about log theft, since they marked every log in every raft with the family log brand, "111." A blacksmith had cut the "111" mark in the back of a poleax, and the Allens not only struck each log in the butt end to brand it but also chopped three notches in the top of the log so that it could be easily identified while floating in the water.

The camp block always followed all the others. When the crewmen came around a bend and saw a stranded block ahead of them, they ran a line to it with the paddle boat as they approached; after they passed, the momentum of the big camp block would jerk the stranded block loose. Sometimes they simply allowed the camp block to follow the same course in the current and strike the stranded block, like one billiard ball striking another, freeing up the first one and sending both on their way. Occasionally, hang-ups were trickier, and the winchlike "bull wheel" or rassle jack was used to get the block loose. The rassle jack was portable and could be set up on the bank or another block; the bull wheel was a stationary winch firmly mounted on a steel pin driven into a central log of the camp block. Besides being used to rescue other blocks, the bull wheel ensured that the camp block itself would never get trapped.

During the day, the crewmen of the paddle skiff sometimes worked hundreds of yards ahead of the camp block, searching for stranded rafts. When they found one, they tied the rope at that end and waited to run the other out to the camp block when it came by so that the camp block would jerk the raft loose. The camp block always tied up at night, and when the Allens landed it at the end of the day, they had to be careful not to allow the enormous momentum of the raft to break their rope. They snubbed the line—allowed it to slide around two or three pens set in the deck—as they played the big block into the bank.

Evening meals, cooked on the open fire in a dutch oven, resembled those of the Binghams and included eggs, biscuits, pork and beans, and the occasional fish, squirrels, or ducks caught or shot along the way. Usually the Allens took about two weeks to float their camp block from Rockland to the Beaumont boom, though some of the unmanned blocks made it down in half that time. One of the family always attended the tallying and scaling of their logs at the boom, just to keep an eye on things.[47]

By the late 1920s, when the Allen and Bingham families ceased their raft drives and shifted to stock raising and commercial fishing, running logs on the river had long since become an anachronism. The heydays of Beaumont and Orange as major centers of southeastern Texas lumbering ended around the turn of the century. By 1910 some of the largest sawmills the world had yet seen were operating in the pine uplands above the river valleys, and all of these got their logs by railroad.

Other northern lumbermen and land speculators followed swiftly on the heels of Lutcher and Moore, drawn by the Homestead Act of 1876, which threw open millions of acres of public lands for sale at ridiculously low prices. Southern legislatures desperately wanted economic development and regarded the great virgin forests as more of an impediment to progress than anything else, hence their willingness to let the lands go for a song. Northern investors and lumber companies (the first lumbermen acted like investors, so great were the perceived profits) rushed south to buy land. More than one company discovered that its trusted land agent had gone "rogue" soon after reaching the southern forests, purchasing land for himself and planning to resell it later. The temptation certainly was very great. Hundreds of thousands of acres of virgin southern pine lands carrying six thousand to twelve thousand board feet an acre sold for $1.25 an acre at a time when quality lumber brought $10 per thousand board feet. Land purchased for $1.25 held timber potentially worth $120. Northern land speculators rushed to county courthouses to locate acreages of privately held timberlands that could be obtained for no more than the payment of back taxes. They also set about financing railroads, since the State of Texas awarded sixteen sections of land, 10,240 acres, for every mile of track constructed—track of any gauge and in any location. No wonder, then, that by 1885 Texas had sold or given away about 32 million acres of public land, much of it heavily forested.[48]

The railroad builders and the boom-era timbermen were in some cases the same people, but in all cases they were closely linked. As the Sabine and East Texas Railroad built north toward Rockland (reaching the town in 1882), a new sawmill and lumber camp sprang up behind the railroad builders along every mile of track they laid.[49] The Houston, East, and West Texas (H.E.&W.T.) Railway built north from Houston to

Shreveport during the years between 1876 and 1886, and by the time it reached Cleveland, five sawmills with a combined capacity of one hundred thousand board feet a day operated behind it. As the line was built, it gave rise to a string of "railroad towns," several of which, like Lufkin, soon became county seats. People called the narrow-gauge H.E.&W.T. "the Rabbit" because of its bobbing, swaying cars and its tendency to jump track; they also referred to it as "Hell Either Way Taken," but it was no joke. This "lifeline of the Piney Woods" opened the great forests along the middle Neches to swift exploitation. The H.E.&W.T. carried pine timber as its chief commodity, was built of pine (ties and trestles), burned pine in its steam engines, and prepared the way for the huge sawmills that followed closely behind.[50]

Between 1880 and 1930, Texas lumber companies logged off over eighteen million acres of pine timber. The cut peaked in 1907, when the state produced two and one-quarter billion board feet of lumber and ranked third in the nation. Northern lumber interests and northern capital predominated throughout the bonanza period, and most ownership was absentee; of thirty-three major operators, only five were native Texans.[51]

Many companies started small and stayed that way, buying a limited amount of timber next to the railroad, building a mill, and cutting out in only a few years. Some started small and evolved into major enterprises. The Angelina County Lumber Company near Lufkin was one such operation. The company began logging in 1887 close to its mill, hauling the logs to the saws in ox wagons. Then, as the "front," the cutting edge of its lumbering operation, moved farther away around 1900, the company shifted to a primitive form of tramway logging: donkey engines now pulled small flatcars over four-inch wooden rails several miles from woods to mill. By 1930 the Angelina County Lumber Company operated a major railroad system hauling sawlogs from timber camps in four counties. The largest lumber camp was in Tyler County, over sixty miles from the mill. The company owned several sections of virgin longleaf pine between Zavalla and Manning in southern Angelina County, and in these open woods it used steam-powered rehaul skidders operated from tramways to pull the logs in and used steam loaders to load them on the flatcars. The skidder cables could reach out six hundred feet on either side, so the company built tramways at right angles to the main line, about twelve hundred feet apart.[52]

Forty miles to the west in Houston County, the 4-C Mill at Ratcliff had come and gone during those years. The 4-C was an example of the huge mills that arrived with northern capital and state-of-the-art technology, transformed a whole county almost overnight, then cut out and vanished even more swiftly than they had come. The Central Coal and Coke Company of Kansas City, Missouri, the parent organization of the 4-C, bought J. H. Ratcliff's peckerwood sawmill in 1901 and used it to saw lumber to build one of the largest mills in the American South. By 1902 three band saws in the main mill of the 4-C cut pine timber at the rate of three hundred thousand board feet a day, a company railroad ran east to Lufkin, company tramways built out in several directions through the timber, and six logging engines and a passenger train ran on the rails.[53]

Meanwhile, construction crews had been at work around the clock transforming sleepy Ratcliff into a typical "company town." It had a huge commissary store where workers purchased food, clothing, and household supplies with tokens, or "bozos," which the company used for pay in lieu of money. A mile-long, sixteen-foot-high, board-and-batten fence blocked the workers off from private merchants in the village of Ratcliff and made it extremely inconvenient for them to buy supplies outside the commisary or to exchange company tokens for real money at the usual rate of "six bits on the dollar." Every family man who worked for the 4-C had his own company house, and the location and the size of the house were closely calibrated with his ethnicity and his position in the economic pecking order of the mill. The non-English-speaking Europeans, called "Dagos" by the locals, had the smallest houses—inferior even to the houses of the blacks, who, like the Dagos, were strictly segregated to their part of town. The location and quality of the housing for Anglo Americans depended on their jobs at the mill. However, even the poorest of the company houses glowed with electricity from the huge power plant—this at a time when the rest of eastern Houston County was sunk deep in the age of kerosene.

As quickly as the 4-C Mill came, so did it disappear. Angelina County Lumber Company and Southern Pine Lumber Company at Diboll purchased land all around the 4-C holdings, preventing the 4-C from obtaining more than 120,000 acres of timber. In part the efficiency of the 4-C put it out of business, since at three hundred thousand board feet a day it was one of the two or three largest mills in the South.[55] In 1918 the 4-C cut out, and the company whisked away machinery, railroad engines, and Dagos almost overnight. Local people came in from miles around to take their pick of the goats, chickens, and other domestic animals that had been left behind. The passenger train ran to Lufkin for a few months more, then that also disappeared, and the very tracks were pulled up. Around Ratcliff for miles and miles in every direction, only the tangled aftermath of cut-and-get-out logging gave evidence that a big mill had come and gone.[56]

A hundred mills almost as large as the 4-C came and went during the period from 1890 to 1920, leaving behind blasted forests. Most lumbermen approached the virgin forest as miners approach a vein of ore—as a nonrenewable resource to be efficiently exploited and then abandoned. Until the 1920s few companies were interested in attempting to regrow timber on their cutover lands, since they would have to cover replanting costs and wait thirty-five years before new saw timber could be harvested, all the time paying for the land and local taxes and defending the property against fires and razorback hogs. Most companies simply bought rights to all the timber—"stumpage." Others either tried (without much success) to sell their cutover lands to farmers or let the lands revert to the counties for back taxes, abandoning not just mill towns and employees but even the land itself.

Gradually, after the turn of the century, the remaining forests became concentrated in the holdings of fewer and fewer large companies, which were characterized by multiple mills and extensive railway systems connecting the mills to far-flung timber camps. At Diboll in Angelina County, T. L. L. Temple's Southern Pine Lumber Company acquired more lands than it cut for decades after 1893, accumulating over 200,000 acres up and down the Neches counties. Unlike other companies, Southern Pine usually bought land outright, instead of just stumpage, and by 1908 had changed its lumbering policies to encourage regeneration of the forest.[57] Southeast of Temple's empire lay the even larger empire of John Henry Kirby, the "Prince of the Pines." In 1901, with the aid of eastern capital, he organized the Kirby Lumber Company. At the peak of its activities the company operated fourteen major sawmills, thirteen logging camps, more than one hundred miles of tramroad connected with the Santa Fe Railroad, a company-wide hospital, a large commissary warehouse and distribution office in Beaumont, and a company headquarters in Houston. The Kirby Lumber Company owned or had stumpage rights to 1 million acres of timber—over half the longleaf pine in Texas.

Kirby's sawmill towns and lumber camps were highly organized. He operated all the commissary stores at his mills as one chain; products not selling in one were moved to another. Every mill and lumber camp had a resident doctor, every commissary had a pharmacy, and all the towns, mills, and logging fronts had similar regulations, pay scales, and policies. Kirby's permanent work force numbered around five thousand, and his mills had a combined production capacity of over nine hundred thousand board feet a day.[58]

Lumber company treatment of employees was paternalistic but arbitrary, and this was as true of Kirby and Southern Pine as it was of other companies. In Kirbyville and Diboll, as elsewhere, mill policies depended on the whims of management. One Angelina County mill granted the widow of a recently deceased employee free housing and commissary privileges for the rest of her life; another company not only refused compensation to a similar widow but required her to pay for the wood of her husband's coffin.[59]

Kirby sometimes gave his employees free Bibles, and Mr. Wier of Wier Long Leaf Lumber Company came up every year from Houston to shake his employees' hands, but both men usually paid only in coupons, negotiable at full value only at the company stores. For a time the Kirby Lumber Company redeemed coupons for cash only twice a year. Resident deputy sheriffs, constables, and company employees called "quarter bosses," who were empowered as special Texas Rangers, enforced the law in the mill towns. In truth, all of these officers served as "company men," and they came down particularly hard on union organizers for the Brotherhood of Timber Workers, often breaking up union meetings and running members out of town. The Southern Lumber Operators' Association, organized by the companies around 1907 to combat the union, fought the Brotherhood so successfully— with blacklists, yellow-dog contracts, intelligence networks, and strong-arm tactics—that the union fell apart by 1914 without having organized a single Texas mill.[60] The companies' antiunion activities, refusal to pay employees in coin of the realm, and other arbitrary practices led to a 1914 federal investigation of what one *Harper's Weekly* writer called the "feudal towns" of East Texas.[61]

While the sawmills devoured the timber, the mainline railroads and logging tramways reached out farther and farther into the remaining forests. From its base at Diboll on the Southern Pacific line, T. L. L. Temple's Southern Pine Lumber Company built a shortline railroad east to the Neches bottoms, then west to Lufkin, and then north along the Neches Valley, cutting timber as it went. The company began to establish logging camps as soon as this was more economical than transporting loggers back and forth each day from the mill town. From 1900 on, a string of ever-more-distant timber camps grew up along the tracks of the Texas South-Eastern, the T.S.E. ("Tattered, Shattered, and Expired"), as Southern Pine's railroad followed the logging front north. For years at a time, loggers and their families lived in temporary houses or converted boxcars rolled in by the engines of the T.S.E. while they built tramlines and logged off the surrounding forest. Then, the camp cut out and was abandoned, and the front moved on to another timber camp farther up the line. From Rutland to Blix to Blair to Alcedo to a dozen other camps, for two generations, loggers followed their jobs north along the Neches, ultimately ending up at Fastrill, far away in Cherokee County.[62]

Work in the timber fronts was rough and dangerous, though most of the loggers preferred the looser life of the woods to the regimentation of the mill towns. Racial discrimination in jobs and pay scales was somewhat less in the woods, where African Americans working as tree fellers in two-man crosscut saw teams, which were paid by the amount of timber felled, could make more than in any other job in the industry. On the other hand, people were regularly killed or injured in woods work. Sawmill work also was dangerous, and the East Texas mill towns had far more than their share of "three-fingered-Willies." A bad mistake in the woods, however, often cost a man his life. Trees dropped branches or fell in unfortunate directions, "top loader" men failed to get out of the way of rolling logs, and steam-skidder cables snapped and went scything through the woods with such frequency that logging caused more disabling injuries than any other industrial occupation in the early twentieth century—seven times the national average. Mining was second most dangerous, sawmilling third.[63]

Some of the danger resulted from the hurried work of the woods crews—in fact, work in the woods was almost as relentless and schedule-driven as work in the mills. Former logging-camp boss W. Allen Smith recalled that his crews in the 1890s had labored under great time pressure. The woods engine blew reveille for Smith's logging camp before daylight. The workday was supposed to be twelve hours, but it really was from "can see to can't see," except in the winter. Then, work started in the dark, and sawyers built pine-knot fires to see to cut their first trees of the day. The schedule drove all. If the ground got too wet to use big-wheeled carts and log wagons to get the quota of logs for the day to the flatcars, loggers used mud-skids called "toads," but they went on working whatever the weather. Ruthless treatment of the logging animals was regretted but often resorted to. If teams bogged down, the loggers hooked tongs into the yokes of the bogged oxen and used additional draft animals on firm ground to "skid out the bogged ones as if they were logs."[64] Industry journals were silent about the dangers of lumbering and the cruelty to logging animals, but at about the same time that Smith's crew was at work, a Mississippi lumberman summed up his strategy for success: "Kill a mule, buy another'n; kill a nigger, hire another'n." Other companies, particularly in the early days, followed similar philosophies.[65]

Deriving their perspective mainly from lumber company records, timber industry historians have emphasized the docility and "company man" mentality of Texas timber workers (in contrast with the romantic "Paul Bunyans" of the Northeast).[66] But oral testimony from the loggers themselves suggests a somewhat different story. Logging camps were rough places and had their share of free spirits, men who challenged authority and shifted from one logging camp to another whenever they felt like it. One woods boss for Trinity County Lumber Company disgustedly remarked, "I have three sets of workmen; one at work, one going, one coming."[67] W. Allen Smith, the "bull of the woods," survived a number of physical confrontations with his workers, sometimes with his gun in hand. Conflicting with the woods boss, "locking horns with the bull," was a common-enough occurrence to have a folk phrase assigned to it. One Big Thicket operator of a steam loader found it prudent for many years to carry a pistol with him on the job, and another Hardin County man told of a rough saloon near the timber camp where Irishmen from the "steel gang" fought a trained bear for whiskey.[68] Barber Roscoe Crouch rode out to Temple's Steepbank Creek logging camp every Saturday for several years to offer loggers a shave and a haircut for four bits. He provided the following description of the camp and the men in it:

> Some of em didn't get their hair cut ever' three months. I've had them come in out of the woods Saturday night, whiskers a inch long, hair hangin' down, and all I had was a old smoky lamp to cut by. If he had a wart on his face, you cut that off too. . . . Must have been twenty-five cots in there [the sleeping shed], and every one of them men seemed to have an individual jug. I drank a lot of coffee that night and had the big eye, couldn't sleep. Ever' little bit somebody's take a drink from his jug—"glunkety, glunk, glunk," just like a bunch of frogs. . . . Those men didn't have any more sense than an ox, but they was tough. What I mean, them timberjacks could drink all night and work all day, just keep goin'.[69]

In 1904, W. Allen Smith saw his first steam skidder at work in the Texas woods, and by around 1910 many Texas companies had added steam skidders and steam loaders to their logging operations. Tramway logging was rather standardized by that time, and most companies operated in more or less the same fashion, dividing each of their logging crews into subcrews of "buckers and fellers," "skiddermen," "loaders," "tram operators," and men in the "steel gang."

Upland logging of the boom era was based on railroad technology, and the steel gang, perpetually laying side tracks through the virgin forest for new logging "chances" and taking up the tracks afterward, made possible the whole operation. The steel gang laid temporary logging trams at right angles to the main tram at the standard rate of sixty six-hundred-pound rails a day per ten-man crew. Company policy and the length of company skidder cables determined the distance between the parallel side trams on one side of the main track, but it was usually one-quarter to one-half a mile. As soon as the steel gang laid a new side tram, the self-propelled steam loader and skidder rolled into position on the track, and several crews of fellers and buckers moved into the virgin woods on each side and began to cut timber.

Loggers called these two-man crosscut-saw teams "flatheads," naming them for the larvae of a huge flat-headed beetle that also cuts deeply into pine trees. The logging crew could go no faster than the flatheads cut, so the company paid them by the amount of timber they felled instead of a daily wage. "Scalers," sometimes including the woods crew boss himself, followed the flatheads and calculated how much timber each team had cut. The highly skilled flatheads worked so fast that visitors at the logging front often commented on the nearly continuous thunder of falling trees.

As the team moved up to a new tree, the lead sawyer swiftly calculated where he wanted it to fall, taking into consideration the lean of the tree, the shape of its top, the direction of the wind, and the lay of the land. Ideally, the tree would fall where it would be easy to get to for limbing and bucking (sawing into sections), but first and foremost it must not fall where it would "lodge up" in another tree. Lodged trees could not be left in the woods but had to be brought down by cutting the tree or trees in which they had lodged, a highly dangerous operation. Having decided on the direction of the fall, the lead sawyer and his partner "bedded" the tree with a carefully calculated V-shaped cut on the side toward which they wanted it to fall, then began cutting on the opposite side. As the men bent to their work, great spurts of sawdust shot from alternate sides of the trunk with each pull of the saw. From time to time, the flatheads applied coal oil to the saw blade as lubricant, and as soon as the saw was deeply enough imbedded in the trunk, one of them drove a steel wedge in the trunk behind it to keep the saw from being pinched and caught. In an amazingly short time, the tree popped, shuddered, and began to fall—often with such accuracy that flatheads would, on a bet, drive a stake with its trunk. Then, with hardly a pause, the tree was limbed and cut into lengths, and the team of flatheads moved on a few paces to the next tree.

The sawyers were the strongest and most enduring of the woods crew and had to have the cardiovascular fitness of professional athletes. To make sure he would get enough calories to sustain him throughout a long, hard day of work, flathead R. J. Rawls always filled his one-gallon Cristal Lard bucket lunch box entirely full of food, including a pint bottle of ribbon-cane syrup.[70]

Moving behind the fellers and buckers, teams of men fastened steel cables to the logs and skidded them to the tramway; other teams used the steam loader to load the logs on flatcars, and twice daily the tram crew hauled twenty or more flatcars at a time to the mill. Over the years, however, memories of the steam skidder remained most vividly in the minds of former woods crewmen. R. J. Rawls recalled:

> Them re-haul skidders, them was what was dangerous—them lines a-flopping! They had two drums on the skidder there and the line off one of em pulled the other one back out in the woods. They had pulleys out yonder in the woods around stumps, just run them cables through them pulleys. It'd pull the tongs back there and they'd have somebody out there to hook you onto a log. They'd holler, and that skidder would take that log on in. After they got them re-haul skidders, when they'd circle them lines around the block I was cutting on, I'd go cut me the biggest trees I had across them lines to hold em down to keep em from flopping. And chunking them limbs—I've seen em chunk limbs far as from here to that road out yonder.[71]

No one who saw the steam skidder at work in the woods ever forgot it. When the "cable man" or "flagger man" gave the signal to the "drum puller" at the skidder, and he threw his lever, the huge log sprang into life and raced through the woods like a battering ram, gouging up the ground, destroying small timber, and sometimes flipping end over end. Even men who were not afraid of anything else in the dangerous woods operations feared the skidder. Roy Smith, of Trinity County, noted: "Them logs would hit the ground every once in awhile in them woods! They tore the woods up. They'd jerk them trees, sometimes be pretty little old pine that was left there, they'd just tear em all to pieces—knock em down, knock the tops out of em, everything. Course, they knowed they wasn't coming back there no more."[72] Walter Cole, of Jasper County, recalled: "I stayed away from em, I never did work around em. A limb could fall two hundred yards [away from the skidder] and kill an elephant. They'd drag that big log and it'd come across the little ones, [and you'd] just see the timber falling ahead of it. Oh, God, yes, they were powerful—turn the train over!"[73]

Before 1900 the companies used mules or oxen to transport the logs to the tramways with tongs and skid chains, big-wheeled (slip-tongue) carts, or log wagons, and some companies operating in mixed pine and hardwood stands, where the skidders did not work well, continued to so. In the longleaf woods, however, hardwoods were rare, the woods were open, and virtually all the companies used steam skidders after 1900. It was simply a matter of economics; the steam skidders sped up operations. With a regular skidder, big "skidder horses" and mules pulled cable and tongs back out into the woods to be attached to another log. The awesome rehaul skidder returned the cable, cycling it through a second drum attached to a stump several hundred yards away. Such skidders exemplified the cut-and-get-out approach to the forest. Purely extractive tools, they attacked the forest like steam shovels attacking a bed of coal in a strip mine, and as Roy Smith said, the companies "knowed they wasn't coming back there no more." Reforestation pioneer W. Goodrich Jones described the devastation caused by the skidder in Texas longleaf woods around 1920: "[The skidder] is an octopus of steel with several grappling arms running out 300 or more feet. These grapple a tree of any size that has been felled, and drag it through the woods to the tram road. These become enormous battering rams and lay low everything in their way. . . . The remains of the forest [are] like the shell town area of France. Use of the re-haul skidder should never have been allowed by the state."[74]

Two decades later, in 1940, a twenty-six-man crew of the Wier Long Leaf Lumber Company still operated a steam skidder in the last block of virgin longleaf forest in Newton, Sabine, and Jasper counties. Interviewed on the job by young graduate student Hamilton Easton, skidder foreman J. J. Griffin was amazingly forthright about his attitudes toward the steam skidder. He told Easton that he detested it and used it only because he was ordered to and because if he did not, "someone else would." Wier's company doctor F. E. McAlister also spoke out against the skidder, which in his opinion should never have been put in the woods. Easton summed up what he had been told: "In the opinion of Mr. Griffin and many others, only a few men really profited from the lumber resources of East Texas. Labor in general received small wages, while the people of the state let their patrimony in timber resources fall into the hands of the large companies to be exploited without regard for the future welfare of the State. This disproportionate distribution of wealth was accentuated by the use of the steam skidder."[75]

Along the Neches counties, the story of the lumbering of the virgin hardwood bottomlands is more complicated than that of the lumbering of the pure longleaf stands or the mixed pine and hardwood uplands. The bottomland hardwoods were more valuable than pine in the early days, especially such species as cypress, white oak, walnut, and hickory. These were selectively cut—high-graded—for home or commercial use from the time of first settlement, often with little concern for who owned the land. However, for two or three decades most of the boom era timber companies concentrated on the pine uplands and largely ignored their bottomlands, only beginning major hardwood operations in the decade before World War I. As late as 1939, the Texas Forest Service calculated that 454,000 acres of virgin hardwood remained, along with 236,400 acres of virgin pine.[76]

In the beginning, many southeastern Texans regarded the bottom-land cypresses, white oaks, and other valuable hardwood species as free resources of the open range, theirs for the taking. People casually cut the trees, with little thought that they were committing timber theft. Louis Bingham's grandfather originally owned large stands of cy-press trees on his Sabine bottomlands, but other men took most of them before the Binghams' float logging ever began. Bingham ex-plained: "A lot of people in the olden days, they cut them old cypress, and they just run em out of there and carried em to the mill. They didn't belong to nobody—belonged to them, if they got em."[77]

In the 1920s, when Bob Allen's family floated cypress rafts down the Neches, Allen's father kept an eye out for big bankside cypresses with dead tops. Such trees often floated even without benefit of girdling and drying, and Allen sometimes paddled ahead of the log drive, cut a cypress, and prepared it to be jerked out in the river by the camp block to join his raft drive. On one fateful occasion Allen's feet became stuck in the mud when the camp block came by "and that log come over the top of him and buried him in the mud—mashed him plumb down in that mud." The mud saved him, but Allen never fully recovered from his internal injuries.[78] This cypress clearly fell into Louis Bingham's category of hardwood timber that belonged to whoever took the trou-ble to get it, no matter who technically owned the land. The cypress trees along the river and the prime white oak and burr oak stave trees were cut early on, with only the best trees and the clearest logs taken. In the *Texas Almanac* of 1904, writer D. Woodhead, of Beaumont, la-mented the "wasteful gutting of the state's hardwood forests." He noted, "Ninety percent of these staves are exported and the only wealth created for Texas is a bare living for poorly paid stave cutters and a mere pittance for the owner of the land—if the trees are not cut with-out his knowledge and consent, which frequently happens."[79]

At first most of the big lumber companies and absentee landowners ignored their hardwoods, leaving them open to casual exploitation by local woodsmen. Most hardwoods would not float, and the bottom-lands were relatively inaccessible to tramway operations. For decades, companies logged only pine from their mixed upland forests, and much virgin hardwood subsequently was destroyed by fires raging through the discarded pine tops and other logging debris.[80] Aware of these attitudes, local people regarded hardwood timber as free to any man with the energy to take it, and taking it involved little risk. As Dan Lay explained:

It was easy enough for people to go through in a wagon with a crosscut saw and cut a tree here and cut a tree there and sell the staves for a fancy price and not have much volume to haul out and not leave much sign. Managers from Chicago might come down every five years and drive around, but by then the spot where the tree was cut would be grown up in brush, and he might not even notice the old stump. And if it was found it wasn't considered significant, because it didn't hurt the big pine stands that they were primarily holding the land for.[81]

The tradition of timber theft continued into a time when the companies tried hard to protect their hardwood resources. But as a result of the customs of the southern open range, they found this very difficult to accomplish. Timber theft continued because landowners could not—in fact, did not dare—close their land to trespass; one reason they dared not was the threat of forest and sawmill arson. As timber industry historians Robert Maxwell and Robert Baker summed the matter up: "The lumber owners and timber managers [soon] discovered that any attempt to fence the area or protect their property with no-trespass signs was regarded as virtually a declaration of war by the local population. As a result, in the Texas-Louisiana region cattle and hogs continued to graze, and natives continued to fish and hunt in the great forests of the Piney Woods despite the advent of the great lumber companies and the logging bonanza that followed."[82]

Some timber thieves cut a single tree for direct personal use, such as when people from Charlie Havard's community took a cypress and rived it into boards to roof their houses. Other bottomland timber theft was systematic, calculated, relatively large scale, and conducted for profit. The big timber companies were vulnerable to this because they could not keep people off their lands, because their operations were so large, because natives knew the tangled bottoms better than they did, and because the attitudes of local people often favored the timber thieves.

A case in point was the career of Albert Moore, of the Druso community in Houston County. Old-timers remembered Moore as an unscrupulous man who lived by his wits in the border zone between the enormous holdings of the 4-C and the Southern Pine lumber companies.[83] Moore was a powerful, dangerous, and unpredictable individual with a predatory nature, symbolized to local people by his possession of two sets of "natural teeth." He had a small sawmill and a stave-making operation, though he owned very little land. Both Southern Pine and 4-C knew he cut their timber, sawed it in his sawmill, and then with great audacity shipped it out on their railroads, but they could never catch him.

One reason they could not was the fact that Moore customarily operated in the large area of tangled sloughs and side channels where Cochino Bayou meets the Neches. Another was that he generally operated at night. Moore specialized in cutting prime white oak stave trees—going in by day to locate a good tree, fell it, saw it up, and split it into bolts. While Moore worked on the downed tree, his trained dog reportedly took a sentry position on its stump, sniffing the wind for visitors. If the dog barked, Moore dropped his tools and moved out of sight until the coast was clear. The riskier work of wagoning the stolen staves from the woods took place at night. Moore knew the area between Cochino Bayou and Pine Island like the lines of his own palm, and he could find his way back to a stave tree on the darkest night. While he walked through the woods leading the way with a lantern, a trained mule driven by an accomplice followed the light. Once, Southern Pine officials found one of Moore's stave stashes and lay a trap to catch him when he took the timber out. Aware of this, he waited until the river flooded and waded in to build a raft and float his staves out down the Neches.

Although clever and resourceful, Moore was no Robin Hood; old-timers recalled that he cheated and stole from his neighbors as readily as he did from the big companies. Nevertheless, they remembered him, with something like admiration, as a man who had defied the lumber company behemoths and gotten away with it. Anticompany attitudes ran deep for many years in backwoods southeastern Texas and to a degree are still present, even in some people who spent their lives working in the lumber industry. Brown Wiggins, of Hardin County, echoed the comments of others when he said of the companies, "They gobbled up most all of the finest timber in our country, and the sawmills didn't make very much out of it, and we didn't do too well either."[84] People still recount stories of how the big companies allegedly tricked or pressured older relatives out of their land, robbing with a fountain pen instead of (as in the case of Albert Moore) with an ax. Partially as a result of these attitudes, timber theft and forest arson have long plagued the timber companies.[85] As late as the 1940s, Southern Pine still found it expedient to allow a number of "squatters" to continue to live on company lands in return for watching out for thieves and firebugs.[86]

After 1910, hardwood prices began going up, and Texas timber companies paid more and more attention to their hardwood timber. Hickory in particular was in heavy demand for use in automobile wheels, and when Kirby Lumber Company caught another company stealing virgin hickory logs from its land, it billed the culprits at several times the going rate for prime pine timber.[87] White oak and walnut trees remained in demand, and so increasingly were the red oaks and the gums—tupelo, black gum, and sweet gum. In 1916 Texas had twenty billion board feet of standing hardwood, and the annual cut had risen to seventy million feet, about one-tenth the annual cut of pine.[88]

Southern Pine Lumber Company pioneered large-scale hardwood logging in Texas, opening a major mill at Pineland around 1908 and continuing to cut hardwood near its home base of Diboll. Big hardwood mills also started operations at Call Junction, at Bessmay on the Santa Fe Railroad in Jasper County, and elsewhere. In 1917 Sabine Tram Lumber Company began to cut fifty thousand board feet of hardwood a day in one side of its double mill at Deweyville, and the Carter Lumber Company's double mill at Camden soon did the same. Many smaller mills, such as the specialized mill of "Hickory" Jones in Angelina County, also began hardwood operations. The 1920 census reflected the continuing hardwood boom, recording a 1919 cut of over twenty-seven million board feet of oak, eighteen million board feet of gum, and over one million board feet each of cottonwood, tupelo, ash, hickory, and cypress.[89]

Some of the big hardwood mills began to phase out by World War II, having cut large portions of the virgin bottomlands along the Neches, but others found additional timber and cut right through the building boom of the 1950s. These cuts followed earlier high-gradings for white oak, cypress, and other species, but this time the mills took all the commercially valuable timber that was straight and sound. Only hollow trees, crooked trees, and trees of little or no commercial value were left. Companies cut the oaks for flooring, the ashes for handle stock, and the big sweet gums and black gums for furniture building materials, boxes, and crates.[90] By the 1930s, the gum species dominated the inventories of many hardwood companies. In the 1940s the large Angelina County Lumber Company mill at Ewing cut twenty-six species of hardwood and some loblolly pine at the rate of sixty thousand board feet a day, but 60 percent of its cut was sweet gum.[91]

Huge virgin timber still emerged from the bottomland forests even at this late date. Angelina County Lumber Company cut one white oak that measured 72 inches at the stump and scaled twenty-eight hundred board feet and several sweet gums that scaled from twenty-eight hundred to forty-two hundred board feet. Southern Pine sawyer Claude Welch, of Diboll, remembered the day his company hauled an enormous 108-inch-diameter tupelo log to the mill for him to saw—somehow. The base of the log had to be trimmed off to get it into the mill, and the saw guide had to be removed to get it into the saw. The machinery used to pick up the log almost blew out with the strain, and Welch worked at sawing this sixteen-foot log for over two hours.[92]

The great tupelo log had probably been loaded on an eight-wheel

Martin log wagon with a "roll chain" pulled by several teams of mules, then drawn to the tram by mules or oxen. If steam engines, steam loaders, and steam skidders dominated the uplands, the bottoms remained the province of animal power into the 1950s. Long after the log wagons were replaced with trucks, hardwood logs still were skidded and loaded with animal power. In the usual pattern, the hardwood loggers went into the bottoms during the two or three driest months of the year, cut the timber with oversize crosscut saws, then hauled it to the nearest tramway just out of the bottom with big-wheel carts or eight-wheel log wagons. The distance hauled varied from a few hundred yards to two or three miles.

Even in the so-called dry season the bottom was only relatively dry, and companies sometimes resorted to skids called "toads" or "mud boats" to get the logs out. Three yokes or more of oxen could slide logs out with a toad in places where even a big-wheel cart would stick in the mud. The toad never bogged down and "would almost float in the marshes." The loggers worked beside their animals and would "just waller in that mud like a bunch of hogs—you couldn't put your finger on any of [them] where there wasn't mud."[93]

Bottomland loggers divided their loyalties between oxen and mules. The "mule skinners" praised the intelligence, speed, and strength of their animals, noting that good mules did what their driver asked with almost a sixth sense, requiring little direction. "Bull punchers," on the other hand, almost constantly urged their oxen on with whipcracks, curses, and what one man remembered as a sort of "singing to his oxen—giving commands, cursing, and cracking the whip."[94] The whip was very important to the ox driver, and Walter Cole recalled: "I used of could knock a horsefly off a cow with it and never hit the cow— these big old green horseflies—pop him off. They'd go like a gunshot— a big gun, too, a ten-gauge." For years Cole used six-yoke teams to pull his eight-wheel log wagons. He observed, "The bigger the team, the better I liked it."[95]

The Carter Lumber Company, which logged the bottoms where Piney Creek runs into the Neches, was famous for its oxen. The company used oxen to get the logs out of the wet bottoms, then used faster mules to get them to the tram or mill.[96] Even the mule men admitted that oxen were better than mules in extreme mud, since the cloven hooves of oxen spread out and kept them from bogging down as much. At a certain point the mules would lie down and quit, refusing to work because of the mud. Oxen, on the other hand, "would bog up, but they'll just keep a-pullin', gruntin' and groanin', and they'll go on. They don't never get down. . . . The oxen'd be bogged down so deep their bellies be touching the ground but they just keep goin.'"[97] As another bull puncher observed: "Oxen won't stall. Mules will 'shoot crap' [lunge forward and backward]. Oxen will get down on their knees and grunt and pull, first one direction, then another. As soon as they feel the load moving they get going and won't stop until they hit solid ground."[98]

Even with oxen, bottomland logging was highly seasonal, and there were inaccessible places that loggers never reached. At Big Slough Island in Houston County, the Forks of the River area in Jasper County, and other locations, loggers were cut off by sloughs and swamps, and most of the hardwood was never timbered. Logging in the bottoms nearly always was possible in late summer, but as Carl Havard explained: "By the first of October, you needed to be getting ready to get out of the bottom. You built your log roads right up aside of the river bank—don't get away from it, you'll bog down. That was the hardest, driest place you have."[99]

Then, sometime in October or November, the Neches rose to flood its bottomlands, and logging was over for that year. Soon after Harold Snelson moved to Angelina County in 1939, he got a job cutting hardwood timber for the Angelina County Lumber Company in the Neches bottom across from Weaver's Bend. Snelson recalled laboring for hours at one end of a six-foot Simon saw cutting a huge overcup oak. As he said, "It [the saw] had bout six inches of play through that sucker—just rub it off where you ain't got no more pull than that—and I's done give out. I thought we'd never get that sucker down." They finally felled the tree and had "got maybe three eighteen- or twenty-foot cuts" when the rain began. Abandoning the overcup oak, the crew escaped the bottoms just in time. The rains continued, the river rose, and the crew "never did get no pay for that last week's log-cutting."[100]

Other bottomland and upland hardwoods went directly to the tie maker. After Charlie Havard's father sold his timber to the Manning mill, which cut only pine, he gave the rejected hardwood, even the prime white oak, to fourteen-year-old Charlie to make into ties. Charlie explained:

Well, you'd take a tree, saw that thing down, cut you off a eight-foot cut—that's the length of the tie—and you have to look at the end of it to tell how many ties its gonna make. And then you take sledge and wedge and bust that thing out till you got it down nearly to a tie size, then take a doublebit and score hack it, and take a broad ax and hew it. Some of them oaks would make eight and ten ties to a cut—big old white oak. I made one that was so big I couldn't stand on the ground and hit it with a sledge way agin the top of it. Had to get up on it, I was that small. I crawled right up on top of the trunk.[101]

Ties from this fine white oak doubtless went into service in the Manning mill's tramway operations in the longleaf woods. By and large, however, the railroads and lumber companies did not like ties split from such large hardwoods, and their preferences in railroad ties helped to shape a major industry. For many years the companies wanted ties of heart hardwood hewn (not sawed) from smaller timber. Without much evidence to back up their prejudice, the companies believed that hewn ties—ties made by hand with a broadax—resisted rot better and lasted longer than machine-made sawmill ties. From 1880 to 1940, tens of thousands of East Texans found employment as part-time or full-time tie choppers because of this preference.[102]

From 1880 on, the Texas census roles were full of men who listed their occupation as "tie-maker," and no wonder. The railroads that crisscrossed East Texas between 1870 and 1900 got their ties from the forests they passed through, and every mile of track required an average of 2,640 ties. In 1887, forester M. G. Kern estimated that U.S. railroads were consuming forest resources equal to the clearing of three hundred thousand acres of virgin forestland each year. Texas axmen were doing their part. In 1905 alone, Texans made four million ties.[103] As the entrepreneur at the top of a long chain of contractors and subcontractors, even "Prince of the Pines" John Henry Kirby got involved. In 1916 the Kirby Lumber Company closed a deal with the New York Central Railroad to supply several million hewn hardwood and pine ties annually. Kirby already had another large tie contract with the Santa Fe Railroad, so the New York Central deal made his company the "biggest hewn-tie producing firm in the South and probably in the world."[104]

At the bottom of the chain of production were two kinds of tie hacks: the professionals, who made ties for a living and moved like gypsies from tie camp to tie camp, and the part-timers, usually subsistence farmers and stockmen who made ties seasonally for a little ready cash. (Doubtless many jacks-of-all-trades, Neches Valley woodsmen chose to describe themselves as "tie-makers" to the census man because this was their closest approach to formal employment.)

In the backwoods communities along the Neches, someone in almost every family chopped ties. In southern Jasper County, Babe McGalin and his older brother Linn made crude ties hewn on only two sides for logging tramways, receiving ten cents a tie for their labors. They worked fast, and before taking the trouble to score-hack and hew a log, they tested it with a "hard wedge" to see if they could split off a whole side at one time.[105] At Shooks Bluff in Cherokee County, William Chandler supplemented his farming income by tie making to help support a large family, and his neighbor William Mettlen hacked ties most of the time and farmed on the side. At his insistence, Mettlen's family even buried William in 1937 in his customary tie-making outfit of jumper and blue overalls.[106] Even the rare man who did not make ties often involved himself in the industry in other ways. In Trinity County Roy Smith and his brother regularly picked up ties from local tie makers and hauled them to the railroad in a wagon, making fifteen to twenty dollars a load. Each man's ties were identified with a special mark.[107]

George Carpenter, of Angelina County, was typical of thousands of other tie makers along the Neches. When he was only twelve, he began hacking ties with his father after crops were laid by, and he soon graduated from the less-demanding job of score-hacking, cutting shallow diagonal cuts into the side of the log with a double-bit ax, to hewing, following behind with the broadax to "knock off the chunks" between the score hacks. Recognizing talent when he saw it, George's father made the boy a special left-handed hickory handle for the broadax and put him to work at that part of the job. As Carpenter recalled:

So, I got to hewing with that, and I could hew just about as good as anybody else. I was a kid—I wasn't but about twelve or fourteen years old. We'd make about 30 ties the day, that was bout the limit. We'd cut down maybe three or four trees, and make em up. Then we'd cut down some more and make em up. Well, we'd make up maybe 200 ties, and then on a rainy day when it was too wet to work in the field we'd haul em out and put on the track over there [at Old Union]. And then the inspector from the railroad would come along and he'd inspect em and then mail us a check.

Later, during the Great Depression, George Carpenter used his skills with a broadax to hew bridge timbers for WPA projects working in the area, hewing "a sixteen-foot log as straight as you could saw it."[108]

Sometimes, family tie-making teams were not brother and brother or father and son but husband and wife. Congressional commissions investigating industrial occupations sometimes regarded this as a scandal, hearing how "mothers with little babies" had to "get crossties for the railroad company for bread." Sometimes husband-and-wife tie makers even took their children along to the woods. The East Texas play-party song "Old Joe Clark" bemoaned:

> Old Joe Clark is a-cuttin' ties,
> Old Lady Clark is a-haulin'.
> Little Joe Clark in the middle of the road
> Is killin' hisself a-bawlin'.[109]

Undeterred by "Old Joe Clark," Ellen Walker, of Hardin County, made ties with her spouse for decades and often took her children with them. As she recalled, Ellen enjoyed making ties.

> Me and my husband cut ties on the Blake Survey. It was three-and-a-half miles from our house to where we cut. We had a baby then, and I had to take the baby with me. Took my old coat, spread it down and put her on it. She'd set there and I'd watch her. I'd score hack and my husband would take his broad ax and bust the slabs off and level it up. . . . We made about twenty a day. We made switch ties out of oak. They had to be 18 feet long. . . . We got ten cents for the regular ties and twenty cents for them long 'uns. . . . Making ties ain't hard work, just takes time. You cut your tree down, measure 'em end to end, measure 'em in the middle and score hack 'em, then take a broad ax and bust it out. I enjoyed makin' them ties. We sold 'em to the Santa Fe Railroad and they paid off good. . . . I was 53 when we quit making ties.[110]

The Walkers, the Carpenters, and the Smiths were part-time participants in the tie industry, but other men were professional tie choppers, moving from tie camp to tie camp and job to job. Although linked to the railroads and the lumber companies through their profession, they were free spirits on the outer edges of southern industrial society. Tie choppers were paid by the tie, worked at their own speeds, and went where they wanted. One man who knew them observed: "They are nomads, the very nature of their calling makes them so, and being nomads, they are spendthrifts. They wander to every point where railroads run and timber grows. . . . Very small causes start them traveling, and it is commonly said that a jug of whiskey and a copy of the St. Louis *Globe-Democrat* will break up any tie camp in the world. The *Globe-Democrat* is the tie makers bible. All the big jobs are advertised in it."[111]

Solomon Wright, of Jasper County, became one such professional tie maker. After rambling around doing different things, he took up his lifelong career of tie cutting at a camp on the Neches River in February 1900. He got the few tools of the trade, apprenticed himself for a time to an experienced tie maker who showed him how to chop, and he was on his own. Within a few days he was known as one of the best men on the job. About the middle of March, a tie job opened up at Ford's Bluff, where the Santa Fe Railroad crossed the Neches, and Wright went there. He noted of the tie-chopping life:

> I was "set." I could make pretty good money and ramble all I wanted to and always be sure of a job. There was tie-making every place there was timber, and there was always room for one more. Best of

all, I didn't have to work under a boss. I could work as little or as much as I pleased, and if I wanted to sit down and rest it was nobody's business. I really worked harder and longer hours than I could have worked if I had been working by the day. I got paid for every lick I struck. If a man knows he can quit or sit down and rest any time he wants to, he feels comfortable with himself. Then, tie-making is nice, clean work. Cutting the ties, a fellow never thinks about time's passing. The trouble is, it passes too fast.[112]

Many subsistence farmers and stockmen along the Neches valued their personal independence as much as Solomon Wright, and they often chose to supplement their cash incomes with timber occupations that avoided direct employment by the big companies. After the timber industry failed during the Great Depression, these minor trades became even more important. Besides stock raising, small farming, tie making, fur trapping, and commercial fishing, people made and sold white oak staves, cypress or pine shingles, charcoal, and white oak or hickory baskets. They also made money by recovering from the river sinker logs lost since log-floating days and by collecting pine knots, wild honey, red oak bark, or gray moss from the woods. Just after 1900, a few people—or perhaps rather more than a few—waded Neches sandbars searching for mussels containing freshwater pearls. After the Eighteenth Amendment passed in 1919, Neches Valley whiskey makers were legion. As more than one man told me, "They practically had to wear tags down there to keep from selling it to one another."[113]

The making of staves and shingles for the market was as old as settlement times and lasted as long as the prime white oaks and heart cypresses. Stave makers wasted a lot of timber, since only the first cut or two off the bottom would do for staves; the rest of the tree was left to rot. Most of the staves went to the French wine industry, which, until modern times, refused to use anything but prime, hand-split, white oak staves for barrels or wine tanks. Workers felled the tree, sawed cuts of certain lengths off the bottom, and split and "bolted up" the cuts into square pieces, from which the staves were rived. The East Texas stave trade peaked around 1900, when over 7 million staves were produced, and by 1916 was on the decline. The international demand for white oak staves was still there, but the big stave trees were "running out."[114]

Stave making was rough, hot work, performed in the deep woods, and when John Bevil visited his father at an isolated stave camp around 1900, he found the men at work with nothing on but their broad-brimmed hats and heavy shoes. As he said: "They were making these big tank staves—be eight or ten, twelve feet long. They split them out and then they took the broad ax and smoothed them, and they could

Cutting virgin white oak to make barrel staves in the bottoms near Roganville, Jasper County, c. 1900. (Jasper County Historical Commission, Jasper, Texas)

smooth them just as clean as you could with a plane."[115] In later times many of the stave camps along the lower Neches were manned by skilled European immigrants from Croatia, an area now partly in Austria and partly in what was once Yugoslavia. Confused locals called these people "Slavonians," "Slabolians," or simply "Germans," but they were impressed by the Europeans' woodworking skills, capacity for hard work, and ability to drink whiskey. Pete Racki, one of their number who remained in the United States, recalled that the Croatians often used an assembly-line method in which one member of the crew did the splitting, another the riving, and another the smoothing with a drawknife.[116]

Two stave camps operating in the Neches bottoms near Buna around World War I felled the choicest white oak, cut the trunks into lengths, bolted them up, then shipped the bolts out by the wagonload. In this case the bolts were made into staves somewhere else, probably overseas. Babe McGalin's father, accompanied by one of the stave men, ran the weekly supply wagon of food and whiskey to the camp, and by the time the two got there, "they'd all be 'bout drunk." Sometimes the stave makers bought a whole rooter hog from Mr. McGalin, cleaned it, spitted it on an iron pole connected to a homemade crank, and "turned that hog two days and two nights" over a slow fire. The McGalins regarded this practice as highly eccentric but still thought the "Slabolian stave makers" were "nice people."[117]

Shingle making was probably even more widespread and economically important than stave making. In 1900, the same year in which 7 million Texas staves were made, no less than 210 million shingles were produced. George Carpenter and his father sold shingles and pickets as well as ties and were typical of many small makers. The shingle maker split a section of cypress trunk into halves, then the halves into quarters, then the quarters into eighths; then they split out the heartwood. With most logs the wood was then "bolted up," ready for "barking" and riving off the shingles. After riving, shingles were dressed with a drawknife on a shaving horse. It took around five thousand shingles to cover a forty-foot-long barn, and a good shingle maker could make over one thousand per day.

By World War I, some backcountry shingle makers had mechanized their operations with shingle mills. Jess Wells's family, in Houston County, operated a small shingle mill that was rigged up from a mule-powered cotton gin. Pine blocks were boiled in a tank to soften them, then they were "fed to the knife." Powered by the mule, the knife cranked up and then snapped down, cutting the shingle. Whether they wanted to or not, five of the seven Wells children worked in this mill on days when it was literally "too wet to plow."[118]

Charcoal making and basketmaking were other minor woods industries practiced along the Neches. Fount Simmons, of Hardin County, made excellent hickory and white oak baskets, selling all he could produce, and other people did the same. Commercial charcoal operations differed from folk methods only in scale. In Angelina County, Oscar Allen's father made charcoal on his own land and hauled it to Lufkin in wagons, and Beaumont native Daniel Lay recalled a larger charcoal enterprise on the lower Neches: "As late as the 1920s, there was a commercial charcoal operation in the Neches River bottom near Beaumont. Hardwood trees were cut and split into pieces suitable for piling in a tight teepee shape. The pile was covered with soil and ignited at the bottom. It smoldered for days, filling the bottom with smoke, in the slow production of a pure form of carbon. When ignited and fanned it produced more heat than any wood fire."[119]

Other people made money by collecting raw materials directly from the woods, often taking full advantage of the customary usufruct rights of the free range. By accepted custom, pine knots, gray moss, wild honey, and other things (but not stave trees) were there for any person to take. Dave Gandy had mastered the mysteries involved in tracing bees to their hives from their watering spots along spring creeks or from his bait cans of sugar water. Gandy found twenty or so bee trees a year in the Neches bottoms; he marked the trees as his own with an "X" or "III," cut them at his leisure, and sold the honey in town.[120] Other people, often whole families working together, gathered Spanish moss during the winter, processed it, and sold the wiry fiber as stuffing for chairs, saddles, and automobile seats. This was not easy; one man who used to collect it recalled, "That stuff is so light that you work hard for a whole week and you won't have even 100 pounds."[121] Often, the easiest and most economical way to collect moss was to look both ways for the landowner, then cut down the tree in which it grew. As one man remembered: "When cattle hear an ax hit a tree over there in that oak country, they just come running. That's ice cream for them, Spanish moss."[122]

Most materials that people collected from the woods to sell had older folk uses, including the moss, which had long been used to stuff mattresses and saddle pads and to serve the functions of paper towels and toilet paper. Another was fat pine, so necessary for starting fires and boiling water in big iron pots. The timber companies used pine knots to fuel the steam boilers of their woods locomotives, skidders, and loaders, and for several decades local people made money by going through the woods in wagons, picking up fat pine, and piling it beside the tracks. During the winter of 1918, Roy Smith, of Trinity County, camped out on Pine Island with his father and brother and collected pine knots for the Southern Pine tramways. They got $2.75 a cord for the fat pine stacked along the tracks, and the pickings were good. The Smiths were working the remains of the original virgin longleaf timber, cut perhaps thirty years before, and as Smith noted, "Them old tops would rot and maybe you could get a cord of pine knots right in one top."[123] Demand for fat-pine fuel was high, since the companies used prodigious quantities of the resinous heart of pine to power the engines with which they demolished the present forest. According to one professional forester, "The volume of fuel wood consumed could amount to 140 cords per track mile per year."[124]

Other minor woods industries of the first half of the twentieth century also made money by scavenging in the leavings of the wasteful cut-and-get-out era. Some of the virgin cypresses on the lower river had been cut from boats at times of high water, and stumps up to sixteen feet high had been left in the woods. A half century after the five-hundred- to one-thousand-year-old trees were felled, people went into the bottoms with log wagons during the dry seasons and cut the trees, usually finding them perfectly sound after all those years of standing in the woods.[125] By the 1920s and 1930s, lumber from the stumps of these ancient heart cypresses far surpassed anything obtainable from living forests.

At about the same time, other people up and down the Neches launched salvage operations to recover other virgin timber that had gone to the bottom of sloughs and the river as sinkers. The river transport era of East Texas logging had been based on the availability of centuries-old cypress and pine trees full of resinous heartwood that resisted penetration by water. The loggers' usual rule of thumb was that a tree needed to be at least two-thirds heart to float; some that failed to meet this minimum were left to lie in the woods after being cut. Even good logs of heart cypress, pine, and sweet gum needed a long season of drying before loggers could raft them up to float them to Beaumont, and even with these there were always surprises. Some logs, after being skidded into the river at a bluff bank, went immediately to the bottom; others barely floated for a while, took on water, and then sank. Still others in loose-log drives made it halfway to Beaumont before becoming sinkers. Gradually, all up and down the Neches, at log landings, bluff banks, and the mouths of creeks where logs were often rafted up, more and more sinkers accumulated on the river bottom.

From 1920 on, by way of various Rube Goldberg devices, people raised the sinkers from their watery graves and sold them to the mills. On the upper river at low water, people used cables and mule-powered stump pullers to crank logs from the river, and later they used truck winches and tractors. The Sadler family from Polk County for a time supplied Southern Pine's "box factory" at Diboll with Neches sinkers, cranking them out by stump puller. Most of these made "pretty lumber." Claude Welch explained, "That thing had a drum on it, and gears—the mule [would] go round and round and cable that log out of the river." In another typical operation, a man simply walked out in the river up to his armpits to put tongs on a log, then the log was dragged out "by a gasoline skid rig powered by a Fordson tractor."[126]

Farther downstream, more sinkers littered the bottom, and salvage operations took place on a larger scale. During the depression, the Strawther family of Jasper County invented a pontoon boat to raise sinkers at Cow Creek on the Sabine, an operation that other people quickly imitated on the Neches. Simple but effective, the Strawther sinker boat had two wooden pontoons eight feet apart with a hand windlass, cable, and tongs located between them. James Strawther recalled, "We'd move those pontoon boats over those logs a-laying down there, and drop those tongs down there and catch em, and use that hand windlass and bring em up." Once they were loosed from the sand on the bottom, many of these huge logs were only slightly heavier than water, and two men could easily hold a log on the surface. After eight or ten logs were accumulated, the sinker boat moved to the bank and unloaded to trucks.[127]

Some of the cypress logs raised by the Strawthers were enormous—eighty feet long—and so old they had been felled with axes, but their wood was still sound. Mills did not pay much for anyone's timber during the depression days of the 1930s, but the Strawthers' rig was simple, cheap, and easy to operate, and the sinkers themselves were free for the taking. So many people imitated the Strawthers that, when they moved their operations over to the Neches around 1935, they found that most of the prime logs were already gone.

Sinker salvaging, gray moss gathering, and a dozen other minor woods industries received new impetus during the depression as people newly out of work from sawmills and lumber camps tried to find other ways to make a living. Many bonanza-era logging operations had cut out in the 1920s, and many more succumbed during the 1930s. The price of high-quality pine timber dropped from $42 per thousand board feet in 1930 to $14.25 per thousand board feet in 1932—and this at a time when it cost the companies about $24 to produce it.[128] Mills shut down or went on extremely limited schedules, and thousands of people fell back on the survival skills of hunting, fishing, gardening, and stock raising skills learned from their grandparents, and began walking the roads looking for work.

One of these was tie maker George Carpenter, of Angelina County. The price of ties in 1932 hardly made the trade worthwhile, and Carpenter looked for other work. Every day he went out, found nothing to do, then came home and shot squirrels for his family's supper, making every .22 shell count. Gradually, things got tighter and tighter for the Carpenter family, and one day after George had walked four miles to a farm, chopped cotton all day for seventy-five cents, and then walked four miles home, he decided to try another way to make money. The outlaw career of George Carpenter, moonshiner, had begun.

Illegal whiskey making was an old British proclivity, based on techniques—and antigovernment attitudes—several hundreds of years old. The name "moonshiner" had its origin in Scotland in the eighteenth century as a term of reference for traditional family whiskey distillers who chose to avoid the British excise tax by making their product at night. These people's descendants came to North America with the basic knowledge of how to build and operate a simple "pot still" to make whiskey from a variety of grains, and that knowledge survived in folk tradition well into the twentieth century.[129]

Traditional whiskey making was a simple process, though some people were much better at its nuances than were others, and it was really more an art or a craft than a science. The whiskey maker put the grain—in the southern United States usually corn "chops"—into a barrel with a certain amount of water and yeast, heated it, then allowed it to cool and ferment into "mash" (also called "jack" or "buck"). Then he put the mash into a copper still over a wood fire and heated the mixture above the boiling point of alcohol but below the boiling point of water. The pot still was sealed with a copper "cap" that fed the gaseous alcohol (mixed with some water vapor) through a copper "cap arm" into a long copper tube called a "worm," which usually coiled around through a barrel of cool water. By the time the gaseous alcohol reached the end of the worm, it had condensed into a white liquid— raw, "first-run" corn whiskey. The traditional maker did not drink this first-run product but cleaned out his still, put the whiskey back in, and repeated the process. "Double-run" whiskey emerged from the worm at 90 to 95 percent alcohol, or 180 to 190 proof—"hot whiskey," some people called it. The maker cut it to 100 proof or so with rainwater, aged it for a while if he was so inclined, and then drank it or sold it.

After Prohibition arrived in 1919, the methods of making whiskey changed. Unlike some of his neighbors, who made it for a living, Charlie Havard, of Angelina County, made only a little double-run whiskey for personal consumption at a spring branch not far from his home. Meanwhile, however, ten or fifteen miles upriver from Charlie's operation, tenants and owners at a big cotton farm had set aside their plows and were making whiskey on a grand scale, shipping it out to the Kilgore oil fields in several-hundred-gallon tank trucks. Mash tanks, stills, and the rest of their equipment were on the scale of a small sawmill. This operation ran all night under lights powered by its own electric generator and trucked the whiskey over its own asphalt roads. Clearly, at least in this part of the Neches country, moonshining had modernized.[130]

Illegal whiskey making did not disappear after the repeal of Prohibition in 1933, but waxed and waned with the rise and fall of the federal tax rate on legal liquor. George Carpenter and thousands of other people began making whiskey for the first time during the depression in the 1930s, even though prices fell drastically after 1933. Sold for as low as two to three dollars a gallon, moonshine was still the "poor man's drunk," and during the previous decade many people had developed a liking for its raw, fiery taste. In 1930s Jasper County, as elsewhere up and down the Neches, moonshiners and moonshine were everywhere. C. W. Gandy recalled: "You used to go to dances around here, and when you'd drive up it'd look like headlights. Ever treetop around that place had a gallon of whiskey under it. Well, if you didn't drink with everybody it'd make em mad and you'd have to fight with em. And we'd generally get so drunk to keep from fighting em, we'd end up sleeping on the porch at night all night long."[131]

With little doubt, the stockmen-farmers in the little communities along the Neches participated in a big way in the moonshine era, though most of them were small makers like Charlie Havard or George Carpenter. Somebody made whiskey in nearly every community, and in places like Black Creek in Hardin County, Weaver's Bend in Angelina County, and Dogtown in Cherokee County, the "somebodys" included nearly everyone. Remote settlements along the Neches were strategically located for moonshining operations: they were a long way from the county seat, on the edge of the semiwilderness of the river bottoms, and always just across the river from a different county. They were, in other words, remote from the law, in a good place to hide stills, and close to another whiskey market. In addition, they were often at the dead end of a country road with only one way into the community, a fact that made it hard for the law to approach unobserved. Former Sheriff Frank Brunt, of Cherokee County, explained:

> On that Buckshot Road back in the moonshining days, most of the bridges then was built out of this heavy oak timber. They'd get a little loose anyhow, but they'd help em to get loose. I've driven over a many an old bridge, and it'd rattle, you know. You hit one of them old bridges and it'd make quite a noise. Well, that would cause the first neighbors close to the bridge to look and see who's coming. Maybe you wasn't gonna stop at their house at all, but they'd see you. And if they recognized you, when you passed they'd go out there and shoot a gun. And you'd go on down about a mile or so and maybe hear another gun. And that was just a signal that there was officers in the community.[132]

Sometimes, as others affirmed, neighbors would also sound their "blowing horns," honk their car horns, or simply pick up their crank telephones. In any case, it was hard to approach the Neches communities unannounced.

Two things were most critical to the situation of the Neches Valley moonshiner: the attitudes of his neighbors in the community and the law-and-order disposition of his county sheriff. The neighbors knew the area as intimately as the moonshiner and often moved about the open range working their livestock or hunting squirrels for the pot. Consequently, they usually knew where the moonshiner's still was— in fact, knew where all the local stills were. Whiskey-drinking neighbors might drop in for a social call, a glass of "buck," or a sample of the product, and teetotal neighbors might just look the other way, but for most people, community loyalties took precedence over attitudes about

the use of alcohol. A man running a still was a temptation to his enemies (or to his competitors), but few community members would dare
to turn him in. As Aubrey Cole, of Jasper County, put it, people usually
"honored your whiskey still." In whiskey-making communities like
Black Creek, people that did not drink or make whiskey usually went
out of their way to demonstrate support and approval of community
members that did. Nobody wanted to be known as a "pimp," an informer.

The other critical factor for the Neches moonshiner was the liquor-
law attitudes of his county sheriff, which ranged on a continuum from
collusion with local moonshiners, to cooperation, to neutrality, to ada-
mant opposition. With little doubt, the Angelina County sheriff in
office at the time of the big Strain Farm whiskey operation upriver
from Charlie Havard knew all about it. In fact, local people with good
reason to know affirm that this sheriff—like many others—was "on
the take." Sometimes the sheriffs and the moonshiners were virtually
one and the same. According to one ex-sheriff, "Up in the north end of
Newton County, old man Beaver Bishop was a known whiskey man;
he was sheriff of the county."[133] In Cherokee County before Sheriff
Frank Brunt's time, county whiskey makers "had the sheriff's office
taken care of. If the federals come in, it's customary to get with the
sheriff to raid the still, if you both trusted one another. It got to where,
when the federals come into the county, the sheriff would get on the
telephone and call the main bootleggers and tell em, 'You better bring
your clothes off the line, it looks like it gonna rain.' That was the
signal. Everybody went and hid their whiskey and shut their stills
down."[134]

Sometimes, as former Texas Ranger Carl Busch contended, not just
the sheriff but the whole county power structure seemed in collusion
with the outlaws.

I was sent into Trinity County in 1928, and it was a terribly bad
bootleg-whiskey making county. Everybody was related from river
to river—first, second, or third cousins. We caught a man who had
five stills set up in a row. He had twenty fifty-gallon gasoline drums
that he was cooking his mash in. Then, he had a gallon can of
concentrated lye sitting there that he put into the mash to make it
cook quicker—wasn't satisfied to let nature do it—and that was
being sold by a hotel in Lufkin. That would eat the lining of your
stomach up! That would kill you! The man should have been hung
right there under a limb for that, cause he had no regard for human
beings at all. . . . We never could get this man indicted [though] it
was a penitentiary offense for making bootleg whiskey in those
days, because he was a first cousin to the county judge, the county
attorney, and to the sheriff.[135]

Most commonly, however, the sheriff took a neutral position toward his county moonshiners—not joining them, probably not taking their money, perhaps seeking them out when someone informed on them, but otherwise not going out of his way to look for them. Especially during the 1930s, a sheriff well knew that many locals made whiskey out of acute financial need and that some of them had voted for him in the last election. In fact, some of them were probably his own friends and family. The whiskey maker, on the other hand, recognized that the sheriff was just doing his job. These attitudes often resulted in a strange kind of friendly rivalry. The moonshiner did everything to avoid capture, but if caught, he usually interacted in a friendly way with the sheriff and gave him no trouble. For his part, the sheriff usually treated the whiskey maker with respect and courtesy, often taking his word that he would come in to the courthouse to post bond the next day. George Carpenter said of his long-term adversary Sheriff Henry Billingsley, "He was a good sheriff, he never did mistreat nobody that he caught running whiskey." Honest sheriffs who played the game this way were even admired. The operator of the Strain Farm distillery told Charlie Havard: "Henry Billingsley would not sell out. We ain't got enough money to buy him. He won't sell."[136]

At the opposite end of the continuum from the sheriff and whiskey makers were the lawmen who fought county moonshiners tooth and nail. Sheriff Frank Brunt in Cherokee County numbered among these, and he had a personal grudge. Brunt's brother Bill had been sheriff just before him, and Bill and a well-known county whiskey man had shot and killed each other during a midnight confrontation on a county highway. Brunt pursued his local moonshiners without mercy, even the ones related to him, and used direct methods. When he caught a whiskey maker, he took the man into the woods and "put a little pressure" on the moonshiner with a persimmon limb, then went after whomever the man had informed on. Brunt employed one local "who was just like an Indian in the woods—knew every pig trail back in that 40,000 acres of open range"—to find stills for him, and he lay in wait for bootleggers in his souped-up Ford at every hour of the day or night. Brunt recalled: "Some of em had their car tuned up professional, but I had mine thataway, too. I give em a pretty good race. I like to got killed chasing em—get on those dirty roads in summertime and that dust fogging up, it was worst than driving in the dark. On that slough bridge going over into Nacogdoches County there's a curve where we wrecked two or three. That's a good place to catch em—crowd em on that curve and wreck em."[137]

The game of cat and mouse between moonshiner and sheriff often pitted woodsman against woodsman. In the days of the open range,

Lawmen displaying captured whiskey still from Buna area, Jasper County, 1920s. (The Museum of East Texas, Lufkin, Texas)

people living in the little communities along the Neches had detailed knowledge of many square miles of landscape and made full use of this knowledge to hide their stills. Sheriffs, on the other hand, prided themselves on how well they knew every nook and cranny of their counties and hired deputies from the same woods-wise communities that the moonshiners came from. The moonshiners' determination to hide was matched by the lawmen's determination to catch them in the act "on their still."

Whiskey makers used many strategies to avoid detection, often setting up operations in the most inaccessible areas they could get to. They might crawl into the densest thicket they could find and cut out a place in the middle to set up their still. Or, they might wait until the river rose in the fall and then wade or paddle out to one of the maze of islands in the backwater to set up there. Still others dug their operations into cutbanks on the bends of creeks, put them under brush heaps, pulled green saplings over them to hide them and dissipate telltale smoke, set them up in the shattered forests just behind logging fronts, or dug them completely into the ground.

A few old hands operated at several locations scattered throughout the woods, moving their stills around from site to site like an MX missile moving from silo to silo. If they got the idea that the law was watching one location, they moved a few miles away to another. The open range facilitated this mobile strategy, since a man had the right to go anywhere he wanted and there was no reason at all to run whiskey on one's own land—in fact, quite the opposite. A moonshiner in the Hudson community followed this strategy, often operating on the land of Oscar Allen's family because, as Allen said, "Nobody suspected my father because he worked all the time."[138] Moonshiners so commonly set up in the no-man's-land of the national forests that foresters made it a practice of going around to country stores the week before they planned to work an area and talking loudly about their intentions. This gave the whiskey men time to hide their stills.[139]

No matter how far back in the woods he set up operations, a moonshiner still had to market his product, and this raised other dangers. Some protected themselves by selling only to known bootleggers at a lower price, and others relied on systems of dumb barter. Following directions, a customer might drive to a certain bridge over a back slough and stomp his foot loudly three times, or go to a certain spot along a road and honk his horn, and then leave money in a hollow tree. Thirty minutes later he would return and pick up his whiskey, the moonshiner having come and gone unseen.

Whiskey makers operating in the deep woods guarded against the signs that might give them away—the smell of smoke, the ring of metal on metal, or the telltale traces of corn chops along a trail. Meanwhile, their woodsmen competitors in the sheriff's office or the Internal Revenue Service, the IRS, watched for just these things. They staked out remote roads, sniffed the wind, listened for careless sounds, and walked the banks of spring creeks.

Moonshiners and lawmen played a game of strategy and counterstrategy. The whiskey makers had to have a good source of water, preferably from a spring or spring creek, and the sheriff and his men often searched these places for stills. Knowing that, the moonshiners sometimes piped water in from some distance away or used "pop augurs" to drill shallow wells so that they could locate somewhere else. When a moonshiner walked into the woods to his still from a county road, he took care to leave the road from a different point every time, only after some distance joining his main trail. Knowing this, deputies and IRS agents often walked parallel to a county road about a hundred yards out, trying to pick up the moonshiner's primary trail after all his little subtrails had come together.

Tiring of this game after a while, many whiskey makers decided to hide their operations much closer to home. As Dudley Denmon, of Jasper County, eloquently explained:

How in the hell you gonna hide from the people when you're selling whiskey? If you went in the woods twenty miles you just had the pleasure of toting your damn liquor and all your damn supplies in the woods and toting it out. So, you might as well go in the damn smokehouse. Everything you drug back yonder in the woods had to be drug there. I got scars on my shoulders and on my back right now—scars from toting liquor! Son, you want to see em? And one hundred and fifty pounds of sugar on my shoulders at one time—I toted it six miles without setting that son-of-a-bitch down. If I ever set it down I couldn't get it back up, cause I had to get somebody to put that fifty pounds on top of that hundred pounds to start with. And bogging in the mud plumb knee deep, and rolling and wrastling through them damn baygalls and titi bushes and what have you. Hell, you might as well set up there beside the goddamn highway. Cause, if they want you they gonna get you![140]

In keeping with this philosophy, some men set up under their own houses and vented the wood smoke through their household chimneys. One moonshiner of Carl Havard's acquaintance piped his smoke some distance away and vented it through the top of a hollow tree. The first time Havard visited this man, he assumed the tree had been struck by lightning, and he paid it little attention, but when he came back two months later the tree was still smoking. More and more, however, the people who set up in and around their own homes in smokehouses, barns, and house lofts used smokeless homemade gasoline stoves to fire their stills. As Dudley Denmon described, the moonshiner could rig up an excellent stove from a twenty-gallon drum with a valve welded on it, a bicycle pump, and the burner from a water heater. With one of these, you could indeed "go in the damn smokehouse."

In every community along the Neches, there were small operators like Dudley Denmon and George Carpenter, large operators like the Strain Farm and "old man Preston Barnes," and sometimes a relationship between them. Former sheriff Aubrey Cole explained the situation in Jasper County:

There were three people in Jasper County that was the big whiskey men. They had the big rigs. They set up more or less like a small sawmill operation, worked a lot of people, ordered their grain, rye and corn and sugar shipped in on the train. They went in wagons and unloaded it at the depot and hauled it out in the woods to their rig. Now, there was lots of people, topwater whiskey makers, that had a little old rig, little old thirty-gallon rig, ten-gallon thumping kegs, and they just might make a run or two of whiskey after the crop was laid by, mostly to get the baby a new pair of shoes with, and to drink themselves. Most of them would sell their whiskey to these three big whiskey men—one was in Evadale, one was in Buna, and one was out next to the Neches River—and they'd carry this raw-made whiskey to Beaumont.[141]

In Angelina County, George Carpenter fell into Cole's category of "topwater whiskey makers," and Carpenter's whiskey-making career typified that of many people along the Neches. Unfortunately for Carpenter, the bulk of his professional moonshining coincided with the terms in office of Sheriff Henry Billingsley, who seems to have been not only an honest man but also an excellent woodsman. Billingsley caught Carpenter twice during the years between 1932 and 1938, and Carpenter escaped from him on several other occasions by the narrowest of margins.

Tiring of chopping cotton for "six bits a day," Carpenter had begun helping at his brother's still in 1932 and soon branched out on his own. In 1934 he was siphoning two gallons of whiskey from his fifty-gallon storage barrel for a customer at about dusk one day when he heard "some weeds a-popping."

> I said, "Aw, I guess it's an armadillo," but it was Henry Billingsley, he was slipping up on me in the night while I was drawing it out. He flashed his light on and says, "Alright, George, I've got you this time." I said, "Yeah, you sure have." He taken and poured this other whiskey out of the barrel and carried these two gallons with him, but he didn't take me in, [just] told me to come in the next morning. So, I went up there the next morning, and boy, he just ripped me up. He was mad, I mean, he was got mad! Fined me $123.[142]

For a time Carpenter retired, but he soon renewed his operations, and in 1936 Sheriff Billingsley caught him at his still a second time. Once again, Carpenter was politely requested to show up at the courthouse the next day and did so, this time paying a fine of $223. Undeterred and now even more in need of money, Carpenter set up operations far back in the woods, but a near-miss from Billingsley led him to relocate his operations much closer to his home—to a spring branch he could see from one of the windows of his house. As he remembered: "[I] dug a hole in the ground and put my [buck] barrels down in it, and then I'd cover em over with some planks and tin and whatever, and put leaves and straw over it, and you could walk right by it and wouldn't even notice it. But somebody found it. I went down there one evening and found where somebody had kneeled down and made a toe track in the dirt."[143]

Billingsley had a line on him once again, and Carpenter avoided his still for several days. Nevertheless, he noted: "[The sheriff] went down there and chopped my barrels down there, and stuff, and the mash just poured out in this hole. He told me to come up there [to the courthouse] the next morning. Well, after they left, I went down there and got my rig set up, and I dipped up that mash out of this hole and I run ten gallons of whiskey out of it. Boy, it sure was good!"[144]

Nor did Carpenter plead guilty. "What hair Henry had, he's almost bald-headed, he pulled out nearly all of his hair, and he just walked the floor and cussed and just raised hell. I just set there listening at him." Billingsley filed the usual charge of "possession of a still," but this time George had a friend in the county attorney's office who made a small change in the indictment, rubbing out the last digit of the date "1938." Later at county court, the judge read the indictment: "George Carpenter is here indicted for a possession of a whiskey still in the year 193. Stand up. That's the oldest man I know of. Case dismissed." For Carpenter, this last narrow escape was the sign to get out of the moonshine trade, a retirement he explained as follows:

I quit in 1938. Billingsley asked me one day, says, "Why don't you quit making that stuff?" I says, "Well, I ain't got nothing else to do, I can't get a job. I'm gonna tell you something, Henry. If I ever do get a job I can make a living at I'm gonna quit. I'll let you know." So, I got a job and worked at it a week and got a payday and I come in to town. I went to the jail house and went in there, and I says, "I got news for you, Mr. Billingsley, I've quit making whiskey, I got me a job." I showed him my check from my payday, says, "I done quit making whiskey. You'll have to quit worrying about me, now."[145]

5
HUNTING, TRAPPING AND FISHING

The subsistence life-style of herding, small-farming, hunting, trapping, and fishing persisted well into the mid-twentieth century along the Neches, and in 1990 many elderly southeastern Texans recalled the bay of the hounds and the call of the hunting horn from among their first memories. Aubrey Cole remembered: "We lived four miles from an outside slough on the Neches River, and one evening my mother and I was at home, I was real small, and she said, "Listen, son. I hear your daddy a-blowing his horn for the dogs." And he was a-standing on the creek bridge four miles from our house. Course, the wind was just right, but he had a blowing horn. He really had a blowing horn."[1]

When the first settlers came to southeastern Texas, more often than not from Alabama or Mississippi, they brought with them the customs of the southern free range and certain basic tools of the woodsman's trade. These included, among other things, the rifle, the ax, the black-mouthed cur stock dog, and the blowing horn. Carefully carved from the horn of a cow or steer, the blowing horn was a long-range communication device for use in the big woods. Its sound carried for miles across the still bottoms, much farther than a man could shout and even farther than the bay of a hound. People used their blowing horns to call dogs and to communicate with other people across great distances. The horns were valued tools of the hunting and herding life.

As in the instance remembered by Aubrey Cole, the most basic use of the blowing horn was in hunting, and its most important function in hunting was to call dogs. Across miles of woods, sloughs, and creek bottoms, only the faint, far sound of the blowing horn could reach out to bring a family's valued hunting hounds or stock dogs back home. To call his dogs, the hunter or stockman used short, rapid blasts of the horn. This "bugling" or "tooting" differed from the rest of the horn language, which signaled from hunter to hunter. Long blasts on the horn always identified human communication, and horn language was uniform throughout the South. Two long blows meant "Where are you?" One long blow meant "Here I am." Three long blows meant "Come to me," and as Aubrey Cole recalled, "Four long blows indicated that I have shot and wounded a deer, I'm follering blood, and I'm a-gonna go on with the hounds, so don't worry about me."[2]

Blowing horns had other important uses. For many years, Aubrey Cole's mother walked out on the family's front porch, poured a dipper of water through the blowing horn (to rinse out residual snuff and tobacco juices), then sounded the "dinner horn" to bring her husband in from the field. Horns also brought aid in emergencies. Rural homesteads usually were dispersed across considerable distances, and the blowing horn was used to communicate between them and—if needed— to call for help in case of sickness, fire, or other disasters. Cole explained: "At 12 o'clock at night, if you heard your neighbor's blowing horn blowing three long blows, he was in trouble, and all the neighbors rolled out and went to him. And of course they answered him with two long blows to let him know, 'I heard you and I'm a-coming to you.'" Horns also functioned as emergency homing devices—as beacons for people lost in the woods. The miles-wide Neches bottom was flat, heavily wooded, and often crossed by a confusing maze of twisting sloughs; at night or on a dark and cloudy day, even competent woodsmen could get "turned around." For a century, many people heard with great relief the repeated horn signal for "Come to me" reverberating across the dark bottoms and walked toward it to escape. As Aubrey Cole told, "I've blowed a-many a lost man out of the woods."[3]

Not every man could make a good blowing horn, and the best of them were handed down across the generations as valued family possessions. Aubrey Cole's horn had been found in the Neches bottom west of Kirbyville by Aubrey's father, Providence Walter Cole, when he was a young man. Evidently lost in the woods for many years, it carried the name of John Jackson, a hunter and ferryboat operator old-timers remembered from during the Civil War. This horn had a pure tone and great carrying power. Walter covered it with skin from the leg of a deer and used it for many decades before passing it on to his son.

Other men also possessed famous horns. In 1992, ninety-year-old Hinkle Shillings, of Shelby County, still had his grandfather's horn, engraved with a date of 1857 by its South Carolina maker and with the likeness of Hinkle's champion foxhound, Dawson Stride, dated 1941. It was a small blowing horn, with a clear, piercing, tenor sound. Hinkle stood on a stump with this horn to win the horn-blowing contest at the Texas state foxhound meet every year from 1934 to 1956, retiring only after he lost his "natural teeth."[4]

The blowing horn was the symbol—and perhaps the most valued

artifact—of the subsistence life-style. In the rural communities along the Neches, most people ran stock in the woods, farmed, hunted, and fished, but they differed in the relative importance they placed on these activities. The Neches stockmen-farmers had their biblical "Jacobs," who tended to business and struggled to get ahead, and their "hairy Esaus," who lived to hunt and fish and disappeared for days or weeks at a time into the river bottoms.[5] Hinkle Shillings never missed a Sunday service at his rural church, but fox hunting took precedence over farming, stock raising, and most of his other activities. Oscar Allen's father farmed, ran stock, operated a small sawmill, and occasionally went hunting or fishing, but Oscar's uncle spent most of his time camped out on the Neches and worked only when he felt like it. Jake Cole's father and his Uncle Bud demonstrated the same basic disagreement of life-styles. A hard-working farmer, Sharp Cole tended to his hogs and cotton, but his sister's husband, Bud Levine, spent much of his time keeping up with the whereabouts of local deer and turkeys and was always ready to go fishing. Jake Cole recalled of his Uncle Bud:

> Somebody come along one time, he was a-plowing up there and somebody come along. "Bud, do you want to go a-fishing?" "Whoa!" He stopped the old mule right there and unharnessed him and carried him to the house. He's getting his fishing material ready, you know. And Aunt Vycie mentioned it to Uncle Bud, said, "Bud, don't think we're getting in the grass a little too much to take off and go a-fishing?" Says, "Woman, you knowed when you married me that I was a hunter and a fisherman, and you just hush." He went on a-fishing.[6]

In settlement times hunting, trapping, fishing, and the gathering of wild plant foods were not only recreational but also essential to a family's survival. In later years these activities rose again to predominance whenever times grew hard, crops failed, or the mills closed. Pioneer diets ran heavily to wild meats, often preserved by smoking or drying. Settlers cured bear "bacon" and venison "hams" in smokehouses and dried venison and turkey breasts over slow fires and on tin roofs. When Noah Smithwick arrived in Texas in the late 1820s, his first meal in the new land was entirely typical—venison "jerky" dipped in wild honey. A century later, Ellen Walker's family in the Big Thicket still heavily depended on dried venison, smoked bear meat, squirrel, rabbit, and raccoon for their daily fare. Walker recalled: "We'd cut venison up in strips and dry it on a scaffold in the sun, jerky. When it dried, put in a sack and hang it up."[7]

Other wild meats, such as beef and fish, could not be so readily preserved. When settlers first came to southeastern Texas, they found wild cattle roaming the woods alongside the herds of deer and flocks of wild turkeys. These cattle were free for the taking, as Ellen Walker noted, but their meat needed to be shared: "Anybody could go and kill one when he wanted to, be wild just like a wild fox. They'd go out and kill a wild beef, kill one and divide it with the neighbors. Didn't everybody have a gun, and a lot of em that did have guns didn't have enough money to buy lead to make bullets." The custom of sharing surplus game with friends and extended family (what Charlie Havard called "taking care of the neighbors") was a logical adaptation to the abundance of wildlife resources and the limitations of food-preservation techniques. However, the custom survived well into the twentieth century—long after most of the wildlife had been "shot out."[8]

Many early sources attest to the original richness of fish, fur, and game in southeastern Texas. A story passed down in one family was typical. Sometime before the Civil War, the family of Dolly Davis went on a fishing trip to the Neches as a reward at the end of a long period of weeding corn and chopping cotton. They traveled several miles to the river in an ox wagon, taking along quilts for bedding and a white-oak cotton basket packed with hams from the smokehouse, sweet potatoes, and gourd containers of lard, syrup, salt, coffee, and cornmeal. While at the river, they caught some large catfish, and the father also killed a bear and a buffalo. After returning home with a wagon full of meat, the man sounded his blowing horn (three long blows) to summon the neighbors to share the riches.[9]

Game was so thick in the early days that the first method of hunting deer, turkey, and other species was really "no method." People often shot what they needed from their porches or after short stalks of fifteen to thirty minutes. Settlers put bells on their horses and let them out to graze at night, but sometimes in the mornings they "could hardly hear the bells for the turkeys gobbling."[10] Deer sometimes tried to follow family milk cows into the cow shed at night and had to be shooed away.[11] Rankin Laird, of Polk County, said: "I grew up where herds of deer roamed to our door, and I didn't have to hunt them. I just took my gun out in the yard and shot one. And wild turkeys waked us every morning with their gobble, gobble."[12] N. B. G. Frazier, of Trinity County, recalled: "Many a time have I stood in the door of my father's home and seen great droves of deer quietly grazing nearby. I have gone out near the farm hunting and have seen as many as 75 deer in one herd. All I had to do was take my choice and kill it."[13] In Hardin County, Pearl Wiggins's father hunted in a way entirely typical. "Papa would say, 'Well, Carrie, are we without fresh meat?' He'd get his gun and ride off and in about an hour he'd come back with a deer, or whatever we wanted."[14]

Nineteenth-century woodsmen termed these early methods of taking deer "still hunting," but by this they did not mean the modern technique of sitting motionless in a tree stand waiting for a deer to come by. Early still hunting was stalking—a slow, stealthy, slipping along through the woods, looking for deer and other game. As Frank Herrington, of Hardin County, explained, "We always walked while hunting, calling it still hunting."[15]

Hunters stalked deer by several techniques. Two hunters sometimes walked parallel courses out of sight of each other on both sides of a creek or slough. They sounded blowing horns at intervals to keep roughly abreast and used another horn signal when they "jumped" a deer heading the other's way. Each man had a chance to "walk up" on a deer and get a shot, but if the deer detected him and ran off, his partner might kill it. Thus, each man both stalked alone and served as a "driver" for the other.[16] On the other hand, if the wind was up and the woods were wet, a lone hunter might move quietly upwind or across the wind. Deer could not smell him under these circumstances or easily hear him; the wet leaves of the forest floor muffled his footsteps, and the wind covered what little sound he did make. Once a deer was in sight, a hunter might attempt a direct stalk or a crawl-up through grass. In a direct stalk the hunter stealthily walked toward the deer while its head was down feeding, and he froze still when it raised up to look around. A shake of its tail often signaled that it was about to do so. After a while, if the stalker was skillful or lucky, he got close enough to try a rifle shot, and in muzzle-loader days many hunters believed that this point was reached when the stalker could clearly distinguish the deer's eyes. If the deer was browsing at the edge of an opening and the wind and ground conditions were right, a hunter might try a crawl-up through deep grass. Other hunters stalked deer on foot using trained horses or oxen as "blinds" between them and the prey, and still others hunted entirely on horseback.[17]

Commercial hunter Fount Simmons, of Hardin County, used the latter technique with great success for many years. A polio victim at an early age, Simmons was paralyzed from the waist down, but he had killed over three thousand deer by the time he stopped bothering to count.[18] He sold venison and bear oil to railroad construction crews in the late nineteenth century, just as commercial hunters before him had sold to log raftsmen, steamboat crews, and plantations. Game was unprotected, free for the taking, and seemingly inexhaustible, and from the beginning people harvested it relentlessly. As early as 1830, tens of thousands of deer hides were reaching Nacogdoches merchants each year.[19] Solomon Wright's father recalled that in the 1840s and 1850s, "Men would kill deer just for their skins and leave the carcasses in the woods for the buzzards and the wolves."[20] A generation or so later, people like Fount Simmons peddled fresh game to railroads and logging camps, and after ice became available around the turn of the century, hunters packed untold numbers of waterfowl, deer, turkeys, and quail in ice barrels and shipped them by railroad to urban markets.

As deer herds began to diminish under this onslaught, and the casual daytime stalk no longer worked as well, people wanting venison turned more and more to "fire-hunting" at night. This was a deadly method, and commercial hunters sometimes killed ten or more deer an hour using it, marking each carcass with flags so that it could be picked up early the next day. Probably of Indian origin, fire-hunting was one of the woodsman's tricks of the trade that settlers brought with them to the counties along the Neches. English visitor William Bollaert observed Texas fire-hunters in action in the 1840s and offered this unmatched description of the technique—one still in use in exactly the same way over a century later.

A party of three or four would in a day or so shoot down some 20 to 30 deer. . . . The hunter being on foot or horseback, carries the fire pan full of lighted pine wood over his left shoulder, left handed people the reverse, proceeding cautiously through the woods. Should there be any deer about they look towards the pan of fire, and in a moment the hunter sees a reflection of the light in the eyes of the deer. This is called "shining the eyes." . . . Deer's eyes may be shined at a 100 yards or more, then they look like a horizontal streak of dim light, but on nearing the deer both eyes will be seen distinctly of a bright light bluish colour. Horses, cats, or human eye did not succeed with us. . . . The hunter generally approaches to within 40 or 50 yards of the game, so managing his pan of fire that he preserves "the shining" of the eye or eyes; he then draws the long wooden handle of the pan forward and makes it a rest for his rifle; aim being taken, the animal seldom escapes.[21]

Fire-hunting took advantage of the behavior of the white-tailed deer, a species that looks fixedly at a light source at night, often allowing the hunter to approach within fifty yards before taking alarm. Perhaps because unchoked, muzzle-loading shotguns could not consistently kill at a forty-yard range, Solomon Wright and most early fire-hunters used rifles. The hunter shot six inches below the deer's eyes, before its body was visible, intending to break its neck if the animal faced toward him or to cut its jugular vein if it stood sideways. As soon as the choked, breech-loading shotgun appeared, this became the weapon of choice for fire-hunting, and the night-hunter's rule of thumb was to approach the deer until he could "part its eyes." With either an old-time fire pan or a newfangled carbide headlamp, the thin, horizontal line of the deer's eyes became two separate spots of light at around forty-five yards—close enough to shoot.

People still fire-hunt for deer in southeastern Texas, though like many other traditional hunting and fishing methods, this has long been illegal. For many decades, only the light sources changed; the technique remained the same. At first, people "shined" deer with torches of fat-pine splinters, then they used "fire pans of thin, narrow strips of iron made in the shape of a round basket, about six inches deep and about seven or eight inches across the top." One hunter often carried the long-handled fire pan, filled with burning pine chips from a "green catface" longleaf pine, while a second one carried the gun and did the shooting.[22] As late as the 1930s, African Americans from the Cairo Springs area of Jasper County used a different—and perhaps a much older—kind of fire pan, one that was really a torch holder. A long wooden handle was enlarged at one end into a flat, plate-sized piece of wood with a hole in its center and a semicircle backing of bright, reflective tin. In the course of the hunt, a succession of pine-splinter torches were thrust into the hole to burn themselves out, while the bright tin directed the light forward.[23]

The use of fire pans continued as a "poor boy" method into the 1950s, but long before then most night-hunters had progressed to headlights.[24] At first, these often used kerosene; later, they used carbide. Although the carbide light often was cranky in operation and sometimes even exploded on a hunter's head, it came into wide use along the Neches. The carbide headlamp cast a bright, diffuse light, similar in quality and intensity to that thrown by a brightly burning fire pan. The same old hunter's rule applied: you could "drop the hammer" when you "parted the eyes." By the 1920s, the standard night-hunter's outfit up and down the Neches consisted of a carbide headlight jury-rigged with a heavy-duty replacement reflector taken from a junked Model T Ford. Hunters polished these large, brass Model T reflectors to throw a golden light that deer thought was "like the moon"—or so hunters believed.[25]

Hunters told many cautionary tales about night-hunting, all based on cases of mistaken identity. An old black night-hunter told C. W. Gandy, "You don't want a bright light to hunt deer—if you'll get a dim light, you'll kill more deer." Perhaps so, but by the dim light of the fire pan or the carbide headlamp, night-hunters shot colts, sheep, mules, horses, and other mistaken targets with some regularity. Sometimes they lost track of where they were and shot their own "slow-track" deer dogs tied in the vicinity to help trail wounded deer, and sometimes they shot each other. Carl Havard noted: "We had some old gentlemen that was old fire hunters. Four of em went off a-deer hunting. And they had an old gentleman along that had arthritis, so he got tired, he went back to the car and sit down. They fooled around out there hunting and got lost and shined a tail light and shot it and hit him in the back with four buckshot. Had to rush him to the hospital. My uncle was in that bunch."[26]

Besides deer, early hunters sought squirrels, ducks, and turkeys. Many southeastern Texans liked the taste of squirrel, though the small animal required a large outlay of costly lead and powder to produce a negligible amount of meat. However, squirrels—and especially the cat squirrel—were the traditional rifle targets by which every woodsman judged his skill. Men competed informally with other men to see how many squirrels they could kill, how many they could bring down with head shots, or how many they could bark. A creature of the hardwood bottoms, the cat squirrel could "limb" from tree to tree almost as fast as a man could run; as Harold Snelson noted, the squirrel looked "like a tail flying through the trees." However, Snelson prided himself that he rarely missed this difficult target with his .22. He told me, "If I could see an ear or an eyeball, he was mine."[27]

Waterfowl—mallards, wood ducks, and other species—were another important wildlife resource for people along the Neches, and this was especially true in the early days. Charlie Havard, of Angelina County, recalled: "Oh, man, the ducks that used to come in here! They used to wrap that bottom up, every year. If the river was out in the backwater you could hear em a-hollering all over that bottom."[28] Charlie lived on the edge of the Neches bottoms and used every traditional hunting method to put ducks on his family's "eating table." Charlie hunted for meat, and the game law had little to do with how he operated. His foster son, W. B. Harris, recalled him setting off for the river on a winter afternoon. Charlie would have on his old leather coat (the only coat he had), and he would take nothing with him but his Model 12 Winchester and a leather string. After about thirty minutes, W. B. would hear Charlie shoot—often very fast, since Charlie was a quick, expert shot. Soon thereafter he would come home with his self-imposed limit of five ducks on the leather string. Five ducks were all that his family could eat before the meat spoiled, and Charlie took care not to waste anything. More often than not, the ducks had been taken by Charlie's standard "crawl-up" method. He knew where the ducks would be, the pin oak trees they would be feeding under, and he would watch for the water moving and would crawl up on them. He shot some on the water and some on the rise—a highly efficient method. Whether it was duck season or not did not matter. Charlie sought meat, not sport.[29]

Charlie Havard and the other Havard men knew every slough, pin oak flat, and backwater pool for miles up and down their stretch of the Neches, and they used this detailed knowledge in duck-hunting. One of their techniques was to set up on the edge of the river at a roost site and wait for the ducks to fly in to roost at dusk. The ducks often landed in the river, then swam back into the woods to their roosting place, and the trick was to be at exactly the right place on the river when this began to happen.

Other duck-hunting techniques of the Havards required the use of a basic tool of the Neches Valley hunter, trapper, fisherman, and stockman: the "paddle boat." Neches woodsmen used one-person, cypress, dugout canoes in the early days, but by World War I many of them had shifted to a two-man version of the *chaland* sometimes termed a "double-ender," an Acadian folk boat sometimes made entirely of four wide planks.[30] This craft, invariably called a paddle boat along the Neches, had a length of around fourteen feet, a beam of about thirty-four inches, squared-off ends perhaps eighteen inches wide, and a depth amidships of only ten inches or so. The paddle boat had a rockered ("raked") bottom for maneuverability and a narrow waterline width for speed—absolutely essential in a craft that from time to time had to be paddled several miles upriver against a strong current. For several months of the year, the Neches flooded its bottomland woods, and only a small, narrow, and agile paddle boat could give access to the river and bottoms. Charlie Havard and his older brothers used their paddle boats for hunting, trapping, fishing, and even stock raising, since from time to time animals had to be rescued from bottomland islands surrounded by the backwater. Some Neches paddle boats were carefully constructed by skilled boat builders from milled cypress lumber; others—virtually as functional, though they might leak a little more—were swiftly nailed together from four pine planks. Charlie's older brothers knew how to make a paddle boat and knew how to make one quickly. Sometimes they traveled by wagon to the nearby Manning mill, purchased four one-by-twelve-inch pine boards, returned home, and "had that boat ready to go in the woods that evening."[31]

Using their long six-foot paddles to pole off the bottom in the shallows, the Havards stealthily worked their paddle boats through miles of backwaters to pot-shoot and "jump shoot" ducks. They also hunted the river, drifting down from miles upstream. In these drift hunts, two gunners perched precariously on the seat amidships while a third man in the stern controlled the boat. The sternman did not paddle or make any noise, but just drifted with the current and kept the boat straight. Every time the boat floated around a sharp bend, the gunners got ready to shoot. If they saw ducks in the river a long way ahead, all hands lay flat out of sight while they drifted down. Sometimes Charlie would order the boat to the bank and walk through the woods to investigate a certain pool under a certain pin oak, and as often as not they would hear him shoot. W. B. Harris often preferred to paddle the boat during these expeditions. He did not mind competing against his brothers, but he disliked shooting alongside Charlie; Charlie rarely missed.

The wild turkey was another important game species, and after the early period of still hunting passed and the turkey populations shrank, people often hunted them during their mating season in the spring of the year. Sometimes hunters used direct methods. One day in the spring of 1885, Solomon Wright and his brother went to the river bottom well before daylight and waited for the turkeys to begin to gobble at the first, faint light of dawn. "All of a sudden they tore loose. They were about fifty in the bunch, a dozen or more old gobblers and the rest hens and young gobblers. They all seemed to gobble and yelp at the same time." The turkeys roosted back in the bottoms about half a mile away, and the Wrights rushed in on foot to get there before the birds flew from the roost. Moving under the trees in the dark woods, the two men picked out the black shapes of the roosting turkeys outlined against the lightening sky and shot several of them.[32]

Thirty years later, when P. O. Eason hunted in Hardin County, turkeys were fewer and wilder, and such crude tactics no longer sufficed. Eason often rode in to his turkey-hunting range the day before, made camp, listened for the gobbling of turkeys as they settled to the roost at dusk, and planned his hunt for the next day. The February woods were cold, so he often made a fire of leaves and small twigs, let it burn down, then swept the embers aside and made his bed on the warm ground. Eason needed to rise well before the first light, and in those days he did not have a watch, but this was no problem. As he recalled: "The owls know when the day begins to break before you do. Along about four o'clock in the morning, every owl in the woods starts just raring; they'd just jar the ground they'd be so many of em, just go wild! You could tell it was fixing to come daylight."[33]

After this barred owl reveille, Eason quickly brewed his morning coffee, then left camp to take up a position about two hundred yards away from where he thought turkeys were roosting. Sitting absolutely still against a big tree in the dark woods, he readied his twelve-gauge shotgun, held a doubled-up peach leaf between his lips, and began to yelp like a turkey hen.

Other men preferred turkey calls made of turkey wing bones, turkey quills, new corncob pipes, thin wooden boxes used by drawing whetstones across the tops, and plugged cow horns with nails protruding from the wooden plug. In the last case, the hunter drew a whetstone across the nail to make the yelp, and the horn magnified the sound.

Whatever the hunter used as a turkey caller, it was important not to yelp too much. A foolish young gobbler might rush in "half yelping and gobbling" to any call and be easy to shoot—Eason preferred a shot at the head—but the old gobblers were different. Eason recalled: "Those old gobblers are smart. You had to know how to yelp for one and how to sit for one. That's why I liked to turkey hunt, because when you killed an old white-headed gobbler, you had accomplished something!"[34]

Packs of red wolves sometimes came around Eason's turkey camps at night—close enough for him to hear them "snap and snarl at one another." As long as he sat by his campfire, he "never had any fear of anything like that," but on other occasions, when he walked home across miles of dark countryside after singings and syrup pulls, he worried about wolf packs, bears, and panthers that "sided" people along the road.[35] Like Lance Rosier's Aunt Dose, people in the Neches counties simply had to get used to big predators. Stockmen, in particular, found these animals a direct challenge to their livelihood.

Wolves, bears, and cougers—the latter always called panthers in southeastern Texas—were numerous in the early days and seemed to show less fear of people than in later times. Families still pass down stories about panthers following people through the woods, stopping only to rend and claw articles of clothing thrown behind to delay them, or about panthers pacing on the board roofs of log houses, scratching and clawing to get inside. Folklorists usually consider such accounts to be "traveling folk tales," but it seems possible that at least some of the stories document actual panther behavior and that in times of few people and many panthers, the latter were a good bit bolder. More than one southeastern Texan stepped outside at night to relieve himself and found a panther in the "dog run," or was "sided" by one along a road at night, or recalled the time one caught a hog "in the chimney corner." Brown Wiggins remembered: "They'd side you on the road, the panther would. You could hear them out there in the bushes. We'd camp a lot and the first thing we'd do [was] tote up enough wood to keep a burning fire all night. Those varmints, they won't come to a fire, but they'll circle that camp all night. Those old panthers will holler and meow."[36]

Not only were there many panthers in the early days, but the panthers showed an unsettling interest in people, their habitations, and their livestock. Hardin County pioneer Hampton Herrington told his sons that the first year after he came to Texas in 1850, he and his neighbors killed thirteen panthers within three-quarters of a mile from the Herrington homeplace. "One night, a panther caught a pig in the chimney corner. My father turned his varmint dogs loose. He and the dogs killed the panther."[37]

Panthers, bears, and wolves all preyed on the stockmen's hogs and cattle, and the wolves liked nothing better than to catch, kill, and consume the settlers' valuable stock dogs. One person recalled, "In them days, when you saw one hog you saw seventy-five—for protection, you know—and we'd tie our dogs or the wolves would eat em up."[38] Sometimes stockmen tried to thin out local wolf populations by holding communal wolf hunts involving dozens of neighbors and scores of dogs.[39] Sometimes they built wolf traps made of slanting logs with a square hole about five feet high in the middle. The wolf smelled the bait inside the trap, walked up the slanting poles to the central hole, jumped down inside, then could not make the vertical leap back out.[40]

Bears often preyed on the settler's stock, especially his woods hogs, and in retaliation, the hogs' owner trapped or shot the bear. Large steel traps, trip-wire gun sets, and log-pen traps all were used, though most people regarded the first two with distaste, since they also could prove deadly for dogs and men. In some ways the log-pen bear trap resembled a twentieth-century hog trap. Built like a small, unchinked log cabin with a flat roof and often a log floor, the trap was six to eight feet square, four to five feet high, and made of hewn logs firmly spiked at the notched corners. A heavy plank door was at one end, set in vertical log "runners." To ready the trap, the trapper raised the door and ran a rope or chain from its top down to a stake at the back of the pen. Then he attached a bait, often hog meat, to the stake on a short rope. If all went well, the bear entered the trap, pulled on the bait, and released the stake, and the door dropped behind him. Displeased with this indignity, the bear then exerted its full powers in an attempt to escape—a real test of the trap's structural integrity. It is no wonder, then, that the old phrase "strong as a bear trap" applied only to log construction of the highest order.[41]

Black bears ranged through the canebrakes and bottoms of all the Neches counties at the time of first settlement, but they were probably most numerous in the thickets of Polk, Jasper, and Hardin counties. During the 1840s, a chain carrier helping surveyors establish the first county lines reported seeing "bear tracks as numerous as hog tracks in a hog pasture."[42]

Bears loved pork, and they regularly came around settlers' houses to attack hogs in chimney corners and hogpens. In Polk County, bears besieged the Bailey household during the time Mr. Bailey served in the Confederate army. Mrs. Bailey poured hot grease on the head of one aggressive bear as it dug under the wall of their dirt-floored cabin trying to get to the lard barrel, and on another occasion she released hogs from the hogpen "so they could bunch together and fight the bears off."[43] Bears might be important game animals, highly valued for their flesh and oil, but they were also stock-killing "varmints," as Vinson Collins of Hardin County testified.

> Our family's only source of living was the hogs that roamed the woods and got fat and the wild game that my father killed in the forest and brought home for food. . . . Thousands of wild bear lived in the Big Thicket and got very fat every winter on the mast that grew on the oak trees in the forest. In the summer they would come out of the Thicket to the piney woods and prey on the hogs that ranged there. My father was one of the few men who lived in Hardin County, and during the summer months he and his neighbors spent much time hunting the wild bear that came out in the open woods to kill their hogs. In the winter when the bear were fat they made very fine meat, and my father used to go back in the Thicket to kill them and bring them home for food.[44]

Like many early stockmen, Vinson Collins's father engaged in two kinds of bear hunting: varmint hunting in the summer when the bears (hungry, poor of flesh, and inedible) pursued his hogs to the uplands, and meat hunting in the winter to replenish family supplies of bear flesh and bear fat.

Evie Brown remembered: "My husband's daddy, Warren Brown, he wanted to raise hogs. That's how come him to work on the bear so much, cause the bear eat all his hogs up."[45] As in this instance, no sooner did a stockman move into an area than he became a bear and panther hunter by sheer economic necessity. Likewise, his stock dogs were turned to double duty as bear and panther hounds. Most early stockmen lacked the resources to maintain a separate pack of dogs to use only on bears; this meant that many times, when men went out to work hogs or cattle, their dogs would jump a bear, and the men went on a bear hunt instead. Predators had to be hunted, but stockmen could not tolerate their dogs running deer. Pioneer Frank Herrington explained: "Yes, we had dogs, but we did not let them run anything but vermin. If a dog chased a deer, his owner caught him, then gave the dog about forty hard lashes with a switch about three feet long."[46]

In truth, many stockmen loved to hunt bears and panthers and, like Solomon Wright's grandfather, were ready to rise up and join the hunt at whatever hour of the day or night that the dogs barked "treed." West of the Neches country in the Trinity bottoms, Buck Barry found "it necessary to keep a yard full of dogs" to protect his hogs from the bears and panthers. As he described, this quickly fell into a pattern. When his hogs came in "looking frightened and disturbed I would put my dogs on their back trail, [and] by the time I would find a dead hog,

Valentine "Bear Tine" Withers as an old man. He is mounted on his favorite riding mule with a bear hound on a rope. The stockman's omnipresent wallet of corn is behind the saddle. (Jasper County Historical Commission, Jasper, Texas)

the dogs would have a panther or a bear up a tree ready for me to kill."[47] Big-predator hunting was a heady business, and other stockmen did the same. Farther south on the Trinity, hog raiser Ab Carter trained a special pack of bear dogs and killed 182 bears between 1883 and 1885.[48]

Near Kountze in Hardin County, stockmen Bud Brackin and Jake Lloyd also were serious hunters of big predators. Brackin trained his dogs to run nothing but bears. Frank Herrington recalled, "Most every winter they would kill about forty."[49] Brackin is said to have killed 305 bears during his lifetime, virtually all from his "hog range" in the vicinity of Kountze. He began hunting in the fall after bears stopped eating the acorn in its hull and began eating just the acorn—at that point he judged them fat enough to hunt. Bears killed several of his hounds, and his best dog, Joe, once was ripped wide open by one. Brackin pushed Joe's entrails back into place, sewed him up with a rawhide string, and nursed him back to health. In later years Brackin liked to say of Joe, "He fought many another bear before he upped and died natural like." At age seventy (or so the story goes), Bud Brackin killed his last bear, cured its hide, hung the hide on his garden fence, and quit bear hunting.[50] The main reason he stopped was neither conservation nor physical infirmity, but a lack of game. Not even Big Thicket bear populations could withstand this kind of hunting pressure.

By the 1890s, as the number of bears diminished due to hunting, habitat destruction from lumbering, and increased food competition by livestock, the rare black bear became an exotic big-game animal, and bear hunting became a famous sport. Sawmill owners, county judges, oilmen, and President Theodore Roosevelt all rushed to take part before all the bears were gone. Bud and Ben Hooks, of Hardin County, led one group of bear hunters. The Hooks had made their money in the Saratoga oil fields, but no sooner had this been accomplished than the brothers turned to the serious business of bear hunting.

The Hooks had a bear camp near a tornado swath called "the hurricane," and this served as their base of operations for years. Over time, their hunts took on a characteristic pattern, one typical of bear hunting all across the American South. The Hooks brothers and their friends traveled to the camp the day before the hunt with a wagon full of groceries, dog feed, and horse feed. The hunters rode horseback, with the dogs trotting alongside. The next morning, they saddled the horses, necked up the dogs in pairs (all but Dandy, the "strike" dog), and proceeded to the hunting area to begin the hunt. Dandy, a redbone hound, was extremely valuable for two reasons: he would run nothing but bears, and—as Carter Hart, one of the hunters, said—"he could smell a trail so cold that no other dog could smell it." The Hooks used Dandy to start the trail, then when the trail got hot enough, they released the other dogs, two at a time.[51]

If the Hooks had a larger party of hunters including some inexperienced ones, the brothers often placed them on "stands"—designated hunting locations—and told them to stay there no matter which way the bear went. If only experienced regulars were present, each hunter moved on horseback to whatever location he thought most strategic to intercept bear and dogs. Hunters equipped themselves with repeating rifles, blowing horns, heavy "hack knives" (often made from recycled crosscut saws and used to cut a way through canebrakes and brush), and sometimes big hunting knives as well. The last had been absolutely essential as backup weapons for self-defense and for "finishing off" game during the days of single-shot muzzle-loaders, and some men still felt uncomfortable without one.[52] Farther west, earlier hunters had even carried short "bear spears."[53] Loaded down with all this gear, in the deep mud and dense thickets of southeastern Texas, the bear hunter engaged in exhausting work. Carter Hart recalled: "Bear hunting is the hardest work a man ever did on earth. We would ride if we could, but lots of times a horse would bog down, bog down anywhere. You had to walk all day in mud, water, and you were in the sloughs, canebrakes, baygalls, and palmetto swamps a lot. I've left early in the morning and come in after dark, and not have a bite to eat all day."[54]

Dandy, the pure-bred redbone hound, was the exception in the Hooks brothers' pack: most of the "fighter dogs" were crossbreeds, with a lot of black-mouthed cur in their ancestries. These dogs were vicious, and needed to be, because they had to fight the bear and delay it long enough for hunters to reach the scene. They were released two at a time after Dandy "struck," since releasing them all at once could result in a monumental dogfight. Fast and powerful, bears often chose to run through thickets and canebrakes that bruised and lacerated the dogs and wore them down. When dogs caught up with the bear, or the bear decided to stop, they had to be extremely careful how they fought it. The bear dog had to bite and jump back, bite and jump back; if it bit and held, as a stock dog did to control a feral hog, the bear would twist around, catch the dog, and often kill it. A. L. Bevil explained what the dogs had to do: "They [had to] know how to fight that bear. Some of them would be in front fighting him, and one would catch him from behind, and when the bear would wheel to catch that dog, another one would get him. And they would just keep warting him and warting him until he would finally go up a tree, or they'd hold him there until someone could get there to shoot him. We all used cur dogs."[55]

The Hooks tried many dogs on bear, and not all of them worked out. Some dogs actually ran the other direction, away from their bear, after being released. As Hart said, "After a dog finds out a bear has teeth, if he goes back, he's a bear dog."[56] At the end of the hunt, when the bear treed or when he stopped to fight the dogs, the nearest hunter rushed in to get a shot before the dogs could be injured, and a man had to be willing to take this chance. Dogs were in the most danger at this point, when they tended to lose all caution and throw themselves on the bear. On one occasion, Carter Hart was frantically crawling a log through an impenetrable thicket trying to reach the fight when he met the bear coming the other way. He killed it just before it got to him—a bear that weighed 640 pounds on the scales of a Kountze feedstore.[57]

Some novice bear hunters found themselves ultimately unwilling to "crawl the log." One man had long pestered Bill Warren to take him bear hunting, so finally Warren took him. The bear bayed in a "real tight thicket," and Warren told the man, "Now, if you want to kill you a bear, just crawl in there where them dogs is and kill him." The man started off, then stopped to remark, "I'm gonna carry that foot to my wife, this is the first bear I ever killed in my life!" Warren replied, "You

Hardin County bear hunter equipped with rifle, blowing horn, and hack knife, c. 1902. (Texas State Historical Association, Center for American History, The University of Texas at Austin)

ain't killed one yet." The man "crawled in there a little piece, and directly he come back and said, 'Josh, you better go in there, I don't believe I'm going in there.'"[58]

In December 1906, the Hooks held one of the last bear hunts at their Hurricane camp; the bears were almost gone. A Kansas City newspaper man and a photographer were present to record the occasion, as was famous bear and panther hunter Benjamin Vernon Lilly. Ben Lilly was an extreme example of the stockman-turned-bear-hunter phenomenon. An Alabaman by birth and a stock drover by profession, Lilly had long ago left livestock, wife, and children behind to follow the thrill of the chase, gradually moving west after the vanishing bears and panthers. He came to Hardin County to renew a friendship with Ben Hooks and to procure a specimen bear for the U.S. government's Biological Survey Project. Two bears were killed during this hunt, one of them by the big city newsman—somewhat to the chagrin of veteran local bear hunters. By this time bear hunting was nearly at an end in southeastern Texas; Lilly estimated that no more than fifteen bears ranged in the area.[59] President Theodore Roosevelt had been supposed to come down for a Big Thicket bear hunt at about this time, but to the lifelong sorrow of the Hooks, he failed to make the trip. A year later in 1907 Roosevelt joined in a bear hunt on the other side of the Sabine and penned this evocative account of what it felt like for a stander to await the coming of bear and hounds.

We waited long hours on likely stands. We rode around the canebrakes through the swampy jungle, or threaded our way across them on trails cut by the heavy wood-knives of my companions; but we found nothing. Until the trails were cut the canebrakes were impenetrable to a horse and were difficult enough to a man on foot. On going through them it seemed as if we must be in the tropics; the silence, the stillness, the heat, and the obscurity, all combining to give a certain eeriness to the task, as we chopped our winding way slowly through the dense mass of close-growing, feather-fronded stalks. Each of the hunters prided himself on his skill with the horn, which was an essential adjunct of the hunt, used both to summon and control the hounds, and for signalling among the hunters themselves. The tones of many of the horns were full and musical; and it was pleasant to hear them as they wailed to one another, backwards and forwards, across the great stretches of lonely swamp and forest.[60]

Sometimes, a hunter's emotional attachment to an outstanding hound like Dandy became almost as strong as his bond to human members of his family. An early resident of Cherokee County named Martin Palmer once summoned a Nacogdoches clergyman fifty miles to preach a eulogy at the funeral of his favorite bear dog. Assuming the occasion was a death in Palmer's human family, the preacher made the trip, and when he got there he found Palmer and all his neighbors gathered around the deceased. Assessing the mood of the crowd, the clergyman did his duty.[61]

The historian who reported this occasion in *Farm and Ranch* magazine in 1900 assumed Martin Palmer staged this affair in jest, but he was probably wrong. Links between hunter and hound could be far stronger than most people understood. In 1941 Hinkle Shillings's champion foxhound Dawson Stride ran itself to death in a fox hunt. Shillings said: "Dawson Stride overdid hisself and died in a race; it'd be a good way for a person to die."[62] Shillings was not a wealthy man, but fox hunters who knew him and Dawson Stride contributed money for a large pink granite monument for his hound, a marker that became the nucleus for the National Hall of Fame Cemetery of Fox Hounds in Shelby County. There, under granite and marble monuments, were gathered several score of hunting hounds from across the United States. Their number included Choctaw ("tough hound, he always gave it all he had"), Climber H ("a running hound with a running heart"), and Dawson Stride himself ("he will be remembered and appreciated as long as the chase exists").

Southerners' attitudes toward the foxhound were a special case of their attitudes toward the dog. As geographer Terry Jordan demonstrated in his history of southern stock raising, *Trails to Texas,* the lifeway of the stockmen-farmers developed in South Carolina and spread westward across the upland South. It was a way of life adapted to the big woods, and in these woods the dog was an essential tool—probably *the* essential tool. In the service of man, the dog's sense of smell complemented and extended the human's sense of sight—which in the woods reached only as far as the nearest thicket. Dogs were absolutely necessary to locate and work hogs and cattle in the forest and—rather often—to step in to protect the drover from his feral beasts. Dogs defended the isolated farmstead from intruders, animal and human, and they served in the hunt—probably their oldest relationship with the human species.

Hinkle Shillings's experiences with dogs were typical of many rural southerners. His father kept stock dogs, and as Hinkle grew up he began using them for hunting—first for possums, then raccoons. He recalled a fateful day in 1916:

I heard my first fox race, rode right through the streets of Center a-horseback and hounds from people that I knew and neighbors. I didn't have a hound at that time. The streets of Center was dusty roads going out to Crockett, that's six miles out from Center. Got out there and trailed all night but never did jump. Some of em, just fore day, they give it up, spread their saddle blankets down, took a nap, but I never did take no nap. Then we run back through Center the next morning, up in the morning, with the hounds a-follering us. From then on, I lost my taste for coon hunting.[63]

Having followed the foxhounds one night in 1916, Shillings then followed them all the rest of his life. He won his first foxhound, Christmas Dawson, as a "premium puppy" for selling subscriptions to *Hunter's Horn* magazine, and he later shipped the dog to Birmington, Alabama, to be bred to a noted stud dog named Hub Stride. Then, Hinkle hit the jackpot: the first dog born in the first litter was Dawson Stride, by general consensus one of the best hounds to ever bay a fox. At that point Shillings began a fifty-year career of fox hunting, dog breeding, field-trial competition, and farming on the side. As he said, "I had a good hound business, I shipped everywhere the foxes run." He kept, on the average, ten or twelve "brood gyps" and about eighteen dogs in all. As Dawson Stride's reputation grew, strangers arrived two or three times a week to meet Shillings and to go hunting with him and Dawson Stride. He was a poor man, but even at the end of a long day of work on his farm, he never declined a hunt. He added, "I never did refuse to take Dawson Stride." Later, people from fourteen states would contribute money for the Dawson Stride memorial.[64]

Twice a week for several decades, Shillings took part in an informal hilltop fox hunt characteristic of hundreds of others across the Neches country. Late on Tuesday and Friday afternoons, hunters from the Good Hope, Sardis, and Antioch communities walked or rode over with their hounds to a place known as Bone Hill. Then the hunt began. Like all the fox hunters before them, they built a fire, loosed or "cast" their hounds, and listened for the first dog to bay.

Only gray foxes lived in the woods around Bone Hill, and the hunters (and doubtless their dogs as well) knew many of them individually. They knew a given fox's territory, the tactics it probably would use to try to "throw" the dogs, and approximately how long it would run before it treed. Fox hunters liked and protected their foxes, often putting out meat scraps along the roads or planting crops that foxes liked. They also discouraged fox trappers and imported foxes from outside for local release. This approval was conditional, however, since hunters distinguished between "good foxes" and "bad foxes." A good gray fox gave dogs and hunters a satisfying two- to three-hour "fox race" before the hounds; a bad fox went up a tree in a half hour. Dogs were normally called off when the fox treed or after a certain amount of time had passed, leaving the fox unharmed. However, after a bad fox had shortened the race by premature treeing several times in a row, hunters might lose patience, go to the treed fox, and "jump it out" for the dogs to catch.

As the Bone Hill fox men stood around their fire listening, somewhere out in the dark woods a hound "made a pick-up"—it "struck" a hot trail and "opened," began to "give tongue." Its owner knew instantly that the hound was his. As J. R. Cockrell noted, "Something happens to a man inside when he hears his dog bark."[65] The other hounds "honored" this dog, rushed to it, and began to "pack up." Soon, the fox "jumped," and the full clamor of hound voices began to drift up from the bottoms. Each hound had its own characteristic bark or bay, its own "mouth," which was well-known to its owner and often to other men as well. Some hounds had "chop mouths," others "squalling mouths," and still others "squealing mouths." For an hour, or two, or three, hunters stood and listened as the gray fox ducked and twisted through woods, thickets, and creek bottoms. If the hunt went on long enough, a few hounds got tired and fell behind, "potlickered," then "howled out" and slunk back to the camp. Usually no one said anything, but the hounds' owners shared their shame. Eventually, the fox ran up a "stooping tree," the hounds bayed "treed," and the hunters raised their horns to "blow them off." Nothing remained but to ride home, feed the dogs, eat breakfast, and go to work; fox hunters often could be distinguished from the general rural population by the dark circles beneath their eyes.

A gray fox normally circled "from one bad thicket and briar patch to another" within a couple of miles of where it was jumped, so a fox race involving a gray usually never went out of hearing. This was not so in a chase of the imported European red fox, the "red ranger." A red fox might run for miles and take the hounds out of the hunters' hearing for hours at a time. Weighing from eight to twenty-two pounds, the red fox was built for both speed and endurance; it could easily run in front of an onrushing pack of baying foxhounds all night and put on sudden bursts of speed of up to forty-five miles per hour.[66] A red fox presented an extreme challenge to any hounds, some of which died of exhaustion trying to keep up with it. Aubrey Cole observed, "Hounds ain't really supposed to catch up with a red fox." Hinkle Shillings added, "You can tell more what you're feeding a-running a red fox than any other game."[67]

During the 1840s and 1850s, red foxes spread into Kentucky, and fox hunters soon found that the older breeds of hounds—redbones, blueticks, and black and tans—could not catch them. Determined to breed a dog that could stay with the red ranger, John W. Walker and Wash

Maupin imported large English foxhounds and crossed them with local dogs to produce a slimmed-down American foxhound, which was called the Walker hound.[68] The Walker was fast and enduring, with a "cold nose," able to smell out a cold trail, but its most characteristic trait was its determination. As Hinkle Shillings said, the men who created the Walker "didn't tolerate a quittin' hound." When a man launched a Walker on the trail of a fox or a deer, it might run all day and run all night, and it might never come back. Walkers got lost with some regularity, and—like Dawson Stride—sometimes ran themselves to death on the trail. After the Civil War, members of the Walker family migrated to Texas, and in a classic double stroke of houndman one-upsmanship, they introduced not only the red fox, which local "pot-lickers" could not catch, but also the dog that could catch it. For many Texas dog men, their redbones, blueticks, and the like were immediately demoted to "coon hounds."[69]

There were other gospels in the foxhound religion. Some hunters favored the Trigg hound, the Hudspeth, the July, the Goodman, or the Birdsong—all swift, enduring American foxhounds—but most Neches Valley hunters were Walker-dog men. They valued the Walker's determination above all things, and they were ready to pay the price of time spent waiting for it to come back. Aubrey Cole summed up the Walker's character: "Endurance, don't quit, don't give up, hustle hard when they made a little lose to regain the trail and continue on and not fumble the ball. Just get up on his tail, get up there and get him! . . . And my daddy said that he could stay as long as a hound can run. He was pretty much in favor of "Let's wait for the dog." I've watched the sun go down a-many a night waiting for hounds and hearing my daddy blow his blowing horn."[70]

If the foxhound's virtues were a cold nose, speed, endurance, a good mouth, "fox sense," and determination, its potential sins were "bab-bling," "potlickering," "trashing," and "cunning-running." At the periodic field-trial competitions, hounds were graded down or eliminated for these things, and since the failures of the dog reflected directly on its owner, some erring hounds were swiftly eliminated in the ultimate sense. Field execution was something of a tradition among zealous fox men.[71] A babbling foxhound barked when there was nothing to bark at, a potlickering hound simply quit and gave up, a trashing dog went off after deer, and a cunning-running (or "skirting") hound anticipated the direction of the fox and cut across to take an unfair lead on other dogs. Cunning-running was a characteristic Walker-dog sin, a fault of overcompetence. None of these sins were tolerated, at least not for very long, and most houndmen believed they had an obligation to purge evil from the holy bloodlines.

Field trials took place over three days. Hounds (with big numbers painted on their sides) were released before dawn each day, and by daylight, judges stationed themselves across the countryside to observe the passing of the pack. They "scratched" dogs for serious misbehaviors, awarded demerits for minor ones, and gave positive points for doing good work. At the end of the three days, judges totaled the scores and announced the winners.[72] Field trials were major affairs. On October 28–31, 1940, the annual hunt of the Texas Fox and Wolf Hunters Association took place near Jasper. Three hundred prize hounds competed (including Dawson Stride), and well over three thousand spectators attended.[73]

Field trials offered formal competitions among men working through their dogs, but the common hilltop fox hunt was also such a competition. Hunters always spoke of it as a "fox race"—a highly significant choice of words. Aubrey Cole eloquently explained this aspect of the game of fox hunting:

The thing is to be able to run that man's dog out, make him quit. Your dog stayed till the race was over, but they made that other one "potlicker," they called it. When that dog came out, he showed his stripe whenever you made him quit. That was the real big thing in fox hunting, is my dog outdo your dog. We referred to it as, "My dogs is a-turning that brush loose so fast in your dog's face that he just can't stay there." Usually, when a dog quit, when he'd pot-lickered, he'd hush. You wouldn't hear him any more. And in a minute you'd hear him go to howling. You'd say, "Uh oh! Old so-and-so has potlickered. They've set the hair on him. He's come out."[74]

Of Hinkle Shillings's thousands of fox hunts, his most memorable was a one-on-one competition between his dogs and those of a rich, Lufkin houndman named Carl Dupree. In 1936 Dupree invited Hinkle to bring his dogs down to southern Angelina County along the Neches to help hunt a long-running fox. Dupree had run this red fox many times and assured Hinkle that it not only would go all night but would "run off and leave the hounds" the next morning. Then Dupree began praising his "bragging dogs," Cochran Chief and Calamity Jane, as hounds that had never been outrun except by this super-fox—thus setting up the competition with Hinkle's Dawson Stride and Dawson's sister Pearl S. Of course Hinkle politely let it be known that he thought his dogs were the best.

The race for the super-fox started before dark in the open long-straw pine forests near Weaver's Bend and went on throughout a long autumn night. By three o'clock in the morning, all of Dupree's dogs had quit except his champion bitch, Calamity Jane. As Hinkle recalled, "Them hounds of ours, I'll say, was just getting ripe, they was a-running that red fox." In the first light of dawn, the men cut the race off at a farmstead on a country road and waited for fox and hounds. Soon, they saw the dogs approaching through the open longleaf woods to the north. "And we seen that red fox break cover and start down that hill. And the hounds was part-time looking at him. And it was just our hounds a-running, Jane had done quit." Desperate, the super-fox ran between the farm garden and the yard fence and into a field of corn, with Dawson Stride and Pearl S on his tail, "and they caught the fox just fore he went into the woods."

Dupree proved a good loser: he had the fox mounted and kept it displayed in his Lufkin Chevrolet dealership for the rest of his life. Hinkle explained that fox hunters hunt "for the pleasure of hunting, they don't hunt for the kill," but this epic race had been an endurance contest to the bitter end. Dawson Stride's death of exhaustion in a similar race occurred five years later.[75]

Although fox hunters normally stopped short of the kill, fox hunting was nevertheless a blood sport, like bear, bobcat, and deer hunting. The deepest aspect of the game was an ancient identification of men with hounds as they pressed to the kill. Some fox hunters had to get closer to their hounds than a distant hilltop. As Walter Cole noted: "I've hunted fox a-many a night all night long by myself, nobody in the woods but me. Just turn my dogs out and ride my horse all night long running a fox. I could ride as fast as a pack—could ride right in the middle of em. They would stretch that fox on the ground."[76] During deer drives, some "drivers" also ran with the dogs, sometimes on foot. "Buck" Vaughn's descendants still tell about how Vaughn, running with the hounds, used to cross the line of deer "standers."[77] Other men liked to hunt bobcats because the bobcat ran a more restricted race than the fox, and the hunter sometimes managed to get in on the fight to the finish. Dogs or hunters customarily killed the bobcats, since they were regarded as major predators of pigs and fawns. People once said that if someone killed a big bobcat on a man's hog range, the stockman owed the hunter a "range claim" on a sow and six pigs.[78]

More often than not, however, the hunter failed to reach the bitter end of the hunt because of brush or thickets or crosscutting creeks. Under these circumstances, his identification with the hounds—his link to the kill—came through his hounds' voices. Bobcat hunter Floyd Warren explained:

It's most fun just before they catch him, and they're got the body scent. When he gets real hot and gets real tired he puts off more scent, then the dogs run him faster, by body scent. Then they start changing their voice; they're running to catch him, they're running for blood. They get more and more excited, scream and raise all kinds of fuss. Sometimes you think that they've done caught him, he's stinking so loud the dogs just scream. It's awful pretty to hear them just before they catch the cat. They squeal like people were beating em with sticks—they just go wild."[79]

Houndman Aubrey Cole said:

When a pack of dogs has run a fox about two hours, and they get him down to about ten acres of ground, and he's a-doing everything he can to shed em, he's just ducking here and ducking there and ducking here and ducking there, old fox hunters call it, "he's a-dragging his tail"—he's putting off lots of scent. And a hound, they don't have to hunt him, they just go with that scent. They boil him down to where they've got up in seventy-five yards of him, and they can look at him every once in a while, its just "Yap! Yap! Yap! Who can and who can't! Who can and who can't!" That last fifteen minutes of that fox race, if you've got it in your system, is just like smoking marijuana. You can't forget that, you can't quit it.[80]

Deer hunters felt much the same. When using dogs to hunt deer became illegal in the Neches counties in 1990, an older generation of deer hunters became reluctant converts to modern still hunting for deer—"tree sitting" or "setting in a box," as they contemptuously referred to it. Others quit deer hunting altogether or became "outlaw hunters," affirming ancient social traditions by breaking the law. Like Q. R. King, of Polk County, a number of men emphasized the many ways in which the use of dogs in deer hunting resembled the sport of fox hunting. King said, "I don't care anything about killing a deer, long as I can hear that dog run." Sometimes he went out without a gun, just to listen to the hounds. King added: "And there's a lot of competition in dog hunting. You've got a dog, I've got a dog. It's like running horses, who's got the best dog."[81]

In 1992 King and his friends still kept their old deer lease and hunted together, but the hunting was not the same. As he said, "The camp life is no good anymore." Ten men could go out still hunting and come into camp in the late morning, not having killed a deer, "all sour." Hunting with dogs, on the other hand, was always fun; you always got to listen to the "deer race." The deer hunters who used dogs had hunted as a unit in a way that the still hunters did not. They had participated in a group experience that combined a meat hunt, a dog race (a competition), a ritual, and a social occasion. Still hunters, even old friends sharing the same camp, did not hunt *together* anymore.

The practice of setting "standers," then driving deer down on them with dogs, was at least a century old at the time of the settling of southeastern Texas. In the American South, the planter class and the "better sort of people" preferred this hunting method up to and after the Civil War.[82] After Anglo Americans came to Texas, using dogs to hunt for deer waxed and waned with the abundance of deer, though the relationship was inverse. In the beginning deer were so numerous as to be virtually a pest. They could easily be killed by stalking, and dogs were badly needed to work stock and to hunt the big predators. Consequently, settlers commonly "broke off" their dogs from running deer—not an easy task, since dogs chase deer more naturally than any other game. Then, varying from locality to locality but sometime around the turn of the century, deer became so scarce that dog drives again became the most practical way to hunt them, and the old southern tradition of the "deer race" was revived.

Deer drives followed a common pattern. The "driver," the person who made the "dog drive," usually ran the hunt. He placed the standers on their "deer stands" and "lined the hunt up." From long experience, the driver knew the named "drives" in a certain territory, knew the customary lines of travel of deer across the landscape, and knew by name the stands—the customary hunting locations—on these "deer crossings." Stands were usually located on rural roads, old tramways, pipelines, and other places where a hunter had a field of view of fifty yards in at least two directions. Drives and stands had names accrued by long association: the "Black Creek Drive," "Fuzzy Stump Stand," "Buck Flat Switch Stand," and the "Old Mouldy Stand." Such names were part of local tradition, having taken on meaning from a thousand hunts. J. R. Cockrell said: "I know at least a hundred people now, that if I call em on the telephone and tell them to go to the Pisspot Stand, they'd know exactly where to go. They'd all be standing within forty yards of each other at a place fifteen miles back in the woods."[83]

The driver masterminded the hunt. He usually tried to put the better hunters on the better stands; the inexperienced or poorly armed drivers got the "wouldn't hurt" stands—the locations where "it wouldn't hurt to have somebody," though the chances the deer would go that way seemed small. He might schedule a second drive over the same territory, with people staying on their stands. Or, he might tell standers to stay on their stands until they heard a horn signal, then to move to other designated stands in a second drive area. Sometimes the hunt was not prearranged, and the driver adjusted to circumstances. Standers were instructed to stay on their stands until the driver came to get them. He might make a drive, and if the deer jumped quickly and ran straight out of the drive area, he might go back to camp, get another dog, and make another drive. Conversely, if the deer ran around in the area a half an hour before coming out, the driver might assume all the deer had run out, go get the standers, and take them someplace else to set up another drive.[84] Eventually, all the strategies were laid out and all the pieces in the game were in place. The driver gave the standers time to get situated on their assigned stands. Then, as Aubrey Cole explained: "You'd usually hear him when he started the drive, you'd hear him go to tooting his horn. He'd blow his horn four or five times and whoop to his dogs, and in the woods he'd go."[85]

Miles away, the standers waited on their stands in the silent woods. After a while, they heard the dogs jump a deer and begin to bay. At this point, each stander readied his shotgun for a quick shot at a running deer—the deer might "run out over him" as easily as anybody else. As time passed and the deer doubled around, circled, and changed directions in front of the dogs, minute by minute the stander's tension grew. Aubrey Cole noted: "Of course it's brush country, and you don't see anything until its within a hundred or so yards at you. To hear em a-coming to you, and you knowing every minute that a big deer's gonna pop out over you, and the dogs just a-crying ever breath—there's a excitement that you don't get out of hardly anything else."[86]

Sometimes, the stander became so overwrought that the dreaded "buck ague" struck, and he "took a chill and went to jerking all over." One man heard the annoying drumming of a woodpecker as the hunt approached, only to realize that it was his own foot "a-jumping up and down on a holler log." Another forgot to shoot and pumped all the shells from his shotgun as the deer passed. When the first deer came out over Aubrey Cole as a boy, he shot way behind it as it crossed the road, then, as he pumped the spent round from the chamber, he accidentally kept his finger on the trigger and the gun went off again, blowing a hole in the ground just in front of his hunting boots. The adult hunters later praised Cole for his slow, methodical rate of fire, denoting the absence of panic, even though he had missed the deer. They remarked, "That boy didn't kill it, but he shore was shooting purty." It was ten years before Cole told the older hunters what had actually happened.[87]

More rituals were associated with dog drives for deer than with most other Anglo-Saxon activities outside of church or fraternity hall. In an unmistakable symbolism, the stander who missed his deer had his shirttail cut off by the other hunters. The hunters would walk about, looking for the least drop of blood; if no blood was found, somebody would perform the amputation. A young hunter who missed a long shot might get only a couple of inches cut off the bottom; an experienced man who missed at close range might have the back of his shirt cut out in a giant "V" right up to his shoulder blades. Depending on local traditions, hunters hung their disgraced companion's severed shirttail in a tree over the deer stand (sometimes to hang there for years), ran it up a makeshift flagpole back at the deer camp, or displayed it in some other prominent place. Sometimes they even sent it home to the man's wife. When the hunter killed his first deer, another ancient ritual was performed: the other hunters smeared him with blood. This might be just a stripe on the forehead, but not necessarily. Q. R. King noted that at his deer camp, they "got to baptize him in blood." They would "open up that old deer and take handfuls of blood and rub it all over him—his clothes, his hair, everywhere." Sometimes they had to "run him down" to do this.[88]

More often than not, however, the deer got away. Assertions by hunters that the deer "liked" to be run by dogs seem dubious, but many "wise old bucks" certainly had experienced the deer drive many times before. Deer were faster than dogs, and hunters affirmed that the deer usually just loped along in front of the hounds, running only fast enough to stay out of sight. They doubled back and forth and "played" with the dogs. If other deer or cattle were in the area, they ran through them to try to "switch the dogs off" on the other animals. Drives were commonly made downwind, so that the deer would not be able to scent the line of standers ahead of them, but many experienced deer approached a road or other opening with great caution. They hung back and tried to spot the standers; then, if they smelled or spotted the standers, they passed through the line between two hunters or else refused to cross it and went off at right angles to escape. A large number of pursuing dogs, unusually fast dogs, or dogs that did not bark might panic a deer, but this was rare. J. R. Cockrell said: "I've stood in a place where you could see the dogs and the deer both. I've seen a deer stop and watch a dog for fifteen minutes and wait until he gets fifty yards of him and then bounce on off."[89] Deer even seemed to have some instinct, or knowledge, about how to manipulate their own scent. Game biologist Charles Boyd once observed a buck approach a road, stop, jump sideways as far as he could jump, tiptoe off parallel to the road for a certain distance, then cross the road and run on. "I watched the dogs, and when the dogs got there to where he started tip-toeing, I mean it was just like you put up a brick wall. There was just very little, if any, scent."[90]

There were tactics and countertactics in this ancient contest between deer, dogs, and men. Local woodsmen sometimes knew the habits of neighborhood bucks so well that they could set up a precision drive involving only one dog, one driver, and one stander. C. W. Gandy's father killed his first deer with the help of Uncle Dave Crockett, a freed slave. Crockett accompanied Gandy to the bottoms with a single dog tied to his belt by a rope. He told the boy exactly where to stand, then went out to drive a particular deer. The deer came by just as Uncle Dave had said, and Gandy shot it.[91] At a much later date, newspaperman Ralph Ramos took former Appellate Justice L. B. Hightower deer hunting with woodsman Uncle Boy Dykes. Before Dykes took his dogs out to make a drive, he put Hightower on a certain stand and told him: "Five minutes after you hear my dogs start be ready. The deer will come from thataway, he'll be a good, big buck. He'll turn at that stump [about thirty feet away], then he'll jump that branch. When he jumps you get him." The judge thought this was nonsense and so was unprepared to shoot when the deer did exactly as Uncle Boy had predicted.[92]

Some hunters preferred to use slow dogs like coonhounds or beagles to make the drive and dispensed with standers altogether. Deer usually chose to jog along only fast enough to stay ahead of such dogs, and they often cut back and forth. Under these conditions the driver sometimes had a chance to anticipate the deer's movements and make the kill himself. When he was a young man and unusually fleet of foot, Harold Snelson often tried to accomplish this by running behind the family coonhound.[93] "Abreast hunting," as Aubrey Cole called it, was another strategy requiring no standers. In this method, driver and dogs were flanked by two moving hunters who stayed off to the sides and somewhat in front and watched for a shot when the deer circled or doubled back.[94] With experienced hunters, abreast hunting could be an effective method; otherwise, it was a good way to get someone killed.

Although some hunters considered the method unsporting, men occasionally ran a deer with relays of dogs. In Houston County, Frank Ashby and another man pursued a legendary old buck with two Walker hounds, two cur dogs, and two mongrel stock dogs. The enduring Walkers stayed on the deer all the time. The others joined the chase at certain road crossings for a short, fast run; then they were pulled off, driven around, rested up, and sent after the deer again. Despite pursuit by the two men in automobiles and by their whole kennel, the big buck still escaped, though slightly peppered with shot by a local duck hunter when the deer swam the Neches.[95]

Walter and Aubrey Cole reacted characteristically to the tactics of the wise old bucks: they used Walker dogs all the way. Aubrey Cole contended that deer running before a good Walker pack had little time to sniff out standers or play tricks. "If you got a pack of hounds that's a-churning one, really giving him a fit, he'll run over a train. He's not a-smelling, he's a-getting away!"[96]

Throughout the first half of the twentieth century, in the early fall of each year, a significant portion of the male population of the Neches counties left their homes for the deer camps, there to reside, off and on, for weeks and even months. Hunters set up operations at traditional sites on spring creeks and at places like Holly Bluff along the river—anywhere there were deer, good water, and plenty of firewood. Often, hunters established camps even before the season started, sometimes even building dog pens and horse corrals. At the Cockrell family's camp in Polk County, the most essential item in the camp was the tarpaulin. Stretched over a pole, or poles, and tethered to stakes, it formed the main protection from the weather. People slept in wagon beds or on the ground under smaller tarpaulins called "wagon sheets." Some of the Cockrell men came to the camp on the weekends, staying for longer periods at the beginning, at Thanksgiving, and at Christmas; others stayed in camp for weeks at a time. Dogs, horses, tents, and other gear remained in place the whole season, and hunters did not worry about having anything stolen. In those days, as Aubrey Cole said, "People honored your deer camp."[97]

Camps of men who customarily hunted deer together developed special traditions. Q. R. King's group collected severed shirttails at the top of an impromptu cane flagpole; one year they had twenty-eight "flags" flying from it at the end of the season. They rolled a huge hardwood "back log" into place on the first day of the hunt and built their campfires in front of it all season. Like the Caddos, they preferred their hunting fire to never go entirely out. As in many other camps, King and his friends consumed much of the venison killed in the hunt while in the woods; at a minimum, the rule was "the camp gets a ham." The camp also got a one-dollar contribution from the hunters for every shot they missed at deer. King's camp began with kerosene lanterns and sleeping on the ground and ended with electric generators and Airstream trailers, but its essential atmosphere never changed.[98]

Usually, someone remained in camp all the time to feed the dogs and keep an eye on things—a person who was not working or who had few responsibilities. Others showed up from time to time during the week and then en masse on weekends and holidays. Traditionally, the deer season began about the time the crops were gathered, and it continued until the end of the year. Whole families might camp out and stay two or three weeks, but more commonly the deer camp was a man's domain. Cockrell women and children rarely showed up at the family camp and never participated in the hunting. J. R. Cockrell explained: "I was forty years old before I ever saw a women in the woods deer hunting. It wasn't forbidden, they just didn't do it. As a kid, there was a lot missing from the atmosphere when the womenfolks were there. But when they went to the house, and when it was all men, that's when, man, there's not anything I'd rather do in the world than that! To go out there to that camp and stay and stay and stay, and follow em around!"[99]

In the 1920s and 1930s, as deer became harder to find, some "men only" deer camps began to substitute indoor sports for the thrills of the chase. In his senior essay of 1921, seventeen-year-old Robert Hooks recorded this description of a Hardin County deer camp he had just attended. His high-school English teacher may have been a little taken aback.

> Every year on November the first about 150 men meet out in the middle of the Big Thicket to have their annual deer hunt and get on a big drunk. In the day time they hunt and in the night time they shoot craps, play poker, and drink all the shinney they want. The poker table and crap table are located in a tent which has electric lights and chairs in it. The crap game usually lasts until about three o'clock in the morning, while the poker game does not break up until daylight.[100]

Doubtless, not many of the poker players rolled out of bed for the deer drive early the next morning. The statistics of this November 1920 deer camp clearly revealed its priorities: 187 men signed in as attending the camp (and more were present); sixteen hundred biscuits were set out on the table for breakfast, along with coffee in "common large wash pots"; and in two weeks, three deer were killed.[101]

As the twentieth century wore on, the deer camps became islands of traditional hunting practices in the rising tide of the game law. Standers adjusted with difficulty to the "bucks only" law, since they specialized in snap shots at running deer. As one man confessed to a game warden years later, his camp of hunters often began with a fine resolve to shoot only bucks, but after several days of unsuccessful hunting, with dogs lost and no venison in camp, the driver's rule of the day often changed to "shoot anything that moves."[102]

Walter Cole gave somewhat conflicting instructions to his son regarding the conservation of deer, and this ambivalence characterized many other hunters. One of Cole's self-devised rules (having nothing at all to do with the official game law) was to limit his deer hunting to the months of August through December. By August 1, he reasoned, "the fawns, yearling deer, was big enough to get out of the way of a hound, and they were big enough and good enough to eat"—presumably, if they failed to get out of the way. However, Walter Cole also told his son, "There wasn't but two seasons for deer, and that was salt and pepper."[103]

J. R. Cockrell noted his family's attitude: "They didn't go [to camp] because the season opened, they didn't come back because the season closed. They went when they got the crops in and when it was convenient for them to go." Not surprisingly, when Polk County closed its deer season in the 1930s, the Cockrell hunting camp went on operating as if nothing had happened. J. R. Cockrell's grandfather sometimes told him at the beginning of the yearly hunt: "Boy, don't you kill one of them old bucks. You can't eat them horns. If you gonna kill a deer, kill one we can eat. If I can't fry it, I don't want it."[104]

Participation in deer camps and deer drives normally was restricted to adults or older boys. In most cases, younger boys (and, in rare instances, girls) began their careers as woodsmen with the casual hunting and trapping of possums, rabbits, and other animals around the homeplace. The "no gun" methods they used were much the same throughout the Neches country. These techniques survived from earlier times, when some people were too poor to waste expensive powder and ball on small game, and many of the methods probably had Native American origins. During the Great Depression, people resorted to some of these techniques again.

Nocturnal hunters often targeted the Virginia opossum. It was regular in its habits, feeding in certain areas (for example, persimmon groves) at certain seasons of the year, and could be taken with only a dog, a lantern, and an ax. Once shaken out of a tree, the possum conveniently "sulled"—went into a trance-like stupor that made it easy to carry home alive, put under an overturned washtub, and fatten for the pot. Even the people who habitually ate possums believed in controlling the animals' diet ("cleaning them out") for a few days beforehand. Like the rooter hog, the possum was an opportunistic omnivore that ate almost everything, including carrion. Rural people who chanced on a possum foraging in the body cavity of a long-dead cow or horse sometimes refused to eat possums ever again, regardless of whether or not they had been "cleaned out."

Any sort of dog was adequate for possums, but especially favored were the small, terrier-like dogs that southerners call "feist dogs." As C. P. Petri explained: "They could smell alright—they could smell a hot squirrel trail or a hot possum trail. We climbed for them possums; I clumb a lots of trees. You'd climb up there and fool around with him and get him out on a limb, and if he got out too far I'd shake him out. If he didn't, if he stayed on the tree, I could reach up there and get that tail and jerk him loose and throw him to the ground. And course, that little old feist would jump on him and he'd just sull."[105]

Avy Joe Havard, of Angelina County, another of the legion of boyhood possum hunters along the Neches, went out so often that he regularly dozed off in school. As a consequence, the teacher whipped him with a four-foot switch cane. Avy Joe and his "neighbor boys" hunted possums on moonless nights along "hardwood branches through the Piney Woods." The family's black-mouthed cur treed the possums, then, if the boys could not shake them out or get them in any other way, the boys cut down the trees with axes. Once a tree was felled, the stock dog often seized and killed the possum. Or as Havard noted: "We taken that ax handle, lay it on the back of his neck, stand on that ax handle, and break his neck—pop it. We had more fun than anything in the world."[106]

During the day, boy hunters "sicced" or "hissed" their dogs on squirrels, cottontails, and swamp rabbits. With their feist dogs, C. P. Petri and his friends located squirrels in the trees, then ran under the fleeing animals, whooping and shouting, while the squirrel limbed frantically through the trees above. Fairly often, the squirrel panicked and fell or jumped to the ground, and the feist dogs grabbed it. If the squirrel "holed up," a boy might climb the tree to the hollow and poke a long, flexible switch cane down the hole, forcing the squirrel to jump out. In a similar technique, dogs pursued rabbits until they took refuge in hollow trees or logs, then the boys used flexible forked sticks to reach in and "twist em out." The rabbit had loose skin, and the forked stick hung in the skin, allowing the extraction of the rabbit. Once it was out of the log, a boy executed the small creature with a chopped blow to the back of its head, the original "rabbit punch"[107] The swamp rabbit, as its name suggests, was a creature of the bottomlands. When the river rose rapidly in early winter, the water often trapped large numbers of swamp rabbits on islands in the backwater, and groups of boys and men went out in paddle boats and killed them with clubs.

Probably the possum and the cottontail rabbit were the most important of the no-gun game animals. Cottontails roamed everywhere in the altered woodlands and fields around settlements, and some boys hunted them with clubs in the tall grass. A hunter of sharp eye and stealthy tread could spot a rabbit in its "form," or bed, before it jumped and could kill it with a club.

Until the 1870s, night-hunters went to the roost sites of wild pigeons with pine torches and thrashed large numbers of birds to death with long poles. Present in limb-shattering numbers and confused by the fiery torches, the pigeons made easy prey for the "bird thrashers." Hunters often cleaned the pigeons and preserved them with salt in large barrels—sometimes for the market.[108] In later decades, bird thrashing of other communally roosting species, mainly blackbirds and robins, became a boy's sport. Many men interviewed around 1990 had gone on bird thrashings in their youth, either in parties of boys or in mixed-sex "courting" expeditions. Jake Cole and others recalled romantic bird thrashings that culminated in "robin roasts" around campfires, where everybody sang.[109] Walter Cole (no relation) explained:

A man would clear up a big new ground, say eight or ten acres, any size, and make brush heaps, and birds would go in there in the wintertime, cold nights, to roost. They'll get in them brush heaps, tight places, and they was cold and about half froze-down. And you take a big coon torch with a brush in your hand and surround that brush heap, and shine that light over the top of it, and tromp the brush heap, and you thrash the birds down when they fly out of that. You hit em with that brush you got in your hand like a brush broom, thrash em down.

To increase his sport, Walter Cole sometimes extinguished his torch, climbed a tree, and caught birds by hand. He explained: "The boys with lights out yonder, you can see a bird a-coming. I've caught birds in the air a-flying in my hat, like catching a baseball."[110]

During depression times, many no-gun hunting and trapping techniques remembered from boyhood came into use again to provide families with food. Four or five strategically placed "box traps" for cottontails kept a family in rabbit meat, and rived-board pen traps effectively caught turkeys or quail. The pen traps for these ground-foraging bird species differed only in scale. In each case a shallow trench baited with corn led the birds under one side of the trap, to surface on the inside. Quails or turkeys moved through the trench pecking the corn, but once inside they refused to reenter the dark hole.[111] Many other kinds of traps, snares, deadfalls, and no-gun hunting techniques soon came back into practice at this time to provide game for the pot. Wanda Gipson DuBose remembered wrapping her shoes in burlap sacks against the cold and holding the pine torch for her father, Herman, on unarmed nocturnal stalks for rabbits and possums. After a snowfall, Herman Gipson tracked rabbits to their lairs in hollow trees, reached bare-handed into the hollows, and extracted the animals.[112]

Gipson also went out at night on fire hunts for raccoons, but at these times he carried a gun. Raccoon pelts were worth several dollars at a time when the standard agricultural wage was about one dollar a day. Out of work, out of money, and even out of food, Oscar Allen's older brother Garnet and his new bride went night-hunting for venison just before Christmas in the 1930s. Spotting an animal's eye in the light of his carbide headlamp, Allen fired his shotgun, but when he went to the location he found not a deer but a huge dead mink on a stump. He said: "Looky here, Pauline, what a mink! Ain't no use to go any further, this'll be enough for our Christmas." Nor was Allen exaggerating; carefully skinned and cured, this mink pelt brought twenty-five dollars.[113]

Hunting and trapping for furbearing animals had a long history along the Neches; as an economic exploitation of the wilderness, closely linked to world markets, it long predated the coming of the Anglo Americans. French, Indian, and Hispanic trappers and hunters dominated the early fur trade, producing an impressive volume of furs and hides. Around 1830, no less than forty thousand deer hides, fifteen hundred bearskins, twelve hundred otter pelts, and six hundred beaver pelts passed into the hands of Nacogdoches merchants in only a few months.[114]

From 1830 to 1990, the fur trade in southeastern Texas waxed and waned with shifts in world fashion and the rise and fall of fur prices in international markets, but some species almost always brought enough to keep hunters and trappers in the fur game. People living along the Neches never quite forgot the intricate folk techniques and knowledge used to trap and hunt mink, raccoon, bobcat, and fox, and they passed these methods down through the generations. Trapping and hunting skills were suddenly at a premium during the "coon boom" of 1975 to 1985. In 1979, the height of the fur boom, any kind of good raccoon hide brought $25 (with some going for $30), and a bobcat pelt brought over $100. By the winter of 1991, the boom had thoroughly busted; raccoons were worth $2.50 and bobcats $5 to $10—not enough to pay people to trap them.[115] It was an old story; world fur fashions had changed, this time accelerated by the complaints of animal rights' activists. At least for a while, nobody wanted East Texas "blue coon" pelts.

For two centuries, techniques for taking furbearers varied little, if at all. Some people preferred to hunt instead of trap for fur, and raccoons were particularly suited for this approach. In the 1930s, Herman Gipson stalked his prey at night along spring creeks by the light of a fatpine "coon torch." Raccoons' eyes are highly adapted for night vision; they shone so brightly in the light of a torch or headlight that the raccoon's head seemed to have an internal light source. Like Gipson, Charlie Havard night-hunted for raccoon during the 1940s, and both Charlie and James May also hunted by drifting the Neches at night and sweeping the banks with headlights. May, a skillful adventurer on hunting club properties, used the classic East Texas poacher's weapon, a .22 rifle with a large, light-gathering telescopic sight.[116] As a high school boy, Charles Wells began headlighting raccoons along spring creeks in the mid-1970s. After a while, newly married and in need of additional money, Wells trained a redbone-cur crossbreed that a friend had given him and began using the dog to hunt for raccoons.[117]

Hunting for raccoons with dogs was an old sport, though somewhat disparaged by fox hunters and other elite followers of the Walker hound. One of the old breeds—a bluetick, a redbone, or a black and tan—worked well for raccoon hunting, as did the Walker variant called a "treeing Walker." Raccoons were smart and might twist and turn around and play some tricks, but they rarely ran great distances before they treed. The raccoon hunter wanted a dog that could trail them, jump them, tree them, and then bark "treed" so that the raccoon hunter could come up and shoot them out. Charles Wells walked old logging roads and creeks with his dog, jumping raccoons and going to the dog when the raccoon treed. Each night's catch was "sack skinned" in the modern fashion—the carcass removed from its sack-like hide, which was left intact. The the hide was stored "green," uncured, in the deep-freeze to await the fur buyer. The raccoon carcasses were eaten or sold for meat; nothing was wasted. Wells's half-breed hound stood him in good stead over the years of the fur boom, during which he took somewhere between fifteen hundred and two thousand raccoons.[118]

A law-abiding citizen, Charles Wells hunted either on national forest land or with the permission of the landowners, but others did their raccoon hunting on private hunting clubs. During the 1930s, Oscar Allen's older brother Garnet trained a special dog to catch raccoons and minks for fur, and the brothers hunted with him for over a decade. This dog, named Old Hound, silently accompanied the Allens to their nocturnal hunting grounds, then began to circle, searching for raccoons or minks—and only these animals. When it found and treed one, Old Hound barked about three times, then barked no more. The brothers carefully calculated his direction and walked toward him. When Old Hound smelled his masters, he whined to let them know where he was, but otherwise he would not make a sound, even if someone passed right by him. This meant that potential dog and fur thieves, landowners, or pasture riders could not locate the scene of the action.[119]

Although many people used dogs to take raccoon, and some used them for mink and bobcat, more woodsmen preferred to trap for fur. Sometimes an initial squeamishness had to be overcome, especially for raccoons, though it was considered unmanly to in any way admit this. Trapping raccoons in steel traps could be uncomfortably like trapping monkeys; raccoons might "whine like a dog" in the trap, and "cover their eyes with their hands" as the trapper approached. Even professional trapper Dudley Denmon, of Jasper County, disliked this aspect of raccoon trapping, though he specialized in catching the animals.

Boys began casual raccoon and possum trapping along creeks and bottoms close to home. Pelts were stretched on cane or cypress frames, dried and smoked, then mailed to various fur buyers—even to Sears and Roebuck. Boys spent their profits on candy, ammunition, and school supplies, among other things. Students often walked beelines through the woods to the rural schools they attended, running their traplines along the way. This was efficient and saved time, but the practice sometimes resulted in a student showing up for school smelling of the "polecat."

Then, usually in their late teen-age years, some boys became serious trappers. In Hardin County, A. Randolph Fillingim and his brother laid a five-mile trapline that they ran every day; sometimes they spent the night at the end of their trapline in a special "trapping camp."[120] At about the same time, Charlie Havard and his brother in Angelina County were "trying to make a living" by trapping. The Havards favored "log sets" for their traps in the flooded bottoms, and their paddle boat was basic to their operations. Charlie said: "There wasn't ary log in that bottom we didn't know where it was at! We was trying to make a living trapping; we were running about sixty traps. We'd get in a boat down here back of my field 'bout sunrise, and we'd get out of it 'bout sundown that evening. Go down this side of that river bottom across the bottom, cross the river, and come back up the other side."[121]

In Shelby County and later in Angelina County, Harold Snelson and his brothers did the same. Born in 1920, Snelson began trapping at age ten and continued until "fur fell" in the middle 1980s—nearly sixty years later. Snelson ran a trapline on the way to Harmony School, and one day he noticed the tracks of a very large mink along a little creek. He had the confidence to go home and make an extra large "stretching board" for this big mink. "Sure enough, in about three days I caught him." He shipped the mink hide to Sears and Roebuck and received fourteen dollars at a time when a man might work from sunup to sundown for one dollar. Snelson recalled, "Fourteen dollars then look like a thousand to me now."[122]

Over the years, by trial and error and by the careful study of animal tracks and other "sign," Snelson became a master trapper. He specialized in "water trapping" for minks and raccoons, and he preferred to make "blind sets"—unbaited traps that catch the animal by precise positioning. In keeping with his preference for blind sets, Snelson liked to set for mink in "little old spring branches and little draws," constricted places where the trapper could read sign and set an unbaited trap exactly where the animal had been traveling. To catch mink or any other animal, the trapper had to think like the quarry. As Harold explained, trapping a mink could be "downright hard—he's the next thing to a coyote." Snelson added: "He's so light and little, you got to set that trap on a hair trigger to catch him. A mink, he likes to go in drifts and hollow logs and everything thataway—he'll go in a hole the size of a peckerwood hole, a mink will. A mink ain't much on big bottoms, they like little streams."[123]

Snelson sometimes used bait when he trapped in the open Neches bottoms, but he preferred to trap for both minks and raccoons on these small, restricted branches where he could calculate exactly the animals' travel paths and could thus use an unbaited blind set, placed precisely two inches beneath the water. Snelson explained (articulating the credo of the elite blind-set trapper), "I can walk up and down that [creek], and usually in a hundred yards somewhere I can find me a place that I can make him put his foot." This was not guesswork but was based on a careful reading of the animal's tracks. "You can see where he's been going, he just put his foot there, all you got to do is put your trap there." Wading in the creek, the trapper looked for places that naturally channeled the animal into a single line of travel. Or, he carefully changed the positions of brush and twigs to better direct, or "wing," the animal into his trap. This winging had to be careful. The trapper could easily "mess things up" with his placement of the trap, rearranging the landscape in a clumsy way; he had to be subtle, making minimal changes. Snelson said: "You can wing a raccoon or a mink either one in easy, but you don't get stuff big as your arm; you use little bitty twigs the size of a matchstem. Them the size of a matchstem will turn a raccoon or a mink, either one; just leave him a little opening there."[124]

The trapper had to think not only like a mink but also like other mink trappers. As Harold explained: "I learnt to trap hiding it from what I's trapping for and the thieves, too. And when you've learned to best both of em, well, you've made a pretty good trapper." Snelson could hide eighty traps across miles of landscape, then unerringly go back to each of them. Some men could not do this and were forced to leave locators for themselves in the forms of ribbons or even soft-drink cans. Snelson asserted that he had never tampered with any man's traps, though he could have. "I can get out there and find where somebody's trap set. [If] I can find as many as three of em, I can get his pattern, see what kind of places, I can find 90 percent of his traps if I wanted to. You find three or four traps, and its just like reading a book; I done got his pattern."[125]

Serious trappers developed personal preferences for prey species and for kinds of sets. Harold Snelson often set for raccoons along the same creeks where he set for minks, making only small adjustments in the placement of traps and in the size of the wings directing the animal into them. Oscar Allen's uncle often made mink sets in much the same way, although he was not so purely a blind-set man as Snelson and sometimes scattered small river perch around on the nearby bank to attract the mink. Former U.S. Senator Ralph Yarborough and his older brother trapped for mink along the Neches River, placing a dead bird impaled on a stick three or four feet out in the water, then setting up brush wings leading out to it with a water-set trap in the middle. Charlie Havard favored a "log set" for both mink and raccoon. Both species walked logs across the flooded bottoms, to stay dry-footed, and Havard had prepared trap logs scattered across both sides of the river bottom for miles. He cut a notch or square in the top of the log deep enough to set his trap in, then covered the trap to the surface of the unaltered log on either side with "bug dust" from wood-boring beetles. "Job sticks" were often placed on the top of the log on either side of the trap to make the animal step squarely in it. Just as the Havard brothers knew every fallen log, so did the McGalin brothers know every hollow tree. Lynn McGalin and his brother Babe liked to make water sets inside hollow trees standing in the backwater. The raccoon or mink would smell the bait and enter the hollow trunk to investigate.[126] A common water set used for raccoon by Snelson, Havard, Dudley Denmon, and many others was located at the edge of the backwater. The trapper set his trap beside a tree in three or four inches of water, then rubbed some bait or scent on the trunk to attract the raccoon. The trap did not have to be covered with much. As Snelson said, "Just lay you one or two of them old black leaves over the top of it." Charlie Havard and others sometimes used a "sight bait" in these circumstances, something shiny on the pan of the trap to attract the curious raccoon. Havard so commonly used white buttons from his long underwear for this purpose that he got in trouble with his wife.

As the years passed, Harold Snelson also mastered the techniques of "dirt trapping" for fox and bobcats. As the name suggests, the dirt trapper buried his trap in the ground a few feet from a game trail or old logging road, then used scent bait of various kinds to attract the passing predators. Scent baits included both "gland baits" and "urine baits," in many combinations. The same scent bait might attract fox, bobcats, and—in later years—coyotes, but the trapper subtly altered the placement of the trap relative to the scent to aim at one predator or another. He visualized—virtually choreographed in his mind—the fox's or bobcat's feet approaching the trap and set the trap accordingly. With a "walk in" set, the animal could approach the trap from only one direction; the "walk through" set was designed to catch a predator coming from either side of the trap.[127]

Harold Snelson and his professional trapper son, Ed, honed their trapping skills by walking miles and miles of sandy roads and reading the animal behaviors tracked into the dust. Around 1955 the prints of a new animal began to appear. The coyote, *Canis latrans*, the superpredator, had arrived in southeastern Texas, moving in from the west. The coyote presented the ultimate challenge for the dirt trapper. As both Harold and Ed told me, using exactly the same words, "Everything else is retarded compared to a coyote."[128]

Coyotes spread rapidly across East Texas, occasionally hybridizing with dogs and with the last of the red wolves. When the Snelsons first started trapping coyotes, the men caught some that had wolf-like features—short ears, big heads, and reddish coats. In later years they occasionally caught coyote-dog crosses with one or two white feet, white rings around the necks, and even—on one occasion—the "glass eyes" of a stock dog.

Whatever their ancestry, coyotes were hard to catch, and trapping for them could be a humbling experience. A novice trapper, with clumsy sets using food baits and rusty traps, might catch one or two in an area, but then the word got around, and the amateur trapper caught no more. Catching coyotes required careful sets and the use of scent baits of great subtlety and variation, since the coyotes were forever learning to associate a certain scent with the trap. If a coyote "made" a trap, it might go around to all of them set by the trapper—scratching, urinating, defecating in their vicinities, and otherwise "leaving a calling card" that it knew what the trapper was up to.

Coyotes were the ultimate survivors. As Ed Snelson noted, they would go into the Neches bottoms to catch frogs or into the city limits of Lufkin and Jasper to catch house cats.

> The sucker will eat sweet potatoes, he'll eat out of garbage cans, he'll eat anything. He's gonna adjust. I trapped three [hunting] clubs this summer, and there was nothing there to eat but muscadines and grasshoppers—that's all they had to eat, muscadines and grasshoppers. They eat persimmons, pears, you name it! You've heard the old theory that when everything on this earth is gone they'll be three things here, a cockroach, a crow, and coyote? That's the God's truth. I don't know about the crow, but the coyote will be here.[129]

Most of the woodsmen who trapped and hunted the Neches bottoms in the fall and winter shifted to fishing the river in the spring. Not surprisingly, Harold Snelson's preferred fishing method in later years was an unbaited "hoop net," the aquatic equivalent of the trapper's blind set. A hoop net is a long, conical fish trap held in shape by big hoops spaced along its length. Fish move into the open end of the hoop net, pass through two internal "throats," then are trapped at the back of the net. In the old days, fishermen tied their own netting, constructed hoops from muscadine grapevines or rived white-oak splits, and built their own hoop nets in keeping with personal theories of what worked best. Sometimes they baited their nets with cottonseed cake or other materials to catch buffalo and other scale fish. However, if the fisherman wanted catfish, especially the big opelousas, or "op," he usually set an unbaited net facing downstream "in one of the trails where they run."[130]

Snelson's hoop-net sets for op showed the same precision, attention to detail, and concern with secrecy as his blind sets for mink. He preferred to use hoop nets when the river was at two-thirds banks, or higher, and preferably when it was on the rise. "That's when your nets will fill up." Precise location of the net was critical for success. As Snelson noted: "You got to know where to set it. You can have it three foot out from where it ought to be, and it may set there a month and not catch as many fish as you can eat. But if you had it over three foot, you might catch a hundred pounds in one lick."[131]

Snelson usually chose bankside sets, with the hoop net dropped down into the right angle between the "second bank" and the horizontal bottom. Like many old-time net or line fishermen, he often went down to the Neches at extreme low water and studied the riverbed, determining exactly where he planned to place his nets. Sometimes he marked a tree twenty or thirty yards out in the woods with some unobtrusive mark exactly opposite the point where he wanted the mouth of his hoop net to end up; sometimes he just committed the location to memory. When Snelson came back to this place at high water, he might let his net down several times before getting it exactly where he wanted it to go. Each time, he dropped the anchor on the "tail rope" of the net, pulled the net out tight with the boat, then released it and allowed it to swing into line with the current, its mouth facing downstream. Like other Neches hoop-netters, Snelson set his net in the mainline current, where the water was "running straight" just outside of the line of "eddy water." Also, like many other fishermen, he made sure that the mouth of his net ended up angling slightly toward the bank.

If positioning the mouth of a hoop net was a matter of inches (like placing a Victor #2 steel trap in a blind set), so was it a matter of concealment. Some men ran lines to the bank from the tail and mouth ends of their nets, but not Harold Snelson; this made them too easy for other people to find. Snelson relied on his trapper's memory to return to the exact sites of his nets and used a hooked "drag" on a rope to bring them up. In setting and running a net, he took care not to nudge the bank with the boat, break branches, or leave any other signs to give away its location. Charlie Havard, another master hoop-net fisherman, also took precautions. His tail and mouth lines were made of hard-to-see black cord, and he tied them under the water with counterclock-wise knots. Right-handed people normally tied knots the other way, and this allowed Charlie to detect if someone was running his nets. He also relied on tradition to protect his nets, since many of the people who fished the Neches in southern Angelina County had their own proprietary sets, handed down across the generations and widely rec-ognized by others. Many of Charlie's prize sets had been his father's and his grandfather's.[132] As fishermen noted, people "honored a man's nets" and were more neighborly in earlier times, but they were also more afraid of getting caught. A half century ago, to be discovered running a man's net in the remote river bottoms could lead to a very unpleasant, even life-threatening, experience.

When Charlie Havard, Harold Snelson, or James May raised one of their hoop nets to the surface, they never quite knew what they would find inside. Snelson set his nets for op, and he once pulled up a net with seven ops, weighing a total of 168 pounds. He struggled for a time before he got them into the boat. As he said: "Biggest one in that bunch weighed 45 pounds. Where you got several of em thataway, one will flop and make that other'n flop, and you'll think they gonna knock the side of that boat off."[133] Market fishermen sometimes set baited hoop nets for buffalo in deep holes, occasionally catching five hundred or six hundred pounds of fish at a time—so many that they had to cut holes in their net and remove the fish one by one until the net was light enough to roll into the boat.

As many men attested, the fish caught in the hoop nets depended in part on the size of the netting. For every legal, three-inch mesh net in the Neches, there were several illegal ones. Many fishermen made their hoop nets of chicken wire or hardware cloth in a bewildering array of sizes and shapes. An occasional wire net might be as large as the room of a house.[134] Charlie Havard and many other people made their own cord-mesh hoop nets, and Charlie preferred to make his the diameter of legal hoop nets but with illegal one-inch mesh. Many fishermen agreed that—for some reason—one-inch mesh nets caught bigger fish than legal-size nets. Some conjectured that this was be-cause the one-inch nets trapped more debris on their surfaces and looked more like hollow logs on the bottom of the river—a known catfish attractor. Others suggested that the small-mesh nets caught little catfish, which the big cannibal ops came in to get.

Other things got into hoop nets as well, usually to the fisherman's displeasure. A hoop-netter might round a bend in the river in his boat and see the hoops of his net sticking above the surface, the net com-pletely full of dead and bloated turtles. Some preferred this to finding the turtles alive, however. Fishermen regarded the loggerhead turtle, the alligator snapper, as one of the authentic monsters of the river bottom. A loggerhead sometimes weighed over one hundred pounds and had jaws "capable of severing fingers and hands" (or so says a sober field manual).[135] Many people told of turtles biting through broomsticks, hoe handles, and cypress boat paddles. Getting such a creature out of a hoop net was a problem, to say the least. One young man of Carl Havard's acquaintance became so overcome with horror at the sight and smell of his first loggerhead that he shot a hole in the bottom of his boat when he killed the turtle.[136] Seasoned net fisherman James May simply turned the hoop net open-side-up in his boat and carefully worked the loggerhead out. As May noted, no loggerhead got into his hoop nets more than once. "I've caught em that weighed a hundred pounds or better. Now, it's a violation of the law to kill em, but I've stuck my knife in a-many a one and just put him back in there—just punch a hole in him and he'll drown—he'll come out on the bank. That water puts pressure on his heart, and his heart won't beat. I've killed a-many a one."[137]

From time to time, alligators or alligator gars also got into hoop nets, though more often than not they tore out. Frank Ashby caught a gar weighing over 250 pounds in one of his nets, and a still-larger alligator gar—called "Felix" by the local people—plagued fisherman for decades downstream from the Highway 7 bridge.[138] Sometimes a fisherman raised his net to find a drowned otter or beaver—though more commonly only a big hole where one had been. Beaver were absent from the Neches for so many years that when riverman C. V. Bishop found one drowned in his net, he did not know what it was. He showed it to an old commercial fisherman who told him: "That's a beaver. You ain't supposed to have that!"[139]

Illegal hoop nets, wire nets, fish-shocking devices, fish poisons, and other methods were part of a long folk tradition of no-holds-barred exploitation of river fish going back to settlement times. Traditional hunters and fishermen along the Neches detested waste and disapproved of people who failed to use what they caught or killed, but their basic dictum was, "God put it all out there for people to get, and we've got a right to get it." Never was this so obvious as in people's use of the resources of the river. In the days of the open range, individuals had specific usufruct rights of trespass, stock ranging, hunting, fishing, and foraging in other people's woods, but the river was different; it was a wilderness and a true commons, belonging to no one and exploited by all. On the river, the rule seemed to be "anything goes." Even fishing shacks along the river banks, illegal structures on private land, long partook of the freedom of the river. For many years, lumber companies and private landowners usually did not ask rivermen to move. Every winter and spring, the river commons flooded across its bottoms from bluff to bluff, vastly expanding its extent. Even if a man chose to fence his bottoms—in the old days, an antisocial act—his fences often failed to withstand the debris carried by the river floods. When southeastern Texans said to each other, "Let's go to the river," they often implied something more than a simple fishing trip. They meant a return to the freedoms of the commons, where you could do anything you pleased.

The trip to the Neches to set out bank lines and camp all night offered an escape from hard work for the children of stockmen-farmers all along the Neches. Claude Welch, of Angelina County, recalled (echoing the testimony of many):

> When I was a little boy, I'd work on the farm and most time we'd quit Saturday at noon. We'd get some flour, meal, lard, and salt and head for that river bottoms. Catch us enough bait to set out Saturday night, catch us a mess of fish, set there and cook em. Them trees used to have lots of green moss on em. We'd get that moss and make us a bed out of it—just lay down on the ground and go to sleep. We was young. We'd use a boat; they'd be old wooden boats all up and down that river.[140]

A thousand Neches "Huck Finns" told similar stories. In Houston County, James May and a black friend trekked cross-country to reach the river at the "Lovell Fish Trap," appropriating farmers' field corn, peanuts, and watermelons along the way; then they camped at the river for two or three days.[141] On leave from work on the family's bottomland farm during the depression, Lester Greenville, of Angelina County, and his brothers rushed to the nearby Neches at high noon on Saturday. The Greenvilles carried a pan of their mother's cornbread, lard, cornmeal, and salt. They caught bait as they traveled—grasshoppers, frogs, anything—it all would work. "Most of the time we'd stay up all night. You didn't have no light excepting we cut some lighter pine. That's what we used for a light to walk the banks of the river. We never had anything but bank hooks, you know, just poles. You wouldn't have but ten or twelve hooks out, and you'd get up the next morning and have nine fish up to seventeen- and eighteen-pound fish. You just wouldn't believe!"[142]

The river was full of fish, and old-time no-boat methods of bank hooks, limb lines, and throw lines usually caught all the fish that family members could eat. The methods still worked in modern times— if a person knew how to use them. Around 1960, an old man in his late eighties named Cole James asked Oscar Allen a favor. Allen owned a fishing camp at a traditional camping site on a Neches bluff in Trinity County, where James had camped as a boy, and the old man asked permission to "go there a-fishing" before he died. Allen readily gave it, and—after refusing the use of Allen's house—James went to the river to "do just like [he] did when [he] was a boy." The old man camped out for days. As Allen described:

> He had holes dug in the ground over there and put his block ice in the ground, and he had his fish staked out in tow sacks. He didn't have no boat. He used hand poles and throw lines, and he probably had 150 pounds of fish. He was a-wading in that water up to here. He had all kind of lines tied to limbs and everything else. He'd have one on a limb and he'd walk out maybe six feet from the bank—if you had a fish on it, the limb be a-shaking—he'd walk out there and get him in the dip net. And everybody else wasn't catching any fish! But that's the last fishing he ever went.[143]

Cole James's last fishing trip showed all the characteristics of the old days and old ways, including the fisherman's use of single-hook "sets" and his willingness to get in the water. Early hook-and-line methods and many other early techniques of fish trapping and fish taking had Native American roots—that much is certain. In the case of the hook and line, gigging, grappling, basket trapping, plant poisoning, and the cross-river fish weir (all described below), the relationship is documented, and Native American origins seem likely for other methods as well.[144] The southeastern Indians lived along southern rivers for millennia, and over many lifetimes they accumulated an impressive array of fish-taking techniques. At a thousand places and times now forgotten, they passed this knowledge on to Anglo and African Americans.

The Neches thronged with buffalo, a species of giant sucker, and though the fish rarely bit a baited hook, it could be taken in other ways, especially during its spring spawn. On the first river rise after the first full moon in March or April, or so the old fishermen said, the "buffalo will float," crowding into drifts along the shallow edges of backwaters to spawn. J. L. Bingham recalled: "I've seen em in them palmetto flats, near all them palmetto be just raising cain in the water. They run right out on a drift or anything, they just go wild. And them eggs just spraying, hanging to ever bush, driftwood, and everything." Frank Ashby added, "They knock them eggs out, a-flouncing. Them old she fish will lay the eggs and the old boars will come by there and spray their spawn. Just thousands of em! You could hear em. First time I ever heard em in my life I thought it was a bunch of hogs in the water. My God almighty, there was fish everwhere!"[145]

Native Americans shot spawning buffalo in the backwaters with bows and arrows, speared them, and took them with clubs, and Anglo Americans did the same. Frank Ashby's father sometimes clubbed buffalo, and other Anglos harpooned them with switch-cane spears shot from muzzle-loaders or else simply shot them with powder and ball.

Giggers with fire pans stalked buffalo and other river fish from boats at night, and other men stealthily waded Neches sandbars and white-sand creeks on the same mission. Besides fish, fire-panners gigged bullfrogs and soft-shelled turtles.

Some people chose to catch bullfrogs with their hands. In daylight, "grabblers" felt around under logs and in holes in bluff banks for catfish, then seized them and brought them out. Especially large ones could be taken by jerking a "grab hook" into the fish by hand or with a "noodling pole," with the line from the big hook handled by someone on the bank. The alternative was to reach into the mouth of the catfish and grab it by the gills, but this could be dangerous; if the catfish weighed forty pounds or more, there might be a real question of who (or what) had whom.

Many twentieth-century rivermen knew of the technique of grabbling, and some had watched others doing it, but most agreed with Frank Ashby when he said, "I never would stick my hand in no hole I couldn't see." Besides the catfish, water moccasins and loggerhead turtles lurked down there under logs and in holes in the bank. Grabbling was the fishing technique of the young, the brave (the foolhardy, many would say), or the inebriated. George Tull, of Angelina County, grabbled for years while under the influence of "pinetop whiskey" until one occasion when he soberly examined the body of a 150-pound loggerhead turtle that had been shot by another man and had crawled out on the bank to die. The alligator snapper's head was as large as Tull's own. After that, Tull quit grabbling, drunk or sober.[146]

As a young man, the intrepid Harold Snelson often went grabbling with parties of friends, who seined and muddied low-water pools, then felt for catfish under logs and brush. Some fish were taken by the seining; others were run to their lairs around logs and banks and became fair game for the grabbler. To grabble, you felt gingerly for the fish in the muddy water with your hands and bare feet. If you touched one on the tail, it shot away, but if you touched the fish from back fin to head, it just "lay there." Harold explained: "And you don't gouge him or nothing but just feel of him slow, rub him on top the head, and he'll lay plumb still there till you get your hand right where you want it. And then, when you clamp down, you better have a monkey's grip!"[147]

According to Snelson, "If you gonna worry about snakes and turtles, you ain't never gonna make a grabbler." Snelson's approach was to feel carefully around and then, when he encountered a snake or a turtle, to remember where it was and not to feel in that place again. Submerged water moccasins felt "just like a man's beard with about a two-days' growth on it." Loggerheads sometimes snapped at Snelson beneath the water when he touched them—he heard them "popping" their beaks—but he "never did get bit by one." He had no illusions about what might happen if his luck ran out: "There's a lot of them suckers can take a finger plumb off, just like you chopped it with an ax."[148]

Every year, the river itself set its own massive "fish trap" in a cycle of flood and withdrawal, and a number of effective fish-taking techniques were based on this. River floods spread across the bottoms in early winter, flushing out and renewing an intricate network of sloughs, side channels, and oxbow lakes and restocking them with river fish. Then, in early summer the river withdrew, leaving many fish trapped in drying pools. When the river rose, some fishermen set special hoop nets, positioning them facing the river in deep sloughs with V-shaped "wing nets" extending to the banks on either side. These caught fish moving out of the river to forage in the flooding woods. Months later, when the river began to fall and fish moved back toward the river, some fishermen reversed the direction of their hoop nets and wings. Other men set posts and nailed rived boards to build "fish fences" completely across sloughs. Fish moved over the tops of these at high water, then were trapped in pools behind them when the river fell.[149] (Southeastern Indians had used this method in tidal creeks.)

The river often created fish traps at such places. Water flowing from sloughs or creeks slowed when it reached the edge of the river, and sediments accumulated at slough mouths. After the river fell, these formed natural dams that sealed off the deeper pools behind. People used various methods to take fish trapped in the slough pools, and sometimes the simpler ones were the most efficient. If conditions were right, a few men with shovels could "ditch a slough"—dig a shallow trench from river to pool and drain enough water to allow fish to be easily caught.[150]

In more shallow slough and creek pools further inland, fishermen used other methods. Sometimes, men or boys built foot-high dams at each end of the pool and dipped buckets of water over the dams until the fish inside could be caught, a simple method that seems to have had no name. In "mudding," a kind of mud poisoning, people muddied a pool with cotton hoes or by walking around on the bottom. Fish soon surfaced, gasping for oxygen, and were readily netted or gigged. West of the Neches on the Navasota River (and probably also on the Neches), settlers used a related method, but with a twist. People rode around in a river pool on horseback until it became extremely muddied, then dragged small, tightly branched brush tops through the pool on ropes to "seine" out the fish.[151]

Other fishing methods in low-water sloughs and creek pools used plant poisons from the walnut, buckeye, or devil's shoestring. Virtually every riverman along the Neches experimented in his youth with green walnut poisoning. The method was simple: the fisherman gathered several partially filled towsacks of green walnuts, carried them to the pool, used clubs to smash them in the sacks into a juicy mess, and sloshed the sacks around in the water. In a short time the fish, their breathing apparatus paralyzed by the poison, would start to "skitter around" and come to the top, where they were dipped or gigged. Too much plant poison in a hole of water could kill everything in it, so many people preferred to use this method in slightly flowing pools. The fishermen blocked the downstream end of the pool with a seine, then pounded green walnuts at a log in the upper end, letting them fall directly into the water. The current distributed the poison down the pool, and paralyzed fish rose to the surface and drifted into the seine. Not surprisingly, some of the rivermen who used the ancient Indian method of walnut poisoning in their youth turned to more drastic fish poisons later on. These included, among other substances, slaked lime, household bleach, and rotenone.

Early Neches fish traps and fish weirs also had Indian antecedents. Catfish loved to go into hollow logs to hide, and if a tantalizing scent bait was present, so much the better. The Choctaw Indians made a conical trap from a fresh cowhide, thus cleverly combining a trap and a blood-bait attractor in one device. After observing the fish move inside the hide, an Indian would then pull a drawstring, sealing the end behind it.[152] Along the Neches, "hollow log" traps occasionally were rigged from white-oak cotton baskets or real hollow logs. Frank Ashby once observed a man trapping fish in a hollow gum log with a flexible throat of white oak "splits" at its mouth. Fish would push their way through the conical throat to get to the bait at the back of the log, then could not get back out. The "Georgia basket trap" or "slat trap" was based on the same hollow-log principle. Such traps were cylindrical and about fourteen inches in diameter; built of narrow, longitudinal, white oak boards, they had one or two flexible wooden throats inside. Fishermen baited these with the nastiest, smelliest, most rancid cheese baits they could concoct, and in optimal circumstances the baits attracted so many channel catfish that they jammed the traps entirely full. Southeastern Indians also sometimes built V-shaped fish traps or fish weirs entirely across small streams, and Anglo Americans on the upper reaches of the Neches did the same. The V-weirs were long gone by 1990, blown up with dynamite by "federal men" sometime in the 1930s, but remnants of their foundations could still be seen at extreme low water. Local people often identified places along the river by the names of early V-weirs that were once located there—the "Lovell Fish Trap" or the "Old Man Ernest Anderson Fish Trap," for example.

As a boy, Frank Ashby accompanied his father to Ernest Anderson's fish weir between Angelina and Houston counties. He offered this excellent description of how it worked:

> They fenced that river with two-by-twelves—they built a fence with little cracks in it where the water and little fish could go through it. It went plumb on to the bottom, and they'd piled rocks and stuff down around the bottom of it [to brace it]. And after he got them two wings built from bank to bank, he built him a chute about six-foot wide right in the center. And that pushed all the water in that chute, and it was swift as hell. And behind that chute, they built some [wooden] fingers. They could raise em—when the water would go up, he'd raise his fingers. And he caught everything that come down that river beside turtles and alligators. He said they'd crawl off. The fish would fall off of that thing and fall over in the fingers, and he had him a big old rake and a fish fork, and he'd rake em off. had a big old box there that he'd put em in.[153]

Ashby's description makes clear that the V-weir worked by creating an artificial rapid to wash amazed river fish down on a fish-catching sieve of wooden fingers located just below. People from all over came down to the river to buy fish from Ernest Anderson's live-box, which was "big as the room of a house." Two of Anderson's brothers also had fish weirs in the area. Buford Anderson told Frank Ashby that he went down to his trap one night with a "road wagon" and a "single wagon," stayed one night, and filled both wagons with fish by first light. He then hauled them to the Southern Pine Lumber Company railroad at Pine Island, packed them in wet moss in a boxcar, and shipped them alive to Tyler to sell. Clearly, the V-weirs could catch a lot of fish.[154]

Frank Ashby later became a commercial fisherman himself, basing his operations in Angelina County at the river bridge on the Lufkin-Crockett highway. Over the years, he tried nearly every method to fish the river, legal or illegal, including such ultimate measures as telephoning and dynamiting. People began to dynamite the big holes along the river at about the time the railroads and lumbering operations moved in. The companies used large amounts of dynamite to blow stumps in tramway construction, and workmen often pilfered some and headed for the river on a lark. As amateurs, they sometimes overestimated how much they needed to do the job. People living nearby in Angelina and Trinity counties still recalled the night that dynamiters set off twenty or thirty sticks at once in the deep hole below the Highway 94 bridge. The blast rattled the windows of Oscar Allen's house two miles away, caused a massive bank slump at the site of the explosion, and pulverized all the river fish in the hole—a classic case of Anglo-Saxon overkill.[155]

As a young man, Frank Ashby and his friends sometimes dynamited the big hole of water at the mouth of Hickory Creek in Houston County. As he explained, capturing the general spirit of these affairs, "Seven or eight of us old boys on weekends, we'd get fish hungry, get us a jug of Haggerville whiskey [and] four or five sticks of dynamite." The fishermen put half their dynamite on a ten-foot cord with a weight at the other end, then rolled the cord and weight around the dynamite. The other half was rigged to another cord and weight. They lit the two charges at the same time and tossed them in the river some thirty feet apart. Each weight unrolled and went to the bottom, dragging the buoyant dynamite down with it to detonate in the water above at the calculated depth. "God a-mighty, them old buffalo and drum turn that river white!" The Haggerville whiskey may have facilitated recovery of the fish, since the "old boys" swam for them in the dark, despite the known presence of alligators. There was only one game warden in Houston County in those days, but the sound of a dynamite explosion carried a long way. Frank observed: "Ah, wonder they hadn't of caught us, shit! We was young then, we didn't give a shit. We take two or three skillets, a five-gallon can of hog lard, sacks of salt, two or three bottles of ketchup, and we'd have the dandiest fish fry you ever saw."[156]

Fishermen willing to dynamite the river had no inhibitions about using five-bar crank telephones to shock fish and "turn them up." This was a restrained—even a conservationist—approach to illegal fishing compared with using dynamite. Dynamite seemed to kill mostly "scale fish" like drum and buffalo (or at least those were the only kinds that surfaced), but electroshock devices were deadly on catfish—as Carl Havard theorized, on "everything that has whiskers." Frank Ashby used this method with some regularity and recalled his introduction to it by another fisherman. They had visited two or three fishy places along the river, thrown the wires overboard, and cranked the telephone, but nothing had happened. Ashby decided he was the victim of a hoax but agreed to try one more place. The man cranked. As Ashby recalled: "Goddamn! I think there's a hundred damn fish, them fish going everywhere. Some of em was all out of the water but their tails. Some of em run out on the bank. I had to get out of the boat to get a blue cat, weigh seven or eight pounds. Man, he got out of there—he run out on a sandbar!"[157]

Ashby later perfected a method using two boats, each with a telephone rig. The telephoners positioned the boats a few feet apart at a likely spot and cranked at the same time. This seemed to increase the electroshock effect on fish. On one occasion, Ashby's electroshock crew targeted a huge op known to frequent a certain place, brought him up, and snag-hooked him on a big hook at the end of a strong nylon line attached to the boat. Then passed a few anxious moments. Frank noted: "Some one said, 'He's gonna sink the boat! He's gonna sink the boat!' I said, 'When this damn motor goes under, I'll swim out.'" This op weighed sixty-two pounds.[158] Unfortunately for the Neches fish, many other rivermen, like Ashby, enjoyed using a telephone. As Harold Snelson described: "It's more fun than anything you ever done in your life! Have you a dip net, and you may start after one over here and he may change direction three time and another one over yonder may run over you fore you get to this one. You got to get after it just like fighting fire, cause they don't stay up."[159]

When Harold Snelson's family went to the river when he was a boy, no such high technology was available, and the fishers made do with bank hooks. However, a willingness to try anything was indicated in a favorite saying of Harold's father, "Pop" Snelson, who liked to remark, "If we don't get em one way, we'll get em another." The Snelsons were poor, and the Snelson family fishing trip was spartan. As Harold explained: "We's so poor we couldn't even afford to buy a loaf of light bread. We taken a can of meal, can of flour, grease, salt, pepper, a jug of syrup, and maybe a side of bacon—and a pound of coffee, you didn't get off without that coffee. That's all you taken to the river. You killed or caught whatever you eat, and you might near eat whatever it was you killed or caught! You killed it or caught it or went hungry."[160]

For more than a century, families went to the river as a reward for hard work after crops were laid by. They set up camp, put out lines, and stayed a few days to enjoy the freedom of the river. Since fish could not be preserved, most of the catch was eaten on the spot to satisfy an accumulated "fish hunger." During the same years as the Snelson family fishing trips, the Lowery family, of Angelina County, often went to the Neches. Mr. Lowery was a wealthy Shawnee Prairie cotton farmer with an automobile, and his family rode in style to the edge of the bottom, then took a wagon down rutted roads to the river. As they traveled, Lowery's young daughters marveled at the "river folk" homes they passed along the way in the Bellview and Weaver's Bend communities—the dog runs and gardens out back, the many dogs, and the "pale-faced, tow-headed children." Unlike the Snelsons, the well-off Lowerys carried plenty to eat and were not so dependent on fishing success, but their camp resembled everybody else's. Like thousands of other families up and down the Neches, they cooked over coals in a dutch oven and slept on mattresses in the wagon under wagon sheets. Like the rest, they carefully placed food, supplies, and even bedding in tarpaulin bags well out of reach of the ground. Rooter hogs were ravenous by early summer, when crops were laid by and people went on fishing trips. Hogs attacked the unattended fishing camps of rich and poor alike, even wading into the river to devour stringers of fish.[161]

After a few days on the river, the Lowerys and the Snelsons and a thousand other families packed tarpaulins, bedding, cypress paddle boats, and other gear in their wagons and rolled home. But some men camped on the Neches one night and never left again. As Roy Smith said of one of their number, a man he knew only as "Tomcat Red," "He camped down there on the river and fished till he died."[162] There were many such men along the Neches—dropouts from rural society who lived on the river for years or decades, sometimes building rived-board shacks on the bank, sometimes possessing little more than a "tarp and a coffee pot." Few men's names were attached to sloughs, bluffs, eddies, and other features in the no-man's-land along the river, but when features were thus named, they most often were named for these men. Scurlock's Slough, Bill Evan's Island, Stirtle Eddy, and a hundred similar names testify to places claimed and named not by legal document but by long use and constant association.

For many years, timber companies ignored "nesters" like "Old Man Scurlock" or Oscar Allen's uncle, Jimmy Stephens. Southern Pine let Stephens live in his mudcat fishing shack "because he was pretty protective and never did bother nothing that would be good for the mill." The owner of the Houston County land on which Scurlock squatted did the same.[163] Scurlock caught fish and shot ducks to eat, had a small garden, and butchered an occasional wandering rooter hog. He sold fish and charged stud fees for the services of his stallion to bring in enough money for ammunition and a few odds and ends—all that he needed. Scurlock's Camp on Scurlock's Slough was a favorite camping and fishing spot for decades, and older locals were not happy when the U.S. Forest Service summarily changed its name to "Big Slough." Like Jimmy Stephens and a hundred others, Scurlock, a kindly old man with a long white beard, lived on the river and fished until he died.[164]

By the 1930s some companies had changed their minds about tolerating the trespasses of these river rats, and Tomcat Red often had to make his camp on the river side of the "second bank" after the river fell. This was arguably "government land," part of the public domain of the river bottom. By long association with his stretch of river above the Highway 94 crossing, Red was an excellent fisherman, and people often came out in buggies from nearby communities to buy his fish.

Like many others, he developed his own theories of fish behavior and how to fish. Roy Smith often purchased fish from Red and sometimes hauled Red's fish out by wagon for public sale. He recalled: "Sometimes when I's hog hunting I'd come to him. He'd have all his fishing tackle stacked up a-sunning, you know, and airing out. And I'd say, 'Red, what you doing with your fishing tackles out?' He said, 'The moon's not right.'"[165]

There were no manuals for how to fish the river, and fishermen like James May, Oscar Allen, C. V. Bishop, Charlie Havard, Louis Bingham, Dudley Denmon, and many others learned their trade from older rivermen of the premotorboat era. Some of these master fishermen were true river rats, like Tomcat Red; others had homes and families—somewhere—but still spent much of their time fishing the Neches.

The master fishermen were individualistic to a fault. In 1950 a man called "Termite," with a high silk hat perched on his head, still ran the lower Neches in a twenty-foot cypress dugout. Another fisherman lived in a hollow tree. But all the old rivermen had certain things in common.[166] Since they used paddle boats, they specialized in fishing limited stretches of the river, and because of this they were highly secretive about their customary sets for trotlines and nets. Many returned to their net sites after the river fell to erase the telltale imprints of their hoop nets from the river bottom. These sets had been discovered after long periods of trial and error and were highly prized, but the rivermen were always looking for new ones. When the river was at its lowest, they studied the riverbed, committing its features to memory and planning new sets. They developed elaborate theories of fish behavior and put these theories into practice with fishing methods that were also closely guarded secrets. Many of them fished with relatively few lines or few nets but in a highly precise way. Some used only limb lines, others short trotlines with only a few hooks. Almost to a man, they went in and out of the river with the nonchalance of otters—wading out to limb lines, going hand-over-hand down snagged trotlines at night to the bottom of the river to get them loose, and engaging in similar watery enterprises.

By the time he died, master riverman Butler Rice had revealed most of his secrets to young Oscar Allen and C. V. Bishop, but another local fisherman carried his knowledge to the grave. "Old Man Glen Tillery" did most of his fishing and line moving at night so that no one could observe what he did. Oscar Allen told me (in the manner of someone revealing a considerable secret):

I've seen his lines. I caught him fishing a time or two down at the Bonner pasture. And he would be fishing under logs—fish with about five or six hooks on his line—and real short lines, let his line go under a log. He'd go to the bank about half way and drive him a stob in the river, and tie that thing, you wouldn't know where. I caught him one time in the boat, he didn't have no motor, he wouldn't use a motor, and he had three or four stobs in there four or five feet long.[167]

One gathers that on this occasion Tillery was considerably chagrined to be caught with his secret fishing accoutrements revealed in broad daylight. Butler Rice, however, was more forthcoming and served as fishing mentor for both Allen and Bishop. Unlike Tillery, Rice stretched his trotlines all the way across the river, but he was extremely chary with hooks. He might have only five of them on a thirty-yard line, each placed with surgical precision according to his reading of the surface currents and his memory of the river bottom. He often waded about at extreme low water to check the exact locations of logs and other bottom features. Rice believed that fish moved in "trails" on the bottom, that these trails changed with the river level, and that the placement of his hooks must change accordingly. The proof of theory was in practice, and Bishop found Rice to be an awesomely effective fisherman. As he said, "I could set out a hundred red perch as big as my hand, and he could use just five, and he'd catch more fish than I could, because he knew just where to put them five red perch." Rice usually set out five lines with a handful of hooks on each one, all close enough for him to watch from a sandbar. He ran a line only when he saw it had a fish on it, "and he'd have his minner jars out on the sandbar, catching shiners—he'd be setting there with a little old fishing pole catching perch of all types." When the river was at its highest in the spring, Rice paddled far out into the backwater and put out "tight-lines" near the edge of the overflow. He stretched these lines as "tight as a clothesline" a few inches above the water, then let hooks baited with soap dangle down five or six inches under the water. This was a deadly method for channel cat, but the obvious problem was how to avoid getting lost in the dark woods. Butler's technique was at first little comfort to Bishop. Butler told him to "pick you out a tree, go to it, then pick you out another tree," and so on; on the way back to the river, you simply reversed the process.[168]

Frank Ashby learned many fishing tricks from an older commercial fisherman and trotline specialist named Jewel Francis. Francis, from Cherokee County, was so good that "he sent two or three girls to college, a-fishing." Francis fished longer stretches of the river than Rice or Tillery, and at the end of his career he used a small motorboat. Ashby ran the motor for him one night and noticed that he was leaving most of his hooks unbaited. He asked why, and Jewel told him: "I just bait the ones they'll bite on, fish don't bite on every bait. I find out where they're running." In other words, this line had been out for several days and Francis now had hard data on that location. Jewel Francis often went out by himself all night with only a syrup bucket, a loaf of bread, a dozen eggs, and his hooks and line. Once or twice during the night, he got out on the bank, built a fire, boiled two or three eggs, and used the water for coffee. Francis caught most of his bait by hand along the edge of the river at night, and his preference was jackfish. He would spot one with his light in the shallow water, jam a length of stovepipe down on top of it, then reach into the pipe for the jackfish. Francis was not only good but also eccentric. He wore cut-off pants at a time when no respectable southern male wore shorts. The pants had a special pocket for a big clasp knife. One night Frank was wading after Jewel up a creek watching him catch perch and jackfish for bait when they came on a huge water moccasin. Frank said, "Watch out!" but Jewel calmly took his knife out and stabbed the snake behind its head. It began coiling and thrashing, and Jewel kicked it out on the bank with his bare foot. At that point Frank got out of the creek. "I said, 'I ain't no snake hunter!' I went to the house."[169]

Jewel Francis once told Frank Ashby that he had banked ten thousand dollars of fishing profits by the end of that year's fishing season, and Frank confirmed this remarkable sum from a trustee of Jewel's bank. This placed Jewel Francis in an elite company of commercial fishermen—at least on the upper Neches. Frank Ashby never made that kind of money fishing, and neither did Charlie Havard, though they both managed to make a seasonal living at the trade.

In the late winter, Havard and his brother took up their trapline and began to tie hoop nets, preparatory to the spring buffalo run. Cotton netting never lasted for more than a season, even if heavily tarred, and nets had to be made anew every year. At first the Havards caught mainly buffalo, piling their paddle boat above the gunwales with fish and on a few occasions with a few fish too many; an occasional tip-over was to be expected during the paddle-boat era. Then they loaded their wagons with buffalo, covered the fish with sweet gum branches to keep off sun and flies, and drove the wagons to the "quarters" at the Manning mill to sell the fish to African Americans. East Texas blacks liked buffalo, and whites liked catfish, and some people believed this difference was deeply rooted in racial biology—ignoring the fact that farther north these preferences were reversed. After their operations were motorized, the Havards sometimes made gill-net "fish drives" for buffalo. One boat remained stationary at one end of the gill net while the other boat slowly motored the other end of the net around in a big circle. This trapped fish inside the closing circle of the net and panicked them into it, where they caught their gills. Fishermen like the Havards also panicked buffalo into gill nets by striking the water with paddles, making commotion with toilet plungers, ringing bells under the surface, plunging red-hot iron rods into the water, or wading on foot. After the spring buffalo run was over, the Havard brothers shifted to fishing hoop nets and trotlines for catfish and selling them in Lufkin. Especially in later years, Charlie Havard sold large numbers of catfish to the Angelina Hotel and the Ruby Cafe.[170]

Occasionally, in the early spring, the Havards' hoop nets filled up with a strange, primitive, duck-billed fish locals called the "spoon-billed cat." These were paddlefish, a form of small sturgeon and one of the most ancient fish species in the river. A semicartilaginous fish akin to ancient gars and bowfins, spoon-billed cats swam through murky backwaters with mouths agape, filtering out plankton from the water. Since the Havards had no local market for paddlefish, they were not happy when they found the fish jamming their nets; the Havards knew of nothing to do with the paddlefish except haul them out in wagons and feed them to the hogs. At the same time, however, farther down-river in Jasper County, Louis Bingham and his father had better information about paddlefish. During the same time, the depression 1930s, the enterprising Binghams peddled paddlefish roe to Yankees at five dollars a pound.[171]

After Louis Bingham and his father left the log rafting business, they turned to full-time commercial fishing on the Sabine and lower Neches. The Binghams' yearly round followed a constant pattern, beginning in the spring with trotlining for catfish. They fished three days of the week, accumulating their catch in big rived-cypress live-boxes. Then, on Wednesday night, they cleaned the fish by carbide headlamps on a river sandbar and carried them in wagons to the Santa Fe depot at Buna. Here, they iced them down in layers in recycled starch barrels or handmade gum boxes and shipped them "express" to Dallas at two o'clock the next afternoon. This got the fresh fish to Dallas markets in time for the prime Catholic fish day of Friday. Often going in with other commercial fishermen to lower their freight costs, the Binghams shipped from six hundred to twelve hundred pounds of dressed cat-fish each week, usually receiving fifteen cents a pound for their catch, less the cost of shipping. The biggest op they ever caught weighed 89 pounds fully dressed and perhaps 130 pounds in the river. After a day or two off, the Binghams' weekly trotlining cycle began again.

In late summer the game changed, and the Binghams shifted to gill-net fishing in the river bottom lakes for buffalo and spoon-billed cat. Their special territory was the maze of lakes and side channels along the Neches west of Buna and Kirbyville. A fisherman could not look at a backwater lake and discern if it was full of buffalo, but he could tell if paddlefish were present. Paddlefish were big, often over 40 pounds, and long for their weight, and in the autumn they put on a show. As Louis Bingham recalled: "I could walk up to an old lake in the fall of the year, and when it turn cool, first norther a-blowing, it'd be a sight to see—them big paddlefish coming out of the water like a swordfish or something in the air and hitting the water and just knock a big hole in the water. You'd see em from one end of the lake to the other, you'd know they was in there."[172]

In late afternoon, the Binghams arrived with nets and paddle boats at the backwater lake that was their target for that night's fishing. The four-board paddle boats were of their own manufacture, and their linen gill nets were the best money could buy—durable enough to last an entire fishing season. The nets came in 150-foot sections, 8 to 9 feet deep. As Bingham said, "We'd start at one end of the lake a-stretching them nets, and we'd go to V-ing it back and forth across that lake." After several sections of the nets had been placed crisscrossing a portion of the lake, the Binghams waited a while for the fish to get in the nets. Then they removed the fish, took the nets up, and moved down the lake forty yards or so to do the same thing again. They repeated the process over and over as the night wore on until the Binghams approached the far end of the lake. There, large numbers of buffalo and paddlefish would have accumulated in the last stretch of water, having fled the commotion of the nets as the Binghams methodically moved down the lake. Then, the fishermen set their nets for the last time and paddled to the end of the lake. At that point, as Bingham said, "You'd get in there with a big limb or an big old oar and start whupping the water, and you'd see corks just a-popping" as the big fish hit the nets. "By daylight, we was gone." As a self-imposed conservation measure, the Binghams never fished a backwater lake for more than one night. However, as Bingham remembered, "It wasn't nothing to catch two thousand pounds of fish in one night with gill nets."[173]

The buffalo and paddlefish trades were much more lucrative than the trade in catfish. The Binghams received twenty-five cents a pound for the buffalo and thirty-five cents a pound for the paddlefish in Chicago and New York—shipping the fish north in ice barrels just like the catfish. The Eastside Market in Chicago purchased large amounts of fish, especially paddlefish, which then were smoked. Paddlefish roe—caviar—was a special case and highly profitable. In the fall of the year, a single thirty-pound paddlefish might yield seven pounds of roe. After carefully cleaning the paddlefish roe and preserving it with salt, the Binghams shipped it north packed in syrup cans and sold it for four to five dollars a pound. The Binghams had their overhead: fine linen gill nets were costly and had to be replaced every year, and occasionally otters and alligator gars got into and tore up their nets, but they still made a good income in hard economic times. As Louis Bingham recalled: "Wrap a lake up with webbing, and in three or four hours you could have that lake fished out. Then you'd go on to another lake. We made money at it, and bought new trucks and stuff like that."[174]

Upriver of the Binghams, a more eccentric riverman ran the Neches for almost a half century. From the late 1930s on, Dudley Denmon, of Hardin and Jasper counties, ranged woods hogs, gardened, trapped, made whiskey, and fished the river. As Denmon said: "I done a lots of net fishing when net fishing was open—hoop nets, trammel nets, and gill nets—and all kind of damn net stuff. The most fish I ever caught in one day is 1,786 pounds, but, hell, I had 37 hoop nets and a thousand feet of gill net and 650 feet of trammel net!" One day Denmon was fishing gill nets in the backwater on the Hardin County side when he caught an alligator—not an uncommon occurrence but this time an omen of things to come. Denmon recalled: "I pulled on the net and got him up there and kept flipping them strings off his teeth and turned the son-of-gun a-loose. Then I said, 'Now, if you get back in there you gonna mess around and make me mad. I'll go to the house and get the gun and shoot hell out of you!'" The next day when he came back, something huge was in the net. Denmon remembered, "It would run out with the tail of that net and throw water ten foot high!" Denmon went for help and a .30-30 rifle and returned to shoot the backwater monster three times through the head. It was an alligator gar, eleven feet eight inches long and just under three hundred pounds.[175]

As a fisherman, Denmon specialized in scale fish, some of which he claimed to locate by smelling the water churned up by his motorboat. He explained: "I could open that boat wide open and go down one part of that river and I could tell you there's no scale fish there. Then you'll hit another section of the river and I'll tell you, 'Yessir! There's buffalos in this river.' I smell them son-of-a-bitches, you see! I smell for em."[176]

Denmon was unusual among Neches fishermen in his compassion for buffalos and other river fish. He initiated a long-running feud with the U.S. Corps of Engineers at B. Steinhagen Reservoir because the Corps' water releases in spawning season lured the buffalos into the backwaters to spawn and then, when the water suddenly cut off, left them high and dry. As he explained:

Buffalo fish was going up in the woods and spawning, they was spawning all over everthing. And these goddamn peckerwoods that worked here at Dam B, they'd run that water up high and them fish would all run out of the river down there and mate and they'd go in there and spawn their eggs all over the bushes and things, then them son-of-a-bitches would cut the dam off! I've seen three fish of spawn on one bush with the sun shining on it. I told em, I said, "Now, by God, them eggs not gonna be sun dried. You people are gonna leave your water on and you gonna leave it on long enough for them to spawn and hatch."[177]

Denmon heartily disliked game wardens and "government men" in general, but he hated telephoners—he called them "lectro men"—even more. After moving to his last home on the Neches, north of Forks of the River, he became acquainted with a certain giant blue catfish, the biggest he had ever seen. On one memorable occasion in 1986, he preached the following sermon on the big blue, the abusers of the river commons, and the need to preserve wild things for "coming-up" generations. Denmon's ideas about conservation owed little to the Texas Parks and Wildlife Department or the Sierra Club, both of which he disliked; his ideas seemed to have been rigged up whole cloth, in keeping with the traditions of the "river-bottom strain."

When me and my wife first come here, I didn't have no motor, didn't have nothing. Had my bed in this old panel-body truck, and we camped right here. I hung that big blue for the first time on the point of a sandbar over here, and he broke my hook. He's a bullheaded blue. That blue cat, no telling how many hundred hooks he's got in his mouth. The rows of teeth he's got in the upper part of his jaws would be about two inches wide. The fins that goes down his back is six, eight inches wide, and its head is a big old chuckleheaded rascal. He takes these old little bitty hooks and eats them every morning for breakfast—he don't pay em no mind, it's not nothing to him. He can straighten them eight-ought hooks just as straight as your finger, and nobody ever was able to hold that fish.
    He moved from up here where I hung him and went down about four bends from here. I located him down there. I was with my kids on a sandbar with some minnow jars catching some minnows to bait up with, and I kept seeing him churning around in the water. So, I recognized that old friend of mine, and we set out a line for him and baited that line with sun perch. And we hung him. He decided he wanted one, I guess. And he straightened that eight-ought hooks just as straight as your finger. I caught him and led him up to the boat one time, and he is one hell of a monstrous fish! I'd say he would go from ninety to one hundred ten pounds. But now listen, I want to tell you something. I haven't seen that fish this whole year. See, he ranges around, he roams around. He'll stay up here at this bend awhile, then he'll go back down about three or four bends

from here. But I have not seen that fish in two years. So, somebody could have paralyzed him.

Them big fish they stay in a deep hole until it rains. He's strong enough that an electro or a microwave wouldn't get him there. The times that he's out of that hole, out in the open, that's the only time they'd get to him. They could have caught him out in the open and knocked all the oxygen out of his wind, his oxygen bags. That's all the hell them electros do anyway, them telephones and microwaves. That's why all the little fish, they'll get right up using their tail and go just like hell. They'll jump, or get out on the bank, or anywhere— lay their head up on a stick or on the bank or just anyway. Them son-of-a-bitches! I'm glad when they get caught.

I'm gonna tell you something. Anything that's an interest and a benefit to the children of this earth, the ones that's here, the ones that's growing up—it's a dirty shame for people to disregard and disrespect the creation of all these beautiful things that have been made, that people have privilege and opportunity to use, during their trip on this planet. They should think about them little fellows that is coming up and allow them the same privilege. If we don't respect this stuff and defend it, they won't never know. They'll just say: "There ain't no more of that. That's just an old story told by some of the old generation."

I say that everything that the Great Master created is entitled to a certain amount of respect—that's what I tell em. I'm not a Christian, I'm just a hard-head, but I think everything is entitled to a certain amount of respect. I'm a-hoping that the things that people love in this world is gonna provide food for all the growing generations so that they can have a little fun and squirrel hunt and stuff. That's for the coming-up generations, not for me. I've got my face pushed up against the door of time.[178]

6

ROOTER HOGS AND WOODS CATTLE

Although they farmed, hunted and fished to make a living, many people residing in the communities along the Neches regarded themselves as stockmen, first and foremost. They practiced a southern, forest-adapted tradition of stock raising very different from the open-country tradition established farther west, and most of them began very young.

Babe McGalin recalled that, from boyhood, he "had rather run a cow than eat." At age six, Dudley Denmon purchased his first rooter hog from his grandfather for the bargain price of five cents, but he had to show his nerve to take possession: Denmon's pig was in a pen guarded by a vicious "biting sow." As he said, "I jumped down off that fence and run through there and picked up that little bitty pig and climbed out on the other side of that fence with that old sow biting right at my rumble, and my granddaddy just died a-laughing." Jude Hart, of Hardin County, and Avy Joe Havard, of Angelina County, began riding to the woods behind their fathers on "hog hunts" and "cow hunts" when they were about the same age as Denmon when he claimed his first hog. Havard was so small that his "feet stuck straight out" across the rump of his father's big black horse. While still a boy, Havard "throwed a fit" when his grandmother went out of the hog business and gave her registered earmark to Havard's brother. Mollified after being allowed to use the same mark in the reversed ear, Havard noted: "That made a pretty mark. I'd see a hog of mine as far as I could see him, that long ear sticking up there, those underbits a-shining in it."[1]

Thirty years later, Avy Joe Havard still loosed his cur stock dogs from the "dog yard" and rode out almost every day to check his rooter hogs and woods cattle across two hundred square miles of Neches bottoms. Like Pres Conner, of Houston County, Roy Smith, of Trinity County, and others, Havard was a significant landowner, with considerable acreages of corn, cotton, and sugarcane, but he let tenant farmers work his crops. While they tilled the fields, he took his stock dogs and rode to the bottoms. Sometimes, Havard identified a neighborhood boy that he thought had "a little bit of that wood's blood, that hog's blood, in him" and allowed him to go along to watch the field castration of a dangerous boar hog. While the yellow cur firmly held the enraged hog by its ear, Havard swiftly dismounted, jerking his "pigging string" from its fast-draw configuration behind the front of his belt. With skills honed by decades of practice, he quickly caught the big boar by its hind legs, threw it, and whipped the pigging string around its feet to immobilize it. Amazed, the neighbor boy would say, "I never seen nothing like that in my life!"[2]

Feral woods cattle and rooter hogs fought fiercely, and sometimes dog and stockman lost the battle. By the end of his career, several of Avy Joe Havard's stock dogs lay in honored graves, having been killed in the line of duty by vicious livestock. The "bad hog," quick as a cat and capable of eviscerating a dog (or crippling a horse or a man) with one speed-blurred swing of a massive head, haunted the dreams of many. C. W. Gandy's father was present when a dying man cried out in delirium toward the end: "The blue boar is a-coming for me! Look out for the blue boar!"[3]

The southern tradition of stock raising practiced by Avy Joe Havard was of uncertain origins, though it was firmly established in Georgia and the Carolinas by the early eighteenth century. In part, southern stock raising reasserted older European practices—the use of the woods as common range for every man's livestock and of herder dogs to work cattle and hogs, the marking and branding of stock, and the periodic burning of the range to encourage the growth of new grass. In part, the southern livestock tradition was an adaptation to social and environmental circumstances of the New World. Labor was lacking to build the extensive closed pastures to which stockmen had become accustomed in parts of southern England, and older British free-range practices seemed more appropriate. Nor were stock enclosures necessary; as settlers quickly discovered, domestic hogs and cattle swiftly adapted to life in the American wilderness.[4] Left to run free and forage for their own food in the woods, they not only survived but prospered—swiftly increasing their numbers until they became a threat to settlers' crops. Soon, in restatements of livestock laws as old as the fifth-century Germanic tribes, colonial legislatures passed "fence them out" statutes requiring landowners to properly fence cultivated fields to exclude wandering cattle, hogs, and other "great cattell." In 1642, the Massachusetts Court asserted the general principle that was followed also in other colonies and in southern states well into the twentieth century: "Every man must secure his corne and medowe against great cattell. If any damage bee done, it shall bee borne by him through whose insuficient fence the cattell did enter."[5]

By "great cattell," the court meant hogs as well as bovines. A forest-adapted animal, the European domestic swine flourished in the American wilderness and quickly became a mainstay of the settlers' diet. After only a few generations in the wild, the pink, docile barnyard swine became black, fast, and fierce feral hogs, often coming to resemble their parent stock, the European wild boar. This transformation occurred with almost alarming speed. In 1658 the Massachusetts Court reported, "Many children are exposed to great daingers of losse of life or limbe through the ravenousness of swyne, and elder persons no smale inconveniencies."[6]

In many parts of the American South (including East Texas), settlers found feral hogs already present when they arrived. The source of these wild swine was probably the expedition of Hernando de Soto, who had traveled through the South between 1538 and 1542. Hardy and fierce, feral hogs thrived on the abundant mast of the primal forests. Called "razorbacks," "rake-straw hogs," "pineywood rooters," or "rooter hogs" by southerners, these animals provided a semiwild and inexpensive source of protein for pioneer families from the very beginning of settlement, and pork was the most widely used meat in the United States until the last decades of the nineteenth century. Southerners in particular ate a huge amount of pork; one historian of the Old South estimated nineteenth-century consumption at about 150 pounds per person each year—2.2 hogs.[7]

The utilization of the forest for swine was not a new practice that arose in America. As historian Michael Williams noted:

[The practice] went back to biblical and classical times in the Middle East and Europe. In medieval Europe woodland was often measured according to the number of swine it would support rather than according to its acreage. The right of pasture for swine—or pannage, as it was called—was a privilege that the medieval peasant valued highly, and in a like manner it was a highly prized resource for the American farmer during the seventeenth and eighteenth centuries, and indeed, even much later in the South.[8]

By 1800 (and probably much before then), practices of open-range hog raising had become firmly established. In 1802, French botanist Francois Michaux traveled through Kentucky and recorded the following account—every word of which equally well described the practices of Neches Valley stockmen into the 1950s.

Of all domestic animals, hogs are the most numerous; they are kept by all the inhabitants; several of them feed 150 to 200. These animals never leave the woods, where they always find a sufficiency of food, especially in Autumn and Winter. They grow extremely wild, and generally go in herds. Whenever they are surprised, or attacked by a dog or any other animal, they either make their escape or flock together in the form of a circle to defend themselves. They are of a bulky shape, middling size, and straight-eared. Every inhabitant recognizes those that belong to him by the particular manner in which their ears are cut. They stray sometimes in the forests, and do not make their appearance again for several months. They accustom them, notwithstanding, to return every now and then to the plantation by throwing them Indian corn once or twice a week.[9]

As Terry Jordan noted in his history of the southern stock-raising tradition, stockmen in the South customarily ran both hogs and cattle on the same wooded range and worked them with stock dogs in much the same way. Derived from mixed British, African, and Hispanic roots, the southern tradition of stock raising emerged in South Carolina and Georgia in the eighteenth century, then spread westward across the Pine Barrens of the Upper South with the moving frontier.[10]

In its essentials, southern stock raising was an adaptation to the great forest that covered most of the upland South until well into the nineteenth century. As historian Grady McWhiney aptly noted: "The Old South, it must be understood, was not one big plantation; it was, for the most part, a vast wilderness with relatively few cleared and planted acres and with relatively few inhabitants, where cows and hogs and other livestock roamed the woods unattended. Of the antebellum South's nearly 557 million total acres, fewer than 10 percent were improved in 1850."[11]

Hogs—forest animals—were more important than cattle to many southern stockmen, though both species used the same range and though southern "woods cattle" were very well adapted to the forest. Two or more times a year, southern stockmen took stock dogs and went out on a "hog hunt" or "cow hunt" to locate the stock, drive them to pens scattered across the unfenced range, and then mark, neuter, or process them for butchering or sale. In the wooded landscape, dogs were absolutely essential for locating and controlling stock: a stockman's hogs and cows were scattered across miles of pine forests, thickets, and hardwood bottoms, and the dog's acute sense of smell was needed to find the animals, and its predatory instincts were necessary to control them. Semiferal woods cattle and rooter hogs reacted to a dog much as they did to a wolf or other woods predator; they "rallied," bunched up for defense, and the stock dog used this behavior and the feral livestock's aggressive nature to control and move them.

As many stockmen attested, trying to drive wild cattle and hogs through the woods with only men on horseback—no matter how many men— was an exercise in futility.

Stockmen in the southern tradition treated their hogs and cattle in a similar manner and even seemed to think about them alike; for example, the adjectives "woods," "rooter," and "rakestraw" often were applied to both hogs and cattle. Stockmen left the animals to run semi-feral on the open range and to fend for themselves, though they were kept in tenuous domestication by occasional bayings with dogs and periodic handouts of salt (to the cattle) and corn (to the hogs). Stock dogs drove cattle and hogs in much the same manner to the same stock pens, where both species were worked by men on foot. Stockmen used horses primarily for transport and to help them keep away from their dangerous livestock. At the stock pen and during the drive, lassoing was a little-known skill, but not so the use of the southern stockwhip. The stockman popped his whip to encourage his dogs and to help control overly aggressive livestock, and he sometimes reversed his grip to use the heavy whipstock as a club. When an adult animal needed to be caught and held for castration or other work, the southern stockman turned not to his rope and horse but to his dog. At the command, "Get him!," the trained "catch dog" grabbed the cow by the nose, or the hog by the ear, snout, shoulder, or tail, and the animal was immobilized. Finally, southern stockmen often drove both cattle and hogs long distances to market—a practice especially common before the Civil War. Major stock trails crisscrossed the antebellum South from pine uplands to agricultural lowlands. "Stock stands" were spaced out every few miles, with pens and food for the stock and with lodging and food for the drovers. Driving hogs cross-country took a lot of patience but was entirely practical, and early statistics bear this out. In 1843 alone, 52,642 hogs (and 3,333 cattle) were driven south through the French Broad River valley, one of the major north-south droving routes; and in the last fifteen years of the antebellum era, southern stockmen marketed an average of 4,468,400 hogs a year. (By comparison, Texas cowboys drove an average of 280,000 cattle north to market each year during the period from 1866 to 1880.)[12]

Although the southern stockmen were a numerous and important group, historians gave them little attention until recently. Major early scholars of the antebellum South, such as Ulrich Bonnell Phillips and Julian A. C. Chandler, focused on the plantation economy and the institution of black slavery and developed a model of southern society composed of slaves, plantation owners, and "yeoman farmers" who wanted to become slaveholders and plantation owners themselves. There was little room in this model for the stockmen, who were either ignored or dismissed in terms similar to the popular stereotypes. The stockmen were "poor whites," "white trash," "hillbillies," "crackers" (a term that derived from their use of the stockwhip), "pineys," or "sand-hillers" and were of little importance in the economic and social scheme of things.[13]

The fact remains, however, that these people marketed 67,026,000 hogs and untold millions of cattle during the last fifteen years of the antebellum period. In 1860 two-thirds of the nation's hogs were raised in the South, and hogs and other southern livestock were worth over half a billion dollars—more than twice the value of the year's cotton crop.[14]

Historians relied on early travelers like Frederick Law Olmsted for their interpretations of the stockmen-farmers, and the travelers were often misled by appearances. They would come on a log cabin or hewn-log house in the woods. The family would have a few acres of weedy corn, patches of sweet potatoes, cabbage, collards, and peas, and maybe a few rows of cotton and tobacco in a "deadening" in the forest. The travelers would see a milk cow, two or three scrubby horses, a few rooter hogs in a pole pen or roaming the yard, and a few emaciated hounds. The man of the family would be sitting on the porch, working on some small task or just smoking and taking his ease.

This scene led Olmsted, other early observers, and latter-day historians to drastically misinterpret a whole social class. Considered as agriculturists, these folks looked like "poor white trash," but they were stockmen, not agriculturalists. The weedy corn was intended for their animals. The men seen taking their ease on their porches often had hundreds, perhaps thousands, of hogs and cattle on the open range. Their real wealth was invisible. Typically, they owned only a hundred acres or so because they did not need to own more. The homeplace the traveler observed was only the stockman's base of operations. The woods were open to any man's stock and would remain that way for a century, so why own more land than was needed?

A century after Olmsted passed by in 1843, similar scenes could still be observed in many of the small communities scattered along the Neches Valley; the lifeway of the stockman-farmer lasted as long as the free range, which did not end in these counties until the 1950s. C. W. Gandy's Uncle Dave was typical of many such men along the Neches. Gandy farmed only twenty acres; he had a garden, a small cornfield, a sweet-potato bed, and a patch of "hog goobers" (peanuts) to be "hogged out" when he fattened his meat hogs. He owned, however, an excellent stock dog with which to find and work the several hundred hogs and cattle he had scattered along the Neches bottom for miles in either direction. Gandy was both rich and free in the reckoning of the southern stockmen; he had a good house, a good garden, a smokehouse full of meat, plenty of hogs and cattle in the woods, and a lot of time to do what he wanted to do. Nor did he waste his time: he was often observed sitting on his front porch carving hickory ax handles and crafting fine blowing horns.[15]

Dave Gandy's cattle, roaming the switch-cane thickets along the edge of the Neches bottoms, differed from modern livestock. They were small cattle, of mixed British and Spanish ancestry. Wild Spanish and Indian cattle were present in southeastern Texas when settlers arrived; the first were lost from the herd of two hundred driven by the expedition of Captain Alonso de León in 1690. As Fray Francisco Celiz recorded, De León "left a cow and a bull at each river crossing north of the Rio Grande, [and] this is the reason there are so many cattle unbranded and wild."[16] Many additional cattle later strayed (or were stolen) from mission herds. In the early nineteenth century, settlers from the United States called these "Spanish," "mustang," or "black" cattle.[17] The wild Spanish longhorns quickly mixed and merged with the nondescript British stock brought in by Anglo Americans and released on the open range, forming the free-range livestock that East Texans commonly termed "woods cattle."

The name was appropriate. Small, generally short-horned, of variable color and configuration, the cattle were masters of survival in the woods. In the summer, they moved into the pine uplands to graze on "woods grass" growing under the pines; in the winter, they trekked to the edge of the bottoms to eat switch cane, American holly, gray moss, and palmetto. Stockmen like Babe McGalin often went to the winter bottoms to cut down holly bushes and small trees laden with moss so that the cattle could more easily get to them, and the woods cattle well knew to come to the sound of an ax. However, even without this help, woods cattle were able to survive. They scavenged for miles across the open range to get the nutrients and minerals they needed from the mineral-poor East Texas grasses, and they were resourceful—sometimes swimming into flooded bottoms in the spring to forage on palmetto in "palmetto flats." As Babe McGalin noted, "Them old woods cows, they'd get pore, look like they was gonna die—we call em old Piney Woods rooters—like a Piney Woods hog—but they'd get just any little old thing to eat, [and] they'd live."[18]

Woods cattle were also wild, fierce, and dangerous to horses and men. Generations of fending for themselves in the wild in the face of heavy predation by bears, cougers, red wolves, and even jaguars had made them so. According to Brown Wiggins, such cattle would rally to the scent of blood or trouble, attempting to overawe the predator. "When we killed a beef in the woods, cattle would come from all directions. There would be two, three hundred head of cattle come from all directions—running, hollering—and when they get there, they'd scrape and paw and fight, nearly kill one another. . . . This was a rake-straw cow, and I think they had it in their mind that a varmint had killed that cow. They'd smell that blood, and if one found it and hollered, just as far as they could hear, they knew what it was."[19]

As Wiggins affirmed, woods cows also fiercely defended their calves—staying with their young "till they nearly starved to death" and refusing to leave the calves unguarded. In the fall of the year, the bulls would bellow and fight. Carl Havard said: "You could hear one a mile up the river and a mile down the river. They'd start bellowing and go to coming together. Then some more from up in there would come. I've seen as high as seven a-fighting in one place, and don't try to separate em."[20]

The inbred wildness and ferocity of the woods cattle had obvious consequences for the stockman. Men stayed on horseback to work these cattle, except in the controlled circumstances of the cow pen, and they made heavy use of whips and stock dogs. As Carl recalled: "A lot of them cattle back in them days, now, if you was out there in the woods a-hunting, and he was sort of upset about something, he'd fight you like a tiger right out in the middle of the woods! The cattle today don't do that." Driving such cattle through the thickets was an adventure. Havard said, "Them cows would fight your horse, they'd hook your horse just like they would you."[21] Solomon Wright participated in several cattle drives in the late nineteenth century, and his family's wild woods cattle regularly tore out of stock stands and spooked and stampeded for miles after scares from alligators or the sound of their own feet popping out of black mud.[22] A half century later, Babe Mc-Galin worked similar cattle in southern Jasper County. He recalled: "Let me tell you something. That river bottom was so thickety you couldn't hardly drive them cows. You had to have whips. These cows we had, you had to get something to stop em, not to move em. They'd go! And we all had a big old long-tailed whip with a stock on it. Use your whip first, then run up beside one and beat him over the head with your whipstock. I done that."[23]

In the late 1970s, Carl Havard purchased some oldtime woods cattle from remaining wild herds in the Forks of the River, but the nostalgic experiment was not a success. The cattle did well enough in fenced pastures, "so long as they had some woods to go in," but when Havard and his sons tried to work them, they jumped six-strand barbed-wire fences and took off. "We had cattle all over Shawnee Prairie—they didn't pay a bobwire fence no mind at all." Latter-day attempts to improve woods cattle by admixture with blooded bulls did not work well either. As Carl noted: "[The woods bull] would get to him and kill him just like that, because he had long, keen horns, and he had fought all of his life. He was kind of like the rooter hogs, he had come up a-fighting."[24]

Feral hogs probably had been in East Texas even longer than feral cows; the hogs had descended from stock lost from a 1542 expedition of one of De Soto's men and from La Salle's failed settlement of Fort St. Louis in 1685. Even more forest-adapted than the woods cattle, they flourished unattended in the virgin hardwood bottoms and pine uplands of southeastern Texas and were a mainstay of the Anglo American diet from settlement times on.

Hogs were a favorite food of many other predators besides man, but sows and boars were armed with formidable fighting teeth, and in the confrontations with bears, wolves, and bobcats, the hogs sometimes won. Stockmen occasionally found dead bobcats near former hog beds, and more than one man reported finding dead bears that had been killed by hogs.[25] Woods hogs were fierce individual fighters, sometimes weighing as much as five hundred pounds, but they also made use of their strength in numbers. Not only did they "bed up" in self-defense at night, but they "rallied," came running from all directions, at the sound of a hog squealing in distress.

More than anything, however, rooter hogs were prolific. Sows began breeding at six to nine months and had two litters of four to eight pigs each year. If bobcats and other predators caught a few pigs here and there, this mattered little; rooter hog numbers still increased rapidly. Many stockmen told stories like that of Babe and Lynn McGalin, whose family migrated to the edge of the Neches bottoms in Jasper County around 1915 with one "piggy sow" (pregnant female) and in a decade had hundreds of hogs in the woods.

One reason for the rooter hog's success was its eclectic diet: the hog was the ultimate omnivore, consuming an enormous range of plant and animal foods. Stockmen usually kept a few "tame" hogs around the house to recycle household wastes, feeding them whatever excess organic material was on hand. Hogs devoured commercial fishermen's "trash" fish and the overkill of wild pigeons after pigeon thrashings. When asked what rooter hogs ate in the woods, stockmen generally responded, "Well, it's easier to say what they didn't eat."

Hogs were well aware of the ripening sequence of "sweet mast" and "bitter mast" acorns in the fall, trekking miles across the bottoms to find acorn-bearing oaks. Hogs ate the acorns of sweet-mast white oak species as soon as they fell. The tannin-filled red oak acorns and other bitter mast often were left to lie in the backwater through the winter; then, leached of their tannic acid, they were consumed in the spring. After the river went down, hogs found these acorns drifted into windrows against the trunks of fallen trees, or the hogs waded backwater pools to bring them up in big mouthfuls from the bottom—sometimes disappearing completely beneath the surface to do so.

In the fall of the year—the rich season—hogs ate the mast of several species of Neches Valley hickories, persimmons, and pecans and got so fat on their favorite pin oak acorns that they could hardly run. After they consumed the accumulated windrows of water-deposited acorns in the spring, hogs began their lean season of late spring and summer. They moved into the uplands to eat grass, earthworms, several species of blackberries, haws, and grapes, and (to the forester's sorrow) the starchy roots of longleaf pine seedlings. When the newborn fawns of white-tailed deer were encountered, hogs caught and ate them (farther west, in the Texas hill country, hogs showed a similar fondness for young goats and sheep). Hogs also ate the eggs of wild turkeys.[26] As the summer progressed, the rotund hogs of winter grew lean and desperate—looking more and more like their "razorback" nickname. If they found a dead cow or horse (or, on one occasion in Hardin County, two murdered men), they devoured the carrion with relish. After the Neches River fell, hogs moved back into the river bottoms to catch crawfish, frogs, and river fish in drying backwater pools and to raid the camps of fishermen. Avy Joe Havard saw hogs on "outside sloughs" eating freshwater mussels. "You'd see the water waving—it wouldn't be that much of a back sticking out. And they get the mussels, mussel shells, they eat them. Boy, they come up and you hear the crack when they burst those mussel."[27] Curious to find the reason for a furious squealing of hogs, Frank Ashby rode his horse up to a backwater slough. "And them old Piney Woods rooter sows and them shoats was catching them old grennel gar out of there. They'd get him up to the bank, knock him out on the bank, and grab him and run off, two or three after em. That's where all that squealing come from. I guess they caught everything out of there."[28]

These opportunistic omnivores were also dangerous. As Jess Wells said: "They'd just hit [a dog] with them tushes, you know, and they'd cut em just like you take a pocket knife and cut em. They'd cut a dog's entrails out of him, they'd cut his throat. They'd eat you up if you messed with em."[29] Many stockmen attested to the aggressive nature and fighting ability of the feral hog. During the 1930s, various sportsmen began to introduce Eurasian wild swine to East Texas. These were the same species as the feral hog, and some men who knew both subspecies (which readily interbreed) attested that the "Russian boars" were no more dangerous to man or dog than the feral boars of the Neches bottoms.[30] Some people called such native animals "rake-straw hogs" because "they'd rake up a pile of pine straw to make their bed, rake it walking backwards."[31] A herd of hogs (invariably called a "bunch" in southeastern Texas) always did this at dark, as a protective measure against predators. The younger animals positioned themselves on the inside and the adults on the perimeter in "a pile of hogs as big as a common house."[32]

Hogs normally went about in groups of twenty to thirty, composed of two or three sows, usually siblings, with their pigs of the year and their older offspring. The home range of the group might be as small as two thousand acres or as large as seventy thousand. Boars left their natal bunch as soon as they became sexually mature, and other boars joined only when the leader sows were in heat. At other times boars wandered the woods in solitary fashion, fighting other mature males when they chanced upon them.[33] Boars' fighting teeth extended as much as six inches above their lower gums, and Brown Wiggins believed that such hogs got meaner with age: "Sometimes they'd meet up in the woods and they'll kill each other—they have a sideways lick that they make the cut with, and you'd find a hog with a whole shoulder cut to pieces."[34] Through a hundred fights, boars developed inch-thick "shields" of scar tissue on their shoulders. A bad hog backed into a tight place was a chilling sight. Wildlife biologists confirm the old stockmen's assertion that a hog sharpens its deadly lower tusks by abrasion with his upper ones, and this behavior also is used as a threat display. Jude Hart recalled: "An old boar, when he gets ready to cut, is just like a barber sharpening his razor. They sharpen their teeth, and they'll go to snapping em. You can see that old dust flying off his tusks."[35]

The innate aggressiveness of the wild hog almost needs to be seen to be believed. In 1992, I assisted a game warden and a "pasture rider" (a hunting club watchman) in the field castration of two young boar hogs caught in a hog trap at a Neches Valley hunting club. After the fight was over and the deed was done, a younger shoat—probably a sibling of the neutered boars—was hogtied and taken by pickup to the pasture rider's home to be used in the training of the game warden's half-grown black-mouthed cur stock dog. This small hog, about the size of a cocker spaniel and virtually harmless, was tethered by one leg to the pole of a purple martin house in the pasture rider's garden, and the dog was allowed to bark at it. This shoat, which had witnessed the neutering of its older brothers, had been trapped, trussed up, ridden in a pickup, tied in an open field, and bayed by a dog; its response was characteristic. Popping harmless teeth, the little hog repeatedly charged the stock dog, which was twice its size, and the game warden, who repeatedly jumped over it. The innate biological dictum of the wild hog was very clear: "When threatened, attack!"

From first to last, the use of stock dogs to bay, drive, and pen woods hogs was based on this innate feral aggressiveness. When Charlie Havard sent his dogs out to "bay em up" and they found a few hogs, all the other hogs within hearing would rally to the attack. The scene at the baying was not what the uninitiated might expect. As Charlie explained: "All the old hogs would rally, you could hear em half a mile, all that was round there would rally in there at that bunch. They'd just run in together and get after that dog—a-running, trying to catch him. They just get in a circle and go to running that dog. They'll cover probably an acre of land trying to catch him. They're going around and around!"[36]

Early one morning in the fall of 1934, Avy Joe Havard (a distant relation of "Little Charlie") got ready to check his stock, as he had on a thousand other mornings. He packed his "wallet"—a voluminous saddlebag made of a recycled canvas cotton sack—with the accoutrements of the southern stockman's trade: quantities of corn and salt to be doled out to maintain the tenuous domestication of hogs and cattle, used motor oil to treat hogs for lice, turpentine for "wormy sows," screw-worm medicine, a "hoof nipper" to defang big "meat hogs" and boars, a strong, noosed fishing cord to catch pigs and pull them up to the saddle for field castration and earmarking, a long-tailed "riding slicker" to keep off the frequent East Texas rains, a sack lunch and army canteens of water and coffee, and a needle and thread to stitch up dogs cut by hogs. On his saddle or on his person he carried a pigging string for tying hogs, his stockwhip, a machete-like hack knife for disentangling man and horse from viney thickets, and a pistol for the field execution of "bad boars." Then, as Havard recalled: "I'd get it on that horse and go out there and open that dog gate. They're gone! At the road out my back gate you hit the woods, four miles to the Neches River. And I had hogs all the way the whole four miles, over here and over there. Them dogs, if the wind was out of the south, they'd just run hard as they could with their heads up until they found a bunch of hogs."[37]

Until they were shown differently, Havard's dogs assumed he was after hogs. Havard ran both cattle and hogs in the river bottoms and probably derived more of his yearly income from cattle sales, but he was more interested in his hogs. Hogs were tricky, dangerous, and challenging to work, and their tasty flesh filled his big smokehouse after the yearly ritual of "hog killing day." As the bison was to the Plains Indian, so was the rooter hog to the rural southerner—the staff of life. A full smokehouse was a basic security; an empty smokehouse (or, farther north, "getting to the bottom of the [pork] barrel") was just the opposite.

On any particular morning, Avy Joe Havard might ride up to the bayed hogs, look them over, throw them a few ears of corn, and then signal his dogs to "Go ahead" and search for another bunch of animals. Avy Joe was a hard-working stockman who prided himself on how well he watched over his animals. This baying and feeding episode further accustomed the hogs to being worked and associated the baying dogs with the handout of corn. After a while, several different bunches of hogs or cattle voluntarily came to the sound of the stockman's blowing horn or the dogs' bay—and sometimes to a particular dog's bay. (The McGalin's hogs, for example, came only to the sound of their long-haired stock dog, Pudo.)

The frequent working and feeding of hogs and cattle made them easier to find, drive, and pen, safer for the dogs, and easier and less dangerous to handle for neutering, earmarking, and butchering; however, southern stockmen differed in how closely they monitored their free-range livestock and how concerned they were to maintain domestication. Some people—Charlie Havard's father, for example—paid their stock minimal attention and more or less let the animals go "wild as bucks."[38] Such men went out with dogs in the late fall, waited until the hogs had been "bayed solid," then reached into the bunch with fish-cord loops on cane poles to snag the unmarked male pigs and pull them out. Then a stockman hoisted the pigs across a saddle, castrated them, and cut their ears with his earmark, registered in the county courthouse. After field castration and marking might come field butchering as the stockmen took out their rifles and proceeded to shoot all the meat hogs they wanted from that particular bunch. Needless to say, this procedure did not make for tame hogs. After the rest of the bunch had run off, the dead hogs were transported from the woods in a wagon or dragged out with horses. Sometimes, they were even scalded in a barrel set in the ground, scraped, and field dressed before leaving the woods.

Dudley Denmon's methods were even more minimalist than this, and as a stockman, he represented the opposite extreme from the diligent Avy Joe Havard. Partly to hide his animals from stock thieves, which had plagued him in his early years, Denmon scattered his herds of hogs on bluffs located along many miles of the Neches River. He waited until the river rose in the late fall and his hogs became concentrated on the high ground, then took his dogs and went by boat to work them. He had trained his dogs to search each hammock or bluff for hogs and to bring any they found to where he waited at the boat. Denmon then shot any hogs that he wanted and slid them into his boat; it was as simple as that. The eccentric Denmon also left many of his male hogs as boars—a practice that did not endear him to other stockmen, who claimed that these long-tusked hogs often injured their dogs. Normally, a boar cannot be killed without rupturing a musk sack at the base of the penis, releasing a foul-smelling substance that taints the meat. However, Denmon had trained his dogs to drive boars into the backwater, where they could be shot while swimming; this meant no rupture of the musk sack and a floating carcass easy to tow to the boat.[39]

Even careful stockmen like Avy Joe Havard often had occasion to mark and neuter some of their stock in the woods. As Roy Smith did one day, a man might come on a bed of newborn pigs in a hollow black gum tree, catch them by hand, and mark their ears. If Avy Joe Havard found young pigs in a bunch that his dog had bayed, he might ride up close and drop the fish-cord loop over each pig's head to pull it to the saddle. This was particularly likely if Havard had penned and worked this bunch in the recent past and planned no further action for several months. Little pigs were much easier to mark and castrate than sixty-pound shoats.

Sometimes a stockman like Avy Joe Havard shot a hog in the woods for fresh meat, and sometimes he castrated or killed a boar. If he found an unmarked boar roaming the woods, he might give it a complimentary castration as a gesture of cooperation with other stockmen. Thus put out of business, the castrated boar (now a barrow or barr) almost always went home to his natal band and rightful owner to receive his proper mark. Some men trusted their catch dogs enough to castrate a boar with the dog holding it by the ear or nose. Others bayed the boar with the dog, roped it, perhaps "choked it down," tied the rope to a tree or handed it to another horseman, and approached the boar from behind. Lynn McGalin recalled that as he neared a hog at this point, the stock dog Pudo stood close by to protect him and to await a reward. No sooner were the boar's severed gonads tossed aside than the dog gobbled them up.[40]

Boars or bulls marked with a man's own mark might be field castrated or even executed for bad behavior as part of the domestication process that went on all the time. The stockman needed hogs and cattle that could fend for themselves in the woods. He might try to improve his hogs with Hampshire boars and his cattle with Brahma bulls, but he could not afford to go too far; too much "good blood" in either hogs or cattle caused the animals to lose their abilities to scavenge for food and fight off predators. Conversely, the stockman could not afford wild or hyperaggressive males that killed his dogs or "broke the bunch." An adult boar that repeatedly fought the dogs and refused to bay needed to be purged from the herds. If such a boar could still be handled, it was often castrated to become a "stag hog." As Carl Havard noted, that

Catch dog and feral hog. (Author's collection)

would make it "simmer down considerable." If the boar seemed too dangerous, it was shot and left to lie in the woods.[41]

Frank Ashby's black mongrel stock dog often held a big hog while Frank castrated it. As Frank described: "He'd catch the biggest boar in that bottom—he'd go right up aside of em and get him right there by his ear. I don't give a damn where he turned around, he [the hog] couldn't cut him cause he's too close up to him. I got down and cut a-many a one with him a-holding him." One day, however, something went wrong. Ashby's dogs bayed a Russian boar, but Ashby had never seen one before and did not know what it was at the time. For a man accustomed to feral hogs, the big boar seemed strangely built, with a big head and massive shoulders covered with scar-tissue shields sloping to narrow hindquarters. The hog was unmarked, just walking along and almost ignoring the dogs, when Ashby decided to do his stockman's duty and castrate him. "I said, 'Catch him, Rip!' And, hell, old Rip caught him but Rip didn't hold him. He throwed that dog as high as that ceiling there. He cut that dog quicker than anything I ever seen. I put one of them .30-30 balls up behind his ear and let him lay there. But I had to pick my dog up and carry him on my horse. Hell, that boar hog would have whupped a bear, but he couldn't whup a .30-30 ball."[42]

Like most other serious stockmen, Avy Joe Havard had hog pens and cattle pens scattered across miles of open range, and every year he used his dogs to find the stock and drive them to the pens to be marked, branded, neutered, and readied for market. Sometimes finding them was easy, but not always. Havard knew in a general way where the different bunches of stock were ranging at any particular time, though the hogs were to a degree more unpredictable than the cattle and much more willing to swim the river. After his dogs bayed the hogs or cattle, Havard rode up to make sure they were his stock and the animals he intended to work. Then he gave the dogs the command to take the stock to the pen, moved back a little, and let the dogs begin to do their work.

Driving semiferal rooter hogs or woods cattle with stock dogs was a strange process, very unlike driving properly domesticated animals such as sheep or modern cattle. "Drive dogs" and "catch dogs" served important functions for the southern stockman, but the "lead dog" was even more critical. Leak Bevil, of Hardin County, offered the best succinct description of how the lead dog worked. When the hogs or cattle were bunched up and ready to drive to the pen, Bevil would tell his dog, "Go around, Joe." At this command the dog (who in some uncanny way knew which pen the stockman wanted the animals to be driven to) would circle the herd and lead out for them to follow. Then, as Bevil said: "If they didn't follow, he'd circle and lead out again. And if they still didn't follow him, he'd come in pretty close and get to fighting them and maybe nip one on the end of the nose. He'd get that animal to fighting him, and then he'd run from it; and he'd keep running until he got that bunch of cattle or hogs to follow him. When you got to the pen where you wanted to pen them, he went in the gate and they just followed on in, and he'd jump out the other side and you'd close the gate."[43]

The lead dog did not drive hogs or cattle as dogs drive sheep; it led them. It barked and nipped at the leaders, arousing their aggressive instincts, and then, as they advanced to attack it, the dog backed away. Eventually the dog had backed away enough to lure the hogs or cattle to where they were supposed to go. Moving feral stock through the woods took advantage of the stock's inbred aggressive reaction to predators. The dog aggravated them, they advanced to attack it, and eventually the whole process got somewhere. As Bevil further explained: "My dogs are lead dogs. They won't work anywhere except in the lead. They lead your cattle or your hogs. You can't hardly drive cattle with your dogs behind them or on the side of them. Any bunch of hogs or cattle that you can keep together, you can drive yourself."[44] (I listened to several detailed descriptions of how dogs moved hogs and cattle before I began to understand the process; asked if the "drive" worked by the lead dog offering itself as "bait" to the feral livestock, the old stockmen invariably said, "Yes!")

In practice, there could be extraordinary complications, most of which the dogs had to work out for themselves. Moving very wild hogs was based entirely on hog aggression, and sometimes things got too rough for a single lead dog to handle. The McGalins customarily used two dogs, one that led and one that usually stayed behind; when the drive dog heard the lead dog's voice change in a certain way at the threat from the hogs, it moved up to help. No command from the stockman was given or needed. Conversely, moving hogs accustomed to being driven and rewarded with corn (such as those of Avy Joe Havard) could be rather easy. The leader sows followed the dog half in a desire to catch and kill it and half in anticipation of corn at the pen.

Driving hogs required more patience from dogs and men than did driving cattle. The Havard stockmen customarily held a bunch of hogs for a few minutes after the dogs had them "bayed solid" and rode around and around them while popping stockwhips—by way of intimidation. Only then did the dogs get the order to move the hogs out. In any case, the important thing when driving hogs was to accustom them to being driven—at all. The initial direction did not matter and could be anywhere the hogs were willing to go. After circling around for a while, the hogs more readily followed the dog, which could take firmer control and lead the hogs off in the direction of the pen.

Wild cattle offered dogs a different set of problems to solve; for one thing, they were faster than most dogs, especially in thick brush. Once again, however, the dogs used the stock's feral instincts to get them under control. The process could be very subtle and could take some time. When James Womack's dogs first began to work a herd of wild cattle, the cattle ran like deer through the brush and would not allow the dogs to get ahead of them. Then, while the stockman hung back, the dogs would

> go in there ever now and then and you'd hear em catch one of them little calves—see, a cow would mill and mill and that would weaken the run. Sometimes they'd have to catch three or four of them calves. See, a dog couldn't outrun the whole bunch in them thickets and get out there and bark em up—he had to have open places. What he'd do is wind around directly and he'd catch one them little old calves. Well, them cows would come around him, and directly that dog would get ahead of em. Maybe it'd take an hour, maybe two hours.[45]

Womack's dogs, in effect, used one instinctive reaction of feral cattle—their rallying to a bovine distress call—to "weaken the run," slow them up, and get ahead of them; then the dogs used another instinctive reaction, aggression to a predator, to lead them to the pen.

Sometimes the communication between dog and man in driving stock verged on the uncanny. At some point in the interview, each of the old stockmen usually said something similar to Charlie Havard's statement: "I can't explain it, and you ain't gonna believe it, but them dogs knew what you said." When he was a young man, Frank Ashby witnessed the extraordinary dog control of one Houston County stockman, "old man Arthur Lee." Ashby accompanied Lee and his son on a hog hunt. In the beginning, Lee's several brindle curs assembled in his front yard, and he gave verbal commands for two of them, Big Bony and Little Bony, to "Go along." They did this, and before Ashby's unbelieving eyes, the other dogs, looking very sad, resignedly lay down in the unfenced yard and watched their master ride away. Frank had reasonable control over his own stock dogs, but nothing like this. At the end of this hunt, several hogs were killed to be carried to Ratcliff to the man who was buying them. Lee did not want Big Bony and Little Bony to accompany the wagon. "He took a wad of them liver and lights and heart and all that—laid a wad over there and a wad over there—and he told them dogs that he hunted with, 'Stay there.' That's all he ever said. Them dogs would set right there maybe two or three days." In fact, they stayed until Lee came back to get them.[46]

On another occasion, Ashby saw Arthur Lee drive seventy-five head of wild hogs—a large group for one man and three dogs to handle—by the Ratcliff School. The school was easily avoided, and very possibly Lee was doing a little "showing out." Lee used a small red gyp as lead dog and two big brindle curs as drive and catch dogs—enforcers for the stock that tried to escape the bunch. The hogs panicked when they saw the playground full of running and screaming schoolchildren, but his dogs were equal to the challenge. As Ashby recalled:

> One of them old big barrs would start off, he's going back to the big woods. That old brindle dog would run up there and catch him by the ear and jerk him around, pinch him on the ass! He'd go back in the bunch. I guess he set there on his horse ten minutes letting them dogs put them hogs all back in the bunch, carried em up there, and put em in the pen. Them dogs know what they's doing. And he wasn't a-hollering or a-whooping and a-telling em nothing; they already knew what to do.

Asked how Lee had trained his dogs, Ashby remarked: "I don't know—that's what I'm telling you! They're just dog men. There wasn't many of em, but there was a few of em."[47]

Even the dogs of Arthur Lee suffered casualties, however—mostly from the rooter hogs. Woods cattle were also dangerous, and many stockmen had horses gored by them, but stock dogs were cut by hogs almost on a daily basis. Like many men, Frank Ashby always carried a canine first-aid kit with him when he worked hogs in the woods. "I got me a can of Vienna sausage—you know, they got a little key on em? Well, that was my eye in one end and I sharpened it off real sharp on the other end with a file, and I put it in a corncob, and I'd carry it in my corn wallet. I sewed that white dog up so much till I could lay him down and roll him out just like a sack of meal! I had a good silk line to sew him up with. He'd be alright."[48]

This was not always true, however; sometimes stockmen's first-aid measures were not enough. James Womack had several dogs killed by hogs, and in his opinion (the opinion of many), "the most dangerous hog was a little young hog." Womack explained, "See, his tushes was young, just like a cat's claws, and he'd just touch you and bring blood." Sows tended to bite and boars or barrs, with their longer teeth, to slash and stab. Avy Joe Havard said: "We've had dogs' throats cut, and they die in two minutes. If the hog cuts that google vein or stabs him in the heart, all he'd do is get away from the hog back out there, and he'd be dead." Nor were the stockmen's horses immune from hog attack. Babe McGalin recalled, "I had a big old boar to cut my horse right across the ham hock, cut way up high; he never did get over that real good." In 1992, Babe himself still bore a long, livid scar down one forearm from an ancient cut by a hog.[49]

With either hogs or cattle, the catch dog did the most dangerous duty. Dogs could not be taught how and where to catch hogs and cattle but worked this out on their own, and some chose procedures that were safer than others. Dogs often "heeled" cattle or "hammed" hogs trying to "break the bunch" during a drive, but this was transitory punishment and not a true catch. In a true catch, a dog caught the animal and held it while the stockman dismounted and approached it on foot. Dogs usually caught a cow by the nose, but they differed in their approaches to the more dangerous hog. Some caught the hog by the ear, some by the snout, some on the animal's side immediately behind the front leg, and some by the root of the tail. Some even changed their catch points over time. A dog of Houston County stockman Pres Conner caught hogs by their ears for a decade until his teeth wore down too much; then, as Frank Ashby noted, the dog shifted his strategy. "You know, the old hogs got a flap round his dick down there? He'd run his head under that hog and catch him by that damn flap back here with these jaw teeth and turned him over. He'd lay him down on the flat of his back!"[50]

Over time, dogs that were too "nervy" or that caught hogs in a dangerous place tended to run out of luck. Across a time span of half a century, Bob Allen still vividly remembered the day one of his best stock dogs came swimming back to him through the backwater, its mangled intestines streaming out behind.[51] This dog could not be saved, but many men told of sewing up disemboweled dogs and nursing them back to health. A friend of Frank Ashby's had a big brindle cur that would get right in the face of a big hog, bark at him, and then— when the hog charged—"catch him right over the end of the nose." Frank told the friend, Jew Conner, "'Jew, if old Culp ever misses one, he's a goner, cause that hog will kill him sure as hell.' He said, 'I ain't never seen him miss one.'" One day, however, Culp's luck ran out. "That hog cut the shit out of that dog—I mean, you could see his heart a-beating down in there. I didn't have my needle that day. We took some horsehair out of a horse's tail and took our pocketknife and cut through that hide and tied him up tight with that hair in bout two or three places." The men left Culp in an old camp house in the bottoms, coming back to check on the dog from time to time, and like many others, Culp eventually recovered.[52]

Another dangerous time for the dogs came as the herd of hogs or cattle approached the pen. Some of the stock recognized the location as the site of previous unpleasant experiences and began to hang back. To counteract this, the lead dog redoubled its efforts, barking at the animals, running up to nip and infuriate the leaders, and backing away toward the pen. Sometimes the stockmen had tried to facilitate the process by riding ahead to lay a trail of corn leading to the gate. Most Neches Valley stock pens had long "wings" of hog wire or rived boards extending out to each side to funnel the animals toward the gate as they approached. These wings were often disguised in downed trees or brush so that the woods-loving livestock would think they were getting away. Finally, as the stock approached the gate, the lead dog barked and nipped, the hogs or cattle squealed or bawled, and the stockmen—crowding from behind—popped their whips. The animals charged into the pen after the lead dog, who leaped over the back fence to escape them. Sometimes the stockmen built a special "dog step" at the back of the pen to aid the lead dog in jumping out, and sometimes they took other measures. As Charlie Harber recalled: "This brother-in-law of mine had a big old red black-mouthed cur dog. He'd go in the pen ahead of the hogs and go out the back side—jump the fence—until he got so old we'd have to help him. He'd ball up in a corner of that pen and fight them hogs off him, and we'd get him by the nap of the neck and the tail and pick him up over the fence."[53]

After all the animals entered the pen, Avy Joe Havard dropped the gate by remote control, loosening the end of a long wire that stretched for two hundred feet into the woods, then he rode up to work his stock. Now it was the stockman's turn to face the angry animals on foot.[54]

He did this with a matter-of-fact confidence based on long practice. Avy Joe's pens were constructed so that the small pigs could be crowded under the side of the main pen into a special holding pen, away from the furious sows, where they could be castrated, earmarked, and inoculated for hog cholera. Charlie Havard and other men built simpler stock pens, and they worked their pigs by reaching into the group with fish-cord loops on long cane poles and hauling the squealing pigs outside; once again, the underlying principle was to minimize contact with the dangerous adult livestock. Some male shoats had grown too large for this process and were roped and pulled to the edge of the pen or held by catch dogs while the stockman marked and castrated them. Some stockmen spayed many young sows to join the barrs as "meat hogs," though this took an exercise in veterinary medicine with which not all people were comfortable.[55]

After the primary business of marking, neutering, inoculating, and separating out animals for home butchering or live sale had been accomplished, Avy Joe Havard and other diligent stockmen took care of incidentals. If they were working cattle, they checked for screw-worms. If they were working hogs, they doused the animals with used motor oil or kerosene to combat hog lice, treated wormy sows with ears of corn soaked in turpentine, and defanged dangerous barrs with hoof nippers or ball-peen hammers. These various treatments required stockmen to move around on foot inside the pen and frequently elicited hog aggressions. As Avy Joe Havard said, "They'd run right from over yonder all the way cross that pen—make the awfulest racket you ever seen—like a bear 'Uhhhh! Uhhhh!'" Havard, a sensible man, worked inside the hog pen behind a tailgate shield taken from a pickup truck. When a sow charged him, he slammed it down in front of him to take the brunt of the attack. As he said, "Them big old sows would hit that board but couldn't get you." Other men went unencumbered, relying on their athletic abilities and stock sense to escape injury. Some caught the charging hog by its ears (a dangerous business), others jumped the hog and let it run under them, and still others braced themselves and delivered a hard kick to its nose. Any of these things avoided a hog attack if properly executed, but "if he hit you one time, you was ruined."[56]

Hogs and cattle destined for market were pushed through a gate in the back of Avy Joe Havard's main pen to a loading area, then run up a chute into a pickup or trailer. Havard and other stockmen regularly trucked stock to auctions at Huntington, Livingston, Lufkin, Beaumont, and other places. Stockmen sold cattle as calves or as two- or three-year-olds. Swine were almost always sold in the fall as fattened meat hogs, though stockmen differed in whether they bothered to first ply the hogs with yellow corn. Some people held the hogs in pens and fed them corn to improve the quality of the meat, whereas others sold them "acorn fat" right out of the woods. In truth, many East Texas customers preferred the taste of mast-fattened meat. Sometimes the stock operations had special arrangements with area retail outlets. As a young man, R. J. Rawls worked for a Jasper meat market owner who ran extensive hogs and cattle along the Neches. Rawls and another man butchered rooter hogs and woods cattle on a weekly basis to supply fresh meat to the meat market, and in the fall of the year they smoked up to twenty-five hogs at a time in the owner's big smokehouse. Farther upriver in Trinity County, Roy Smith, who had hundreds of hogs and cattle in the bottoms, was the exclusive supplier of woods-fattened stock to the Lufkin Q-P Store.[57]

In earlier times, long-distance drives to market had been common, and shorter-distance cattle and hog drives to railroad shipping points and urban areas persisted well into the twentieth century. Until the coming of the railroads in the 1870s and 1880s, the primary market for cattle in the area between the Neches and the Sabine was Louisiana. Texas cattlemen like Solomon Wright and his father took their cattle up the old Beef Trail to Louisiana. The Beef Trail crossed the Neches, came through Jasper, passed close to the Wright's homeplace, and then crossed the Sabine at Nix's Ferry. Various people living along the Beef Trail kept "beef stands." As Wright explained: "These were pens of stout logs for drovers to hold their cattle in over night, also chuck and beds for men who did not pack their own bedding and provisions. The beef stands made a small charge for accommodations."[58] By 1870, when

Wright was five or six years old, his father and other local cattlemen sold steers "mostly to the sugar planters of Louisiana, or to their representatives." The usual place for delivery was in the open pinewoods on the Louisiana side of the Sabine. The Texas drovers not only had to cross the river but also had to get the semiferal animals that Wright described as "wild cattle," "mossyhorns," and "swampers" out of the bottomland and brush.[59] Other stockmen along the Neches did the same. At around the same time, Charlie Havard's great-grandfather and other men gathered up around five hundred wild cattle from Shawnee Prairie in southern Angelina County and drove them east to Natchez.[60]

Short-range cattle drives to railroads and market towns continued into the 1930s. Bill Warren's family gathered woods cattle from the Big Thicket between Black Creek and Pine Island Bayou and pushed them south to China, a shipping point near Beaumont; in Trinity County James Womack and his father regularly made drives to Lufkin. The Womacks' main problem was how to get their wild cattle across the old iron bridge over the Neches. Cows and calves had to be tied along the bridge every fifty feet or so before the others would allow themselves to be driven across.[61]

All up and down the Neches, men like Howard Odom's father in Houston County and Walter Cole in southern Jasper County regularly bought cattle from farmers and drove them to local shipping points. Walter Cole would be out for a week at a time, going from house to house dickering with stockmen and small farmers to buy cattle, then returning to pick them up and drive them to the railroad at Brooklyn in Sabine County. Cole's methods and gear merged elements from both the southern and the western cattle cultures. He rode a trained cutting horse on a western saddle and carried a lasso, but three stock dogs ran alongside, and he made regular use of his whip. Cole put a special "road brand" on the cattle to make them easy to identify. As he said: "I branded a-many of em with a wagon rod. Take about two days driving on the road to get a bunch of cattle road-broke." Like most southern stockmen and drovers, Cole valued his stock dogs above all else. He recalled: "I had an old shepherd dog—a big dog, lion-head shepherd, full-blood—and I would talk to him like a man. He walked right behind my horse. I could catch the wildest brimmer bull, any kind there was in the country, with him and tie him [the bull] down by myself."[62]

The old southern practice of driving hogs to market also continued along the Neches counties. Although Solomon Wright made no mention of this, the Beef Trail would have been very atypical of southern drove roads if it had not seen the occasional passage of herds of swine.

James Ewing, of Angelina County, made yearly hog drives east to Louisiana before the Civil War, and doubtless many others did the same.[63] Shorter-range hog drives continued into the 1930s. Walter Cole recalled that Jasper County stockman Will Wright "drove hogs a-horseback from here to Orange and shipped em, two or three hundred head of em at a time—they had places along the road there ever eight or ten miles, pens they built to put em in."[64] Using very similar methods, Charlie Havard, of Angelina County, and Jude Hart, of Hardin County, also took part in several-day hog drives of around fifty miles. Three or four men and boys and several dogs would first gather the hogs in a field and drive them around the area for some hours to accustom them to being driven, then would set off with them across country. At night, drovers penned the hogs or held them with dogs in a bunch. A wagon accompanied these expeditions to pick up the big, fat hogs that had "burned out."[65]

Still, getting feral hogs to market was tedious and could be a problem—unless the market came to you. Stockman Pres Conner, of Houston County, was one of those well-off landowners who nonetheless preferred the life of the woods. He had many hundreds—probably thousands—of rooter hogs along the Neches, and when the 4-C Mill came to Ratcliff, he got the contract to supply pork to its commissary. Beginning just after the turn of the century, Conner and his sons regularly drove large hog herds to Ratcliff. Sometimes they marked hundreds of pigs in one day, often working from dawn to dusk and well into the night. As Avy Joe Havard recalled, "Working by the light of the moon didn't bother dogs at all." Conner eventually made so much money selling his hogs to the 4-C Mill that he opened a bank in Ratcliff.[66]

Occasionally, the big mills cut out the middlemen and set up their own hog and cattle operations. During the 1920s, the Southern Pine Lumber Company of Diboll opened a huge stock-raising operation in the Boggy Slough area west of the Neches along the Trinity-Houston county line. The company bought out the resident farmers and stockmen, purchasing not only their lands but also their "hog claims," their earmarked stock in the woods. Then the company put up a hog-proof perimeter fence around thirty-seven thousand acres of land—the first such fence in the area—and stocked the range with additional hogs, several thousand cattle, and ten thousand West Texas goats (which soon died of disease in the swamps and miasmas of the Neches bottoms) to begin operations. The company railroad, the Texas South-Eastern, ran right through the property, and beside it Southern Pine built pens, chutes, and a slaughterhouse and began to ship numerous cattle and twelve hundred hogs a year to the company town of Diboll.[67]

Pasture rider Charlie Harber, who worked with the Southern Pine ranch as a young man, reported that it was not the economic success the company had hoped it to be. Perhaps it was mismanaged—certainly the goat-raising experiment did not work out. Harber's uncle spent all one unpleasant summer piling dead goats and burning them. The company stockmen brought in blooded hogs and cattle to improve the woods breeds, but they could never fence the Neches River, and other men's stock continued to wander into Boggy Slough. The company practiced a modified free-range operation right until the end, working stock with dogs, doling out corn, and earmarking in the usual way. Finally, it gave up on the ranch and founded the Boggy Slough Hunting Club, the first private game preserve in southeastern Texas. Despite efforts to remove or eradicate the Boggy Slough hogs, many remained, too wary or nocturnal to be caught or killed. Much good blood had been mixed with the native stock, but it had disappeared. By the 1930s, the Boggy Slough hogs were as black, long-tusked, wary, and mean as any "rake-straw rooters" along the Neches, though perhaps a little bigger and stronger.[68]

Most stockmen along the Neches operated on a far smaller scale than Southern Pine, Pres Conner, or even Avy Joe Havard, although their rooter hogs and woods cattle remained very important to their way of life. For one thing, from the 1830s to the 1950s, whenever hard times came—when the mill closed or the cotton dried up—a man's free-range livestock often pulled his family through. In the cash-poor 1930s, many people made a little money by selling cattle or hogs, or they bartered stock to other poor people for food or services. Every family with cattle in the woods killed a few beeves during the year, kept what it could immediately use, and shared the rest with neighbors. In a week or a month, the neighbors would do the same thing.

Since pork could be smoked and preserved, hogs were even more important than cattle for the stockmen-farmers along the Neches, and every year in the late fall, after the first hard cold spell, hog-killing time came around. As in the case of thousands of other families, the Gandy clan gathered at the homeplace of Grandmother Gandy for the yearly event. In the week before, Dave Gandy would have gone into the Neches bottoms with his dogs to find, bay, drive, and pen the hogs. Dave's nephew, C. W. Gandy, explained:

> When it would come time to drive those hogs up—hog killing time—
> we'd go in there and cut out fourteen barr. We'd drive em up. He
> had pulled his sweet potatoes and had planted about an acre and a
> half of hog peanuts, big old peanuts, what's called hog goobers.
> And he'd bring them hogs up and I'd run em in them peanuts and

in the corn to get the nubbins where he pulled the corn. Then he'd take em and put in a big old *pieux* pen out there, and he'd start pouring that yellow dent corn to em.

And when it come time to butcher, well, he had a big old syrup kettle, and we had to go put the fire under that old syrup kettle and get that water hot, and get that tin out there to lay the hogs out. And all the boys in the family and my uncles would all congregate up there early in the morning to eat breakfast. Us boys had to go out and build a fire and get everything ready. The men would talk about what they were gonna do and how they were gonna do it. Then we'd kill all them hogs, and dress em, cut em up, put that salt on em, and put em in the smokehouse. And a couple of us boys had to cut bear grass to hang that meat up with. One piece would hang a big ham up on a smoke rack. We had to cut enough of that to get ahead to be ready when they got ready to hang up the meat. And we used hickory and a little big of sassafras in our smoke wood to give it a better flavor.[69]

Like the Gandys, Avy Joe Havard's family in Angelina County were prodigious hog butcherers and pork users, and their smokehouse was as big as the room of a house. Each year the family killed a large number of hogs, cut them up, salted down the meat using two hundred pounds of salt, then stacked it around on shelves in the smokehouse to drain. After twelve days, no more and no less, the Havards put bear-grass strings through each ham or side of bacon, dipped it in a washtub of boiling water, and hung it in the smokehouse. At that point, a hickory-and-sassafras fire was kindled, and the Havard children were assigned to take turns keeping the fire going for twelve long days and nights.[70]

Like other Neches Valley countrymen, the Havards prided themselves on using "all of the hog but the squeal." Hams and bacon sides went to the smokehouse, shoulder meat and trimmings were made into sausage (which then went to the smokehouse), selected segments of small intestine were fried as "chitlins," fat from the hog was cut into pieces and cooked in a washpot to make lard and "cracklins," and ribs and backstrap were eaten fresh. The Havards processed the hooves into pickled pig's feet, cooked the meat from the head for headcheese, and scrambled the brains with eggs for breakfast. Even the bladder was pressed into service: Avy Joe and his brothers inflated it with a quill, hung it in a tree to dry, then used it as a kickball or volleyball.

Like many southerners, the Havards preferred all their vegetables heavily seasoned with salty pork—in fact, Avy Joe's mother used one whole side of a hog jaw when she cooked a "mess" of snap beans or peas. The Havards gave a lot of pork away, but sometimes, as Avy Joe

Hog-killing time at the Lucius Smith place, Beech Grove Community, Jasper County. (Jasper County Historical Commission, Jasper, Texas)

recalled, they had the misfortune to eat with the family of a hog-deficient neighbor. "We'd go to a neighbor or somewhere and eat with em and couldn't hardly eat—just be clear water, you know. Wouldn't be enough season, wouldn't be no meat. We'd eat a little of it but we'd just starve to death to get back home. I've heard mama say lots of times, 'Oh, my God, them poor people, they don't even season their food! They might eat it, but we used to high-season food.'"[71]

Neches Valley stockmen not only shared meat and worked together in cattle and hog drives but often cooperated in many other ways. They could hardly have done otherwise, given the nature of the open range. At any point along the Neches bottoms, several families' stock mixed and merged across many square miles of landscape, and the river was no real barrier. Hogs and cattle waded it or swam it at will, and men like Charlie Havard sometimes had as many animals across the river as in their home counties. From Weaver's Bend to Rockland, the Havard and Weaver clans on the Angelina County side shared the range with the Barnes and Lewis clans in Polk County. It was in every man's best interest to maintain good relations with every other stockman, whether or not he liked a given individual personally. Hogmen and cattlemen cooperated by taking part in communal predator hunts, building and maintaining fences around cultivated fields, burning the range to encourage the growth of new grass, exchanging information about the whereabouts of each other's livestock, conducting emergency expeditions to save stock from river floods, and marking, castrating, inoculating, and butchering each other's animals.

On the open range, practicality joined Christian ethics in promoting cooperation. Jake Cole explained: "We'd help each other. Sombaugh Robinson had the woods full of hogs, and if I had a hog running with them that I didn't find, he'd kill it for me. I'd do the same thing for him if I got one of his with mine—I'd kill it, clean it, take it to him. That's neighborly love. That ain't here now!"[72] By the 1920s, communal predator hunts had mostly ceased, though red wolves and bobcats still took a toll of stockmen's animals. Stockmen still needed to cooperate about fires and fences, however.

Burning the woods was an old southern stockmen's tradition and the most extreme expression of a man's free-range usufruct rights over other people's land. Stockmen usually burned the range in late winter to encourage a maximum growth of woods grass for their cattle in early spring. The carrying capacity of the pine uplands for cattle was decidedly marginal, so this recycling of nutrients for the upland grasses had a significant effect. Fires benefited stockmen's hogs to a lesser degree and rarely intruded on the moist bottoms, though they did encourage the growth of upland blackberries and other lean-season hog foods.

The setting of woods fires was every man's right, though stockmen sometimes cooperated in the process and often exchanged information about their intentions. A man might tell a neighbor he planned to burn the range between two creeks on a certain weekend, giving the other man a chance to burn a portion of his cattle range at about the same time. Cattle would trek for miles to the new grass of burned-over woods, so most men liked to offer their own herds new grass nearby. "Neighborly love" may have been the stockmen's policy, but it seemed prudent not to tempt distant neighbors (or strangers) with the presence of one's unbranded calves.

The problem with woods fires was that they often burned out of control, far beyond the stockmen's original target areas, and this necessitated additional cooperation. Stockmen sometimes worked together to set backfires to burn off firebreaks adjacent to the fences around their cultivated fields. In the open-range era, when numerous stock wandered the woods, a man's rail or *pieux* fences protecting his crops had to be strong and unbroken. If one untimely woods fire destroyed a fence, a man might find cows (or hogs) in the corn virtually overnight, with disastrous results.

The burned fence was a common rural emergency, and neighbors often turned out for a fence building or "rail mauling" to help the stricken family save its crops. Walter Cole, of Jasper County, and George Carpenter, of Angelina County, recalled taking part in a number of these communal work events, lasting from one to three days, with big dinners, dances, and other social events at night.[73] In 1898 when a fire destroyed the rail fences of a Cherokee County man named Pies Hill, who was away from home on jury duty, twenty-four neighborhood men showed up at the Hill farm the next morning with crosscut saws, axes, and wedges. Mrs. Hill cooked the noon meal in a washtub to feed the volunteers. This group of men cut and split three thousand rails that day, and in short order Hill had his fence rebuilt and his crop planted.[74] To the twenty-four participants, this was social insurance, since no man, not even one with several sons and sons-in-law, could replace all of his rail fence quickly enough to keep the stock from destroying his crops. Helping Pies Hill obligated Hill to reciprocate when disaster struck their fences.

At the best of times, cultivated fields were under siege from hungry hogs and cattle wandering the open range. Householders, most of them also stockmen, often walked their fences looking for a weak link and sent their cur dogs out on patrol. Cows would pass readily through a gap in a fence, but hogs were even more of a problem. Certain ones learned to use their snouts to lift off the top rails of a fence until it was low enough to scramble over, then they rooted and gorged their way "right down the row." Oscar Allen and his brothers recalled many nights spent keeping watch over cornfields, trying to catch outlaw sows and boars in the act.[75]

Fence-breaking and crop-destroying swine sometimes were shot, though this was not supposed to happen. In southeastern Texas, as in Robert Frost's New England, "good fences made good neighbors," but the Texas fences were supposed to fence stock out, not in. As Carl Havard explained, it was the farmer's moral responsibility to build and maintain his fences so that nothing could get in; if it did get in, the fault was his—a fault doubly compounded if he harmed the livestock. In the etiquette of the open range, farmers were supposed to notify the stockman of the incursion, the stockman was to immediately come and remove his animals and offer the injured farmer a courtesy hog or cow, and the farmer was to refuse.[76] Sometimes things actually worked like that, especially since the injured farmers usually were open-range stockmen themselves and could not afford a holier-than-thou attitude. There were also more practical concerns; if a man summarily executed another man's cow in his field, and the herder found out about it, what might happen to the farmer's cows out there in the woods?

The situation was fraught with social peril, and American courts were full of herdsman-farmer squabbles for three hundred years, from colonial times until the end of the open-range era. Small wonder, then, that most southeastern Texans kept their fences up with great diligence. Split-oak rails were stacked nine or ten high in "fence worms" so tight they resisted not only outlaw hogs but also river floods. Eight-foot cypress *pieux* boards were rived off big horizontal cypress logs (turned after each riving with a peavy) and nailed between strong posts. As soon as people could afford "bobwire," they placed strands of it across the tops of both rail and *pieux* fences to further "fence em out."

As elsewhere along the Neches, stockmen in southern Angelina and northern Polk counties exchanged information and cooperated in working each other's stock. Charlie Havard lived directly across the river from Johnny Barnes, and the two men's hogs and cattle crossed the Neches all the time, especially when the river was low. Havard and Barnes vaccinated, marked, and castrated each other's hogs, often using each other's pens, then compared notes to settle up. Havard's foster son, W. B. Harris, recalled: "Every year—we was both poor folks, Johnny and us—we'd go down to the river, didn't have a boat, and they'd talk, holler at each other across the river. Well, they'd tally up the list for whoever owed the other one, they'd wrap the money on a rock and throw it across the river."[77]

Other families of the Havard, Weaver, Barnes, and Lewis clans also cooperated. Charlie Havard's nephew, Carl Havard, recalled that every so often someone would be dispatched to town to the nearest telephone to communicate with Polk County and relay information about how many hogs had been marked, castrated, and inoculated, and by whom, and whose hogs had been seen in what location. This information exchange about wandering hogs became especially important as hog-killing season approached. As Carl noted, the Barnes might say: "'Well, you got six or seven big barrs in here at the Hell's Neck.' Everybody know'd every place. And we might say, 'Yeah, you got three or four barrs needs killing in here at the Mayer Old Field, Oliver Fish Hole, Robbin's Camp'—wherever they was at and the location. Ever place on that river had a name. Then the hog man on the other side might say, 'Would there be a possible chance of a couple of y'all meeting us at the river at Hell's Neck—boat come in there?'" The Havards would say, "no problem," and a date would be set. "We'd get our wagons, our horses, our dogs, our wash pots. We'd bail out down there, and we'd carry an extra horse or two. And they'd come to the river, well, we'd have a boat in there. They'd get in the boat and come over and use our horses. We'd kill the barrs, build a fire, scrape em right there on the river. Load em in the boat and carry em over there and they'd put em in the wagon and carry em on home."[78]

All of the information exchange about the locations and status of different kinds of livestock relied on an intricacy of shared place-names across many miles of river bottoms. For the hunter, trapper, and riverman, knowledge of the bottoms was a great advantage, but for the free-range stockman, it was an absolute necessity. A man's stock roamed for miles up and down the river valley, and his livelihood depended on knowing the local range in great detail and accuracy. The old stockmen prided themselves on their knowledge of the landscape, their ability to communicate locations, and their inability to get lost—to be able to "come out" of the bottoms no matter what the weather conditions, time of day or night, or stage of the river. After the Neches rose to flood its valley in the winter, these skills became especially critical. As Lynn McGalin noted: "If a man's coming through there regular, he better know ever bit of it—ever tree, everthing else. And when the river gets up, it ain't the same country no more, cause you up high. But you still got to know it."[79]

The Neches Valley stockmen also cooperated to save each other's animals from the yearly river floods, although there was a desperate, every-man-for-himself quality about these episodes. Just as the river set a yearly trap for river fish in drying sloughs and backwaters, so did it set a trap of a different order for men and livestock. Gradually, as fall moved into winter, the Neches rose in its channel until it flowed to the tops of its banks. At this point, heavy rains and a swift rise of an additional two or three feet often sent water coursing up backwater sloughs in the shallow valley to flood miles of bottoms. Hogs and cattle had moved into the bottoms in the late fall in search of acorns and switch cane; now, they were threatened by the swiftly rising water.

The cattle were more at risk, and stockmen often rode into the bottoms at first news of the rise in the river to try to get them out—a haste that in the rain, cold water, and flooded woods sometimes led to tragedy. Devil's Bayou in northwestern Angelina County is only one of the places along the Neches associated with lost livestock and drowned men. On November 19, 1907, Mack and Joe Bowman were trying to get cattle out of the backwater in the Devil's Bayou after the Neches had risen to flood stage. Mack's horse came back without him, and later his body was found near a ford on the Bayou. As a local historian noted, "It was believed that the horn of the saddle struck the boy in the stomach and caused him to fall off in the swift water." Fifteen years later, in 1922, another big rain had swollen the Neches, and Reagan Simmons drowned. He and several other men, all on horseback, had been trying to rescue their cattle trapped by the rising floodwaters near Pine Island. Simmons's body was found thirty-six hours later; in the swift floods of early winter, the river could be cruel.[80]

For every death, there were many narrow escapes. Jess Wells knew an old man who became trapped in the bottom while trying to get his cattle out. The man was a feeble swimmer, but when he and his cattle came to a deep place, he would grab the tail of one of the cows and let himself be pulled across. "He'd kick enough to stay on top of the water, and when the cow went out, why he'd go out." On one occasion, Wells almost drowned. He and an old stockman were in a flooding bottom, and the older man said: "Well, we're getting lots of water in here. Can you see any land over that way?" Wells said, "No, it's all water," and the old man replied, "We better get out of here!" They barely escaped in time, swimming their horses at the deep places.[81]

Every year, the bottoms were full of hogs and cattle when the river went on its sudden rise. Carl Havard recalled, "I've seen it down there time and time again, a fast rise from above come down, you'd go down to that river and you'd hear hogs squealing in ever direction." More cattle drowned in the river floods than adult hogs, since the latter were good swimmers, but this was not true for pigs. Jess Wells said: "Now, with pigs, a world of pigs got drowned. That old sow would have a bed in the bottom, you know, and the river come up. She'd go to the hills and leave them pigs in there. I know a man stayed in them woods all the time. Me and him was in there when the river was rising, and he said, 'They'll be a thousand pigs drowned between Anderson Crossing and [Highway 21] on both sides of the river tonight.' That river was sure coming."[82]

Most of the wood-wise livestock made it out of the bottom without being trapped by the floodwaters, but not all; every year some cattle or hogs drowned or became stranded on hammocks out in the backwater. In the wide lower valley west of Buna, sometimes these higher locations were separated by miles of swift water from the edge of the swollen Neches. Here, livestock might be stranded for weeks or months, devouring every possible food source, even the bark off the trees, and eventually starving to death. So, down two hundred winding miles of the Neches "as the river flows," stockmen mounted the rare saddle horses that did not mind swimming the backwater and launched paddle boats and dugouts to save their stranded livestock and those of other men.

Some men, including Charlie Havard, believed that "you couldn't hardly drown a hog" and advocated letting the hogs swim out on their own. As Charlie noted: "Some of em would try to go in there and boat em out, but they'd drown more hogs than they'd save. Generally there was an old sow or two in the bunch that knowed the nearest way out. If you just let em alone, that old sow would walk around on that hammock, you'd hear her groan, directly, she'd lay down in that water and every one of em foller her—I mean, just fast as they could hop in there behind her."[83]

Lynn McGalin and his father once followed the watery course of a sow that had finally made the decision to swim out with its young shoats; as they paddled in the direction they thought the sow had gone, they found dead shoats, one after another, floating motionless in the cold water. Or at least the animals seemed to be dead. McGalin said: "I'd pull the boat up there, my dad take em by the heels, shake the water out of em, put em down in the boat. They was alive!"[84]

Other men took advantage of the hogs trapped on hammocks to get their winter meat—it was, after all, hog-killing time. Jude Hart recalled: "I've swum out with two hogs tied to the saddle and one to the horse's tail. You can put a rope round a hog's neck and a half hitch in his mouth and tie the other end to his hind feet—dead or alive. Then tie the rope to the horse's tail and he'll come right on out." Jess Wells's father helped Pres Conner do this in Houston County, sounding a blowing horn from time to time so Conner could find his way out of the flooded bottoms. Finally, Conner came "chugging in" out of the gathering dark, riding his old "swimming mare" and floating two dead hogs tied to the mare's tail.[85]

In the wide bottoms west of Buna and Kirbyville, the McGalins and their neighbors regularly went in to save their cattle trapped on hammocks, normally taking two or three dogs and two paddle boats. The dogs ran the cattle off the islands and started them swimming toward the closest dry land on the edge of the bottoms. Often, one boat would lead the cattle, and the other would follow behind them. The McGalins accompanied their stock until they saw that the cattle had made it safely, then they turned around to pick up the dogs, who had been swimming after the cows but had "burnt out" (or, if the water was cold, "froze down"). As Babe explained: "Them dogs burn out, but we couldn't fool with em, we have to go keep them cows a-coming. We come on till we seen they was gonna go to the hill, and we went back and hunt that dog, and he'd clumb up a little tree—just set there a-howling." In a previous generation, Jasper and Newton county stockmen had used seventeen-by-four-foot cypress dugouts to rescue cattle from the backwaters of the Neches and the Sabine. These were ponderous craft, designed only for this purpose and capable of hauling out five or six dead hogs or two or three live cows "that was pore and couldn't go."[86]

With little doubt, the river floods acted as the greatest brake on the increase of stockmen's herds. Every year, the grass died in the uplands, the mast fell in the bottomlands, and woods cattle and rooter hogs moved toward the Neches in search of succulent switch cane and "sweet mast" acorns. The river had set its trap, and then one day the rains came, and the trap was closed.

This is not to say that the stockmen did not have other problems:

from the earliest times, various predators and pests, animal and human, plagued their herds. Wild pigeons troubled Neches Valley stockmen up until their disappearance around 1880. In flocks so vast they eclipsed the sun, the pigeons settled into bottomland woods and stayed until they had devoured the mast over entire areas. In the 1930s, old Houston County settlers told ornithologist H. C. Oberholser that they had dreaded the coming of the mast-destroying flocks and had thrashed pigeons to death in huge numbers at the roosts at night in attempts to save food for their hogs.[87] In Anderson County, farther up the Neches, settlers did the same. Charles Yarborough told his son Ralph: "The passenger pigeons ate the mast or acorns from trees—it was their favorite food—and settlers went to their roost in Anderson County and killed them in great numbers, leaving them on the ground. They killed them to keep the pigeons from eating the acorns they wanted the hogs to have."[88]

Bears and panthers caught a good many stock in the early days, though they had been eliminated from most of the Neches country by 1900. Bobcats and red wolves remained, and they took a steady toll of pigs and young calves. Occasionally, southeastern Texas stockmen lobbied the state for predator control measures—especially for the wolves, which also liked to catch and eat the settlers' stock dogs.

Alligators also were common along the Neches, and some stockmen believed they caught far greater numbers of free-range livestock than most people recognized. An alligator would surge out of the murky water to catch a drinking shoat or calf by the nose or would sweep the animal into the slough with its tail. Some men actually saw this happen. Lester Greenville's brother saw an alligator catch a hog, take it under, pull it out on a sandbar to get a better grip, then take it under again. Many men were close enough to the attack to hear the hog's squeal and the splash. Pasture rider Charlie Harber's experience was typical. He was up on Cochino Bayou near a big slough one day and observed a seventy-five-pound hog at the edge of the water. "I watched him, and he went down to get a drink of water. Well, I looked off back up the river, and I heard this hog squeal, and just make one squeal, and there's a big splash. I rode down there and wasn't nothing but blood on at the top of the water. I never did see the alligator or the hog no more."[89]

Neches alligators grew to formidable size. Hunters killed one that was thirteen feet three inches long and weighed 1,040 pounds in the Forks of the River around 1960—statistics that give credence to the stories several men told of catching or killing fourteen- and fifteen-footers.[90] Neches Valley woodsmen shot every alligator they could, and they had deeper reasons than the animals' predations on their livestock. At Pine Island Hunting Club, pasture rider Alvin Dark killed scores of alligators and followed the policy that "the only good one is a dead one." He found their bankside dens, called "underhouses" by the rivermen, then probed down through the overlying ground with a sharp rod until he drove them out. Then he shot them.[91] At a much earlier time they were also shot by frontiersman Buck Barry, who once observed an alligator catch a swimming black bear. Barry's reasons for shooting alligators were probably similar to Dark's. As Barry explained, "The alligators were so deadly to our dogs that we never let one escape if we had a chance to kill it."[92]

Many people affirmed the alligator's fondness for dog meat. Pioneer Noah Smithwick wrote of the early Texas settlers, "Dogs, of which every well-regulated family had several, were their special weakness, and many thirsty canine drank and never thirsted more." Alligators would come to investigate a well-imitated dog's bark or hog's grunt, and Ralph Jackson and other boys along Double Bayou often threw a dog into their favorite swimming hole a few times to test out the water before they went in themselves. According to Frank Ashby, Pres Conner once lost a favorite stock dog to an alligator at a Neches river ford. Returning the next day for revenge, Conner staked a yapping feist at the edge of the water, then took a position with his rifle on the over-looking bank. As Frank told the story: "That old dog went to barking, and that old alligator [came] swimming right up there to that dog. And he shot him in the eye with a Winchester—killed him." Sometimes, if even some of the many stories passed down are true, alligators caught more than dogs. Around World War I, two brothers were swimming in the big river hole at the tip of Pine Island when an alligator caught one boy, pulled him out on a sandbar, then took him under. Many men from the area participated in a search for the boy's body, but although they killed several alligators, they never found the right one.[93]

Despite the prevalence of cooperation and "neighborly love" among stockmen, hogs and cattle also suffered from human predators. Live-stock roaming far and wide in the woods were always a temptation, and the southern stock thief was as old as the southern free range. In 1741, a North Carolina writer complained, "Many Wicked Men in this Province make it their business to ride in the Woods and steal Cattle and Hogs, and alter and eface [sic] the Marks and Brands and others, and mismark and misbrand Horses, Cattle, and Hogs." A 1786 statute affirmed the truth of this and provided for ferocious punishment: the North Carolina stock thief was to be pilloried, whipped, branded with a hot iron on both cheeks, and relieved of his ears with a sharp knife. No sooner had Frederick Law Olmsted crossed the Sabine into Texas at Gaines Ferry in 1843 than he began to hear about stock thieves. The owner of the ferry, a Mr. Strawther, complained of a special plague of hog stealers thereabouts. Olmsted wrote: "No slave country, new or old, is free from this exasperating pest of poor whites. In his neighborhood were several who ostensibly had a little patch of land to attend to, but who really, he said, derived their whole lazy subsistence from their richer neighbor's hog droves."[94]

The local "poor whites" probably took a somewhat different view of the matter: why should this rich man object if they took a hog to eat from time to time, just for their own use? The underlying ethic governing the taking of a resource from other people's land on the free range focused on how a person planned to use the resource. Taking something for personal consumption or use was permissible; taking something for sale was not. Admittedly this stretched free-range traditions a bit, but a man's taking of an occasional hog to feed his family fell into the permitted category. Rural people clearly distinguished between the occasional, subsistence-motivated stock thief and the professional one. A century after Olmsted crossed the Sabine, George Carpenter observed of a local hog thief: "He was out for the money. Now, a feller go out there and shoot a man's hog, he's out for the meat; I done that myself." Nor should the big stockman begrudge a young man getting started if the latter took a few unmarked shoats to serve as his "seed stock." According to Frank Ashby, the saying current in Houston County at the time he began stock operations was, "The man that had the best dog had the most hogs."[95]

Admittedly, some stock thieves crossed the line into true professionalism. Every rural community had one or two men who ran a few hogs and cattle for the sake of appearances and for an explanation of their peregrinations about the open range but who took other people's livestock on a regular basis. Although stockmen usually looked down on neighbors who did this, they were often tolerated as crosses to be borne and sometimes even regarded with amusement. In about 1840 riverman Andrew Smyth's politician brother George wrote of one such man:

> Some money rules, some scruple not,
> For gain to use deceit
> Though great the crime, it seems the lot
> Of Cameron to love meat.
> His hogs are few in any range,
> His mark, he has forgot,
> In hurry, haste, 'tis true, though strange,
> Are others often shot.[96]

Many local hog thieves were well known (and more than a little admired) among their neighbors for their uncanny skill with stock dogs; they represented Ashby's "best dog, most hogs" dictum carried to its logical extreme. A man well acquainted with the Havard family had dogs so good "that he could steal em out from under your bed with em." Of a famous Hardin County hog thief, one man said:

> There's an old man around here—I won't call his name—he's a thief, and he'll steal hogs. But some folk will steal his hogs, too, but he just laughs about it, because he'll go get em out of the pen at night. He'll take this dog of his, and when he opens the pen, he'll get down and pull the dog's ears, and put that dog ahead of him and he'll never bark. His old red dog was worth a lot to him when he wanted to steal hogs, cause he'd never make a racket. He would hear about someone penning a bunch of hogs, and he'd go there that night and open that gate, get them hogs, and that dog, he'd never bark.[97]

Stock theft often was not very amusing, however, and it became especially serious during the depression in the 1930s. A stockman sometimes knew who was stealing his animals, though he rarely thought it worthwhile to force the issue. As Lynn McGalin observed, "Course, you didn't say nobody was a hog thief!" In rural southeastern Texas, to directly accuse a man of stock theft invited a physical confrontation or even a "killing"—a death that resulted from a "fair fight" between consenting adult males and that was customarily no-billed by the local grand jury. In Hardin County Tom Moye found where someone had been butchering his hogs in the woods, and he trailed the wagon to the home of Tom Lindsey. Moye then disgraced Lindsey, letting it be known in the community who had taken his hogs. This story got back to Lindsey, who later killed Tom Moye in a fight at a community log-rolling.[98]

Sometimes a person confronted a stock thief by accident, with serious consequences. One of the dangers of the open range was the possibility of chancing on some illegal activity as you went about your business—a moonshiner working at his whiskey still, an Albert Moore cutting stave trees, or—in Edgar Womack's case—a man killing one of your hogs. On December 13, 1935, Womack found Henry Lacy slaughtering a hog, and Lacy shot him dead with his .30-30. Later, Henry Lacy, a black man, went to his death in the electric chair.[99] There were many such violent incidents across the three-hundred-year history of the southern open range.

Sometimes stock theft was the way local stockmen informed a newcomer that the range was already filled to capacity. Something like this clearly happened to Charlie Crager and Brown Stephens, of the New Willard community, Polk County, in the early 1950s. Crager complained in the Livingston newspaper: "I had a bunch of cows and hogs and they have all been taken away. A neighbor told me that another neighbor had killed my hogs—then later the hogs showed up with three new marks on them. I cannot have range hogs or gather any of them. One certain individual has stated that there was only room for three people on the so-called open range." Brown Stephens wrote: "This free range is not a free range at all—it is claimed by only a few and when I have attempted to use it I have not got anywhere. I have not got any of my hogs back and have got only a few of my cows back. I had to just quit and forget I had any woods hogs because I did not want to get into trouble over this 'free range.' Some of my hogs were killed and drug within a few hundred yards of my house with their ears cut off."[100]

Evidently, the local stockmen who stole Stephens's and Crager's livestock wanted to make very sure that the two men knew about it—the sooner to discourage them from attempts to participate in the New Willard open range. Such conflicts between established stockmen and hopeful newcomers were probably common. Like the Havards, the Barnes, and the Lewises of Angelina County, the three old-time stockmen around New Willard perhaps cooperated with each other in "neighborly love," but this did not mean they were willing to allow other men to come in and run stock on their traditional range.

When the first stockmen came to southeastern Texas, they settled in rural communities but spaced themselves out some distance apart to allow adequate room for their growing herds. For decades their stock flourished on the rich resources of the virgin range. Gradually, the interstices filled up with additional stockmen, and the open range became crowded with the rooter hogs and woods cattle of many different men. What ecologists have termed the "tragedy of the commons" began. Inexorably, the minerals and nutrients of the primal ecosystem were depleted. It was in the interest of all stockmen to preserve the resources of the open range—living space for livestock, water, grass, switch cane, and mast—undiminished, but it was in every man's personal economic interest to run as many hogs and cattle in the woods as he could. If a stockman acted rationally in his own interest, his actions tended to destroy the carrying capacity of the range for all—including himself. No wonder, then, that such a man might resist the entry of newcomers.

With little doubt, the woods along the Neches were filled to overflowing with feral hogs and cattle in the last decades of the open range. Exactly how many we will never know. Many observers attested that hogs and cattle were everywhere in the 1930s, 1940s, and 1950s—a public nuisance, especially when they got on the highways where automobiles were traveling faster all the time.

When Aubrey Cole camped along the Neches as a boy, he could hear groups of hogs all up and down the river squealing and "pulling cover" at dusk as they prepared to bed down for the night. Most of these hogs were unofficial animals—ones left off the Jasper County tax roles. As Cole and others affirmed, it was customary for local stockmen to grossly underestimate the numbers of free-range livestock they owned when the local tax collector or the worker from the U.S. Census came around. The county tax collector was an elected official, unwilling to anger the voters, and in any case he had little capacity to count a man's animals roaming the remote woods. Consequently, he and the stockmen entered into a tacit conspiracy of underestimation.[101]

Only in one instance did something like a true count of livestock—in this case, cattle—take place in the Neches counties. In 1937 and 1938, the tick eradication program of the Texas Sanitary Livestock Commission (with significant help from the Texas Rangers) forced southeastern Texas stockmen to get cattle out of the woods and bring them in to be dipped. Despite bitter protests, threats, outbreaks of forest arson, and some violence, this was accomplished. According to the *United States Census of Agriculture* for 1935, the county contained 14,257 cattle. However, the *Jasper Newsboy* reported that tick eradication workers dipped 43,000 cattle in Jasper County in June 1937, 23,804 in July, 77,000 in August, 82,635 in September, and 75,453 in October.[102] Although the monthly counts included some re-dippings, the totals for Jasper County were astonishing. Along the Neches and in the pine uplands, free-range cattle and hogs roamed everywhere.

7
CLOSING THE WOODS

The system of customary usufruct rights and land-use practices that southerners commonly termed the "open range," or the "open woods," lasted for many generations in the rural South and was a continual source of astonishment to newcomers. The first things such people usually noticed were the free-range hogs and cattle wandering the woods, public highways, and city streets. As a general rule, municipal laws passed to control livestock existed for decades before serious enforcement began to occur. A female letter-writer to the *Jasper Newsboy* bitterly complained in 1911: "Jasper has a hog law, but it's the biggest farce we know. The hogs roam the streets at will rooting open gates, eating folks' chickens, potatoes, and everything else they can find. The women want the men of the town to repeal the law or see that it is enforced. Enforce the law. That's what you were put in office to do!" Despite this spirited criticism, forty-one years later the county-seat town of Jasper still had a hog problem. A note on the editorial page in 1952 reminded residents, "Pound prices are being increased to $4 for cattle (first offense), $2 for hogs." On the other side of the Neches, the county seat of Kountze and the Hardin County courthouse also had a long association with free-range livestock. In 1888 county commissioners had paid John Bevil ten dollars for "boxing up the Court House to keep out hogs, etc.," but wandering swine still plagued the town square into the 1950s and sometimes broke into the courthouse itself.[1]

Associated with the right to run stock on other people's land were other customary rights, including the privileges of trespass and year-round hunting, which also were strongly maintained, whatever the statutory law might proclaim. Soon after his transfer to Hardin County from Central Texas in 1950, game warden Clarence Beezley arrested two local men for hunting deer with dogs out of season, and he found the response of the citizenry astonishing. One of the hunters had resisted arrest; as Beezley said: "This one, we had to rassle him to take his rifle away from him. I had just come from Halletsville, and I thought, 'Boy, it's really gonna cost these old boys.' So, we went in to Kountze courthouse. I never had been there before, and at that time the main street wasn't paved, and there were hogs laying around on both sides of the street. The people were outside the courthouse waiting for the game warden to come in with these two guys, and they was making fun of us! The only friend we had was that lady j.p. [justice of the peace], and we got one $50 fine."[2]

After experiencing much "culture shock," as he termed it, Clarence Beezley came to understand what was different about rural southeastern Texas. He summed this up in two related points: the survival into the middle twentieth century of a tradition of "living off the land," and the "Indian idea that the land belongs to everybody."[3] In 1887, another scandalized newcomer had put the matter even more succinctly: "The people have been in the habit of using every man's property as their own for so many years that they have come to believe that the land has no owners."[4] Nothing much had changed over the decades.

From 1830 to 1950, local traditions gave southeastern Texans the right to trespass and to range livestock on other people's property. People could, in addition, go on another person's land to hunt, fish, cut firewood, collect hickory nuts, harvest bee trees, build stock pens and fishing shacks, and improve the common range by setting the woods on fire. Needless to say, these customary rights precluded the perimeter fencing of properties by landowners. At the outer limits of generally accepted free-range rights were such practices as fur trapping, stave making, and shingle making—all of which were disapproved by some users of the open range because they were done for profit and not for personal use but which were still common, especially on the lands of absentee landlords.[5]

The tradition of the open woods always had its abusers, its hog thieves and stave thieves; however, the whole system, the way of life of the Neches Valley stockmen-farmers, was based on cooperation and neighborliness. After Dave Gandy found and marked a bee tree in the Neches bottom in the spring, he could be nearly certain he would find the tree unmolested in the fall when he came to cut it, with a season's accumulation of honey in its hollow trunk. As many Neches Valley residents affirmed, in the days of the open range, people generally "honored" other people's marked bee trees, trotline sets, remote fishing shacks, unattended hunting camps, and roaming livestock.

As historian Steven Hahn noted, among the stockmen-farmers the usufruct rights of the open range took their place beside other "habits of mutuality" in a rural society very different from the present: "Common rights, in short, not only enabled small landowners and the landless to own livestock, but they fit comfortably into a setting where social relations were mediated largely by ties of kinship and reciprocity rather than the marketplace."[6] The tradition of the open range was only a part (although perhaps the most important part) of a system of habits of mutuality that set these communities apart. The following were elements of the system: the cooperative use of unenclosed lands as commons for stock raising; usufruct rights to travel, hunt, fish, gather, and collect fuel wood on unenclosed land; cooperative work occasions such as logrollings, fence buildings, syrup makings, and many others; various forms of "swap work" and barter; the sharing of food in an era of primitive food-preservation technologies; and mutual support between members of extended families, church congregations, neighborhoods, and rural communities.

Many people I interviewed groped for some way to describe the lost world of these small communities along the Neches and to explain the vast gulf they saw between then and now. They told of "neighborly love," of family feuds over livestock, and of rural isolation and roads so bad for weeks at a time that only six-ox teams could "pull the mud" into town. More than anything else, however, they spoke of the days of the open range, before the "woods were closed," and of the social conflicts involved in its closing. J. R. Cockrell explained: "The amazing thing about it, the most marked change that you can observe, is that fifty years ago you could go out in the woods and you'd see people all the time. I'd see more people in the woods then that I can see now in town. You know, people had cattle and hogs, and they was hunting and fishing—they was out in the woods all the time. Now, they're places five miles from here that might as well be in China. Nobody goes there, it's in somebody's pasture."[7]

The process of closing the woods—of shutting down the traditional usufruct rights on other people's land—took place over the half century from 1940 to 1990, involved much social conflict, and resulted in a backlash of extreme territoriality. When Oscar Allen's family cut pines on their own property during the 1930s, they took care not to leave any lodged trees in the woods to possibly injure other people's passing livestock or neighbors traveling across the Allens' land on a hundred errands. On his arrival in Jasper County in 1963, game warden Billy Platt found only one large property in the entire county where the owner had dared to erect a perimeter fence. Such fences were anathema to the free-range system, and stock-raising neighbors regarded them as major antisocial acts. Thirty years later, however, everything was behind fences, the woods were closed, the Neches counties had the most fiercely protected property boundaries in Texas, and U.S. Forest Service officials were troubled with a recurrent problem of individuals attempting to stake out and defend personal hunting territories in the government-maintained "commons" of the national forests.[8] Clearly, rural land use along the Neches had passed from one extreme to another; "habits of mutuality" had given way to the most determined assertion of territoriality and common-law property rights. Small wonder, then, that this change was accompanied by a large measure of social conflict.

The origins of the southern commons—the open woods or free range—are obscure, but this system of land use developed very early in the history of the colonial South. In part, it was a natural response to frontier conditions of low population density and seemingly limitless land; in part, it was a reassertion of older traditions of the European commons. When Dave Gandy claimed a bee tree in the Neches bottoms by marking it with a cross or a Roman numeral three, he followed a practice well established in the customary forest laws of northern Europe by A.D. 1000.[9] Likewise, two usufruct rights—"pannage," the right to range hogs in the lord's woods to eat mast, and "windfall," the right to gather firewood—were highly valued by the medieval peasantry. Cultural geographer Clarence Glacken has recorded the intricate customary relationships between medieval Europeans and the forest that once covered most of the landscape. Peasants went into the woods to gather the raw materials for their houses, furniture, treenware utensils, and a thousand everyday objects. Above all, the forest was important for livestock. The barbarian peoples of the Latin West divided trees into two classes according to their grazing value: those producing mast suitable for livestock were classified as productive (*fructiferi*) and the others as nonproductive (*infructosi*).[10] In England after the Norman Conquest of 1066, William I's inventory, the *Domesday Book*, recorded the extent of forest lands on Saxon estates not by acres but by the number of swine each forest could support. Usufruct rights in the woods were so important for the survival of medieval peasants that several other European languages echoed an ancient Swedish saying: "The forest is the mantle of the poor."[11]

In England, during the fourteenth through the sixteenth centuries, the ancient usufruct rights gradually eroded with the growth of royal authority and the assertion of landowner powers under the common law. Enclosures of common lands and strict enforcement of the game laws provoked much conflict. In particular, the poaching of game animals in the king's or the lord's forest became an extreme point of contention between commoners and their betters and was already a capital offense by Norman times.

Both the memory of the old usufruct rights and the modern assertion of fence, stock, and game laws made their way across the Atlantic as part of the cultural baggage of the early settlers. Because of frontier conditions, however, common-law property rights suffered a retrogression, and this was especially true in the American South. As historian Steven Hahn summed up the matter: "Fee-simple landownership prevailed in the antebellum South. Real property could be bought and sold at will, its purchaser entitled to full possession. But from earliest settlement, custom and law circumscribed exclusivity and widened use of rights. Unimproved, and thus unenclosed land, which constituted most of the acreage on Southern farms, won sanction as common property for hunting, fishing, and grazing."[12]

Colonial legislatures made some attempts to pass stock and game laws and to prohibit trespass, but such laws proved largely unenforceable and often provoked a violent response. In 1785 when South Carolina prohibited hogs from running at large in two low-country counties, "some classes" fought back by deliberately setting fire to and destroying fences.[13] Likewise, rural people resisted or ignored North Carolina laws of 1784 and 1810 prohibiting the hunting of deer at night. As Stuart Marks remarked of these early game laws (in words entirely applicable to twentieth-century conflicts along the Neches), "Perhaps the proof in the pudding of wildlife policy was not found in the enactment of laws but in the ways the courts and public sentiments actually operated in the countryside."[14] Increasingly, however, southern courts went on record as preservers of the public rights to game and the customs of the open range. The royal colony of Georgia explicitly reversed the common law in 1755 when it required each planter to have fences of a specified height; otherwise, "any trespass or damage so ever he shall receive or sustain by hogs, cattle, or horses shall be his own loss." Later, the Territories of Mississippi and Alabama, and the Republic of Texas, followed in the same pattern.[15]

In law and in practice, the rights to trespass, range stock, and hunt were closely linked. The comments of wealthy South Carolina planter William Elliot in 1859 accurately described the situation in much of the American South:

Though it is the broad common law maxim, "that everything upon a man's land is his own" . . . and he can shut out his neighbor without any wrong to him, yet custom, with us, forfeited by certain decisions of the court, has gone far to qualify and set limits to the maxim. The right to hunt wild animals is held by the great body of the people, whether landholders or otherwise, as one of their franchises, which they will indulge in at discretion; and to all limitations on which, they submit with the worst possible grace![16]

Then Elliot sarcastically described a court scene from a case of hunter trespass and conflicting landowner and hunter rights. The hunter, on the stand, was being questioned by an attorney.

Counsel — "Would you pursue a deer if he entered your neighbor's enclosure?"
Witness — "Certainly."
Counsel — "What if his fields were planted, and his cotton growing, or his grain ripe?"
Witness — "It would make no difference; I should follow my dogs, go where they might."
Judge — "And pull down your neighbor's fence, and trample on his fields?"
Witness — "I should do it, though I might regret to injure him!"
Judge — "You would commit a trespass; you would be mulcted in damages. There is no law for such an act!"
Witness — "It is hunter's law, however."

Elliot concluded, "And hunter's law is likely somewhat longer to be the governing law of the case in this section of the country, for the prejudices of the people are strong against any exclusive property in game, as every one feels who attempts to keep it to himself." He then told of the experiences of several friends who had sought to protect game on certain parts of their properties. Poachers had killed their game, burned their fences, and proved impossible to convict in the local courts.[17] In some areas—the Neches counties among them—Elliot's observations would remain current for another century. Over the years, his story of poachers would be repeated on the properties of William Crain, James Albert Best, and a hundred other landowners along the Neches Valley. In Neches country, as in other parts of the rural South, "hunter's law" and other free-range traditions lasted a long time.

After the Civil War, during the 1870s and 1880s, reformers renewed their attacks on the traditions of the open range, but now with greater urgency. Southern agricultural journals and newspapers soon were full of their complaints and demands. The old concerns of the reformers were still there—preserving game populations for the "better sort" of people, enacting a stock law, preventing timber depletion, and asserting full common-law rights of the property owner—but behind these concerns lurked the labor problem. The labor-intensive system of cotton agriculture needed freedmen and poor whites at work in the fields as tenants and sharecroppers, but the traditions of the commons gave them a way to avoid participation by growing a little corn, running stock on the open range, fishing, and hunting. As Steven Hahn noted: "Planters recognized that customary use rights, along with the availability of public domain in some states, jeopardized labor supply and discipline and, by extension, the revitalization of the cotton economy. The 'labor question,' therefore, became linked inextricably with the 'land question.'"[18] *Southern Home and Farm* magazine explicitly stated the reformers' agenda for their attack on the southern subsistence life-style when it listed the following under "needed new laws": the increased regulation of hunting, fishing, and foraging; a stock law; laws against "hunting, fishing, trapping, netting, or seining on another's land without permission"; the enforcement of all labor contracts with tenants; a law to severely punish people "tampering with fences"; and (last but not least) a tax on dogs.[19]

In general, the late-nineteenth-century movement for game and stock laws made good progress in Black Belt counties across the South but poor and difficult progress in the Upper South and Pine Barrens. Emphatically, the counties along the Neches must be numbered among the latter, since they had no stock laws, effective game laws, or perimeter fences—let alone dog taxes—well into the twentieth century. As a historian of the southern stock laws noted, the open range lasted longest in counties composed mainly of white independent farmers who owned their own land and were not tied exclusively to cotton production, a description that aptly characterizes most of southeastern Texas. Not surprisingly, there were more hogs and cattle per capita in open-range counties than in stock-law counties, and this difference was especially striking in the case of hogs. In fact, "the greater the number of hogs per capita a county had the greater was the likelihood of that county's remaining open range."[20]

Hogs flourished in the Neches bottomlands in 1920, as did other elements of the southern subsistence life-style. The free range was the linchpin of this way of life, and—for various reasons—it remained firmly in place along the Neches. Elsewhere across the South, state legislatures were ending the free range, county by county, through legislative acts or else were empowering local governments to end it, but in Texas the stock law required a local vote.[21] In counties such as Jasper, Tyler, Hardin, Trinity, and Polk, most of the rural people were stockmen-farmers, the towns (and the urban vote) were small, and citizens defeated stock-law initiatives time after time. Many rural voters well recognized that the stock law was much more than a regulation requiring the fencing of livestock; they knew that it would "close the woods," excluding them from hunting, fishing, gathering, and exercising other usufruct rights they felt they needed to survive, especially in an era of bad roads and rural isolation.

Large property holders and would-be progressive stockmen and farmers might want a stock law, in order to exclude others from their lands, but for many years they rarely dared to express these opinions in public. At best, those who engaged in what local people thought was excessive fencing were ostracized by their communities; at worst, they were likely to find that the agents of "hunter's law" had thrown their fences down (or even burned their barns). In East Texas, as in New England, "good fences made good neighbors," but only those fences around cultivated fields were "good." Enforcers of the open range cut other early fences with wire cutters, felled trees across them, or burned them. Setting the woods on fire each year was an old southern tradition, and along with encouraging the growth of new grass and increasing the ratio of pasture over forest, the practice also enforced the customs of the southern free range. As geographer William Chambers shrewdly observed in 1934, "Fire often destroys wooden fence posts so that the wire falls down, and land that has been fenced against livestock is added to the open range."[22]

By the 1920s, large lumber companies owned most of the land along the Neches, and although the companies sometimes worked behind the scenes for the stock law, for many years they remained officially neutral on the issue. They had long ago learned that southeastern Texans regarded any attempt to fence the woods or to exclude stockmen and hunters from company lands as nothing short of a declaration of war and that local response was predictable—forest arson, or in the companies' preferred euphemism, "fire trespass."[23]

The custom of burning the woods—whether to make the grass grow or to punish one's enemies—ran like a hidden current just beneath the surface of much of the history of rural southeastern Texas (and doubtless that of other parts of the Pine Belt as well). As a general rule, throughout the twentieth century, whenever an individual, lumber company, or government agency violated the old usufruct rights and closed down some aspect of the open range, southeastern Texans retaliated by setting the woods on fire.

The story of burning the forest has many twists and turns that must be understood to grasp the underlying dynamics of the conflict over closing the woods. When the first Anglo Americans arrived in southeastern Texas with their customs of burning the range, they built their homesteads in a natural environment already profoundly shaped by fire. Natural fires set by lightning had swept southern pine uplands for millennia, and when Native American peoples moved into the area around ten thousand years ago, they used fire as a basic tool. The Caddos and other groups set periodic fires to clear stubble from cultivated fields; to eliminate fleas, ticks, and other pests from around their villages; to curb undergrowth and open the woods for travel and hunting; and, by increasing the "edge effect," to encourage the growth of useful plant foods and the presence near the villages of such preferred game species as deer and turkey.[24]

The open, park-like stands of longleaf and other pines that Anglo Americans found when they arrived in southeastern Texas (and that were later so attractive to the timber companies) "are thought to be a man-induced fire sub-climax within the general deciduous region of the eastern woodlands," according to one forest historian.[25] When fire was kept out of the upland forests—an impossibility before the coming of modern fire-control techniques—they tended to change into mixed forests of pine and hardwood in which the latter dominated. Even the Piney Woods wildlife was fire-adapted: their instincts honed by millennia of wildfires, hawks circled along the edge of slow-moving ground fires, waiting for game to flush, and bobwhite quail flew in to the smoking stubble behind the flames to feast on roasted insects. Whether set by lightning, Indians, or Anglo stockmen, the upland fires stopped at the edge of the wet bottoms.[26]

One disapproving visitor from West Texas commented that southeastern Texans, like the Native Americans before them, believed that the land was "better country" if they burned it off.[27] The stockmen-farmers along the Neches Valley burned the woods for many of the same reasons as the Indians. Since burning the woods only improved them, settlers were careless with fires set to clear field stubbles or to boil water in black yard pots, often allowing the fire to escape to the nearby woods. They regularly set fires around their homesteads to remove undergrowth, to kill snakes, ticks, and other vermin, and to "clean the woods"—to eliminate the gaseous miasmas that emanated from rotting vegetation and that were believed to cause malaria, yellow fever, and other deadly diseases.[28]

Anglo stockmen—and in rural southeastern Texas, that included many families in the Neches Valley communities from 1830 to 1950—had additional reasons for burning the woods. Stockmen set ground fires in the late winter or early spring to recycle nutrients and encourage the regrowth of new grass for their cattle. Such areas also served to "congregate cattle" and make them easier to find for rounding up, marking, and branding. As one forest historian noted, these fires were in part necessitated by the fires of neighbors. "To avoid losing the wandering cattle, almost every stockman set the woods in which he ranged his cattle ablaze in self-defense."[29] Stockmen also set other woods fires around their homesteads to create protective firebreaks outside the rail fences surrounding their cultivated fields and the picket fences surrounding their homes. Regularly swept clean of debris by twig brooms, the traditional bare-dirt country yard functioned as a further barrier against the threat of roaming woods fires.

Stockmen also set woods fires to maintain grass-covered openings in the forest, to maintain or improve the ratio of grassland to woodland, and to maintain—even to enforce—the traditions of the open range.[30] A man would think twice about building an expensive perimeter fence if he believed it might be destroyed by fire in a single night. In the face-to-face world of the rural communities along the Neches, Charlie Havard's rule about "taking care of the neighbors" extended to making sure they maintained their good opinions of you. A tradition of revenge arson, of "spite fires" in retaliation for real or perceived wrongs, also was part of the cultural baggage of the first settlers moving in from the Deep South. Nor were a man's fences his only vulnerable property. People accustomed to burning the woods recognized the conditions of low humidity and high wind in which woods fires turned destructive, and as novelist William Faulkner noted, the "barn burner" was a familiar class of southern outlaw.

The first lumbermen, many of them Yankees fresh from the white pine forests of Wisconsin and Minnesota, learned hard lessons about southern traditions of the open range, including those of burning the woods. Beneath the surface and behind the scenes, company land-use policies had to be adjusted to these social realities for almost a century.

In the spring of 1916, when scientific forestry in Texas was in its infancy, State Forester J. H. Foster notified Texas Forestry Association executives at a Houston meeting that more than half the total forest area of East Texas had been burned over within the past sixty days. Foster may have exaggerated a little, but not much. The same year, the Texas A&M forestry department published a research document that reported: "Most of Hardin County burns over annually. Fires are usually started by stockmen under the belief that grazing is improved and the custom meets with general approval."[31]

Presumably, the timber company men were not especially alarmed. During the cut-and-get-out era of lumbering along the Neches, timbermen regarded woods fires as little more than a nuisance. The open-stand virgin longleaf woods, the timbermen's prime target, were unharmed by the periodic fires that swept through them. In the cutover mixed pine-and-hardwood uplands, many virgin hardwoods left behind from the pine loggings suffered a fiery demise in the flames ignited by dried pine tops and other logging debris, but until around World War I the companies were only marginally interested in hardwoods. In any case, stockmen's fires had little effect on the companies' vast hardwood holdings in the river and creek bottoms.

The companies' early lack of concern about fires in their woods did not extend to fires in their sawmills. From first to last, companies like the 4-C Mill in Houston County, which practiced arbitrary or authoritarian policies toward their employees, were much troubled by spite fires in and around their mill towns. The sixteen-foot board fence that 4-C management erected to wall off employees from the nearby community of Ratcliff and force them to trade at the company store suffered repeated arson attacks, and other mysterious mill fires, some of them quite serious, plagued the 4-C. Sawmills were highly combustible workplaces, but—like southeastern Texas courthouses—they burned with suspicious frequency. In 1916, the same year that State Forester Foster addressed the Texas Forest Association, the *Gulf Coast Lumberman* reported that no less than seven lumber mill and lumberyard fires had occurred in East Texas in a single week. The biggest of these fires completely destroyed the 100,000-board-feet-a-day sawmill of the Carter-Kelly Lumber Company at Manning, on the edge of the Neches bottoms.[32]

By the 1930s, cutover lands along the Neches had become concentrated in the hands of a few large timber companies, and these companies joined the newly arrived U.S. Forest Service (USFS) and the Texas Forest Service in a concern for regeneration of the pine woodlands and the suppression of fires. Unlike the first-growth forest, the second-growth forest was vulnerable to fire, and such fires continued to sweep the woods. According to the Texas Forest Service, 6,211 fires burned 527,446 acres of East Texas woodlands in 1932, and most of these were deliberately set.[33] In and around the Davy Crockett, Angelina, Sam Houston, and Sabine national forests, young men of the Civilian Conservation Corps (CCC) labored for the Texas Forest Service at many tasks, most of which were related to the control of woods fires. In their time off from fighting forest fires, the CCC boys built fire roads, fire lookout towers, and fire communication networks. By 1939, the Jasper CCC Camp alone had logged 19,785 man-days in fire suppression.[34]

Despite all this effort, the free range remained in effect, and most of the traditional stockmen along the Neches still believed that "it's better country if you burn it off." They remained unconvinced about the need for fire prevention, and they increasingly resented innovative new policies of the lumber companies, the USFS, and the CCC—policies that, to their mind, threatened the open range. In 1937, for example, the USFS used CCC labor to build a 160-mile hog-proof fence around fifty thousand acres of the Angelina National Forest. The USFS hoped to encourage regeneration of pines by fencing out free-range livestock, especially hogs, but local stockmen were outraged by the actions of the "tree monkeys."[35] CCC boys also joined lumber company workers in a widespread new policy of deadening upland hardwoods to encourage the growth of pines. Traditional stockmen and hunters bitterly resented this innovation as well, believing that it ruined the open range for hogs, squirrels, and deer. Once angered, they turned to traditional retaliation; an ominous verse circulating during the 1930s warned:

> If you've got the money,
> We've got the time,
> You deaden the hardwoods
> And we'll burn the pine.[36]

Nor was the inflammatory poet speaking in jest. During World War II, rural southeastern Texans continued to set the woods on fire for all the old reasons, and timber companies, the USFS, and the Texas Forest Service redoubled their efforts to influence public opinion against the practice. Aware of southerners' respect for the Holy Scriptures, the USFS even published a document citing biblical "admonitions about stewardship of the land," and foresters handed it out in rural schools and carried it door to door across the countryside. Taken from Revelation 22:2, one text read, "In the midst of the street of it, on either side of the river, was there the tree of life, which bore twelve manner of fruits, and yielded her fruit every month: and the leaves of the tree were for the healing of the nations."[37] Having tried the Bible, in 1945 the USFS tried Smokey Bear, launching a much more successful public relations campaign against burning the woods. Gradually, the number of woods fires in the Neches counties declined, though the frequency of arson fires in the woods in these counties remained at around 60 percent, the highest in Texas.[38]

As the stock-law battles of the 1950s approached, the underlying dilemma of the timber companies, USFS officials, and other large landowners was very clear, if paradoxical. For a half century, they sought to answer one abiding question: how do we gain more control over our lands in order to reduce woods arson without arousing the ire of rural traditionalists and causing *more* woods arson? Especially for the timber companies, the horns of the dilemma, the rock and the hard place, seemed very close together. Nor did the problem decrease with time: conversion to selective harvesting practices in the 1950s and to even-aged forest management practices in the 1960s and 1970s made the timber lands of the companies and the national forests *more* vulnerable to arson rather than less. Large landowners moved very carefully, but at every stage of closing the woods—the coming of the stock law, perimeter fencing and stock leasing, the organization of hunting clubs, the assertion of game laws, and the end of using dogs to hunt for deer—some Neches Valley traditionalists set the woods on fire. The 1930s warning about deadening the hardwoods would be followed a half century later by others, equally explicit. "No dogs, no logs," one vowed. Another warned, "Where the dogs can't go, the pines won't grow."[39]

The process of closing the woods, of shutting down the traditional usufruct rights, moved at different speeds in different places along the Neches, but the general pattern was clear. First came the stock laws, then perimeter fencing of large properties for stock leasing, then hunting clubs, and then a protracted struggle to end hunting trespass and dog drives for deer. As game biologist Charles Boyd told me, "The hog wars came first, then came the dog wars." In this assertion he was broadly correct.[40]

To call the conflict over the stock law a "war" may have been a hyperbole, but it was only a slight exaggeration; ending the free range involved a great deal of social conflict. Avy Joe Havard's terse report on the stock-law fight in his neighborhood in Angelina County was typical: "We fought it hard as we could. They had some pretty close arguments about it—could of really gotten bad. None of my friends or neighbors didn't get killed or anything, but we got close to it."[41]

Gradually, between 1920 and 1950, anti-free-range factions in the counties along the Neches gained influence and votes. Townsmen had always disliked livestock wandering their city streets, and the nuisance had continued despite successive generations of municipal ordinances against it. Railroads, legally liable to the stockman for every hog or cow killed on their unfenced rights-of-way, were another old opponent, as were chamber of commerces and other civic boosters, which hated the "hick" image that free-range stock gave their locales. Editors of weekly newspapers in the county-seat towns also opposed the free range, as they had for decades, but most of them took care about what they said in their editorials. The stock law was the hottest issue in local politics, and rural editors usually preferred to limit themselves to factual coverage of upcoming stock-law elections, complete and gory accounts of every car-stock crash on county roads, and special columns on "improved" (fenced) pastures and the kinds of pure-bred livestock that could be raised only behind fences. Photos of prize-winning blooded bulls and boars filled the back pages of the *Jasper Newsboy*, the *Kountze News*, the *Tyler County Booster*, and the *Polk County Enterprise*—photos usually taken far away from rural southeastern Texas, however.

Progressive stockmen and farmers—or those who might have been such, had they dared—also waited to vote down the open range, and during the 1930s powerful allies joined them. The U.S. Forest Service, the Texas Forest Service, and the timber company foresters not only hated the stockmen's range fires but also loathed the roaming rooter hogs for their destruction of pine seedlings, and the USFS made early attempts to restrict the hogs from its timberlands. Another opponent of the free range was the Texas Game and Fish Commission, whose newly graduated research biologists well recognized the hog's impact on wildlife food sources. With the aid of federal funds, in 1940 the state game agency even had the nerve to build a seventeen-thousand-acre hog-proof fence around a portion of the Devil's Pocket in Newton County and to restock the area with deer. The fever tick eradication program of the Texas Sanitary Livestock Commission also affected free-range stockmen in the late 1930s. The repeated dipping of cattle, horses, and mules was compulsory—enforced, if necessary, by armed Texas Rangers—but the cost of hiring people to round up their stock forced a few small cattlemen to sell out. Most embittered stockmen just grumbled about "government interference" and stayed in business, but worse was soon to come. On the dirt highways of southeastern Texas, automobiles traveled faster and faster, and the conflict between woods stock and sixty-mph motorists increased in intensity.

After World War II, the major fight over the stock law began. Many young people who had left rural communities to join the service or to work in war plants did not return, thus weakening the free-range vote, and the failure of cotton prices to revive after the war drove others off the land. County-seat towns grew in population and prosperity during the late 1940s and early 1950s; as more and more people bought cars, more and more motorists came to resent stock on the highways. As stock-law supporters increased in number, election results grew closer and closer until finally, precinct by precinct and county by county, the opponents of the free range began to win.

State statutes governing the closing of the open range clearly favored those who wanted change, so stock-law forces had a variety of election strategies from which to choose. By 1953 stock elections were brought under two laws, one governing the vote for cattle and the other the vote for hogs and all other large domestic animals.[42] The mechanism for requiring a stock-law election was simple: at the petition of a small number of residents of a county or a subdivision of a county, the county commissioner's court was compelled to schedule an election in that jurisdiction. The election could be about cattle, hogs, or any of the other animals. Elections for cattle and elections for hogs had to be petitioned separately and held separately, but they could take place at the same time—the voter simply had to cast two ballots. Votes were by county or by county subdivision (normally the commissioner's precinct), depending on how the petition had been brought. If the stock law suffered a defeat in a jurisdiction, the process could be repeated and another election brought in that same jurisdiction after only a year had passed. A stock issue defeated in a countywide election could be brought immediately in any county subdivision.

Stock-law supporters could try a wide range of electoral strategies within the framework of these laws, and it seems remarkable that the free-range faction held them off as long as it did. The most common strategy of the stock-law forces was obvious—simply to hold elections over and over again until they wore down the resistance of the opposition. If the county-seat town was large enough to swamp the rural vote (as in the case of Lufkin in Angelina County), the stock law might be brought countywide. If it was too small to do this but large enough to swamp its precinct, then the vote might be brought in that precinct, with the expectation that the more rural precincts soon would follow, domino fashion. Sometimes, as in certain Hardin County precincts, a foot-in-the-door approach was used. Few people opposed a stock-law for horses and mules, so a vote on those animals might be brought first. Later, presumably after voters had accustomed themselves to the idea of a stock law, an election for cattle or hogs could be held.

The twists and turns of local stock-law fights were difficult even for participants to follow, let alone for historians working forty years later. Decisive votes often ended in a jumble of lawsuits, challenging election results. Several generalizations can be made, however. Although votes on hogs often were brought countywide, it was most common for votes on cattle to be fought precinct by precinct. Larger numbers of voters favored a stock law for hogs than favored a stock law for cows. Towns of any size invariably voted for the stock law. The presence of animals on the highways was the issue most important to voters and the press. Most precincts of most Neches counties had a stock law for hogs and cattle by 1960. Finally, once voters approved the stock law in a county or precinct, they never reversed their vote—this despite a clear legal procedure for doing so. Closing the free range proved a one-way process.[43]

Probably because of editorial caution, newspapers in the 1950s rarely communicated much of a real sense of the stock-law fights, with one notable exception. Galvanized into action by a local tragedy, editor Joe Lee Kirgan, Jr., of the *Polk County Enterprise*, took the lead in the stock-law battle in his county in 1957 and made the pages of his newspaper a forum for the opinions of both sides. As printed in the pages of the *Enterprise*, the conflicts between town and country, rich and poor, traditionalists and progressives—and the arguments each side used—were typical of other stock-law fights in southeastern Texas. In fact, they closely resembled the opposing sides and the public rhetoric in late-nineteenth-century stock-law battles reported from North Carolina and Georgia.[44]

The events of 1957 culminated the long struggle for a Polk County stock law. The previous countywide stock election had come three years before, in 1954. By that date, a number of earlier elections had already been held, and one or more commissioner's precincts on the western side of Polk County, the ones away from the Neches bottoms, already had hog laws. In 1954, stock-law forces tried once again, bringing two petitions for joint countywide hog and cattle elections in April of that year. At this time editor Kirgan remained carefully noncommittal on the issue, remarking only that although stock-law fights had proved bitterly divisive in surrounding counties, Polk County remained calm.[45] The editor printed letters for and against the stock law in the weeks leading up to the election, including a letter on April 1, 1954, from T. A. "Slim" Jones, of Angelina County, who argued that the stock law had been the ruination of his county. Supporters of the stock law in Angelina County had claimed it would eliminate road accidents, but with no stock on the highways to slow them down and keep them alert, Angelina County motorists were driving faster and faster. More accidents had occurred, rather than less. Moreover, Jones warned, if Polk County voted in the stock law, small farmers in that county would have to sell out, just as they had been forced to do in Angelina County. Jones hoped that Polk County voters would have enough sense to maintain "the benefits of the free range the Good Lord provided."

Two or three rebuttal letters to Jones followed in subsequent weekly editions of the *Enterprise,* and then, on April 15, the day before the stock election, a full-page advertisement with gory photos of dead cows and smashed automobiles appeared, paid for by "owners of small farms and the Stock Law Committee." Although the photos illustrated the townsmen's problem with the open range—stock on the highways— the text of the ad discussed small farmers' experiences with the dark side of "the so-called free range," as several of the accounts spoke of it. In the ad, local people complained about the dangers of free-range stock, about hogs smashing through fences to destroy crops, and about the "dumping" of stock in their area by desperate stockmen from nearby counties where the range was already closed. Most often and most vehemently, however, ad contributors complained about their free-range neighbors, who cut their fences, deliberately let stock into their fields, and—by stealing their animals—refused to let them take part in the "so-called open range." Otis Martone bitterly asserted, "People who think this so-called 'free range' helps the little farmer are wrong—we are not permitted to benefit by it and it is ruining us." Brown Stephens said, "I had to just quit and forget I had any woods hogs because I did not want to get into trouble over this 'free range.'" Wealthy absentee landlords Mr. and Mrs. W. E. Jacks complained:

There is no peace and harmony among the people who have range stock and hogs. Certain range stock and hog owners have told us to fix the fences to keep out their animals and at the same time these people would trespass on our fenced property and stated that if there was a fence where they wanted to go that they would just cut the wire. We have been afraid to have cattle on the range for the last 20 years because of the uncertainty of their welfare because of the "free-range" cattle owners.

How much these sad stories of free-range abuses and the images of blood and destruction on the highway influenced Polk County voters is impossible to say. In any case, on April 16, 1954, the stock law went down to defeat once again. In a county with around 3,000 registered voters, a large percentage of them went to the polls. The vote count was 933 for a stock law for cattle, 1,426 against; 1,109 for a stock law for hogs, 1,258 against. Even though the full-page ad had protested that this was not a town-versus-country issue, the election results followed this pattern: the precincts in the town of Livingston voted overwhelmingly for the stock laws; rural precincts overwhelmingly opposed them. Choosing his words carefully but with an undertone of regret, on April 22 editor Kirgan noted that the election had no effect on the preexisting hog laws in the western precincts, that Polk remained one of the "five or six" counties in Texas without a general stock law, and that there could not be another election for twelve months.

For two years, all was serene in Polk County. Then, on February 21, 1957, editor Kirgan thundered forth in a front-page editorial calling for a new stock-law election. Mary Jo Phillips Davis, Livingston High School valedictorian of the 1956 class, had recently been killed when her husband of seven months hit a cow on the Liberty highway. Kirgan noted: "We have heard many arguments to the need of a stock law and have yet to hear any argument which could uphold the open range as it is now. . . . All the stock on the roads cannot be worth the life of a human being. . . . Can Polk County continue to operate in the fashion of 30 or 40 years ago, or can we try to more or less modernize this county in line with our present civilization?"

In the next weekly edition of the *Enterprise* on February 28, letters from both sides of the stock issue tried to answer the editor's ringing question. Their words were harsh—the sort of language that in deep East Texas often presaged physical violence. The editor himself was somewhat subdued, holding his ground but denying that he was "trying to get anyone to leave his homestead." But the letter writers were not so restrained. Woody Amos, a newcomer to the county who was now leading the stock-law fight, wrote: "I want to say this now, we, the voters of Polk County, killed Mary Jo Phillips Davis, theoretically, back in April, 1954, when we failed to pass the stock law. . . . Now hear this, all that intend to vote against the stock law come to my home and I will take you to the parents of Mary Jo Phillips Davis and we will discuss it with them."

Mrs. Hobby Hendrix, writing in rebuttal to editor Kirgan's previous editorial, was equally on the attack.

There were a great many things in favor of an open range you did not mention. One of these things were that God gave the American people this great country of ours to use, not to be rented or bought or sold to a very few to use, which would certainly happen if we ever voted a stock law in our county. There's not one farmer out of ten who would have the money to lease land, much less to build fences that would hold cattle that had run free all their lives. No one but big farmers could do that, and you know what would happen then. Every little farmer would have to sell their own stock and when they do, that means they have lost their last chance of making any cash at all, unless they leave the farm as so many have to go to public works.

Most of the loose stock today belongs to the little farmer. The big farmer has his penned in his improved pastures. He can afford to do so . . . but the little farmer lives on the most meager living in the world. Oh, sure, they have all the farm produce that they raised in freezers, smoke houses and jars. But have you ever tried, dear editor, to eat peas, potatoes, meat, and other farm produce without a little salt, flour, coffee, and sugar to go with it? And do you know where they get their money to buy those little luxuries? Nine times out of ten they get it from selling one of those loose cows that seem to be bothering you so much.

Nor was this all Mrs. Hendrix had to say. She argued that a stock law in Polk County would finish the job of driving young people off the land, that old people trying to remain independent would not be able to buy medicine, that wrecks on the highway (like the Davis tragedy) were caused not by stock but by recklessness and speed, and that if the townspeople passed the stock law and ruined the countrypeople, the latter would refuse to buy the *Polk County Enterprise* or do business in Livingston.

After this spirited beginning, week by week the debate in the pages of the *Enterprise* grew ever more intense. When Woody Amos called an organizational meeting for the stock-law campaign, Mrs. Hendrix and other opponents showed up to heckle him. (One man rose from the audience to ask, "How fast was Davis's husband going when he hit that cow?")

In a letter on March 7, a free-range supporter evoked the Golden Role in a biblical question: "Some people say if a man is not able to keep his stock up he should not have it, but can we say this and, 'Love Thy Neighbor as Thyself'?" Apparently the question stung. Editor Kirgan responded:

> It seems the greatest criticism to the stock law is that it would keep the small farmer, many who don't even own or lease any land other than the ground their house is built on, from running stock on our "great open ranges." Have you ever stopped to think just whose open ranges your stock is feeding on? These letters say to consider your fellow man and to "Love thy neighbor as thy self." Can you say you are loving your neighbor when you let your stock loose and they get in his land to destroy all he has done toward improving his pastures?

Then the ingenuous editor shifted his attack. Opponents of the stock law claimed that speed, not hogs and cattle, caused wrecks on the highways, but he had visited the radar check station a few miles out of Livingston. Of 755 cars checked on this particular day, only 19 were traveling above the speed limit of sixty miles per hour.

At this time, the editor chose to ignore Mrs. Hendrix, who turned her considerable powers of description to Woody Amos, the point man, along with Kirgan, in the stock-law fight.

> Last night at the City Hall at Livingston, I heard a little man from the great city of Houston [Amos], who obviously didn't know which end of the cow to get the milk from, stand up and have the audacity to try and tell a farmer how to run his business, he told them he wanted them to be his friend, while he called them murderers, ignorant, selfish and fools. . . . He bragged about how educated he was. . . . He made no real point of his speech excepting to the tragedy he kept coming back to like a drowning man to a life raft. From his speech anyone would gather that the farmer has no rights at all, no right to the use of the taxes he helps to pay in, no rights even to use the highways to travel on. This little man would have you believe the farmer was a parasite to be gotten rid of in one way or the other. A farmer that was not needed in the growth of the city, and its pretty plain who is pushing this little man.
>
> Its the big farmer who had every acre he can possibly fence and can't stand the sight of the "dirt farmer," as he called him, "with a few head of cows." Its the man who wants to use the highway as a racetrack every time he gets on it. And perhaps its someone like the little man we heard last night, who wants his name before the public and doesn't have anything to do but stir up trouble.

Here, as before, Mrs. Hendrix threatened an economic boycott of Livingston merchants if the stock law passed. A week later, on March 14,

Amos responded that he already had more than enough signatures on his petitions to require the stock-law elections. He noted: "Those who threaten reprisal against the businessmen were like a snake in a bed of coals, striking everything in reach, whether they be to blame or not. Let us all use this wonderful freedom to voice our convictions at the polls without any fear from the talk of a very few."

Beneath the level of the major debate, less strident voices spoke out for and against the stock law, some even advocating compromise. One man suggested building fences along the roads and leaving the rest of the range open. Another man, who had grown up in a "renter family" in a stock-law county where landowners would not let tenants have more than one or two milk cows, pleaded: "There are thousands and thousands of little children coming up that may need the range ten times more than we do. Please think of someone beside yourself. When I am dead and gone the young people can't blame me for voting such a rotten thing as that on them."

In the last April edition of the *Enterprise* (the stock-law election had been set for May 18), Mrs. Hobby Hendrix renewed her assault on Woody Amos and the stock law in another long letter. Amos clearly did not care how many Livingston businesses he hurt, she said. "It could be the Insurance and Railroad companies that are pushing this law, and there are some big stockmen who would like to get rid of the little rancher so they could corner the beef market and at their own prices." Then she lectured Amos at length on the nature of the East Texas range and the necessity for stock to wander far and wide. She assured him, "The country people are also thankful for the secret ballot your Wandering Boy spoke of, not because they are afraid or ashamed of the way they vote either." She added: "We have a wonderful country that has offered freedom to everyone in it . . . but every time we vote a restraining law like this, it shortens that freedom a little more. In this case, no longer will people be able to fish and hunt for free like they have since the days of the pilgrims. Eventually all the land will be fenced and posted and there won't even be a place to get off the highway without permission from the owner."

By this time, however, editor Kirgan apparently had heard enough from Mrs. Hendrix. Chivalry was dead. In the same issue in which her letter appeared (April 28), he launched a devastating counterattack. Mrs. Hendrix had claimed that the free-range stockmen were being treated unfairly because they paid their county taxes and now were being ignored. However, Kirgan had checked the tax records open to the public in the county clerk's office and had found that the biggest free-range stockmen in the county declared "very few head for county tax purposes!" Then Kirgan lectured Mrs. Hendrix on the issue of patriotism:

> Laws are made to protect the majority of the people of the country. The same may be said of the stock law. And as far as your statement "And wouldn't it be better to take a little from those that have, than all from those that have not?" I'm sure you don't mean that, since you will find the basic point in Marxism (better known as communism) that this is practically their whole belief, and certainly neither you nor I nor anyone else wants a taste of communism in this fine country.

That these words were a palpable hit may be assumed. During the remaining six weeks of acrimonious debate in the pages of the *Polk County Enterprise*, Mrs. Hobby Hendrix contributed no more letters.

Others took up their pens in defense of the free range, however. Mr. and Mrs. T. L. Hammond warned on May 2 that the stock law would be the end of "the freedom of God's great out-of-doors" in Polk County.

> This is God's country and we have a right to enjoy the freedom of the thousands of acres of lush grass and underbrush that was put here for our stock, for our benefit. Open your Bible to Genesis 1:30: "And to every beast of the earth and to every fowl of the air and to everything that creepeth upon the earth, wherein there is life, I have given every green herb for meat, and it is so." And read Psalms 50:10, "For every beast of the forest is mine and the cattle of a thousand hills."

It was perhaps not accidental that the editorial filler immediately following the Hammonds' biblical justifications for the open range read: "When filled with hot water, a thick glass will crack more quickly than a thin one." In any case, one week later on May 9 a theological counterassault occurred, this time from James L. D. Celestine, who observed:

> There were people who quote scriptures to prove that their livestock were given freedom and right by God to run loose as they please. I consulted the Bible, but I could not find where God had sanctioned that . . . "every beast . . . every fowl . . . and everything that creepeth upon the earth . . . " would have dominion over man. Rather it is stated that they must be under man's dominion! Therefore I feel that we, the citizens of Polk County ought to control our livestock.

Two weeks before the fateful May 18 election, either stock-law opponents ceased to submit letters to the *Enterprise* or, as seems more likely, editor Kirgan ceased to publish them. Kirgan's own editorials reiterated all his earlier arguments for the stock law and once again tarred the free-rangers with the brush of Marxism-Leninism. "America was not founded on this belief," Kirgan asserted, "for which we thank the Lord."

Reported in the *Enterprise* on May 2, another event played into the hands of stock-law forces. Perhaps brought to the surface by the furious debate over the stock law, an old quarrel over free-range hogs erupted in the Midway community. After brooding over some ancient disagreement for decades, T. A. "Red" Butler and Henry Lamb settled the matter with shotguns at thirty yards. Lamb shot from his house, Butler from his pickup. Both were hit by buckshot. With one arm broken, Lamb staggered out to the immobilized Butler and administered the coup de grace—a .22 bullet through the head.

How much this killing affected the election results cannot be known, but it may have been critical. On May 18, 1957, voters approved stock laws for hogs and cattle in Polk County by narrow margins. With almost 2,000 votes cast, the cattle law passed by only 105 votes and the hog law by 262. The vote split along town-country lines, as it had in 1954. Immediately after the election, the pages of the *Polk County Enterprise* returned to their erstwhile calm, and editor Joe Kirgan had nothing more to say about the stock law. On June 20, the paper matter-of-factly reported that diehard supporters of the free range had just rallied by the hundreds on the courthouse lawn in Livingston, had hired lawyers, and had launched a lawsuit to declare the election null and void. Like most similar lawsuits contesting stock-law elections on technical grounds, this one lingered in the courts, was delayed, and finally was dismissed. Authorities pronounced that the Polk County free range was to be closed. Late in 1957 came a final irony; the *Enterprise* headlined, "W. W. Amos and Family Escape Injury as Auto, Cows Collide." Two cows were killed in the accident, and the president of the Polk County Stock Law Association insisted that he had been traveling only forty-five to fifty miles per hour.

It would be wrong to think that immediately after the stock-law passed, southeastern Texans rushed out and began building perimeter fences. Doubtless this happened in some places, but not many; in most rural neighborhoods along the Neches, landowners still had to be concerned about the attitudes of their neighbors and the possibilities of property destruction and forest arson. The stock-law crept discreetly into rural precincts, rather than arriving with a blare of trumpets. Five years after a successful stock-law election, Jasper County had only one major perimeter fence.

Stock on the highway was a different matter, however. Most county sheriffs' offices immediately hired special "stock deputies" to catch and impound stock on the public roads, and the state legislature soon passed its closest approximation to a statewide stock law to aid in this process. Beginning in 1959, owners could be fined two hundred dollars a day for every one of their animals found wandering loose on Texas highways.[46]

Yet for years, perhaps for a decade or more in some places, the stock deputies did not intrude overmuch in the affairs of the Neches Valley stockmen-farmers. Animals in the deep bottoms wandered far from roads and the eyes of townsmen, and overzealous enforcement of the stock law (and the game law) was a good way to lose one's reelection for sheriff. Even law-abiding Babe McGalin continued to run hogs and cattle in the Neches bottom for a considerable period after the 1954 passage of the Jasper County stock law, removing them only after hunting club members began to complain. In Hardin County, Dudley Denmon long ignored the stock law and the letters from various lumber companies telling him to remove his hogs from their woods. Denmon marked 120 pigs in 1960, the last year he worked his hogs, then gave up. He simply could not get them out, and now it meant trespassing to try to do so. Many of his estimated fifteen hundred hogs remained in the timber companies' new hunting leases along the Neches to be shot by members. In 1986 the irascible Denmon still bristled at any talk about "wild hogs." They were not wild hogs but his hogs, descended across many generations from the "runty pig" he had snatched from under the nose of the "biting sow" in his grandfather's hog pen. Hard-working Avy Joe Havard labored for months after the Angelina County stock law to remove his hogs, but even he could not find all of them. Like Dudley Denmon, many men resented leaving "their seed in the woods" and felt cheated. As Claude Welch told me, "There's been many a hog killed in the Ryan Lake Club, my friend, belongs to the Sanfords!"[47]

Before and after the coming of the stock law, rural practitioners of the old usufruct rights—users of the open woods—regarded perimeter fences with loathing, and almost every early attempt to fence a major property along the Neches Valley resulted in a local fence war. Stories about fences completed on one day, then cut between every post for miles (or burned, or ruined with acid, etc.) the following night, were told all along the Neches. Arson was the easiest way to reestablish the free range, but most early fence-builders recognized the fire danger and used fire-resistant fence posts of lighter pine when they built their barbed-wire fences. Strangely, the resin-rich pine posts burned and charred on the outside when the fire came through, then self-extinguished, leaving the fence intact.

Far more common than the grand gesture of miles of fence destroyed in one night was the casual cutting of fence wires by passing woodsmen. For years, rural landowners spent much time mending fences. Disregarding the state's stringent fence law, which had made fence cutting a felony in 1884, many rural people carried wire cutters with them as they moved about the woods and cut fences as needed—both for convenience and for a political statement. A traveler on his way to the river might even cut a fence at one point on his way in and at another, a hundred yards away, on his way out. Other trespassers commonly used the fence gaps.

At various places and times across several decades, Neches Valley fence conflicts teetered on the edge of actual violence, sometimes going over the brink. Fence cutters were difficult to catch in the deep woods and thickets of southeastern Texas, but sometimes people informed on them. Pasture rider Charlie Harber told the following story from his personal experience:

> They organized Pine Island [Hunting Club], and they put a fence around it to keep people out of there, but they cut the wire practically between every post after they fenced it. I want you to know, they done a job on that fence! And there was a fellow by the name of Grimes that went to the penitentiary over that. When he got out, they said it was the Harrisons in this Reddtown community that turned him in for cutting that fence. He ended up killing "Cricket" Harrison. He come along and found him and shot him through the door of his pickup. He killed him right at my house in Cochino Creek bottom over there; I heard him when he shot him.[48]

Charlie Harber began his career as pasture rider in 1937 at Boggy Slough Hunting Club, the scene of the first big perimeter fence in that part of the Neches Valley, as noted earlier. Sometime in the early 1920s, Southern Pine Lumber Company in Diboll decided to launch a massive stock operation in the Neches bottoms of Trinity and Houston counties. Boxcar-loads of wire fence soon were rolling in on the company railroad, and hundreds of men began stringing fence around three sides of a 37,000-acre property, with the river as the eastern boundary. The Boggy Slough fence was like no other that local people had ever seen; it was, as the saying went, "boar-proof and bull-strong." Soon, many families who owned small properties along the river found themselves cut off to the west by the Southern Pine's fencing. Frank Ashby, who lived in the area and knew many of these people, told their side of what happened next:

> They built ever one of them people who lived in there an eight-foot lane out to Druso, where the mail route was. They built em all an eight-foot lane and come by and told em, "You get your hogs and

your cattle off my land, and don't go the river, you're trespassing." Well, shit! There old man John Wells was with five hundred head of hogs and cattle and 180 acres of land, he didn't have nowhere to put all that. They cut that damn fence for ten or twelve miles, I don't know, old man John never did tell me how far. I know he's into it. They cut it between every post, all night, I reckon. And he said that damn bunch didn't buy no new wire. They went there and tied every damn place—had hard men out there tying that wire—three or four be tying wire and another standing out there with a .30-30 rifle. And old man John Wells said, "Hell it's time to go, I got to go somewhere!" He sold that 180 acres for four dollars and a quarter an acre, and he was glad to get that. He got his cows out, but the hogs, they just kept em. Wadn't no way—they just give em so long. He couldn't go in there and pen all them hogs and haul em out in a wagon. And that's the reason that Diboll had so much trouble; these people, like old man John Wells, hell, he'd kill a hog in a minute if he seen one, cause he left five hundred head over there.[49]

Others maintained that Southern Pine properly compensated local farmers for their lands and "hog claims" in the woods. In any case, Boggy Slough soon reintroduced deer to the Neches bottoms and began the first large-scale private attempt to build up the deer herds. Local people like John Wells and Frank Ashby, still brooding over the perimeter fence and the original land deals, now had other reasons to challenge Boggy Slough. Small wonder, then, that when Charlie Harber's uncle first began working there as a pasture rider in 1925, "they put ever one of their riders with a .30-30 on his saddle and a six-shooter on his hip, and they told him, 'You protect this thing!'"[50]

Some of the poachers who put a carbide light on their heads and began to challenge the pasture riders by night-hunting on Boggy Slough had not seen a deer until they were grown men. In the period around World War I, recognizing that deer were fast disappearing, some of the river-bottom strain limited their deer hunting to certain months of the year, joined "buck clubs" and resolved to kill only buck deer, or quit hunting altogether to preserve local "seed stocks." As usual, none of these self-imposed conservation measures had much to do with the state game laws. Other hunters did not stop hunting, however, and they pursued East Texas deer to virtual extinction. Around 1916, as Charlie Havard recalled: "There was a little bunch of deer in here, and they got to running em with hounds. They killed all of em. Then there were thirty years you didn't see a deer track in this country. If there was ary of em in here nobody didn't know it." Farther north along the Neches Valley, things were the same; the hunt for the last deer (and bear and turkeys) had been relentless. "They believed in killing whatever they could see," Charlie Harber said. "Them old farmers, if they found a deer track, it may take em two days with three packs of hounds, but they killed it. That's what happened to the deer." Game warden Walter Kirby, a country boy himself, added: "I don't think they realized where they come from or what a gift they'd had, because they would ride the roads on the fenders and look for tracks, and then when they found a track would set the dogs out—total destruction." Small wonder, then, that when young Claude Welch saw some strange animals released from a boxcar on Southern Pine lands around 1930, he did not know what they were. Welch had "roamed the woods like a squirrel" all his life but had to ask his uncle, "What is them things, Uncle Jim?" "Them's deer," the older man told him.[51]

Big timber companies like Southern Pine (later, Temple-Eastex and Temple-Inland) owned most of the property along the Neches Valley, and changes in company land-use policies largely determined each stage of the long conflict over closing the woods. Although local companies assured the editor of the *Jasper Newsboy*, on the eve of the Jasper County stock-law vote, that they had no interest in fencing their lands, timber interests commonly worked behind the scenes for the stock law. Most stockmen knew or suspected this. Avy Joe Havard explained, matter-of-factly, "The companies like Southern Pine and Carter, they's the two biggest companies right in here, then, they got all their employees to vote for it, and they passed it."[52]

After the dust had settled from the stock-law elections and tempers had cooled, Southern Pine, Carter, and Kirby began leasing their lands to stockmen for ten or fifteen cents an acre. Avy Joe Havard struck such a deal with the local companies, sharing with them the expense of perimeter fences and building many miles of internal cattle fencing at his own cost. Hogmen to the end, he and his neighbors tried to stay in the hog business and spent thousands of dollars on experimental "electric hog fences," all to no avail. Too many creeks and sloughs cut the Neches bottoms, and the wily rooter hog proved resistant to fencing in—even with electricity.[53]

Small stockmen could not join in the big company leases, so they sold their animals (the ones they could catch) or—at least for a time—dumped them in nearby free-range areas or let them run on company land unmarked. However, the free range was dead, and local stockmen like Avy Joe Havard, who were paying hard money for the privilege of pasturing their animals, pressured these men to get off the company pastures. Neighborly love was no longer the rule. As Havard explained: "There was some that give us a little trouble in there. They'd come in there with bad dogs that didn't work hogs regularly, and man, you'd find hogs with their heads tore up and their ears all off. Absolutely just eat up! And we'd tell em, 'Now, listen. You keep that dog out of here. The next time I find him in here, I'm gonna put a bullet between his eyes!' My brother and me, we didn't try to be tough, but we was."[54] Clearly, this was not free-range talk; the days of the old cooperation had ended.

As time passed, and depending on how nervous companies were about fire in the woods, hunting clubs grew up from these first stock leases. Sometimes the companies required the stockmen to pay a few cents more an acre to acquire hunting as well as grazing rights, and then the stockmen subleased to hunters. Sometimes companies leased separately to stockmen and hunters—a practice that often caused squabbles between the two groups. In the early days, it was easier to give the stockmen predominance. Dollarhide Hunting Club shared thousands of acres of Temple company lands with Avy Joe Havard and his brother, but the Havards had legal power over all the hunting.

The coming of hunting clubs triggered the dog and deer wars, the last great conflict between traditionalists and modernists over the old usufruct rights of the southern open range, but the real battle did not begin until the deer returned. With the aid of the Texas Game and Fish Commission, seed stocks of deer were reintroduced to the Boggy Slough Club on Southern Pine lands, to other Temple clubs, and later to other private pastures. Soon the deer flourished and began to spread north and south along the Neches bottoms. Adjacent to the Neches counties, state game preserves reintroduced deer to the Devil's Pocket of Newton County in 1940 and the Moore Plantation in the Sabine National Forest in 1950. In the estimate of game biologist Charles Boyd, the state released more than five thousand southern and western Texas deer in East Texas between 1938 and 1967.[55]

Simply releasing deer was not enough, however. Like the administrators of Boggy Slough, who issued rifles and pistols to the pasture riders, state game officials knew they had to defend the deer—night and day. During the 1950s, as rural school closings and stock laws destroyed the cultural underpinnings of the old subsistence way of life, rural traditionalists asserted open-range hunting rights with increased intensity. Perhaps this was a kind of compensation for what was being lost; certainly it involved elements of revenge. Some rural people heeded biologists' pleadings to allow the deer to reestablish themselves and spread, but many did not. Practically from the day the first deer jumped from the first boxcar at Boggy Slough Club, local hunters polished the brass reflectors of their carbide head lamps and took shotguns from the wall.

Many rural people saw the game preserves and hunting clubs as the final assertion of the power of rich townsmen (aided and abetted by the government) over the traditional rights of countrymen, and their appetite for venison (certainly very strong during the 1930s depression) was whetted by a taste for revenge. Pasture rider Charlie Harber, who had been born and raised in and around Boggy Slough, described their attitudes:

> This hunting club we're setting in now [Eason Lake Club, just down river from Boggy Slough], it started out there was only fifteen members in this club. It's like Boggy Slough, see, all them old farmers that was raised over there had to move out after they bought that thing. That just ruined their hunting. They had no place to hunt. They taken all of the river bottom from down here way up in Houston County. And back years ago, these people outside of these clubs they brought their children up, "Son, if you see something, kill it. These rich people have the priority on all of this game, so if you can slip in there and kill something, do it."[56]

At Boggy Slough, Eason Lake, and hunting clubs all up and down the Neches, the sons obeyed, and since poachers and pasture riders both were armed, many dangerous confrontations occurred. Charlie Harber was standing beside another man on a road one night when a rifle bullet passed between them from behind and struck up sparks from the concrete. Under the circumstances, this was an attempt not to frighten but to kill. Many men poached on the 37,000-acre Boggy Slough Club, but two of the most determined were brothers Warren and Cole James. One night, pasture riders and game wardens shot Warren James to death as he walked a tramway with another hunter, and the differing accounts of what happened that night revealed how polarized the countryside had become. There was no middle ground in the interpretations. Depending on whom one spoke to, James was "a rough man, but a good man," who was determined to assert the traditional hunting rights of his people, or he was a sociopathic outlaw, a man who had killed his father-in-law and who was accustomed to beating his wife and bootlegging whiskey on the courthouse square in Groveton. As in the case of many other such incidents, accounts also disagreed about who shot first, the agents of the game law or the poachers. In the end, the result was the same: Warren James lay dead, "nine buckshot between his chin and his navel," and the tree behind which the game wardens had hidden was so scarred with buckshot that "it look like it'd been pecked by a red-headed pecker wood."[57]

Nor would James be the only casualty of the southeastern Texas deer and dog wars. A considerable number of other people were shot or killed over the years on both sides of the conflict. Several "type 1 wildlife areas" later were named for murdered game officers, and when Charles Boyd retired in 1992, he confessed, "I'm glad one didn't end up named after me."[58] For some years during Boyd's earlier career, getting shot had been a distinct possibility. Several wardens told me they survived only because they had been outlaw hunters themselves in their early days and knew how such people thought and acted. Boyd himself credited his survival as defender of the Moore Plantation game preserve in the early 1950s to previous military training. He had been a member of the elite force readied to strike inland to release American POWs from Japanese prison camps on the eve of the invasion of Japan, and this training—never used in Japan—came in handy in Sabine County.

Early game wardens like Enoch Jones, who took part in the Boggy Slough shooting, were lonely, marked men, responsible for enforcing the game law in an unrealistic array of East Texas counties. Only a few of them were as combative as Jones. When his son contemplated getting into law enforcement work, Jones advised, "Don't attempt to arrest a man unless you are legally right, but if you start to arrest him, arrest him or die." Jones never went around in uniform, since that made him even more of a "walking target." On weekends, he patrolled the countryside chauffeured by his son, who also got out of the car to open pasture gates, leaving Jones free to watch out for ambushers.[59]

Most wardens took a more moderate approach, trying to make friends and educate the public about the value of the game law. For decades, this was a hard sell. Wardens newly assigned to southeastern Texas soon discovered (if they had not known these things already) that a great many rural people did not obey the game law, that the ones who might have cooperated with the lawmen were afraid of the outlaws, that the sheriff's office wanted nothing to do with the unpopular wardens, and that the justice of the peace courts—game violations were misdemeanors—usually would not convict. The newly arrived warden had a choice. He could go to war with the traditional hunters and fishermen, or he could take a more pedagogic approach, trying to change people's attitudes and to catch the occasional violator whom local justice of the peace courts would convict—for example, someone from outside the county who was poaching on local territory.

When Larry Williford was growing up in Polk County, the local warden used the educational strategy, paying special attention to Larry's uncle, Zack Williford, the ringleader of the family clan of outlaw hunters. After many friendly visits from this warden, Zack Williford informed his family: "You know, you have a hard time going behind a man's back that'll get on the front porch with you and talk to you and crawl on that bench [at the eating table] with you and eat peas and cornbread with you. I'll tell you fellows, he's just talked me into quitting." Then Williford went around to his erstwhile followers among the family's younger males and gave them fair warning: "I've decided that I'm gonna stop outlaw hunting. We're not gonna have anything if I don't. Y'all can if you want to, but you need to know that from this day forward I'll turn you in if I know about it." According to Larry Williford, about half the family followed his Uncle Zack and observed the game laws, and about half did not, "but, till the day he died, the ones that didn't change, they hid from him more than they did the game warden."[60]

After Billy Platt came to his first assignment as game warden in Jasper County in 1963, he combined the hard-nosed approach with a more conciliatory one. Platt had been an outlaw hunter himself until he "made the turn" at age thirty, so he well understood the problems he faced. He reported: "When I went to work, I had two people in the county that wanted me at their place. One was Mr. Withers at Buna and one was the Garlingtons up here where they had a big shoot-out over dogs, and they killed one and both the boys got shot up bad. I could drive up to a house and stop and meet the people, and they'd start looking down the road, hoping someone wouldn't come by and see me standing in his front yard talking to him."[61]

Elsewhere, in an adjacent county, people refused to sit on the same church pew with the warden's wife and child. After a while, however, Platt began to make some progress. He successfully befriended Link Garlington, one of the most zealous outlaw hunters in the county and—like Zack Williford—a role model for the younger generation. Garlington and his friends at least cut back on their outlawry. This was no small achievement. Link Garlington lived in an old dogtrot house. "[It] had all the walls completely covered with deer horns—I'm talking about with velvet on em, killed in the summer, you know." While Billy was still in game warden school, Garlington had pulled a gun on a Sabine County game officer and told him, "I've always wanted to kill a game warden."[62]

Platt also used a hard-nosed approach to game-law violators. If a man wanted a fistfight when Platt tried to arrest him, Billy accommodated him. After one of these affairs with a man from the Buna area, an informant told Platt, "You better not go back down to that Buna country for a while—they gonna kill you, they gonna bushwhack you." But Platt went on about his business. Recognizing that the justice of the peace courts would not convict local game-law violators even in the presence of conclusive evidence, Platt made sure that many of the outlaws nonetheless spent an unpleasant night in the Jasper County jail. Platt said: "It worried a lot of em. It was harassment, but it was legal harassment; it was the only thing I could do."[63]

Even this ended soon after Aubrey Cole became sheriff. Now when Platt carried "an old night-hunter" into the courthouse, the "dispatcher would give him a blank bond form and say get it signed and bring it back tomorrow." Platt noted, "That violator would beat me down the steps while I was filling out the paperwork." Cole was an old enemy of Platt's: he was the first man Platt had caught illegally hunting deer. The traditional hunters were his political constituency. Soon after Cole was elected sheriff, Platt went to him and suggested a reconciliation: "You've got a badge on, you fixing to put a gun on, you fixing to see a different side of life out here. Any way I can help you, all you got to do is pick up a radio and call me; I'll be there any way I can. Let bygones be bygones." Although noncommittal at the time, Cole did not accept Platt's offer, nor can he entirely be blamed. A political alliance with the local game warden was not a good idea for a Neches Valley sheriff. Cole's predecessor in the sheriff's office, R. C. Pace, had been no friend of the game laws (Platt once had caught *him* outlaw hunting), but Pace at least took a neutral position regarding the wardens. Now, however, things changed. The sheriff's office stopped relaying game-law calls to the wardens' radios. In fact, Cole's chief deputy called Billy Platt one day and told him the county needed the radio units back from the wardens' cars.[64]

If relationships with the sheriff's office deteriorated over Billy Platt's years in Jasper County, relationships with rural communities and the timber companies improved. During the late 1960s and early 1970s, more local people—most of them former traditional hunters like Zack Williford—decided that the best way to bring back the game and continue to enjoy their sport was to lease lands from the companies as hunting clubs.

The timber companies had their own complicated reasons for issuing hunting leases, and only some of these reasons had to do with bringing back the game. In the beginning, companies like Kirby, Carter, or Southern Pine leased their lands to clubs for only a few cents per acre a year. Their main payoff came from improved public relations and increased control of their lands. When a company set up a hunting club, it influenced local opinion in favor of full common-law property rights over land and recruited another body of local people to serve as a countervailing force against the trespassers, traditional hunters, and fence cutters, who refused to recognize the company's exclusive rights to its land. At the very least, the company got a group of locals who would watch out for arsonists and outlaws—people who, if less well disposed, might have engaged in arson and outlawry themselves. However, as always, the key question for a company was this: will we gain more in long-term control of our lands (decreases in trespass, vandalism, and forest arson) than we will lose in retaliatory, short-term increases in trespass, vandalism, and forest arson?

These sometimes difficult cost-benefit decisions continued into the late 1980s, when many companies chose to lease their last "outlaw zones"—previously unleasable areas still dominated by diehard traditional hunters—to the Texas Parks and Wildlife Department as "type 2" public hunting lands, open to the general public for thirty-five dollars a year. Hunting with dogs, long a thorn in the companies' sides, was forbidden in type 2 areas. In 1988, as they had in 1938 when the companies deadened the hardwoods, some forest arsonists struck back. "No dogs, no logs" was spray-painted on company buildings, and letters warned, "Where the dogs can't go, the pines won't grow." The poets were not joking.[65]

During the early 1960s, Champion Lumber Company leased its first tracts to hunting clubs. Q. R. King and his fellow dog hunters got the second lease in Polk County, and King sarcastically noted that "Mother Champion's" policy was to lease one tract, wait to see how much of its woods burned up, and then lease another.[66] Other companies did the same, especially as the deer population increased and membership in hunting clubs became more and more desirable. By the 1980s, tracts that had leased for a token amount or for a few cents an acre in decades past were now worth several dollars an acre a year. As one man explained, "Deer had become a commodity."[67] Nor did leasing lands to hunting clubs in any way cramp companies' modern silvicultural practices. In fact, it turned out that deer rather liked "clear-cuts."

Certain pioneer leasing arrangements showed the way to other companies but were in part cautionary tales. Temple pioneered the hunting club concept at Eason Lake Club in 1928 and at other places, but the company had its share of trouble with traditional users of the open woods. In 1956, in one epic experiment, the East Texas Pulp and Paper Company in Evadale leased a 40,000-acre tract of the Neches bottoms in Tyler, Hardin, and Jasper counties to an organization of reformed outlaw hunters called the East Texas Wildlife Conservation Association. The association leased the enormous tract for one dollar a year but agreed to reestablish and protect the game, to see that all state and national game laws were obeyed, and to recruit no more than four hundred members.[68] The company's motive was simple—to try to gain more control over its land—but many local hunters reacted predictably. Once again, arguments that the protected deer herd soon would multiply and spread to surrounding areas fell on deaf ears. Many locals were more concerned with this "clubbing up" of the open woods, and they found the annual fee of twenty-five dollars not just an affront to their pocketbooks but a violation of their "Indian rights."

One man bluntly told a game warden, "God put em out there for people to eat and I'm gonna eat em!" As at Boggy Slough, armed pasture riders hired by the East Texas Wildlife Conservation Association prowled the bottoms night and day, trying to protect the deer, and the usual confrontations with poachers occurred. One Associated Press news story stated: "The threat of a backwoods war over hunting grounds is hanging over East Texas like a blanket of fog. The old-timers of Orange, Newton, Jasper and Hardin Counties, with threats of woods fires and fence cutting their only weapon, are bitterly opposed to organizations trying to bring game conservation into these piney woods. They can see this only one way: There is a move underway to steal their hunting grounds."[69]

Howard Hargrove, the president of the East Texas Wildlife Conservation Association and the guiding will behind its activities, was harassed, beaten up, and threatened, but he persevered until the battle was essentially won. Then, riven by internal squabbles, the club disbanded into several smaller clubs. It seems dubious that either Hargrove or the Evadale papermill had fully recognized how much trouble would result. One day in the late 1950s, hogman Dudley Denmon, of Hardin County, having been politely requested to remove his illegal swine from the association's lease, paid a visit to Hargrove at association headquarters. The long-suffering president must have had many such visitors.

The president of that outfit told me, "Denmon, you ain't going in them woods." I said, "Boy, don't you be telling me what I'm gonna do. I'll come around there and get you." I said, "You want my damn hogs? I'll get you, boy!" And I went after him, and he went in a room and locked the door and his damn little secretary went under the desk, and his goddamn game wardens, his pistol haulers, all went outside. Right down there in Hardin County I told him, I said, "You ain't gonna tell me what I ain't gonna do. By God, I'm a true-blooded American!"[70]

A lot of men along the Neches got just as mad as Dudley Denmon, and once again, the issue involved more than stock or hunting rights. Step by step—with the passage of the stock laws, the coming of fences, the enforcement of the game laws, and the organization of the bottoms into hunting clubs—agents of the twentieth century destroyed the old subsistence lifeway. This left a legacy of bitterness, which ended up directed at fence builders and hunting clubs and led to many local conflicts during the 1960s, 1970s, and 1980s. As the country "fenced up and clubbed up," deer populations increased even more, and at hundreds of hunting clubs up and down the Neches, night-hunters and dog hunters redoubled their attack.

In southern Angelina County, Charlie Havard, respected leader of the Bellview community, strapped a carbide lamp to his forehead and led his sons on nighttime forays into the "papermill pasture." The Havards often walked many miles and stayed out all night, returning in the first light of morning with the deer they had killed. Taking pride in the fact that nothing was wasted, they kept what they could use as "frying meat" and distributed the rest to the neighbors.[71] Elsewhere in the Bellview community, other night-hunters struck deep into the lands of private hunting club owner William Crain, a man embroiled in a bitter feud with his outlaw hunting neighbors. Crain's woods and pastures were the traditional hunting grounds of the community, and some of the night poachers knew the landscape as well as he did. They timed their expedition to coincide with the rise of the moon, because most felt that the very best time to headlight deer was from moonrise to the first hour after moonrise. After killing a deer, the poacher "laced him up" to carry out. The deer was gutted, its head was cut off, the "leaders was split right behind each leg," then the deer's right back hoof was thrust through its left foreleg and its left back hoof through its right foreleg. At that point the deer could be put on rather like a backpack, its crossed legs under the hunter's chin serving as a handy gun rack. Then the night poacher packed the deer out, sometimes for miles. One man, who wished to remain anonymous, said: "I've toted em till sweat would be sloshing in my shoes and knowed if I laid him down I couldn't pick him up. But I never killed one and left him there, not one in my life."[72]

Some poachers attacked by land, some by water. Farther upriver along the Neches, waterborne night-hunters slipping in from the Highway 7 road crossing plagued the Pine Island Club. Located on a large island created by one of the major "old river and new river" splits, the club provoked local woodsmen by attempting to bar access to the Old River side. Pine Island Club cut down trees across the Neches channel called Old River, blocked it with a steel cable, and ultimately built a low dam. After one man offered to "get a power saw some night and throw some of them thousand-foot pines in there to really block the river," the club hastily removed the trees. Later, local outlaws cut the cable, towed it upstream, and sunk it to the bottom of the river. One man in 1992 recounted an elaborate scheme to do something equally drastic to the Pine Island dam. A fisherman who had his hoop net cut up in Old River across from a club member's camp gave the man a traditional southern warning: "If that net comes up with another hole in it, there ain't no need of you going down to that damn camp house, cause there ain't gonna be no camp house down there. I'll pile them damn pine knots around it and set it afire."

Conflict over fishing access triggered poachers' night attacks by motorboat—or, at least, so they said. Local men slowly cruised the river at night, watching for the reflection of deer's eyes on the bank. Pine Island Club was on the east bank of the Neches, Boggy Slough Club was on the west, and poachers commonly struck at both. Ordinarily, one hunter operated the boat while the other sat in a raised seat or stood on a small stepladder and scanned the banks with his light. Hunters used the classic poacher's weapon, a .22 with a large, light-gathering rifle scope, and tried to hit the deer between the eyes. The hunting method was efficient, and the river poachers were virtually impossible to catch. One man said: "I killed many of em with a .22, don't let anybody kid you. I got an old J. C. Higgins out there that holds twenty-five shorts, and I got a three-quarter-ton Ford truck out there that wouldn't haul or drag all the deer I killed with that." When the pasture riders and game wardens began to "harass him," this man pointed out to one of the riders that things could get a lot worse if they did not back off.

He [the pasture rider] told me one day, "Every time I file on you, you'll pay a fine." I said, "Elmer, let me tell you one thing." I said, "I've got a .22 here." I had me a jeep seat in my boat where I could just set up on the back of it. I said, "I can come up the river and gut-shoot them old does, and they'll just run off out there and lay down and die." And I said, "What do you think them club members are going to do when they start finding them deer out there laying dead? They're gonna run you off." "Oh," he said, "that wouldn't be right." I said, "No, it's not gonna be right if you harass me, either."

Many of the pasture riders were drawn from the same woods-wise communities that the traditional hunters came from, and the poachers sometimes found the riders more formidable foes than the game wardens—especially in the early days when neither side gave much thought to lawsuits and practiced "winning by intimidation." In some cases, as at Pine Island, the clubs chose to fight fire with fire in their recruitment of pasture riders. Sometimes they hired squatters who predated the club and who refused to leave. One man explained, "Old man Brooks Williams had a tent down there when they first fenced it in, and they had to get the sheriff to go down there and get him and make him leave out, and then they hired him for pasture rider." Once on the club payroll, the old woodsman became a stalwart defender of Pine Island, though he sometimes operated beyond the letter of the law. When Williams heard a motorboat coming up Old River, he often stood on the Pine Island bridge swinging a long club as a threat to turn the boat back. One day he got in an argument with two boaters and shot one of them in the leg.

The hunting clubs' biggest problem, however, was hunting with dogs, a traditional method that caused the most severe conflicts during the duel over hunting access. In a practice commonly spoken of as "running dogs against a man's land," the dog hunter did not even have to trespass. Dogs would be carried to one side of the club property and turned loose while standers took up positions just outside the opposite fence lines to await the deer. After the bottoms "clubbed up," nobody was running long-coursing Walkers anymore. The poaching hunter wanted curs or cur-hound crosses, dogs that ran fast for a short time, then came back. Later, for reasons that will become obvious, the poacher often used "throwaway" dogs picked up at the pound.

For game wardens and pasture riders, the dog hunter was hard to deal with. Using dogs to hunt for deer was legal in most southeastern Texas counties until 1990, so as long as the standers in a hunt stayed off the club property to await the deer, they were breaking no law. Nor could the dog be ticketed; as game warden Walter Kirby laconically explained, "You can't file on a dog."[73]

Some counties, like Angelina, had an early law against dog hunting for deer, but loopholes always existed. For a long time, the law read that wounded deer could be pursued with dogs, so the hunters would go out in the morning, fire a gun in the air to simulate a deer wounding, and cast the hounds. After this "doughnut" in the law was closed, others were used. If questioned, hunters said their dogs were coursing "wolves" or rabbits; if the game warden had actually seen the dog pursuing a deer, the owner would say something like: "That so-and-so! He's trashing. I sure will beat the hell out of him when he comes back."[74]

Pasture riders, club members, and perhaps game wardens (though no warden ever admitted this) had only one effective recourse: they shot the dogs. This dog murder—as the dog men saw it—caused endless conflict. To properly evaluate this, the reader should recall the large, granite monuments of the National Hall of Fame Cemetery of Fox Hounds in Shelby County. An old country saying held that it was "better to mess with a man's wife than a man's dog," and this exaggerated only slightly. One man warned Texas Parks and Wildlife officials at a 1986 public hearing in Jasper County: "I got five dogs. They all got a name, you know, for me, just like my kids. And if a man grabs my dogs he might as well grab me, cause that's they way it's gonna come down." Another man remarked of dog-shooting club members: "Could be some killing around here some of these days and it'd be justified.

They ain't got no right to kill a man's dog for going on a club, cause he don't know no better. Come shoot the man, take it out on the man—and maybe you'll get shot!"[75]

Ms. Jonnie McConnico in Angelina County had a reputation, probably well-deserved, for shooting dogs on her Criss-Cross Club and for ordering standers off the nearby county roads at gunpoint. As warden Walter Kirby recalled: "Old lady McConnico toted a .30-30 everywhere she went, would kill a dog in a heartbeat, and would tell a man to kiss it where it feels good—a tough, tough old lady. If you were messing with her property, she was bad!"[76] McConnico developed her methods in the face of formidable opposition, however. One day, Frank Ashby was present when a well-known local badman with two killings to his credit came to call. He had brought his favorite dog to show it to Ms. McConnico, and Frank told what happened next: "He called her out there. And he said, 'Now, you look at that dog good, look it over real good.' Said, 'This is my dog. I raised that dog, and if you kill that dog and I find it out, damn your soul, you'll never kill another!'"[77]

In truth, however, the besieged defenders of deer herds and private properties felt they had little recourse but to shoot the dogs. Boggy Slough Hunting Club and other Temple clubs began by catching people's dogs and notifying them to come and pick the dogs up, but this caused so many confrontations that authorities instructed pasture riders to just make the dogs disappear somewhere on the trackless Neches bottoms. According to one account, hunting club owner William Crain at first also tried to return people's dogs, often tying them at a butane tank on the road for the owners to pick up—until the day one man got his dog, drove off about forty yards, and put a rifle bullet through the butane tank.

The private wildlife defenders—William Crain in Angelina County, James Albert and Bertha Best in Houston County, and a hundred others down the Neches—were in a class by themselves during the dog and deer wars. The game wardens tried to help all that they could, but each family was basically on its own in the remote countryside surrounded by hostile neighbors. James Albert Best told me, "They get mad enough to kill your cow or burn your house, or something nother; you have to get mad with em, is all I can tell you."[78] Jonnie McConnico's fortress-like house was splattered with buckshot from the county road on numerous occasions. According to one game warden, William Crain "was just a little frail-looking man, but he was big as a dynamite stick on his own land."[79] However, Crain suffered for many years from spite fires, cattle shootings, and fence cuttings. On one occasion, when he and his wife were waylaid and beaten up on their way into town, Mrs. Crain had her arm broken. At this point, a Texas Ranger was called in to make a show of force. Crain admitted he shot dogs and was prepared to pay the price. As pasture rider Charlie Harber said: "They killed dogs—dogs didn't go across his property down there. And they killed no telling how many good cattle for him. He told me and the game warden one time, he said, 'Well, as long as they run dogs, they gonna lose some dogs, and I'm gonna lose some cattle.'"[80] As a Bellview man noted, Crain also paid a heavy price in ostracism by his neighbors: "He killed lots of dogs. He didn't just have enough friends for nothing on account of that—he died with no friends."

Back before Billy Platt became a game warden, he and an older companion went dog hunting in Polk County, and their deer hounds failed to return. The next day they found the dogs on a nearby fenced property, and their worst fears were realized.

> There were our dogs, shot dead all of em, with the collars taken off of em, they're just laying there. And that man that was older than me—I was mad but he went berserk. He started crying and cussing. And if someone had driven up that worked this place, they'd have died right there.
>
> I got bad upset. We got the dogs and carried em to the courthouse in Livingston, and we had probably two hundred people around this courthouse there looking at these dogs shot all to pieces. And you talking about people mad! Everybody in the country ran dogs. Everybody! But the next day I got to thinking. I thought, you know, this is not worth it. We would have killed somebody if they'd of drove up there.[81]

At the Garlington Ranch in Jasper County, somebody did drive up. Ranchers Dalphin and Sterling Garlington raised pure-blood Brahma cattle behind a strong fence and for years objected to deer dogs crossing their land. The Garlington brothers told friends of the family that their cattle were skittish and "just lost it" when deer chased by dogs ran through the cattle to throw the dogs off the scent.[82] Everybody in the countryside thought the brothers shot dogs, and indeed trailing hounds did have a way of disappearing around the Garlington Ranch. According to Billy Platt, Dalphin and Sterling's dog hunter older brother Link, with whom they lived in a state of feud, went out of his way to throw gasoline on the flames. The younger Garlingtons killed Link's dogs "just in droves, and every time somebody would lose a dog, a dog hunter, they'd go to Link and say, 'Did you hear our dogs come through here yesterday?' He'd say, 'Yeah, they came through my land, went over into Dalph and them. I heard three shots and the dogs hushed.'"[83]

On Christmas day in 1954, six men went dog hunting for deer near the Garlington Ranch. The drive went off in the direction of the ranch, and shots were heard. Some of the hunters' dogs did not come back, and one that did had a buckshot wound. From this point, the hunters and the Garlington brothers told wildly different stories about what happened next, but the essential facts are clear. The dog hunters and the Garlingtons encountered each other on a road near the perimeter of the ranch and had a fire fight. Over forty shots were fired, both Dalphin and Sterling were severely wounded, several dog hunters were hit, and one—Roy Muench—was killed. Sterling Garlington told Billy Platt that he was lying in the ditch, paralyzed but with his eyes open, when one dog hunter walked up and said, "You son-of-a-bitch, you'll never kill another dog!" The hunter shot him in the head, and then, Garlington told Platt, "My lights went out." Not being accustomed to executing people upside-down at point-blank range, the hunter shot high, the bullet skidded around Garlington's skull without penetrating, and he survived. Then, although in a more elaborate way than usual, the local courts pronounced this whole affair a "killing"—a regrettable but unpunishable act of violence among consenting adults. One grand jury indicted the hunters, who were acquitted; then a second grand jury indicted the Garlingtons, who also were acquitted.[84]

As the 1970s moved into the 1980s, an increasing number of traditional hunters along the Neches gave up the chase, the last vestige of the old free-range days. Deer and deer hounds were incorrigible crossers of fence lines and jurisdictions, and that was no longer acceptable. Still hunting and dog hunting were essentially incompatible, and lumber companies like Champion, tired of the eternal squabbles among its hunting leases, finally forbade dog hunting altogether (then counted the forest fires). Q. V. King and his friends were forced to swallow the bitter pill of conversion to "tree sitting," but J. R. Cockrell quit deer hunting entirely. As Cockrell explained, he had been forced to use "sorrier and sorrier dogs" until it just was no longer worth the trouble. Now his wife provided the family's venison.

In 1988 the Texas Parks and Wildlife Department split the season between still hunting and dog hunting, and in 1990 the agency ended dog hunting altogether. Before the 1988 rule change (which traditional hunters correctly perceived as the beginning of the end), game warden Walter Kirby received the task of chairing the Jasper County hearing about the proposed change in the law. The department solicited public comments, and it certainly got them. The meeting, described by one observer as "three hundred mad, drunk people in one room," verged on getting out of hand. Recent department surveys had proven to the agency's satisfaction that 80 percent of the citizens of the last counties allowing dog hunting for deer were opposed to the practice. On this night, however, only representatives from the other 20 percent were present. One by one, hour after hour, person after person came to the microphone to praise the old ways and the voice of the hound and to make dire warnings, some of them truly chilling, about what might happen to game wardens, timber companies' pine plantations, and stockmen's cattle if the new law was approved. There was much talk of God-given rights, of family hunting traditions, and of dog hunting as a truer exercise of sportsmanship than "tree sitting." At the end of whatever else they had to say, many participants echoed the words of James Mauex, who proclaimed: "There ain't no man gonna come up and tell me that I can't run my hounds. I am forty-seven going on forty-eight years old. I've done lived a lifetime, so don't worry about me. You may get some of them young bucks, but I want to tell you one thing tonight. You can't catch all of us!" One man even rose to inform department officials that he planned to engrave the names of area game wardens in the owner's slot on the collars of his deer hounds.[85]

The vows of defiance, even the blood threats, rang hollow; most of the men in the room at the Jasper County Courthouse knew that dog hunting, like the rest of the old life-style, was all but dead. Exasperated, Walter Kirby finally cut off one man who would not stop talking, telling him Kirby would meet him outside the courthouse after the meeting to discuss the matter as long as he wanted. Kirby recalled: "And basically that's what happened. After we got outside that night, and the old boy just talked on and on, I said: 'You know, all I can tell you is the hound dog is gonna be somewhat like the American Indian. Civilization is just gonna swallow it up—whether I do it, whether you accept it, or what happens, it's gonna go.'"[86]

Walter Kirby bore the double burden of wearing the game warden's uniform as agent of the twentieth century and of understanding—and to a degree sympathizing with—the nineteenth-century life-style he helped to bring to an end. As he summed up the matter: "It's a loss to these people—it's a loss of a way of life. It's a tradition that's gone. They always felt like that all these forests and woods were theirs."[87]

Now the old ways last in memory only as long as the rememberers remain. In 1993, 105-year-old Walter Cole and his son Aubrey still recalled ancient fox hunts on the edge of the Neches bottoms, under the hunters' moon. On one occasion, the Coles had been accompanied by "old man Charlie Daniels," a retired schoolteacher with a "brag dog" named Buck. In the cool of the autumn evening, the hunters loosed their hounds and waited around the fire. "Directly, old man Charlie said: 'Listen! I hear old Buck, he's right in yonder to the left of the moon; he has struck a fox.' Somebody else said, 'Well, I hear old June or old so-and-so right in here, and he's after something.' Old man Charlie said, 'Yes, but old Buck don't run *something*, he's after a *fox!*'"[88]

Then the hounds "packed up," and the hunters began to call the hunt, following the fox across the remembered landscape, calling the web of names that lay upon the land. Down Sam Goode Branch the gray fox ran, then west into the Neches bottoms to Double Slough then south to Palmer Lake and Sand Slough and beyond. As they sat around the fire, listening to the voices of their hounds, the hunters called the old names for places on the land. Locations in the hills were often named for people, but in the Neches bottoms, the names differed; they were woods names, river names, wilderness names: Buck Lake, Lone Pine Ridge, Gourd Vine Eddy, Bear Man's Bluff, Pigeon Creek, Black Water Slough. The Hasinai Caddos had used similar names—forgotten now, as many of the hunters' names will soon be. But even when the names are gone, deep in the Neches bottoms the wilderness will linger. Something of that wilderness will remain as long as the river rises to flood its valley in the spring.

Preface

1. Hoagland, *Notes from the Century Before.*
2. Sonnichsen, *The Grave of John Wesley Hardin*, 26.
3. Baker, *The Peregrine*, 12.

Chapter 1. Introduction

1. Truett and Lay, *Land of Bears and Honey*, 22; Jordan, *Trails to Texas*, 103–7.
2. Martin, "Late Pleistocene Faunal Distribution," 120; Shafer, "Early Lithic Assemblages in Eastern Texas."
3. Gunter, *The Big Thicket*, 43–52.
4. Seale, "River People," 43.
5. Owens, "Big Thicket Balladry," 203. For the most authoritative modern description of the characteristics of the American backwoods life-style, see Jordan and Kaup, *The American Backwoods Frontier*, 1–18.
6. Billington and Ridge, *Westward Expansion*, 50.
7. Ibid., 59.
8. Hudson, *The Southeastern Indians*, 272–499.
9. Williams, *Americans and Their Forests*, 53; Hilliard, *Hogmeat and Hoecake*, 73.
10. Hudson, *The Southeastern Indians*, 272.
11. Clark, *The Greening of the South*, 11–12.
12. Schaadt, *Hardin County History*, 8; Seale, "River People," 43.
13. Daniel W. Lay interview, August 7, 1992.
14. R. J. Rawls's grandfather in Tyler County was typical. He came to the county during the Civil War, tried cotton farming for a while, then turned to stock raising in the Forks of the River country along the Neches and began to prosper. R. J. Rawls interview, April 27, 1986.
15. King, "The Closing of the Southern Range," 53.
16. Ibid.
17. Ibid.
18. Jordan, *Trails to Texas*, 25–58.
19. Owsley, *Plain Folk of the Old South*, 26.
20. From the *Patent Office Report* for 1850, quoted in McDonald and McWhiney, "The Antebellum Southern Herdsman," 159.

21. Jordan, *Trails to Texas*, 1.
22. Wright, *My Rambles*, 10.
23. Caplen, "Camp Big Thicket," 112.
24. Claiborne, "A Trip through the Piney Woods," 514–33.
25. Caplen, "Camp Big Thicket," 110.
26. Olmsted, *The Cotton Kingdom*, 304.
27. Billington, *Westward Expansion*, 315.
28. McDonald and McWhiney, "The Antebellum Southern Herdsman," 147.
29. King, "The Closing of the Southern Range."
30. Hahn, "Hunting, Fishing, and Foraging"; idem, *The Roots of Southern Populism*. See also the acerbic debate between Hahn and his economic-historian critics: Kantor and Kousser, "Common Sense or Commonwealth?"
31. Clarence Beezley interview, May 1, 1992.
32. Abernethy, "Running the Fox"; idem, "The East Texas Communal Hunt."
33. Utley, *Bear, Man, and God*.
34. Swanton, "History and Ethnology of the Caddo Indians," 10.
35. King, "The Closing of the Southern Range," 68.
36. Billy F. Platt interview, July 10, 1992.
37. J. R. Cockrell interview, May 13, 1992.
38. Sitton, *Ringing the Children In*, 141.
39. Charlie Harber interview, February 28, 1992.
40. W. B. Harris interview, May 6, 1992.
41. James W. May interview, May 7, 1992.
42. Parvin, "Bottomland Hardwoods."
43. Ralph W. Yarborough interview, November 26, 1985.

Chapter 2. A Flow in Time

1. Olmsted, *A Journey through Texas*, 83.
2. Strahler, *Introduction to Physical Geography*, 288.
3. Czaya, *Rivers of the World*, 66.
4. Briggs and Smithson, *Fundamentals of Physical Geography*, 349.
5. Chorley, *Geomorphology*, 302.
6. Oberlander, *Essentials of Physical Geography Today*, 349.
7. Czaya, *Rivers of the World*, 184.
8. Neal and Haskins, "Bottomland Hardwoods," 311.
9. Truett and Lay, *Land of Bears and Honey*, 18; Ajilvsgi, *Wildflowers of the Big Thicket, East Texas, and Western Louisiana*, 13–14.
10. Parvin, "Bottomland Hardwoods," 30.
11. Bray, "Vegetation of Texas," 23–24.
12. Harris, *Bottomland Hardwoods*, 4.
13. Ibid., 7.
14. Fentress, "Wildlife of Bottomlands."
15. Oberholser, *The Bird Life of Texas* 1:526–29.
16. Ibid., 419–20.
17. Ibid., 418.
18. Martin, "Late Pleistocene Faunal Distribution and Community Evolution"; Shafer, "Early Lithic Assemblages in Eastern Texas."

19. Lay, "Pristine East Texas"; idem, "The Role of Fire in Forest Management."
20. Lay, "Forks of the River," 28; and Fritz, *Realms of Beauty,* 62.
21. Ippolito, *National Forests of Texas,* 13.
22. Ibid., 18–19.
23. Ibid.
24. Williams, *Americans and Their Forests,* 43–47.
25. Ippolito, *National Forests of Texas,* 20–23.
26. Ibid.
27. Texas Parks, *Caddoan Mounds.*
28. Ibid.
29. Ibid.
30. Ibid.
31. Ippolito, *National Forests of Texas,* 23–25.
32. Swanton, "History and Ethnology of the Caddo Indians," 142.
33. Ibid.
34. Ibid.
35. Newcomb, *The Indians of Texas,* 290–291.
36. Griffith, *The Hasinai Indians of East Texas,* 47.
37. Swanton, "History and Ethnology of the Caddo Indians," 129.
38. Ibid., 158; Griffith, *The Hasinai Indians of East Texas,* 103–4.
39. Swanton, "History and Ethnology of the Caddo Indians," 154–58.
40. Keller, "The Subsistence Paleoecology of the Middle Neches," 156.
41. Swanton, "History and Ethnology of the Caddo Indians," 133–34.
42. Ibid.
43. Hudson, *The Southeastern Indians,* 287.
44. Swanton, "History and Ethnology of the Caddo Indians," 135.
45. Ibid.
46. Ibid., 136.
47. Ibid., 137.
48. Ibid., 136.
49. Hudson, *The Southeastern Indians,* 276.
50. Doughty, *Wildlife and Man in Texas,* 34.
51. Ippolito, *National Forests of Texas,* 26–28.
52. Ibid.
53. Hale, "Mining and Prospecting on the Louisiana-Texas Frontier."
54. Meinig, *Imperial Texas,* 26–27.
55. Keller, "The Subsistence Paleoecology of the Middle Neches," 98.
56. Swanton, "History and Ethnology of the Caddo Indians," 197.
57. Ibid.
58. Cronon, *Changes in the Land,* 85
59. Newcomb, *The Indians of Texas,* 345–47; Glover, "A History of the Caddo Indians."
60. Bowman, *Land of the Little Angel,* 4.
61. Ibid.
62. Cronon, *Changes in the Land,* 67.
63. Woldert, *A History of Tyler and Smith County, Texas,* 77.

Chapter 3. The River-Bottom Strain

1. Meinig, *Imperial Texas*, 33.
2. Zuber, *My Eighty Years in Texas*, 21.
3. Wright, *My Rambles*, 8.
4. Brown Wiggins in Loughmiller and Loughmiller, *Big Thicket Legacy*, 16.
5. Owsley, *Plain Folk of the Old South*, 23.
6. Arden Hooks in Loughmiller and Loughmiller, *Big Thicket Legacy*, 130.
7. Owsley, *Plain Folk of the Old South*, 63.
8. Ibid., 94–95.
9. Olmsted, *A Journey through Texas*, 55.
10. Evans, "Transportation in Early Texas," 2; Wiggins in Loughmiller and Loughmiller, *Big Thicket Legacy*, 16.
11. Walter Cole interview, July 9, 1992.
12. Olmsted, *A Journey through Texas*, 390.
13. Caplen, "Camp Big Thicket," 112.
14. Easton, "The History of the Texas Lumbering Industry," 49.
15. Wiggins in Loughmiller and Loughmiller, *Big Thicket Legacy*, 16; also see P. O. Eason in ibid, 219.
16. Daniel W. Lay interview, August 7, 1992.
17. Wiggins in Loughmiller and Loughmiller, *Big Thicket Legacy*, 15. For a general discussion of the miasmic theory of disease, see Doughty, *Wildlife and Man in Texas*, 18–20.
18. Lance Rosier in Loughmiller and Loughmiller, *Big Thicket Legacy*, 64.
19. Ralph W. Yarborough interview, November 26, 1985.
20. A. Randolph Fillingim in Loughmiller and Loughmiller, *Big Thicket Legacy*, 81.
21. Walter Cole interview, June 9, 1992.
22. Ibid.
23. Jordan, *Texas Log Buildings*, 105.
24. Wiggins in Loughmiller and Loughmiller, *Big Thicket Legacy*, 16.
25. Fillingim in ibid., 86.
26. Jordan, *Texas Log Buildings*, 15.
27. Owsley, *Plain Folk of the Old South*, 108.
28. Charlie Havard interview, April 12, 1986; Overstreet, "Chimney Dobbin' in the Big Thicket."
29. Aubrey Cole interview, July 9, 1992.
30. A. E. McGalin interview, May 14, 1992; Lynn McGalin interview, May 29, 1992.
31. Boon, "The History of Angelina County," 43–49; Bowles, "The History of Trinity County," 19–20.
32. Croom, *When the Pines Grew Tall*, 34.
33. Hilliard, *Hogmeat and Hoecake*, 39.
34. A. L. Bevil in Loughmiller and Loughmiller, *Big Thicket Legacy*, 39.
35. Claiborne, "A Trip through the Piney Woods," 520.
36. Wiggins in Loughmiller and Loughmiller, *Big Thicket Legacy*, 17.
37. Carl Havard interview, March 19, 1992.

38. A. E. McGalin interview, May 14, 1992.
39. Bevil in Loughmiller and Loughmiller, *Big Thicket Legacy,* 31–32.
40. R. J. Rawls interview, April 27, 1986.
41. Hicks and Stephenson, *Woody Plants of the Western Gulf Region;* Peacock, "Folk Medicine in the Big Thicket.
42. Rosier in Loughmiller and Loughmiller, *Big Thicket Legacy,* 59.
43. Daniel W. Lay interview, July 7, 1992.
44. Harold Snelson interview, March 20, 1992.
45. Wright, *My Rambles,* 49.
46. Ibid., 9.
47. Sam Houston Cain in Loughmiller and Loughmiller, *Big Thicket Legacy,* 52.
48. Collins, "Settling the Old Poplar-Tree Place," 63.
49. Hilliard, *Hogmeat and Hoecake,* 73.
50. Hogan, *The Texas Republic,* 32; Clark, *Frontier America,* 214.
51. Wright, *My Rambles,* 2.
52. Ellen Walker in Loughmiller and Loughmiller, *Big Thicket Legacy,* 6–7.
53. C. W. Gandy interview, July 20, 1992.
54. Alpha Omega Havard interview, March 14, 1986.
55. Oscar Allen, personal communication with Thad Sitton, July 20, 1992.
56. Haynes, "The History of Polk County."
57. Walker in Loughmiller and Loughmiller, *Big Thicket Legacy,* 7.
58. Walter Cole interview, July 9, 1992.
59. Posey, "A History of Cherokee County," 60.
60. Wright, *My Rambles,* 5; Odom, "A History of the East Texas Cattle Industry," 37.
61. Mathews, "The Economic Development of Angelina County," 23–26.
62. Walter Cole interview, July 9, 1992.
63. Daniel W. Lay interview, August 7, 1992.
64. William Cronon studied English and Indian place-names in New England and concluded that, whereas the "English frequently created arbitrary place-names which either recalled localities in their homeland or gave a place the name of its owner, the Indians used ecological labels to describe how the land could be used." However, perhaps because of the traditions of the southern free range, most Anglo-American place-names in the Neches bottoms are of the Native American variety—"ecological labels" expressive of usufruct rights. See Cronon, *Changes in the Land,* 65–66.
65. Mathews, "The Economic Development of Angelina County," 23–26.
66. Odom, *Over on Cochino,* 74–77.
67. Hooks, "An Essay on Hardin County Politics," 145.
68. James Addison Moye in Loughmiller and Loughmiller, *Big Thicket Legacy,* 187.
69. Walker in ibid., 7–8.
70. Fillingim in ibid., 84.
71. For example, during the 1934–35 school year only two black schools operated in the ten common-school districts along the Neches in Angelina County, and both of these were located inland at major mill towns. In the other eight

districts only fourteen black "scholastics" (age six to seventeen) resided. "A Report on the Adequacy of Texas Schools," Works Progress Administration, State Board of Education, Project No. 65-66-7752 (October 1937), 141–44.

72. Walker in Loughmiller and Loughmiller, *Big Thicket Legacy*, 9.

73. Owens, "Big Thicket Balladry," 201.

74. Frank Ashby interview, March 16, 1992.

75. Croom, *When the Pines Grew Tall*, 47.

76. Sitton and Rowold, *Ringing the Children In*, 138.

77. Ramos, *Rocking Texas' Cradle*, 200–202.

78. C. W. Gandy interview, July 10, 1992.

79. Ralph W. Yarborough interview, November 26, 1985.

Chapter 4. River Traffic, Timber Work, and Moonshining

1. Sullivan, "Navigation of the Neches and Sabine Rivers," 13.

2. Hogan, *The Texas Republic*, 66.

3. Ibid., 64.

4. Hollon and Butler, *William Bollaert's Texas*, 307.

5. Bowman, *Land of the Little Angel*, 21.

6. McReynolds, "Frontier Towns in Antebellum East Texas," 4.

7. White, *East Texas Riverboat Era*, 7.

8. Seale, *Texas Riverman*, 150.

9. White, *East Texas Riverboat Era*, 61.

10. Houstoun, *Texas and the Gulf of Mexico*, 179; Hogan, *The Texas Republic*, 73.

11. Hogan, *the Texas Republic*, 73.

12. *Sunday Enterprise* (Beaumont, Texas), November 27, 1932.

13. Seale, *Texas Riverman*, 142.

14. Ibid., 68.

15. Ibid., 70.

16. Ibid., 74.

17. Ibid., 75.

18. Ibid., 146.

19. Hill, "Grandma Harrison," 73.

20. Nichols, *Now You Hear My Horn*, 7.

21. Sullivan, "Navigation of the Neches and Sabine Rivers," 43.

22. White, *East Texas Riverboat Era*, 6.

23. R. J. Rawls interview, April 27, 1986.

24. Walker, *The Southern Forest*, 160.

25. Easton, "The History of the Texas Lumbering Industry," 47.

26. Ramos, *Rocking Texas' Cradle*, 51.

27. Zuber, *My Eighty Years in Texas*, 26.

28. Easton, "The History of the Texas Lumbering Industry," 29.

29. Ibid., 31.

30. Ibid., 67.

31. Ibid., 114.

32. Maxwell and Baker, *Sawdust Empire*, 17–33.

33. Easton, "The History of the Texas Lumbering Industry," 171.

34. McReynolds, "Frontier Towns in Antebellum East Texas," 10–11.

35. "Log Brand Records for Hardin and Jefferson Counties."
36. Easton, "The History of the Texas Lumbering Industry," 169.
37. R. R. Allen interview, May 14, 1992.
38. Ibid.
39. W. B. Harris interview, May 6, 1992.
40. Roy Smith interview, January 4, 1986; Carl Havard interview, March 19, 1992.
41. Williams, *Americans and Their Forests*, 248.
42. White, *East Texas Riverboat Era*, 130.
43. Ibid., 132.
44. R. R. Allen interview, May 14, 1992; J. Louis Bingham interview, May 28, 1992.
45. J. Louis Bingham interview, May 28, 1992.
46. The following accounts described rafting practices similar or identical to those of the Allen family: Bert DuBose interview, n.d.; R. J. Rawls interview, April 27, 1986.
47. R. R. Allen interview, May 14, 1992.
48. Williams, *Americans and Their Forests*, 240–43.
49. Schaadt, *Hardin County History*, 58.
50. Maxwell and Baker, *Sawdust Empire*, 36–38.
51. Ibid., 159, 166.
52. Boon, "The History of Angelina County," 91–95.
53. Odom, *Over on Cochino*, 13–15; Maxwell and Baker, *Sawdust Empire*, 157–58.
54. Frank Ashby interview, March 19, 1992.
55. Maxwell and Baker, *Sawdust Empire*, 157.
56. Frank Ashby interview, March 19, 1992.
57. Burka, "The King of the Forest."
58. Maxwell and Baker, *Sawdust Empire*, 98–105.
59. Ibid., 124.
60. Ibid., 162.
61. Creel, "The Feudal Towns of Texas."
62. Biesele, *The Cornbread Whistle*, 27.
63. Maxwell and Baker, *Sawdust Empire*, 124.
64. Easton, "A History of the Texas Lumbering Industry," 154–56.
65. Clark, *The Greening of the South*, 18.
66. Maxwell and Baker, *Sawdust Empire*, 114.
67. Bowles, "The History of Trinity County," 72.
68. Brown Wiggins in Loughmiller and Loughmiller, *Big Thicket Legacy*, 28.
69. Roscoe Crouch in ibid., 170–71.
70. R. J. Rawls interview, April 27, 1986.
71. Ibid.
72. Roy Smith interview, January 18, 1986.
73. Walter Cole interview, July 9, 1992.
74. Quoted in Williams, *Americans and Their Forests*, 252.
75. Easton, "The History of the Texas Lumbering Industry," 330.
76. Ibid., 315.
77. Louis Bingham interview, May 28, 1992.

78. R. R. Allen interview, May 14, 1992.
79. Quoted in Easton, "The History of the Texas Lumbering Industry," 259.
80. Ibid.
81. Daniel W. Lay interview, August 7, 1992.
82. Maxwell and Baker, *Sawdust Empire*, 68.
83. Roy Smith interview, January 4, 1986; Charlie Harber interview, February 21, 1992; Odom, *Over on Cochino*, 21–26.
84. Wiggins in Loughmiller and Loughmiller, *Big Thicket Legacy*, 25.
85. Maxwell and Baker, *Sawdust Empire*, 67.
86. Easton, "The History of the Texas Lumbering Industry," 376.
87. Daniel W. Lay interview, July 23, 1992.
88. Easton, "The History of the Texas Lumbering Industry," 255.
89. Ibid., 256.
90. Daniel W. Lay interview, July 7, 1992.
91. Boon, "The History of Angelina County," 116.
92. Bowman, *The Land of the Little Angel*, 3; Claude Welch interview, January 17, 1986.
93. Brunce Jordan in Loughmiller and Loughmiller, *Big Thicket Legacy*, 44.
94. Allen, *East Texas Timber Workers*, 38.
95. Walter Cole interview, July 9, 1992.
96. Daniel W. Lay interview, July 7, 1992.
97. Brunce Jordan in Loughmiller and Loughmiller, *Big Thicket Legacy*, 44.
98. Ramos, *Rocking Texas' Cradle*, 95.
99. Carl Havard interview, April 10, 1992.
100. Harold Snelson interview, March 20, 1992.
101. Charlie Havard interview, March 14, 1986.
102. Allen, *East Texas Timber Workers*, 40–41.
103. Williams, *Americans and Their Forests*, 347.
104. Easton, "The History of the Texas Lumbering Industry," 222.
105. Babe McGalin interview, May 14, 1992.
106. Cravens, *Between Two Rivers*, 92–93.
107. Roy Smith interview, January 4, 1986.
108. George Carpenter interview, April 4, 1986.
109. Allen, *East Texas Timber Workers*, 60.
110. Ellen Clark in Loughmiller and Loughmiller, *Big Thicket Legacy*, 11–12.
111. Allen, *East Texas Timber Workers*, 41.
112. Wright, *My Rambles*, 94.
113. C. W. Gandy interview, July 10, 1992.
114. Allen, *East Texas Timber Workers*, 22.
115. John R. Bevil in Loughmiller and Loughmiller, *Big Thicket Legacy*, 138.
116. Pete Racki in ibid., 113–14.
117. Babe McGalin interview, May 14, 1992.
118. Jess Wells interview, December 20, 1986.
119. Daniel W. Lay, unpublished manuscript, Nacogdoches, Texas.
120. C. W. Gandy interview, July 10, 1992.
121. Dempsie Henley, quoted in Douglas, *Farewell to Texas*, 14.
122. Clarence Beezley interview, May 1, 1992.

123. Roy Smith interview, January 4, 1986.
124. Walker, *The Southern Forest*, 105.
125. Easton, "The History of the Texas Lumbering Industry," 166.
126. Roy Smith interview, January 18, 1986; Oscar Allen interview, March 15, 1986; Claude Welch interview, January 17, 1986.
127. James Strawther, personal communication to Thad Sitton, June 9, 1992.
128. Maxwell and Baker, *Sawdust Empire*, 200–202.
129. Carr, *The Second Oldest Profession*, 30–35.
130. Charlie Havard interview, April 12, 1986; Carl Havard interview, May 8, 1992.
131. C. W. Gandy interview, July 10, 1992.
132. Quoted in Sitton, *Texas High Sheriffs*, 122.
133. Aubrey Cole interview, July 9, 1992.
134. Brunt in Sitton, *Texas High Sheriffs*, 121.
135. "The Incredible Mr. Busch," 51–52.
136. Charlie Havard interview, March 14, 1986; George Carpenter interview, April 4, 1986.
137. Brunt in Sitton, *Texas High Sheriffs*, 124.
138. Oscar Allen interview, March 15, 1986.
139. Walker, *The Southern Forest*, 191–92.
140. Dudley Denmon interview, January 3, 1986.
141. Aubrey Cole interview, July 9, 1992.
142. George Carpenter interview, April 4, 1986.
143. Ibid.
144. Ibid.
145. Ibid.

Chapter 5. Hunting, Trapping, and Fishing

1. Aubrey Cole interview, May 28, 1992.
2. Ibid.
3. Ibid.
4. Hinkle Shillings interview, July 21, 1992.
5. Dobie, *The Ben Lily Legend*, ix.
6. Jake Cole interview, July 9, 1992.
7. Smithwick, *The Evolution of a State*, 8; Ellen Walker in Loughmiller and Loughmiller, *Big Thicket Legacy*, 6.
8. Walker in Loughmiller and Loughmiller, *Big Thicket Legacy*, 8; Charlie Havard interview, March 14, 1986.
9. Ramos, *Rocking Texas' Cradle*, 103.
10. Wright, *My Rambles*, 2.
11. Ralph Yarborough interview, November 26, 1985.
12. Quoted in Haynes, "The History of Polk County," 37.
13. Bowles, "The History of Trinity County," 13.
14. Pearl Wiggins in Loughmiller and Loughmiller, *Big Thicket Legacy*, 208.
15. Herrington, "Buckshot and Blue Whistler," 96.
16. Ibid., 105; Babe McGalin interview, May 14, 1992.
17. Doughty, *Wildlife and Man in Texas*, 23–26.

18. Rosier, "Late Fount Simmons Rescued Governor Ross from Big Thicket."
19. Doughty, *Wildlife and Man in Texas*, 34.
20. Wright, *My Rambles*, 2.
21. Hollon and Butler, *William Bollaert's Texas*, 277.
22. Wright, *My Rambles*, 9.
23. C. W. Gandy interview, July 10, 1992.
24. Charles Boyd interview, April 8, 1992.
25. W. B. Harris interview, May 6, 1992; Harold Snelson interview, March 20, 1992.
26. Carl Havard, interview, May 8, 1992; C. W. Gandy interview, July 10, 1992.
27. Harold Snelson interview, March 20, 1992.
28. Charlie Havard interview, April 12, 1986.
29. W. B. Harris interview, May 6, 1992.
30. Knipmeyer, "Settlement Succession in Eastern French Louisiana."
31. Charlie Havard interview, March 14, 1986.
32. Wright, *My Rambles*, 71.
33. P. O. Eason in Loughmiller and Loughmiller, *Big Thicket Legacy*, 216.
34. Ibid.
35. Ibid., 220.
36. Brown Wiggins in Loughmiller and Loughmiller, *Big Thicket Legacy*, 22. Temple-Inland wildlife biologist Don Dietz told of recent documented mountain lion attacks on hikers and mountain bikers in the Rocky Mountain West (Don Dietz interview, August 13, 1992).
37. Herrington in Abernethy, *Tales from the Big Thicket*, 99.
38. Brown Wiggins in Loughmiller and Loughmiller, *Big Thicket Legacy*, 22.
39. Boon, "The History of Angelina County," 25.
40. Brown Wiggins in Loughmiller and Loughmiller, *Big Thicket Legacy*, 22.
41. Aubrey Cole, personal communication, October 16, 1992.
42. Quoted in Fleming, "Texas Bear Hunting," 13.
43. Hewett, "From Moss Hill," 224.
44. Collins, "Settling the Old Poplar-Tree Place," 63.
45. Evie Brown in Loughmiller and Loughmiller, *Big Thicket Legacy*, 161.
46. Herrington in Abernethy, *Tales from the Big Thicket*, 96.
47. Barry, *Buck Barry*, 51.
48. Truett and Lay, *Land of Bears and Honey*, 47.
49. Herrington in Abernethy, *Tales from the Big Thicket*, 99.
50. Ramos, *Rocking Texas' Cradle*, 178.
51. Carter Hart in Loughmiller and Loughmiller, *Big Thicket Legacy*, 97–108; Erinstra, "A Family Full of Legends," 181–97.
52. Herrington in Abernethy, *Tales from the Big Thicket*, 105.
53. Hollon and Butler, *William Bollaert's Texas*, 253.
54. Carter Hart in Loughmiller and Loughmiller, *Big Thicket Legacy*, 105.
55. A. L. "Leak" Bevil in ibid., 38.
56. Hart in ibid., 105.
57. Ramos, *Rocking Texas' Cradle*, 183.
58. Loughmiller and Loughmiller, "Bill Warren of the Big Thicket," 63.
59. Ben Hooks, "Ten Days in the Big Thicket"; Kiehne, "Texas Bear Hunt."

60. Roosevelt, "In the Louisiana Canebrakes."
61. White, "Cherokee County Characters."
62. Hinkle Shillings interview, July 21, 1992.
63. Ibid.
64. Ibid.
65. J. R. Cockrell interview, May 15, 1992; Abernethy, "Running the Fox."
66. Stevens, "Crafty Import," 22.
67. Hinkle Shillings interview, July 21, 1992; Aubrey Cole interview, July 9, 1992.
68. Marks, *Southern Hunting in Black and White*, 95.
69. Hinkle Shillings interview, July 21, 1992.
70. Aubrey Cole interview, May 28, 1992
71. J. R. Cockrell interview, May 15, 1992.
72. Hinkle Shillings interview, July 21, 1992; Aubrey Cole interview, July 9, 1992.
73. *Jasper Newsboy*, November 24, 1940.
74. Aubrey Cole interview, May 5, 1992.
75. Hinkle Shillings interview, July 21, 1992.
76. Walter Cole interview, July 9, 1992.
77. Charles Wells interview, March 16, 1992.
78. Aubrey Cole interview, May 5, 1992.
79. Floyd Warren in Loughmiller and Loughmiller, *Big Thicket Legacy*, 200.
80. Aubrey Cole interview, July 9, 1992.
81. Q. R. King interview, May 13, 1992.
82. Marks, *Southern Hunting in Black and White*, 20–22.
83. J. R. Cockrell interview, May 15, 1992.
84. Ibid.
85. Aubrey Cole interview, May 5, 1992.
86. Ibid.
87. Ibid.
88. Q. R. King interview, May 13, 1992; Abernethy, "The East Texas Communal Hunt.
89. J. R. Cockrell interview, May 15, 1992.
90. Charles Boyd interview, April 8, 1992.
91. C. W. Gandy interview, July 10, 1992.
92. Ramos, *Rocking Texas' Cradle*, 201.
93. Harold Snelson interview, March 18, 1992.
94. Aubrey Cole interview, May 5, 1992.
95. Frank Ashby interview, March 16, 1992.
96. Aubrey Cole interview, May 5, 1992.
97. Ibid.; J. R. Cockrell interview, May 15, 1992.
98. Q. R. King interview, May 13, 1992.
99. J. R. Cockrell interview, May 15, 1992.
100. Hooks, "'Shinny' and Gambling Had Big Roles in 1929 Deer Hunt."
101. Ibid.
102. Charles Boyd interview, April 8, 1992.
103. Aubrey Cole interview. May 5, 1992.

104. J. R. Cockrell interview, May 15, 1992.
105. C. P. Petri interview, May 4, 1986.
106. Avy Joe Havard interview, February 22, 1992.
107. Buck McAnulty interview, May 7, 1992.
108. Oberholser, *The Bird Life of Texas*, 418; Doughty, *Wildlife and Man in Texas*, 104.
109. Jake Cole interview, July 9, 1992.
110. Walter Cole interview, July 9, 1992.
111. Brown Wiggins in Loughmiller and Loughmiller, *Big Thicket Legacy*, 17; Hilliard, *Hogmeat and Hoecake*, 80.
112. Wanda Gipson DuBose interview, November 25, 1992.
113. Oscar Allen interview, November 7, 1986.
114. Doughty, *Wildlife and Man in Texas*, 34.
115. Harold Snelson interview, March 18, 1992.
116. James May interview, May 7, 1992.
117. Charles Wells interview, March 16, 1992.
118. Ibid.
119. Oscar Allen interview, November 7, 1986.
120. A. Randolph Fillingim in Loughmiller and Loughmiller, *Big Thicket Legacy*, 86.
121. Charlie Havard interview, March 14, 1986.
122. Harold Snelson interview, March 18, 1992.
123. Ibid.
124. Ibid.
125. Ibid.
126. Ralph Yarborough interview, November 26, 1985; Charlie Havard interview, March 14, 1986; Lynn McGalin interview, May 29, 1992.
127. Harold Snelson interview, March 18, 1992.
128. Ibid.; Ed Snelson interview, March 17, 1992.
129. Ed Snelson interview, March 17, 1992.
130. Harold Snelson interview, March 18, 1992.
131. Ibid.
132. W. B. Harris interview, May 6, 1992.
133. Harold Snelson interview, March 18, 1992.
134. Walter Kirby interview, April 9, 1992.
135. Garrett and Barker, *A Field Guide to the Reptiles and Amphibians of Texas*, 85.
136. Carl Havard interview, May 8, 1992.
137. James May interview, May 7, 1992.
138. Frank Ashby interview, March 16, 1992.
139. C. V. Bishop interview, February 14, 1986.
140. Claude Welch interview, January 17, 1986.
141. James May interview, May 7, 1992.
142. Lester Greenville interview, January 4, 1986.
143. Oscar Allen interview, November 7, 1986.
144. Hudson, *The Southeastern Indians*, 282–84.
145. J. Louis Bingham interview, May 28, 1992; Frank Ashby interview, March 16, 1992.

146. George Tull interview, May 18, 1985.
147. Harold Snelson interview, March 18, 1992.
148. Ibid.
149. Carl Havard interview, April 10, 1992.
150. Roy Smith interview, January 4, 1986.
151. Frank Ashby interview, March 19, 1992.
152. Hudson, *The Southeastern Indians*, 282.
153. Frank Ashby interview, March 19, 1992.
154. Ibid.
155. Oscar Allen interview, March 15, 1986.
156. Frank Ashby interview, March 19, 1992.
157. Ibid; Carl Havard interview, April 10, 1992.
158. Ibid.
159. Harold Snelson interview, March 20, 1992.
160. Ibid.
161. Lowry, *From Shawnee Prairie*, 67–69.
162. Roy Smith interview, January 4, 1986.
163. Oscar Allen interview, November 7, 1986.
164. William Starling interview, December 20, 1986.
165. Roy Smith interview, January 4, 1986.
166. Clarence Beezley interview, May 1, 1992.
167. Oscar Allen interview, March 15, 1986.
168. C. V. Bishop interview, February 14, 1986.
169. Frank Ashby interview, May 6, 1992.
170. Charlie Havard interview, March 14, 1986; Carl Havard interview, April 10, 1992; W. B. Harris interview, May 6, 1992.
171. J. Louis Bingham interview, May 28, 1992.
172. Ibid.
173. Ibid.
174. Ibid.
175. Dudley Denmon interview, January 3, 1986.
176. Ibid.
177. Ibid.
178. Ibid.

Chapter 6. Rooter Hogs and Woods Cattle

1. Dudley Denmon interview, January 3, 1986; Jude Hart in Loughmiller and Loughmiller, *Big Thicket Legacy*, 147; Avy Joe Havard interview, February 22, 1992; Babe McGalin interview, May 14, 1992.
2. Avy Joe Havard interview, February 22, 1992.
3. C. W. Gandy interview, July 10, 1992.
4. Jordan, *Trails to Texas*, 1–50.
5. For the great antiquity of European "fence them out" laws, see August, "Cowboys v. Rancheros," 460; Massachusetts Court quoted in Cronon, *Changes in the Land*, 135.
6. Cronon, *Changes in the Land*, 135.
7. Hilliard, *Hogmeat and Hoecake*, 124–30.

8. Williams, *Americans and Their Forests*, 67.
9. Michaux, in *Early Western Travels*, 246.
10. Jordan, *Trails to Texas*, 1–50.
11. McWhiney, *Cracker Culture*, 62.
12. Ibid., 54.
13. McDonald and McWhiney, "The Antebellum Southern Herdsman."
14. Ibid., 147; McWhiney, *Cracker Culture*, 54.
15. C. W. Gandy interview, July 10, 1992.
16. Odom, "A History of the East Texas Cattle Industry," 6.
17. Hogan, *The Texas Republic*, 20.
18. Babe McGalin interview, May 14, 1992.
19. Brown Wiggins in Loughmiller and Loughmiller, *Big Thicket Legacy*, 25.
20. Carl Havard interview, April 10, 1992.
21. Ibid.
22. Wright, *My Rambles*, 53–56.
23. Babe McGalin interview, May 14, 1992.
24. Carl Havard interview, April 10, 1992.
25. Jude Hart in Loughmiller and Loughmiller, *Big Thicket Legacy*, 155; Wright, *My Rambles*, 6.
26. Don Dietz interview, August 13, 1992; Bigony, "A Javelina Is Not a Pig."
27. Avy Joe Havard interview, February 28, 1992.
28. Frank Ashby interview, March 16, 1992.
29. Jess Wells interview, December 20, 1986.
30. Taylor, *The Feral Hog in Texas*, 2–3; Charlie Harber interview, February 28, 1992.
31. Brown Wiggins in Loughmiller and Loughmiller, *Big Thicket Legacy*, 21.
32. Ibid.
33. Taylor, *The Feral Hog in Texas*, 6.
34. Brown Wiggins in Loughmiller and Loughmiller, *Big Thicket Legacy*, 21.
35. Hart in ibid., 152.
36. Charlie Havard interview, March 14, 1986.
37. Avy Joe Havard interview, February 22, 1992.
38. W. B. Harris interview, May 5, 1992.
39. Dudley Denmon interview, January 3, 1986.
40. Lynn McGalin interview, May 29, 1992.
41. Carl Havard interview, March 19, 1992.
42. Frank Ashby interview, May 6, 1992.
43. Leak Bevil in Loughmiller and Loughmiller, *Big Thicket Legacy*, 34.
44. Ibid.
45. James Womack interview, March 2, 1992.
46. Frank Ashby interview, May 6, 1992; Charlie Havard interview, March 14, 1986.
47. Ibid.
48. Ibid.
49. James Womack interview, March 2, 1992; Babe McGalin interview, May 29, 1992; Avy Joe Havard interview, February 22, 1992.
50. Frank Ashby interview, May 6, 1992.

51. Bob Allen interview, May 14, 1992.
52. Frank Ashby interview, May 6, 1992.
53. Charlie Harber interview, February 21, 1992.
54. Avy Joe Havard interview, February 22, 1992.
55. Carl Havard interview, March 19, 1992.
56. Avy Joe Havard interview, February 22, 1992; Brown Wiggins in Loughmiller and Loughmiller, *Big Thicket Legacy*, 21.
57. R. J. Rawls interview, April 27, 1986.; Roy Smith interview, January 4, 1992.
58. Wright, *My Rambles*, 5.
59. Ibid., 50–56.
60. Charlie Havard interview, March 14, 1986.
61. Loughmiller and Loughmiller, "Bill Warren of the Big Thicket," 67; James Womack interview, March 2, 1992.
62. Walter Cole interview, July 9, 1992.
63. Mathews, "The Economic Development of Angelina County," 23.
64. Walter Cole interview, July 9, 1992.
65. Hart in Loughmiller and Loughmiller, *Big Thicket Legacy*, 151; Charlie Havard interview, March 14, 1986.
66. Frank Ashby interview, May 6, 1992; Avy Joe Havard interview, February 28, 1992.
67. Charlie Harber interviews, February 21, 1992, and February 28, 1992.
68. Ibid.
69. C. W. Gandy interview, July 10, 1992.
70. Avy Joe Havard interview, February 28, 1992.
71. Ibid.
72. Jake L. Cole interview, July 9, 1992.
73. Walter Cole interview, July 9, 1992; George Carpenter interview, November 8, 1986.
74. Cravens, *Between Two Rivers*, 16.
75. Oscar Allen, personal communication, July 20, 1992.
76. Carl Havard interview, March 19, 1992.
77. W. B. Harris interview, May 6, 1992.
78. Carl Havard interview, March 19, 1992.
79. Lynn McGalin interview, May 29, 1992.
80. Cravens, *Three Ghost Towns of East Texas*, 7–9.
81. Jess Wells interview, December 20, 1986.
82. Ibid.
83. Charlie Havard interview, March 14, 1986.
84. Lynn McGalin interview, May 29, 1992.
85. Hart in Loughmiller and Loughmiller, *Big Thicket Legacy*, 156; Jess Wells interview, December 20, 1986.
86. Babe McGalin interview, May 29, 1992; Louis Bingham interview, May 28, 1992.
87. Oberholser, *The Bird Life of Texas*, 1:418–19.
88. Clark, *Chandler*, 37; Ralph Yarborough interview, November 26, 1985.
89. Lester Greenville interview, January 4, 1986; Charlie Harber interview, March 17, 1992.
90. Fentress, "Wildlife of Bottomlands: Species and Status," 49.

91. Charlie Harber interview, March 17, 1992.
92. Barry, *Buck Barry*, 50.
93. Smithwick, *The Evolution of a State*, 5; Jackson, *Home on the Double Bayou*, 106; Frank Ashby interview, March 16, 1992; Oscar Allen interview, November 7, 1986.
94. Quoted in Jordan, *Trails to Texas*, 26; August, "Cowboys v. Rancheros," 480; Olmsted, *A Journey through Texas*, 66.
95. George Carpenter interview, April 4, 1992; Frank Ashby interview, March 16, 1992.
96. Seale, *Texas Riverman*, 108.
97. Hart in Loughmiller and Loughmiller, *Big Thicket Legacy*, 155.
98. James A. Moye in Loughmiller and Loughmiller, *Big Thicket Legacy*, 188; Lynn McGalin interview, May 29, 1992.
99. *Trinity Standard*, February 19, 1937.
100. *Polk County Enterprise* (Livingston, Texas), April 15, 1954.
101. Aubrey Cole, personal communication, October 16, 1992.
102. *United States Census of Agriculture: 1935*, 780; *Jasper Newsboy*, July 8, 1937.

Chapter 7. Closing the Woods

1. *Jasper Newsboy*, May 31, 1911, November 13, 1952; Schaadt, *Hardin County History*, 36.
2. Clarence Beezley interview, May 1, 1992.
3. Ibid.
4. Caplen, "Camp Big Thicket," 112.
5. P. O. Eason in Loughmiller and Loughmiller, *Big Thicket Legacy*, 219.
6. Hahn, "Hunting, Fishing, and Foraging," 42.
7. J. R. Cockrell interview, May 13, 1992.
8. Billy Ball interview, May 27, 1992.
9. Glacken, *Traces on the Rhodian Shore*, 322.
10. Ibid., 320–32.
11. Ibid., 320.
12. Hahn, "Hunting, Fishing, and Foraging," 39.
13. King, "The Closing of the Southern Range," 53–54.
14. Marks, *Southern Hunting in Black and White*, 32.
15. Hahn, "Hunting, Fishing, and Foraging," 41; King, "The Closing of the Southern Range," 53–54.
16. Elliott, *Carolina Sports by Land and Water*, 292.
17. Ibid., 292–93.
18. Hahn, "Hunting, Fishing, and Foraging," 44.
19. Ibid., 46.
20. King, "The Closing of the Southern Range," 68.
21. Ibid., 58–59.
22. Chambers, "The Pine Woods Region," 309.
23. Maxwell and Baker, *Sawdust Empire*, 68; Walker, *The Southern Forest*, 178–81.
24. For recent discussions of the ecological impacts of Native Americans' use of fire, see Williams, *Americans and Their Forests*, 43–47; Hudson, *The Southeastern Indians*, 276–77; Cronon, *Changes in the Land*, 50–51.

25. Williams, *Americans and Their Forests,* 47.
26. Lay, "Pristine East Texas."
27. Hardy Farmer in Loughmiller and Loughmiller, *Big Thicket Legacy,* 179.
28. Maxwell and Baker, *Sawdust Empire,* 66; Walker, *The Southern Forest,* 178–79.
29. Walker, *The Southern Forest,* 179.
30. Chambers, "Divisions of the Pine Belt in Texas," 103.
31. Easton, "The History of the Texas Lumbering Industry," 414; Foster, Krauz, and Johnson, "Forest Resources of Eastern Texas," 24.
32. Easton, "The History of the Texas Lumbering Industry," 249.
33. Maxwell and Baker, *Sawdust Empire,* 66.
34. *Jasper Newsboy,* July 22, 1937, February 3, 1937, February 16, 1937, September 28, 1939.
35. Ibid., July 22, 1937.
36. Maxwell and Baker, *Sawdust Empire,* 68.
37. Quoted in Walker, *The Southern Forest,* 181.
38. Davis, "Southeast Texas Forest Arson," 1.
39. Ibid.; Ron Davis, personal communication, July 20, 1992.
40. Charles Boyd interview, April 8, 1992.
41. Avy Joe Havard interview, February 22, 1992.
42. Texas stock laws are summarized in Chapter 5 ("Stock Law and Limited Range") and Chapter 6 ("Stock Running at Large") in *Vernon's Annotated Revised Civil Statutes.* Art. 6954 pertains to cattle, Art. 6930 to hogs and other livestock.
43. For Hardin County, see *Kountze News,* April 22, 1954, March 7, 1957, June 27, 1957, August 22, 1957, October 31, 1957, November 28, 1957. For Tyler County, see *Tyler County Booster,* July 19, 1956, August 16, 1956, September 20, 1956, October 4, 1956, October 18, 1956, October 25, 1956, February 28, 1957, March 14, 1957, May 2, 1957, June 13, 1957, September 8, 1957, September 19, 1957, October 31, 1957, December 5, 1957. For Jasper County, see *Jasper Newsboy,* November 13, 1952, April 16, 1953, August 27, 1953, August 25, 1955, October 6, 1955, October 13, 1955, October 21, 1955, November 17, 1955, January 12, 1956, January 19, 1956, February 23, 1956, September 13, 1956, March 21, 1957, November 21, 1957, October 9, 1958, December 4, 1958, March 19, 1959.
44. Escott, *Many Excellent People,* 188–90; Hahn, *The Roots of Southern Populism.*
45. *Polk County Enterprise* (Livingston, Texas), March 18, 1954. All additional dates cited in the discussion of the Polk County stock-law conflict refer to the *Enterprise.*
46. Passed by the fifty-sixth legislature, this was titled, "Livestock—Running at Large on Highways" (*Vernon's Annotated Revised Civil Statues,* Art. 1370 A).
47. Babe McGalin interview, May 14, 1992; Dudley Denmon interview, January 3, 1986; Claude Welch interview, January 17, 1986.
48. Charlie Harber interview, February 28, 1992.
49. Frank Ashby interview, March 19, 1992.
50. Charlie Harber interview, February 21, 1992.
51. Charlie Havard interview, , April 12, 1986; Charlie Harber interview, February 28, 1992; Walter Kirby interview, , April 17, 1992; Claude Welch interview, January 17, 1986.

52. *Jasper Newsboy,* August 25, 1955; Avy Joe Havard interview, February 22, 1992.
53. Avy Joe Havard interview, February 22, 1992.
54. Ibid.
55. Boyd, "Of Woods and Wildlife," 7.
56. Charlie Harber interview, February 28, 1992.
57. Oscar Allen interview, November 7, 1986; Charlie Harber interview, February 21, 1992; Leon Jones, personal communication, February 14, 1986.
58. Charles Boyd interview, April 8, 1992.
59. Leon Jones, personal communication, February 14, 1986.
60. Larry Williford interview, July 21, 1992.
61. Billy Platt interview, July 10, 1992.
62. Ibid.
63. Ibid.
64. Ibid.
65. Dan Boone, personal communication, June 10, 1992; Phil Evans, personal communication, June 9, 1992; Davis, "Southeast Texas Forest Arson," 1–6; "Angry East Texas Hunters Setting Fires," *Austin American-Statesman,* December 21, 1992.
66. Q. R. King interview, May 13, 1992.
67. J. R. Cockrell interview, May 13, 1992.
68. *Jasper Newsboy,* December 27, 1956; *Sunday Beaumont Enterprise,* December 23, 1956.
69. *Orange Leader,* 1956.
70. Dudley Denmon interview, January 3, 1986.
71. W. B. Harris interview, May 6, 1992.
72. Henceforth, individuals not named and/or referenced in the text of this chapter remain anonymous by request.
73. Walter Kirby interview, March 17, 1992.
74. Ibid.
75. Tape recordings of public hearings on proposed game law changes, held by the Texas Parks and Wildlife Department in Jasper, Texas, April 8, 1986.
76. Walter Kirby interview, March 17, 1992.
77. Frank Ashby interview, May 6, 1992.
78. James Albert Best interview, July 8, 1992.
79. Walter Kirby interview, March 17, 1992.
80. Charlie Harber interview, February 22, 1992.
81. Billy Platt interview, July 10, 1992.
82. Jake Cole interview, July 9, 1992.
83. Billy Platt interview, July 10, 1992.
84. *Jasper Newsboy,* July 14, 1955, January 5, 1956, February 16, 1956, May 17, 1956, May 24, 1956, February 6, 1958; Billy Platt interview, July 10, 1992.
85. Tape recordings of public hearings on proposed game law changes, Jasper, April 8, 1986.
86. Walter Kirby interview, March 17, 1992.
87. Ibid.
88. Aubrey Cole interview, May 28, 1992.

Written Sources

Abernethy, Francis E. "The East Texas Communal Hunt." In *Hunters and Healers*, edited by Wilson H. Hudson, pp. 3–10. Austin: Encino Press, 1971.
———. "Running the Fox." In *The Sunny Slopes of Long Ago*, edited by Wilson H. Hudson, pp. 146–50. Dallas: Southern Methodist University Press, 1966.
———, ed. *The Bounty of Texas*. Denton: University of North Texas Press, 1991.
———, ed. *Some Still Do: Essays on Texas Customs*. Austin: Encino Press, 1975.
———, ed. *Tales from the Big Thicket*. Austin: University of Texas Press, 1966.
———, ed. *T for Texas*. Dallas: Texas Folklore Society, 1982.
Adams, Arlisha Wortham, et al., eds. *Journey to Jubilee: Groveton, Texas, U.S.A.* Groveton: Groveton Ex-Students Association, 1980.
Ajilvsgi, Geyata. *Wildflowers of the Big Thicket, East Texas, and Western Louisiana.* College Station: Texas A&M University Press, 1979.
Allen, Ruth. *East Texas Timber Workers*. Austin: University of Texas Press, 1961.
Askins, J. M. *Where Oh Where Is Blair?* Lufkin: Best of East Texas Publishers, 1990.
August, Ray. "Cowboys v. Rancheros: The Origins of Western American Livestock Law." *Southwestern Historical Quarterly* 96 (1993): 456–88.
Baker, J. A. *The Peregrine*. London: Penguin, 1970.
Barrett, B. L. "Recollections of a Big Thicket Woodsman." *East Texas Historical Journal* 11 (1973): 59–62.
Barry, James Buchner. *Buck Barry: Texas Ranger and Frontiersman*. Lincoln: University of Nebraska Press, 1978.
Benke, Adrian. "The Ugliest Texans." *Texas Parks and Wildlife* 31 (1973): 6–11.
Biesele, Megan. *The Cornbread Whistle: Oral History of a Texas Timber Town.* Lufkin: Diboll Historical Society, 1986.
Bigony, Mary-Love. "Dark History, Bright Future for Native Wildlife." *Texas Parks and Wildlife* 49 (1991): 4–11.
———. "A Javelina Is Not a Pig . . . but a Feral Hog Is." *Texas Parks and Wildlife* 45 (1987): 34–39.
Billington, Ray Allen. *Westward Expansion: A History of the American Frontier*, 4th ed. New York: Macmillan, 1974.

Billington, Ray Allen, and Martin Ridge. *Westward Expansion: A History of the American Frontier*, 5th ed. New York: Macmillan, 1982.

Boatright, Moody, William Hudson, and Allen Maxwell, eds. *Singers and Storytellers*. Dallas: Southern Methodist University Press, 1961.

————, eds. *Texas Folk and Folklife*. Dallas: Southern Methodist University Press, 1954.

Boon, Effie. "The History of Angelina County." Master's thesis, University of Texas at Austin, 1937.

Bowles, Flora G. "The History of Trinity County." Master's thesis, University of Texas at Austin, 1928.

Bowman, Bob, ed. *Land of the Little Angel: A History of Angelina County*. Lufkin: Angelina County Survey Committee, 1976.

Boyd, Charles E. "Of Woods and Wildlife." *Texas Parks and Wildlife* 25 (1967): 6–9.

Bray, William. "Distribution and Adaptation of the Vegetation of Texas." *Bulletin of the University of Texas No. 82, Scientific Series No. 10* (1906).

Briggs, David J., and Peter Smithson. *Fundamentals of Physical Geography*. London: Hutchison, 1985.

Burka, Paul. "The King of the Forest." *Texas Monthly* 10 (1982): 114–23.

Busch, Carl. "The Incredible Mr. Busch." *Chinquapin* (1980), 48–57.

Caplen, John A. "Camp Big Thicket: Life in the Piney Woods, 1887." In *Tales from the Big Thicket*, edited by Francis E. Abernethy, pp. 107–13. Austin: University of Texas Press, 1966.

Carr, Jess. *The Second Oldest Profession: An Informal History of Moonshining in America*. Englewood Cliffs, N.J.: Prentice-Hall, 1972.

Chambers, William. "Divisions of the Pine Belt in Texas." *Economic Geography* 10 (1930): 94–103.

———— "The Pine Woods Region in Southeastern Texas." *Economic Geography* 10, no. 3 (1934): 309.

Chorley, Richard J. *Geomorphology*. London: Methuen, 1985.

Claiborne, John F. H. "A Trip through the Piney Woods." *Mississippi Historical Society Publications* 9 (1906): 514–38.

Clark, Joy, ed. *Chandler: Its History and People, 1880–1980*. Jacksonville: Chandler Historical Society, 1981.

Clark, Thomas D. *Frontier America*. New York: Charles Scribners Sons, 1969.

————. *The Greening of the South*. Lexington: University Press of Kentucky, 1984.

Collins, Vinson A. "Settling the Old Poplar-Tree Place." In *Tales from the Big Thicket*, edited by Francis E. Abernethy, pp. 58–68. Austin: University of Texas Press, 1966.

Cox, Jim. "More Than a Match for Hunters." *Texas Parks and Wildlife* 39 (1981): 8–10.

Cravens, John N. *Between Two Rivers: A History of Wells, Texas*. Wichita Falls: n.p., 1974.

————. "Kilraven: A Ghost Town in the Southern Part of Cherokee County, Texas." *East Texas Historical Journal* 9 (1971): 162–70.

————. *Three Ghost Towns of East Texas.* Abilene: Abilene Printing Company, n.d.

Creel, George. "The Feudal Towns of Texas." *Harper's Weekly* 69 (1915): 76–78.

Cronon, William. *Changes in the Land.* New York: Hill and Wang, 1983.

Croom, Guy. *When the Pines Grew Tall.* Lufkin: Red Mountain Publishing Co., 1986.

Czaya, Eberhard. *Rivers of the World.* New York: Van Nostrand, 1981.

Davis, Andrew. "Folk Life in Early Texas: The Autobiography of Andrew Davis." *Southwestern Historical Quarterly* 43 (1939–40): 158–75, 321–41.

Davis, Ron. "Southeast Texas Forest Arson." Unpublished Texas Forest Service report prepared for the Federal Bureau of Investigation, n.d.

Day, James M. "Silver Ingots in East Texas." In *Tire Shrinker to Dragster,* edited by Wilson H. Hudson, pp. 37–49. Austin: Encino, 1968.

Dobie, J. Frank. *The Ben Lily Legend.* Boston: Little Brown and Co., 1950.

Doughty, Robin W. *Wildlife and Man in Texas.* College Station: Texas A&M University Press, 1983.

Douglas, William O. *Farewll to Texas: A Vanishing Wilderness.* New York: McGraw-Hill, 1967.

Easton, Hamilton Pratt. "The History of the Texas Lumbering Industry." Ph.D. diss., University of Texas at Austin, 1947.

Elliott, William. *Carolina Sports by Land and Water, Including Incidents of Devil-Fishing, Wild-Cat, Deer and Bear Hunting, Etc.* New York: Derby and Jackson, 1859.

Erinstra, Ellen W. "A Family Full of Legends." In *Tales from the Big Thicket,* edited by Francis E. Abernethy, pp. 181–97. Austin: University of Texas Press, 1966.

Escott, Paul D. *Many Excellent People: Power and Privilege in North Carolina, 1850–1900.* Chapel Hill: University of North Carolina Press, 1985.

Evans, Cleo F. "Transportation in Early Texas." Master's thesis, St. Mary's University of San Antonio, 1940.

Everett, Diana. *The Texas Cherokees.* Norman: University of Oklahoma Press, 1990.

Fentress, Carl D. "Wildlife of Bottomlands: Species and Status." In *Bottomland Hardwoods in Texas,* edited by Craig A. McMahan and Roy G. Frye, pp. 37–57. Austin: Texas Parks and Wildlife Department, 1986.

Fleming, Kay. "Texas Bear Hunting." *Texas Parks and Wildlife* 38 (1980): 12–15.

Foster, J. H., H. B. Krausz, and G. W. Johnson. "Forest Resources of Eastern Texas." *Texas A&M College Department of Forestry Bulletin* 5 (1917).

Fritz, Edward C. *Realms of Beauty: The Wilderness Areas of East Texas.* Austin: University of Texas Press, 1986.

Garrett, Judith M., and David G. Barker. *A Field Guide to the Reptiles and Amphibians of Texas.* Austin: Texas Monthly Press, 1987.

Gaston, Edwin W. "Tall Timber Tales." In *Singers and Storytellers,* edited by Moody Boatright, William Hudson, and Allen Maxwell, pp. 178–184. Dallas: Southern Methodist University Press, 1961.

Glacken, Clarence J. *Traces on the Rhodian Shore: Nature and Culture in Western*

Thought from Ancient Times to the End of the Eighteenth Century. Berkeley: University of California Press, 1967.

Glover, William B. "A History of the Caddo Indians." *Louisiana History Quarterly* 18 (1935): 872–946.

Griffith, William J. *The Hasinai Indians of East Texas As Seen by Europeans, 1687–1772.* New Orleans: Middle American Research Institute, Tulane University, 1954.

Gunter, Pete. *The Big Thicket: A Challenge for Conservation.* Austin: Jenkins Publishing Co., 1971.

Hahn, Steven. "Hunting, Fishing, and Foraging: Common Rights and Class Relations in the Postbellum South." *Radical History Review* 26 (1982): 37–64.

———. *The Roots of Southern Populism: Yeoman Farmers and the Transformation of the Georgia Upcountry, 1850–1890.* New York: Oxford University Press, 1983.

Hale, Duane K. "Mining and Prospecting on the Louisiana-Texas Frontier, 1713–1763." *East Texas Historical Journal* 18 (1980): 41–47.

Harris, Larry D. *Bottomland Hardwoods: Valuable, Vanishing, Vulnerable, 1984.* Gainesville: Florida Cooperative Extension Services, Institute of Food and Agricultural Sciences, University of Florida, 1984.

Haynes, Emma. "The History of Polk County." Manuscript, Barker Texas History Center, University of Texas, Austin, 1937.

Herrington, Frank. "Buckshot and Blue Whistler." In *Tales from the Big Thicket,* edited by Francis E. Abernethy, pp. 93–106. Austin: University of Texas Press, 1966.

Hewett, Margaret L. "From Moss Hill." In *Tales from the Big Thicket,* edited by Francis E. Abernethy, pp. 215–26. Austin: University of Texas Press, 1966.

Hicks, Ray R., and George K. Stephenson. *Woody Plants of the Western Gulf Region.* Dubuque: Kendall/Hunt Publishing Co., 1978.

Hill, Ethel O. "Grandma Harrison: A Day at Drew's Landing." In *Tales from the Big Thicket,* edited by Francis E. Abernethy, pp. 69–74. Austin: University of Texas Press, 1966.

Hilliard, Sam B. *Hogmeat and Hoecake: Food Supply in the Old South.* Carbondale: Southern Illinois University Press, 1972.

Hoagland, Edward. *Notes from the Century Before: A Journal from British Columbia.* New York: Random House, 1969.

Hogan, William Ransom. *The Texas Republic: A Social and Economic History.* Norman: University of Oklahoma Press, 1946.

Hollon, W. Eugene, and Ruth Lapham Butler, eds. *William Bollaert's Texas.* Norman: University of Oklahoma Press, 1956.

Hooks, Ben. "Ten Days in the Big Thicket." Manuscript, Barker Texas History Center, University of Texas, Austin, n.d.

Hooks, H. A. "An Essay on Hardin County Politics." In *Hardin County History,* edited by Robert Schaadt, p. 145. Dallas: Hardin County Historical Commission, 1991.

Hooks, Robert. "'Shinny' and Gambling Had Big Roles in 1929 Deer Hunt." *Kountze News,* August 29, 1957.

Houstoun, Matilda. *Texas and the Gulf of Mexico; or, Yachting in the New World.* London: John Murray, 1844.

Hudson, Charles. *The Southeastern Indians.* Knoxville: University of Tennessee Press, 1976.

Hudson, Wilson H., ed. *Hunters and Healers.* Austin: Encino, 1971.

———, ed. *The Sunny Slopes of Long Ago.* Dallas: Southern Methodist University Press, 1966.

———, ed. *Tire Shrinker to Dragster.* Austin: Encino, 1968.

"The Incredible Mr. Busch." *Chinquapin* (Fall/Winter 1980), 51–52.

Ippolito, John. *A Cultural Resource Overview of the National Forests of Texas.* Lufkin: U.S. Forest Service, 1983.

Jackson, Ralph Semmes. *Home on the Double Bayou: Memories of an East Texas Boyhood.* Austin: University of Texas Press, 1961.

Jordan, Terry G. *Texas Log Buildings: A Folk Architecture.* Austin: University of Texas Press, 1978.

———. *Trails to Texas: Southern Roots of Western Cattle Ranching.* Lincoln: University of Nebraska Press, 1981.

Jordan, Terry G., and Matti Kaup. *The American Backwoods Frontier: An Ethnic and Ecological Interpretation.* Baltimore: Johns Hopkins University Press, 1990.

Kantor, S. E., and J. M. Kousser. "Common Sense or Commonwealth? The Fence Law and Institutional Change in the Postbellum South." *Journal of Southern History* 59 (1993): 201–66.

Keller, John. "The Subsistence Paleoecology of the Middle Neches Valley." Ph.D. diss., University of Texas at Austin, 1974.

Kiehne, A. L. "Texas Bear Hunt, 1906." In *Tales from the Big Thicket,* edited by Francis E. Abernethy, pp. 123–36. Austin: University of Texas Press, 1966.

King, J. Crawford. "The Closing of the Southern Range: An Exploratory Study." *Journal of Southern History* 48 (1982): 53–70.

Kirksey, Guy. "'Hoping Out' in East Texas." In *Texas Folk and Folklife,* edited by Moody Boatright, William Hudson, and Allen Maxwell, pp. 195–202. Dallas: Southern Methodist University Press, 1954.

Knipmeyer, William B. "Settlement Succession in Eastern French Louisiana." Ph.D. diss., Louisiana State University, 1956.

Lay, Daniel W. "Bottomland Hardwoods in East Texas: A Historical Overview." In *Bottomland Hardwoods in Texas,* edited by Craig A. McMahan and Roy G. Frye, pp. 8–19. Austin: Texas Parks and Wildlife Department, 1986.

———. "Forks of the River." *Texas Parks and Wildlife* 41 (1983): 24–29.

———. "Pristine East Texas and Some Impacts of Settlement." Paper prepared for the annual meeting of the Texas Association for Endangered Species, Nacogdoches, Texas, 1987.

———. "The Role of Fire in Forest Management." Paper presented at Big Thicket Association meeting, Beaumont, Texas, October 31, 1987.

"Log Brand Records for Hardin and Jefferson Counties." Manuscript, Texas Forestry Museum, Lufkin, Texas, n.d.

Loughmiller, Campbell, and Lynn Loughmiller, eds. *Big Thicket Legacy.* Austin: University of Texas Press, 1977.

———. "Bill Warren of the Big Thicket." In *T for Texas,* edited by Francis E. Abernethy, pp. 59–78. Dallas: Texas Folklore Society, 1982.

Lowry, Mildred. *From Shawnee Prairie*. New York: Carlton Press, 1990.

McDonald, Forrest, and Grady McWhiney. "The Antebellum Southern Herdsman: A Reinterpretation." *Journal of Southern History* 44 (1975): 147–66.

McMahan, Craig A. "Texas' Bottomland Hardwoods: The Needs of a Diminishing Resource." In *Bottomland Hardwoods in Texas*, edited by Craig A. McMahan and Roy G. Frye, pp. 5–7. Austin: Texas Parks and Wildlife Department, 1986.

McMahan, Craig A., and Roy G. Frye, eds. *Bottomland Hardwoods in Texas*. Austin: Texas Parks and Wildlife Department, 1986.

McReynolds, James M. "Frontier Towns in Antebellum East Texas: Jasper County." *East Texas Historical Journal* 16 (1978): 3–14.

McWhiney, Grady. *Cracker Culture: Celtic Ways in the Old South*. University: University of Alabama Press, 1988.

Marks, Stuart A. *Southern Hunting in Black and White*. Princeton: Princeton University Press, 1991.

Martin, L. D. "Late Pleistocene Faunal Distribution and Community Evolution." *Bulletin of the Ecological Society of America* 61 (1980): 120.

Mathews, Archie B. "The Economic Development of Angelina County." Master's thesis, University of Texas at Austin, 1952.

Maxwell, Robert S. "The Pines of Texas: A Study in Lumbering and Public Policy." *East Texas Historical Journal* 2 (1964): 77–86.

Maxwell, Robert S., and Robert D. Baker. *Sawdust Empire: The Texas Lumber Industry, 1830–1940*. College Station: Texas A&M University Press, 1983.

Mayer, John J., and Lehr Brisbin, Jr. *Wild Pigs in the United States*. Athens: University of Georgia Press, 1991.

Meinig, D. W. *Imperial Texas: An Interpretive Essay in Cultural Geography*. Austin: University of Texas Press, 1969.

Michaux, Francois A. *In Early Western Travels, 1748–1846, Vol. III*, edited by Reuben Gold Thwaites, pp. 243–50. Cleveland: A. H. Clark Co., 1904.

Neal, Jim and Jeff Haskins. "Bottomland Hardwoods: Ecology, Management, and Preservation." In *Wilderness and Natural Areas in the Eastern United States*, edited by David L. Kulhavy and Richard N. Conner. Nacogdoches: School of Forestry, Stephen F. Austin University, n.d.

Newcomb, W. W. *The Indians of Texas*. Austin: University of Texas Press, 1961.

Nichols, James W. *Now You Hear My Horn: The Journals of James Wilson Nichols*. Austin: University of Texas Press, 1967.

Oberholser, Harry C. *The Bird Life of Texas*. 2 vols. Austin: University of Texas Press, 1974.

Oberlander, Theodore. *Essentials of Physical Geography Today*. New York: Random House, 1982.

Odom, Harrell. *Over on Cochino*. Waco: Texian Press, 1980.

Odom, Max. "A History of the East Texas Cattle Industry." Master's thesis, University of Texas at Austin, 1958.

Olmsted, Frederick Law. *The Cotton Kingdom*. 1861. Reprint. New York: Alfred A. Knopf, 1953.

———. *A Journey through Texas; or, A Saddle-Trip on the Southwestern Frontier*. 1857. Reprint. Austin: University of Texas Press, 1978.

Overstreet, Cecil V. "Chimney Dobbin' in the Big Thicket." In *Some Still Do:*

Essays on Texas Customs, edited by Francis E. Abernethy, pp. 77–87. Austin: Encino, 1975.

Owens, William A. "Big Thicket Balladry." In *Tales from the Big Thicket,* edited by Francis E. Abernethy, pp. 199–214. Austin: University of Texas Press, 1966.

Owsley, Frank L. *Plain Folk of the Old South.* Baton Rouge: Louisiana State University Press, 1949.

"Paper Mill Leases 40,000-Acre Plot Free to Outdoors Association." *Beaumont Enterprise,* December 23, 1956.

Parvin, Bob. "Bottomland Hardwoods: Every Acre Counts." *Texas Parks and Wildlife* 44 (1986): 24–37.

Peacock, Howard. "Folk Medicine in the Big Thicket." *The World and I* (1986): 193–209.

Peavy, Josephine C. "A History of Newton County, Texas." Master's thesis, University of Texas at Austin, 1942.

Posey, James B. "A History of Cherokee County." Master's thesis, University of Texas at Austin, 1928.

Ramos, Ralph. "Farmer and Forester Worked Hand-In-Hand." *Sunday Enterprise-Journal* (Beaumont, Texas), August 11, 1974.

———. *Rocking Texas' Cradle.* Beaumont: Enterprise Co., 1974.

Reinstra, Ellen W. "A Family Full of Legends." In *Tales from the Big Thicket,* edited by Francis E. Abernethy, pp. 181–98. Austin: University of Texas Press, 1966.

Roach, Hattie J. *The Hills of Cherokee.* Self published: 1952.

———. *A History of Cherokee County (Texas).* Dallas: Southwest Press, 1934.

Roosevelt, Theodore. "In the Louisiana Canebrakes." *Scribner's Magazine* 43 (1908): 52.

Rosier, Lance. "Late Fount Simmons Rescued Governor Ross from Big Thicket." *Kountze News,* March 7, 1957.

Russell, Richard J. *River Plains and Sea Coasts.* Berkeley: University of California Press, 1967.

Schaadt, Robert, ed. *Hardin County History.* Dallas: Hardin County Historical Commission, 1991.

Seale, William. "River People." *East Texas Historical Journal* 5 (1967): 43–50.

———. *Texas Riverman: The Life and Times of Captain Andrew Smyth.* Austin: University of Texas Press, 1966.

Shafer, Harry J. "Early Lithic Assemblages in Eastern Texas." Paper presented at Paleo-Indian Lifeways Symposium, Lubbock, Texas, 1975.

Sitton, Thad. *Texas High Sheriffs.* Austin: Texas Monthly Press, 1988.

Sitton, Thad, and Lincoln King, eds. *The Loblolly Book: Omnibus Edition.* Austin: Texas Monthly Press, 1986.

Sitton, Thad, and Milam Rowold. *Ringing the Children In: Texas Country Schools.* College Station: Texas A&M University Press, 1987.

Smithwick, Noah. *The Evolution of a State; or, Recollections of Old Texas Days.* 1900. Reprint. Austin: University of Texas Press, 1983.

Sonnichsen, C. L. *The Grave of John Wesley Hardin: Three Essays of Grassroots History.* College Station: Texas A&M University Press, 1979.

Stevens, Joe. "Almost Gone." *Texas Parks and Wildlife* 35 (1977): 2–7.

——. "Crafty Import." *Texas Parks and Wildlife* 27 (1969): 22–24.
——. "The Forks of the Creek." *Texas Parks and Wildlife* 32 (1974): 6–11.
——. "The Fur Trade." *Texas Parks and Wildlife* 36 (1978): 2–5.
Strahler, Arthur N. *Introduction to Physical Geography.* New York: John Wiley, 1969.
Sullivan, John Frederick. "Navigation of the Neches and Sabine Rivers during the Nineteenth Century." Master's research report, University of Texas at Austin, 1967.
Swanton, John R. "Source Material on the History and Ethnology of the Caddo Indians." *Smithsonian Institution Bureau of Ethnology Bulletin 132* (1942).
Tatum, Miriam Havard. *River Road.* Diboll: Angelina Free Press, 1979.
Taylor, Rick. *The Feral Hog in Texas.* Austin: Texas Parks and Wildlife Department, 1991.
The Texas Almanac, 1936. Dallas: A. H. Belo Corporation, 1936.
Texas Parks and Wildlife Department. *Caddoan Mounds: Temples and Tombs of An Ancient People.* Austin: Texas Parks and Wildlife Department, 1984.
Truett, Joe C., and Daniel W. Lay. *Land of Bears and Honey.* Austin: University of Texas Press, 1984.
United States Census of Agriculture: 1935, Volume I, Statistics by Counties. Washington, D.C.: U.S. Government Printing Office, 1936.
U.S. Fish and Wildlife Service. *Texas Bottomland Preservation Program.* Albuquerque: U.S. Fish and Wildlife Service, 1985.
Utley, Francis L. *Bear, Man, and God: Eight Approaches to William Faulkner's "The Bear."* New York: Random House, 1971.
Vernon's Annotated Revised Civil Statutes of the State of Texas, Vol. 19A. Kansas City: Vernon Law Book Co., 1960.
Walker, Laurence C. *The Southern Forest: A Chronicle.* Austin: University of Texas Press, 1991.
White, Dabney. "Cherokee County Characters." *Farm and Ranch* 19 (1900): 1.
White, Edna M. *East Texas Riverboat Era and Its Decline.* Beaumont: LaBelle, 1967.
Williams, Michael. *Americans and Their Forests: A Historical Geography.* Cambridge: Cambridge University Press, 1989.
Woldert, Albert. *A History of Tyler and Smith County, Texas.* San Antonio: Naylor, 1948.
Wright, Solomon A. *My Rambles as East Texas Cowboy, Hunter, Fisherman, Tie-Cutter.* Austin: Texas Folklore Society, 1942.
Zuber, William P. *My Eighty Years in Texas.* Austin: University of Texas Press, 1971.

Oral Sources

Individuals interviewed during the research for *Backwoodsmen* are listed below. Some people were recorded only once, but many had much to tell and were interviewed again and again, eventually contributing several hours of taped recollections. Other than the two exceptions noted below, all the *Backwoodsmen* oral history tapes are on deposit in the East Texas Research Center, Ralph W. Steen Library, at Stephen F. Austin State University, Nacogdoches, Texas.

Allen, Oscar. Taped interviews with Thad Sitton, 1985–86.
Allen, R. R. Taped interview with Thad Sitton, 1992.
Ashby, Frank. Taped interviews with Thad Sitton, 1992.
Ball, Billy S. Taped interview with Thad Sitton, 1992.
Beezley, Clarence. Taped interview with Thad Sitton, 1992.
Best, James Albert. Taped interview with Thad Sitton, 1992.
Bingham, J. Louis. Taped interview with Thad Sitton, 1992.
Bishop, C. V. Taped interview with Thad Sitton, 1986.
Boyd, Charles. Taped interview with Thad Sitton, 1992.
Carpenter, George. Taped interviews with Thad Sitton, 1985–86.
Cockrell, J. R. Taped interview with Thad Sitton, 1992.
Cole, Aubrey. Taped interviews with Thad Sitton, 1992.
Cole, Jake L. Taped interview with Thad Sitton, 1992.
Cole, Walter. Taped interview with Thad Sitton, 1992.
Davis, Ron. Telephone interview with Thad Sitton, 1992.
Denmon, Dudley. Taped interviews with Thad Sitton, 1986.
Dietz, Don. Taped interview with Thad Sitton, 1992.
DuBose, Bert. Taped interview with Jim Hudgins, n.d.
DuBose, Wanda Gipson. Taped interviews with Thad Sitton, 1985–92.
Gandy, C. W. Taped interview with Thad Sitton, 1992.
Greenville, Lester. Taped interview with Thad Sitton, 1986.
Harber, Charlie. Taped interviews with Thad Sitton, 1992.
Harris, W. B. Taped interview with Thad Sitton, 1992.
Havard, Alpha Omega. Taped interview with Sarah C. Sitton, 1986.
Havard, Avy Joe. Taped interviews with Thad Sitton, 1992.
Havard, Carl C. Taped interviews with Thad Sitton, 1992.
Havard, Charlie. Taped interviews with Thad Sitton, 1986.
King, Q. R. Taped interview with Thad Sitton, 1992.
Kirby, Walter. Taped interviews with Thad Sitton, 1992.
Lay, Daniel W. Taped interviews with Thad Sitton, 1989–92.
McAnally, Coy. Taped interview with Thad Sitton, 1992.
McAnulty, M. H. "Buck." Taped interview with Thad Sitton, 1992.
McGalin, A. E. "Babe." Taped interviews with Thad Sitton, 1992.
McGalin, Lynn. Taped interview with Thad Sitton, 1992.
May, James W. Taped interview with Thad Sitton, 1992.
Neal, Jim. Taped interview and a subsequent telephone interview with Thad Sitton, 1992.
Petri, C. P. Taped interview with Thad Sitton, 1986.
Platt, Billy F. Taped interview with Thad Sitton, 1992.
Rawls, R. J. Taped interview with Dan K. Utley, 1986.
Shillings, Hinkle. Taped interview with Thad Sitton, 1992.
Smith, Roy. Taped interviews with Thad Sitton, 1985–86.
Snelson, Edward. Taped interview with Thad Sitton, 1992.
Snelson, Harold. Taped interviews with Thad Sitton, 1992.
Starling, William. Taped interviews with Thad Sitton, 1986.
Tull, George. Taped interview with Thad Sitton, 1985.
Walker, Ed C. Taped interview with Thad Sitton, 1992.

Welch, Claude. Taped interview with Thad Sitton, 1986.
Welch, R. V. Telephone interview with Thad Sitton, 1992.
Wells, Charles. Taped interview with Thad Sitton, 1992.
Wells, Jess. Taped interviews with Thad Sitton, 1986.
Williford, Larry. Taped interviews with Thad Sitton, 1992.
Womack, James. Taped interview with Thad Sitton, 1992.
Yarborough, Ralph W. Taped interview with Thad Sitton, 1985. (Note: In accordance with this interviewee's wishes, these tapes were not placed in a public depository.)

Tape recordings of public hearings on proposed game law changes held by the Texas Parks and Wildlife Department in Jasper, Texas, on April 8, 1986, are on file at Texas Parks and Wildlife Department Headquarters, Austin, Texas.

Abernethy, F. E., 11
African Americans, 14, 230, 279–80n
Alabama, territory and state of, 3, 7, 46, 134, 237
Alabama Creek, 22
Allen, Oscar, 130, 136, 169, 171, 177–78, 183, 185–86, 222, 235
Allen, R. R. ("Bob"), 93, 95–96, 98–100, 110, 213
Alligators, 227–28
Amos, Woody, 249–52, 254
Anderson, Buford, 182
Anderson, Ernest, 182
Angelina, county of, 12, 14, 17, 53, 68, 71, 82, 93, 101, 111, 113, 117, 121, 123–34, 126–27, 130–33, 141, 170, 175, 177, 179, 182, 184, 191, 203, 217, 219–21, 223–24
Angelina County Lumber Company, 101–102, 113
Angelina County National Forest, 243
Angelina River, 23, 83
Archaic cultures, 28–29
Ashby, Frank, 76, 162, 176, 179, 181–84, 187–88, 208–209, 211–13, 228–29, 257, 269
Atakapan speakers (Bidai, Dedose, Patrici, Akokisa), 29–30, 41. See also Indians

Barn buildings. See Communal work events
Barnes, Johnny, 223
Barry, Buck, 147–48, 228
Basket making, 121
Bean, Peter Ellis, 42–44
Bear Man's Bluff (Weiss's Bluff), 68, 83, 87, 273
Bears, black, 25; Hasinai Caddos' hunting methods for, 36; hunted for sport, 148–51; hunted as stock-killing varmints, 145–48; importance to early Anglo-American diet of, 59, 146; as threat to livestock, 61–62, 145–47, 202, 227; traps for, 145

Beaumont, Texas, 90–91, 97, 99, 100, 110, 121, 132
Beavers, 176
Bedias Creek, 42
Beef Trail, 66, 215
Bee Tree Slough, 27
Beezley, Clarence, 233–34
Bellview, Texas, 14, 184
Berlandier, Jean Louis, 37
Bessmay, Texas, 113
Best, James Albert, 238, 269
Bevil, A. L., 149
Bevil, John, 119, 209–10
Bevilport, Texas, 82–83, 85–86
Big Pine Hammock, 68
Big Slough (Scurlock's Slough), 16, 115, 185
Big Thicket, 3–4, 106, 146, 164, 216
Bill Evan's Island, 185
Billingsley, Henry, 128, 132–33
Billington, Ray Allen, 4
Bingham, J. Louis, 93, 98, 110, 186, 189–91
Bird thrashings. See Communal work events
Bishop, C. V., 176, 186–87
Black Creek, Texas, 71, 126–27
Black Water Slough, 273
Blue Buck Shoal, 83
Boats, "paddle," 142–43
Boggy Slough, 217–18, 256–57, 265
Boggy Slough Hunting Club, 256–57, 259–60, 267, 269
Bollaert, William, 82, 139
Bowman, Mack, 224
Boyd, Charles, 161, 245, 259, 261
Boykin, Wesley, 73
Boykin Springs, Texas, 71
Bracken, Bud, 147
Brotherhood of Timber Workers, 104
Brown, Evie, 146
Brown, Warren, 146
Brunt, Frank, 126–28